World Wide Research

Reshaping the Sciences and Humanities

edited by William H. Dutton and Paul W. Jeffreys

with a foreword by Ian Goldin

The MIT Press
Cambridge, Massachusetts
London, England

For information about special quantity discounts, please email special_sales@mitpress.mit.edu

This book was set in Stone Sans and Stone Serif by Graphic Composition, Inc., Bogart, GA. Printed and bound in the United States of America.

Library of Congress Cataloging-in-Publication Data
World wide research : reshaping the sciences and humanities / edited by William H. Dutton and Paul W. Jeffreys ; foreword by Ian Goldin.
    p. cm.
Includes bibliographical references and index.
ISBN 978-0-262-01439-7 (hc. : alk. paper)—ISBN 978-0-262-51373-9 (pbk. : alk. paper)
1. Research—Methodology. 2. Research—Technological innovations.   3. Information technology.
I. Dutton, William H., 1947–   II. Jeffreys, Paul W., 1954–
Q180.55.M4W67   2010
001.4'2—dc22
                                                                                    2009032003

10 9 8 7 6 5 4 3 2 1

Contents

Foreword by Ian Goldin   ix
Preface   xi
Acknowledgments   xiii
Contributors   xv

World Wide Research: An Introduction   1
William H. Dutton and Paul W. Jeffreys

I Foundations   19

1 Reconfiguring Access in Research: Information, Expertise, and Experience   21
William H. Dutton

1.1 The Long Now of Cyberinfrastructure   40
Geoffrey C. Bowker, Paul N. Edwards, Steven J. Jackson, and Cory P. Knobel

1.2 Identifying Winners and Losers: The Role of Webometrics   45
Mike Thelwall

1.3 "Superstar" Concentrations of Scientific Output and Recognition   48
Robert Ackland

2 The Developing Conception of e-Research   51
Paul W. Jeffreys

2.1 Research Platforms in the Cloud   67
Tony Hey, Roger Barga, and Savas Parastatidis

2.2 The New e-Research   72
David De Roure

2.3 The Promises and Threats of e-Research in the Strategies of Firms and Nations   75
John Taylor

II State of the Practice   79

3 Digital Resources and the Future of Libraries   83
Eric T. Meyer, Christine Madsen, and Jenny Fry

3.1 Data Webs for Image Repositories   98
David Shotton

3.2 Digital Technology and Ancient Manuscripts   102
Alan Bowman

4 Key Digital Technologies to Deal with Data   107
Yorick Wilks and Matthijs den Besten

4.1 Embedded Networked Sensing   120
Christine L. Borgman

4.2 Identifying Digital Objects   125
Michael A. Fraser

4.3 Use of the Semantic Web in e-Research   130
Kieron O'Hara, Tim Berners-Lee, Wendy Hall, and Nigel Shadbolt

5 Embedding e-Research Applications: Designing for Usability   135
Grace de la Flor, Marina Jirotka, Sharon Lloyd, and Andrew Warr

5.1 Trusted Computing Platforms   153
Andrew Martin

5.2 Social Networking and e-Research   157
Mike Thelwall

III Social Shaping of Infrastructures and Practices   161

6 Enabling or Mediating the Social Sciences? The Opportunities and Risks of Bottom-up Innovation   165
William H. Dutton and Eric T. Meyer

6.1 An e-Infrastructure for the Social Sciences   185
Rob Procter

6.2 Chinese e–Social Science: A Low-End Approach   188
Jonathan J. H. Zhu and Xiaoming Li

7 Institutional Infrastructures for Global Research Networks in the Public Sector   191
Paul A. David and Michael Spence

7.1 Ownership of Medical Images in e-Science Collaborations: Learning from the Diagnostic Mammography National Database 214
Tina Piper and David Vaver

7.2 The Value of Authorship in the Digital Environment: Producing and Protecting Scientific Information 218
Justine Pila

8 The Politics of Privacy, Confidentiality, and Ethics: Opening Research Methods 223
William H. Dutton and Tina Piper

8.1 Ethical and Moral Dimensions of e-Research 241
Michael Parker

8.2 Data Sharing in Genomics—Is It Lawful? 245
Jane Kaye

8.3 Protecting Confidentiality 249
Julia Lane

IV Implications for Research 253

9 The Changing Disciplinary Landscapes of Research 257
Jenny Fry and Ralph Schroeder

9.1 The Agenda-Setting Role of e-Research 272
Paul Wouters

10 Reshaping Research Collaboration: The Case of Virtual Research Environments 277
Annamaria Carusi and Marina Jirotka

10.1 The Future of Virtual Research Environments 295
Matthew Dovey

11 Will e-Science Be Open Science? 299
Paul A. David, Matthijs den Besten, and Ralph Schroeder

11.1 The Politics of Open Access 317
Gustavo Cardoso, João Caraça, Rita Espanha, and Sandro Mendonça

11.2 Open Access versus "Open Viewing" for a Web of Science: The Neurocommons Example 322
John Wilbanks and Hal Abelson

12 Shaping Research in Developing Areas 325
Marcus Antonius Ynalvez, Ricardo B. Duque, and Wesley Shrum

Coda: The Ends and Means of World Wide Research   343
William H. Dutton and Paul W. Jeffreys

Glossary   349
Abbreviations   355
Index   357

Foreword

The challenges facing the world are immense and wide ranging, and they often arise rapidly and in unanticipated ways. For example, the 2008 global financial crisis and its profound, reverberating economic and social consequences caught most financial experts and politicians by surprise. Climate change threatens our entire way of life and the survival of many species. The potential for swift global spread of infectious diseases requires new ways of thinking about travel, disease control, and health care. Terrorism is becoming a feature of modern societies, with major repercussions on previously taken-for-granted freedoms and ways of doing things. The aging of Europe and many other regions of the world is one of a wide range of issues affecting the shifting profile and movement of people and resources across the globe.

The goal of the James Martin 21st Century School, which nurtured this book, is to develop strategies for responding to these kinds of serious problems. In some cases, such as climate change, there is a developing consensus on the facts of the case and a growing sense of what needs to be done. Consensus does not necessarily translate into action, however, because it is frequently not simply a lack of policy options or political will that prevents action. Rather, the barrier may be a perceived lack of information that can be regarded as sufficiently independent, rigorous, and trusted. In other areas, the analysis of existing information stretches the capacity of our methods in analyzing and modeling complex global interactions to enhance genuine understanding of underlying processes. Elsewhere, researchers have not been able to communicate the results of their work in sufficiently clear and powerful ways.

The 21st Century School is focused on opportunity as well as on risk. There is immense potential in new technologies and in the forces of globalization to improve the quality of life for more people and to mitigate the growing systemic risks. Achieving this potential urgently requires new research and innovative research methods.

Potential and Threats from the Use of Digital Networks in Research

What can advances in research, enabled by new developments around the Internet and other digital technologies, contribute to addressing these challenges and communicating the results? This book explores how what its editors call advanced "e-research" networks can efficiently and reliably gather, analyze, and document research information on a global scale to contribute to informed discussions about developing appropriate solutions. As examined in the volume, new e-research approaches can create more comprehensive and trusted data sets, support larger and more complex analytical and modeling tasks, and help researchers to visualize and communicate their results as well as to collaborate in pooling expertise and resources.

However, the progress of research and its positive contribution to future challenges are not inevitable. Many technical, financial, ethical, institutional, and legal difficulties stand in the way of realizing and exploiting these advances. All of these issues are covered in this book, which captures a valuable, multidisciplinary perspective from those at the forefront of advances in research.

There is real risk that the infrastructures required to move research to this new level will not be built coherently. Access to them might also be unevenly distributed around the world and generate even greater inequalities in access to information. Scholars' skills and training might not keep pace with the innovations in research tools and methods. Advances in technology might be misused in ways that violate the ethical standards that protect the public and the research community's independence. Scholars themselves might employ the technology in ways that distance them from the empirical realities of the twenty-first century, rather than in ways that enable them to gain a more accurate picture of our world.

Research is a window to the world and its future. Nevertheless, the scholarly community has relatively neglected the need to understand how information and communication technologies can be applied to research problems and enhance the range and quality of research across the sciences and humanities. This book seeks to help close that gap. The topics covered are critical to enabling the academic community to help business, industry, government, and society at large to address the major challenges I have outlined.

The volume will be valuable to those scholars developing and practicing new approaches to research as well as to anyone who is curious about the potential for new technologies to transform research. Will new tools distance researchers from their subjects, leaving them engrossed in computer screens or virtual worlds, or will they enable them to build on the tried and true in opening new ways to solve some of the most vexing problems? The answer is not a foregone conclusion because the success of e-research will depend on the wise use of the best tools and a collective will to cooperate and collaborate—an approach that this book seeks to foster.

Ian Goldin
Director, James Martin 21st Century School, University of Oxford

Preface

Uncloaking a Revolution in Research

A revolution is under way in the technologies being developed to support research across all disciplines. It is often cloaked in technical terminology—an alphabet soup of acronyms and obscure articles in specialized conference proceedings. However, its results might fundamentally transform the ways researchers go about their work, just as innovations such as the mobile phone, the Internet, the World Wide Web, and email have altered how we carry out our everyday lives. The consequences of the rise in increasingly powerful and versatile computer-based and networked systems for research—what this book calls "e-research"—will generate waves well beyond the laboratory or the ivory tower because they are more generally changing how we know what we know.

Our edited volume offers authoritative and accessible insights to the nature of this new set of technologies, how these technologies are being applied, and with what consequences in a variety of fields. It explains why major public and private investments are being made in e-research and how they promise to shape the quality of research that underpins policy and practice that are affecting how we work and socialize, as well as how we make once-in-a-lifetime decisions on climate change, medical treatments, urban design, and other strategic issues. The success or failure of e-research is not predetermined, but it is likely to be an assorted mix of some spectacular failures, many incremental improvements, and some as yet undreamed of major successes, much like the creation of the Internet and Web from earlier phases.

Most fields of research have already experienced change in the technologies they use and on which they increasingly depend. For example, the Internet has offered new pathways for researchers to get information and communicate with colleagues. Future advances may introduce an additional step change in the collaborative and computational potential of researchers around the world. This change may be only a chimera or what others see as the dawn of a glittering age of discovery. Will it be for the better or the worse? Who will benefit and who will be disadvantaged? Readers of this book can find informed answers here.

Who Should Read This Book?

The research community, their funders, and the providers of the technologies they use must understand the technological changes taking place in research. This subject is too important to be left to the technical experts and a few tech-savvy researchers in the sciences and humanities. That is why we have edited this book to offer contributions from well-informed authors that can be read by anyone with a serious interest in the future of research and its role in policy and practice.

The authors explain complex technical and substantive areas clearly but without over-simplification, which makes the book of value not only to the growing community of e-researchers, but also to researchers in different domains who are charting their career and planning their training, as well as to managers and professionals involved in research at all levels who need to know the potential risks and opportunities opened up by these innovations. All those with a concern for the quality of research that informs students, business and industry, governments, and civil society should gain much from our contributors. Skeptics and critics as well as enthusiasts and the hopeful regarding e-research will find a balanced approach that treats their views fairly in order to improve understanding of the nature and implications of the expanding and fast-moving set of innovations examined.

Research on the social implications of the Internet and of related information and communication technologies (ICTs) has investigated many sectors, from home uses of the Internet to national and global policymaking. However, it is only beginning to focus on the implications for research itself, perhaps because the subject is too close to home. Social scientists with an interest in science and technology should therefore find this book to be a rich source of material for debate over the social aspects of technical design and implementation as well as their implications for work in an information age.

The technical innovations surrounding ICTs are among the most spectacular transformations of this era, and yet questions still abound over the quality of information that forms the basis of our decisions in banking, finance, international affairs, the sciences, and the humanities. Of course, technology is only one part of a larger complex of factors shaping decisions made by people about how to use technologies to change how they access information and with whom they do and do not collaborate. It is a product of an ecology of choices about information, people, services, and technologies that are constrained by many social and technical factors.

That is what this book is about. It is the outcome of work by a physicist who has led e-science initiatives at the European Organization for Nuclear Research (CERN) and in universities, and by a social scientist who focuses on the social shaping and implications of ICTs. It draws contributions from scholars across a wide range of fields as well as from leaders in the policy world and in business and industry. It is an example of the interdisciplinary collaboration required to conduct and understand the potential of innovations in worldwide research.

Acknowledgments

The editors of this volume led an early project of the James Martin 21st Century School at the University of Oxford. Called "e-Horizons," this project was dedicated to understanding the societal implications of advanced electronic information and communication technologies. It was initially focused on these innovations' implications for research.

The project was critical to launching our collaboration on this book. However, it was through joining forces in several research initiatives and disciplines across the University of Oxford that the editors and their colleagues, including several James Martin Research Fellows, have been able to develop a synthesis of the rise of research-centered computational networks and their global implications for the scope and quality of research across most disciplines. We hope this book fosters a commitment to gaining a better understanding of the broad implications of these developments.

Through e-Horizons, the editors saw the potential of linking the social science base of the Oxford Internet Institute (OII), a department within the Social Sciences Division, with the computational and physical sciences foundation of e-science initiatives at the University.

The OII was founded in 2001 with the mission of investigating the societal implications of the Internet, broadly defined as a network of networks. One of its earliest grants examined the social and institutional aspects of e-science. This project led to a major grant from the U.K. Economic and Social Research Council in support of the Oxford e-Social Science (OeSS) project (RES-149-25-1022), a major node of the U.K. National Centre for e-Social Science. Bill Dutton was a principal investigator of this project, with Marina Jirotka of the Oxford e-Research Centre and Ralph Schroeder at the OII. A second-phase grant for the OeSS was awarded in 2008 (RES-149-25-1082).

Oxford e-science has been supported through a series of grants from the U.K. Engineering and Physical Science Research Council, other U.K. research councils, the U.K. Department of Trade and Industry, investments from companies, as well as the University of Oxford. Through these grants, the Oxford e-Science Centre was established, which in 2007 evolved into the Oxford e-Research Centre (OeRC) within Oxford

University's Mathematics and Physical Sciences Division. The OeRC's remit is to work with research units across the university to enable the use and development of innovative computational and information and communication technologies in multidisciplinary collaborations.

Most chapter authors in this volume were associated with OeSS, and many with other e-science and e-research initiatives across Oxford University. The ability to marshal support from these multiple sources has been essential to the realization of this book. We greatly appreciate the commitment of all those who have sponsored the work that has resulted in this book.

In addition to this institutional support, the editors and authors benefited from the critical reviews and comments of anonymous reviewers for MIT Press as well as of many colleagues around the world who read various essays and chapters while we were preparing the book. It is impossible to mention everyone, but we are particularly grateful to Denis Noble, Martin Kemp, Seamus Ross, Angela Sasse, and Jonathan Zittrain, all of whom participated in the original conference leading to the launch of this book.

Furthermore, our colleagues within e-Horizons and OeSS discussed this book project at each stage in its development, including Annamaria Carusi, Paul David, Matthijs den Besten, Marina Jirotka, Eric Meyer, Michael Parker, Justine Pila, Tina Piper, Lucy Power, Ralph Schroeder, Michael Spence, Anne Trefethen, David Vaver, and Steve Woolgar. Although most focused their contributions on particular chapters and essays, they all were major contributors to the very conception and production of the volume.

Miranda Llewellyn within the Office of the Director of Information Technology at the University of Oxford made a valuable contribution to the management of multiple online and offline versions of dozens of manuscripts over years of their preparation.

Malcolm Peltu, a London-based editorial consultant, helped us to review and edit manuscripts into a uniform style and format, enabling us to provide a far more integrated and coherent volume than would have been possible without his editorial contributions. His work was taken forward by David Sutcliffe, an editor at the OII who put the many manuscripts into shape for MIT Press.

Of course, we are especially grateful to the many contributors to the volume. We initiated their work when we convened an e-Horizons conference in May 2006, followed by an OeSS conference and another e-Horizons conference in 2008. Initial drafts of essays and chapters were generally first developed for these conferences, but they have evolved and been supplemented since then through a continuing series of reviews and revisions. We thank all the authors for their original contributions to this book.

Contributors

Hal Abelson is Class of 1922 professor of computer science and engineering in the Department of Electrical Engineering and Computer Science at MIT.

Robert Ackland is a fellow in the Australian Demographic and Social Research Institute at the Australian National University.

Roger Barga is an architect in external research at the Microsoft Corporation (Redmond, Washington).

Tim Berners-Lee is the director of the World Wide Web Consortium; a senior researcher at the MIT Computer Science and Artificial Intelligence Laboratory; a professor of computer science for the Intelligence, Agents, Multimedia Group in the School of Electronics and Computer Science at the University of Southampton; and a founding director of the Web Science Research Initiative.

Christine L. Borgman is professor and presidential chair in information studies at the University of California, Los Angeles.

Geoffrey C. Bowker is professor and senior scholar in cyberscholarship in the School of Information Studies at the University of Pittsburgh.

Alan Bowman is Camden Professor of Ancient History on the Faculty of Classics at the University of Oxford.

João Caraça is director of the Department of Science of the Fundação Calouste Gulbenkian in Lisbon.

Gustavo Cardoso is a researcher and member of the board of directors of the Centro de Investigação e Estudos de Sociologia and director of the Observatório da Comunicação in Lisbon.

Annamaria Carusi is a senior research associate at the Oxford e-Research Centre.

Paul A. David is professor of economics (emeritus) and senior fellow of the Institute for Economic Policy Research at Stanford University; titular professor of research on the digital economy at l'Ecole Polytechnique and Telecom-ParisTech (Paris); and an emeritus fellow of All Souls College, University of Oxford.

Grace de la Flor is a doctoral student at Linacre College, University of Oxford, and a researcher at the Oxford e-Research Centre.

Matthijs den Besten was a James Martin Research Fellow at the University of Oxford, where he worked with the Oxford Internet Institute, the Oxford e-Research Centre, and the e-Horizons project. He is now at the École Polytechnique, Paris.

David De Roure is professor of computer science in the School of Electronics and Computer Science at the University of Southampton and founding member of the school's Intelligence, Agents, Multimedia Group.

Matthew Dovey is the e-Research program director for the United Kingdom's Joint Information Systems Committee. Prior to holding this position, he worked in the e-Science Centre at the University of Oxford.

Ricardo B. Duque is a professor of Social Studies of Science at the University of Vienna, Austria.

William H. Dutton is director of the Oxford Internet Institute; professor of Internet studies at the University of Oxford; and fellow of Balliol College, University of Oxford.

Paul N. Edwards is an associate professor in the School of Information at the University of Michigan.

Rita Espanha is a researcher at the Centro de Investigação e Estudos de Sociologia and member of the board of directors of the Observatório da Comunicação in Lisbon.

Michael A. Fraser is head of infrastructure systems and services at Oxford University Computing Services.

Jenny Fry is a lecturer in information science at Loughborough University.

Ian Goldin is director of the James Martin 21st Century School at the University of Oxford, where he is a professorial fellow at Balliol College. He came to Oxford from the World Bank, where he was vice president between 2003 and 2006.

Wendy Hall is professor of computer science in the Intelligence, Agents, Multimedia Group of the School of Electronics and Computer Science at the University of Southampton and a founding director of the Web Science Research Initiative.

Tony Hey is corporate vice president of external research at the Microsoft Corporation (Redmond, Washington).

Steven J. Jackson is assistant professor in the School of Information at the University of Michigan.

Paul W. Jeffreys is director of Information Technology at the University of Oxford, professor of computing at the University of Oxford, and professorial fellow of Keble College, University of Oxford.

Marina Jirotka is reader in requirements engineering and director of the Centre for Requirements and Foundations at the Oxford University Computing Laboratory; associate director of the Oxford e-Research Centre; and fellow of St. Cross College at the University of Oxford.

Jane Kaye is Wellcome Trust Fellow in Medical Law at the Ethox Centre of the University of Oxford.

Cory P. Knobel is a doctoral student in the School of Information at the University of Michigan.

Julia Lane is program director of the Science of Science & Innovation Policy Program at the U.S. National Science Foundation.

Xiaoming Li is a professor of computer science and the director of the Institute for Internet Information Studies at Beijing University.

Sharon Lloyd is a research facilitator and project manager at the Oxford University Computing Laboratory.

Christine Madsen is a doctoral student at the Oxford Internet Institute and former manager of the Open Collections Program at the Harvard University Library.

Andrew Martin is deputy director of the University of Oxford Software Engineering Programme; a university lecturer in software engineering; and a fellow of Kellogg College at the University of Oxford.

Sandro Mendonça is a researcher at the Instituto Superior de Ciências do Trabalho e da Empresa and at the Instituto Superior de Economia e Gestão, and a member of the board of directors of the Observatório da Comunicação in Lisbon.

Eric T. Meyer is a research fellow at the Oxford Internet Institute. He received his doctorate in social informatics from Indiana University.

Kieron O'Hara is a senior research fellow in the Intelligence, Agents, Multimedia Group of the School of Electronics and Computer Science at the University of Southampton.

Savas Parastatidis is an architect for technical computing at the Microsoft Corporation (Redmond, Washington).

Michael Parker is a professor of bioethics at the Ethox Centre of the University of Oxford.

Justine Pila is the lecturer in intellectual property law at the University of Oxford; a fellow and senior law tutor at St. Catherine's College, University of Oxford; and senior member of the Oxford Intellectual Property Research Centre.

Tina Piper is an assistant professor and research director of the Centre for Intellectual Property Policy in the Faculty of Law at McGill University, Montreal.

Rob Procter is professor and research director of the Economic and Social Research Council's National Centre for e-Social Science at the University of Manchester.

Ralph Schroeder is a James Martin Research Fellow at the Oxford Internet Institute and course convenor of the institute's master of science in Social Science of the Internet; he was previously a professor in the School of Technology Management and Economics at Chalmers University in Gothenburg, Sweden.

Nigel Shadbolt is a professor of artificial intelligence in the Intelligence, Agents, Multimedia Group of the School of Electronics and Computer Science at the University of Southampton and a founding director of the Web Science Research Initiative.

David Shotton is reader in image bioinformatics and director of the Image Bioinformatics Research Group of the Department of Zoology at the University of Oxford.

Wesley Shrum is a professor of sociology at Louisiana State University, where he focuses on the sociology of science and technology.

Michael Spence is vice chancellor and principal of the University of Sydney and former head of the Social Sciences Division at the University of Oxford.

John Taylor is chairman of Roke Manor Research and chair of the Web Science Trust. He was previously director general of the Research Councils in the U.K. Office of Science and Technology and director of Hewlett-Packard Laboratories Bristol.

Mike Thelwall is professor of information science and leader of the Statistical Cybermetrics Research Group at the University of Wolverhampton; visiting fellow of the Amsterdam Virtual Knowledge Studio; a docent in the Department of Information Studies at Åbo Akademi University; and research associate at the Oxford Internet Institute.

David Vaver is emeritus professor of intellectual property and information technologies law at the University of Oxford and professor of intellectual property law at the Osgoode Hall Law School of York University, Toronto.

Andrew Warr is a researcher at Google.

John Wilbanks is vice president of the Science Commons project at Creative Commons. He came to Creative Commons from a fellowship in Semantic Web for life sciences at the World Wide Web Consortium.

Yorick Wilks is a senior research fellow at the Oxford Internet Institute and professor of computer science at the University of Sheffield.

Paul Wouters is program leader of the Virtual Knowledge Studio for the Humanities and Social Sciences in Amsterdam, and professor of knowledge dynamics at Erasmus University in Rotterdam.

Marcus Antonius Ynalvez is assistant professor of sociology in the Department of Behavioral Sciences at Texas A&M International University.

Jonathan J. H. Zhu is a professor of media and communication at the City University of Hong Kong and a Changjiang chaired professor of communication at the Renmin University of China.

World Wide Research: An Introduction

William H. Dutton and Paul W. Jeffreys

Researchers across all fields of study are being presented with exciting opportunities as well as significant threats by the use of advanced Internet capabilities, innovative computational networks, and related information and communication technologies (ICTs). Such technological resources and applications are enabling a growing spectrum of researchers to join collaborations that share a common network or large-scale sources of data and information.[1] The changes in research practices enabled by these innovations may have widespread and major implications for the quality and value of research.[2]

This book's aim is to assess the implications of these developments in computation and networking that are shaping the practice and outcomes of research—which we refer to generically and discuss more fully in this introduction as "e-research"—from a variety of interrelated social, institutional, and technical perspectives. The volume offers many tangible examples and case studies to help anchor readers in its exploration of the shaping and implications of e-research across different disciplines and institutions in many nations around the world.

The Significance of ICTs for Research and Society

Jacques Ellul (1964) warned his readers decades ago that technologies were a means to an end, but were being viewed as ends in themselves as society became increasingly focused on "technique." This book focuses on the ends and the means in e-research by examining the possible research outcomes and exploring both the potential and the limits of the supporting technologies. The wide significance of the ends being targeted—the improved quality of research and the informing of related theory, policy, and practice—also highlights the importance of the underpinning technologies in achieving that end.

The volume describes the promise of new approaches to research, but we also emphasize that a one-way relationship between technological potential and actual outcomes cannot be assumed. For example, despite the pace of ICT innovation, many still lack trust in the quality of information they are presented with. This refrain has been heard so often that the questions it asks so vividly have become commonplace: "Where is the wisdom we have lost in knowledge? / Where is the knowledge we have lost in information?"

These lines, from the Choruses to T. S. Eliot's 1934 play *The Rock*, are at the heart of a modern conundrum.[3] In an age suffused with information enabled by innovation in ICTs, there is widespread uncertainty across many sectors of society over the quality of information. The global financial crisis that emerged in 2008 painfully illustrated this point, showing that decision makers cannot be complacent about the quality of information on which they make decisions.

Despite advances in ICTs, a critical challenge continues to be our ability to trust knowledge and information drawn from the growing deluge of data available at the fingertips of anyone with access to electronic technologies. Will the technologies be used to enable research to be pursued more effectively, or will they set up significant new barriers? Will innovations in the means result in higher-quality research or in a deterioration of what can be achieved? In examining answers to these kinds of questions, this book offers a critical perspective on the changes described in order to help those who seek to enhance associated policy and practice to chart a course that might avoid the emergence of a world "lost in information."

We show how uses of e-Research innovations can transform—for better or worse—the processes of discovery in ways that might either enhance or hinder our ability to grapple with many substantial problems facing the twenty-first century. In particular, we identify the nature and dynamics of the many factors that shape and constrain advances in e-research and its application.

World Wide Research: Seeking to Create a Virtuous Cycle of Innovation

The e-research developments illustrated in this book encompass activities that use a wide spectrum of sophisticated ICT capabilities, some of which have come under specific classifications such as "e-science" and "e–social science" (chapters 1 and 2). A vision of the enormous potential gains these innovations might bring has led to a broad range of initiatives in many countries. Many chapters discuss major pioneering e-research national initiatives, such as those related to "e-infrastructure" in the United Kingdom's e-Science Programme and to "cyberinfrastructure" in the United States (e.g., chapters 2 and 7). These initiatives typically involve large-scale data sets and are conducted via distributed collaborations that leverage access to powerful computing capabilities and collaborative environments for undertaking research.

A key example of an innovation in computation and networking that has been focused on supporting research is the Grid (see box I.1). The Grid, advanced Internet applications, and other research-centered computational networks (RCNs)[4] have become folded into broad definitions of e-infrastructures for research.

Box I.1

The Grid: A Powerful Distributed-Computing Service

Grid computing harnesses the capabilities of multiple computers to target a common purpose. It has become a well-used core element of e-infrastructures, using software that enables many computers in the same or distributed locations to work together as if they were a more powerful single system. This concept evolved from developments in the 1970s aimed at using "distributed-computing" techniques to make optimum use of available computing resources, such as by coordinating the deployment of processing and storage resources at places other than at the physical location of a researcher seeking an answer to a problem.

The pioneers of this technique (Foster and Kesselman 2004) coined the name "Grid" to indicate their vision of providing a computing utility equivalent to an electricity grid, into which users can "plug" their own systems. This utility offers enormous potential for giving many people access to virtually unbounded computational capacity (Foster 2003). Its emergence was one of the driving forces behind early e-research initiatives (Berman, Fox, and Hey 2003; see also chapter 2 in this volume). A related form of providing distributed-computing power of much value to support research has emerged through what is called the "Cloud" (essay 2.1).

The use of a growing range of RCNs might break the technical, geographical, institutional, and disciplinary boundaries that constrain research creativity and productivity. If implemented effectively, RCNs might offer flexible and sustained support for increased participation, improved access, and new ways to combine resources and skills. These results would have an impact on shrinking or expanding psychological as well as physical distances among colleagues around the world (Friedman 2005), but not necessarily spelling the "death of distance" (Cairncross 1997). In fact, the opposite might well be the case. New technologies can also create new centers of worldwide expertise. These centers might lead to a concentration of related resources and know-how, where geography would matter even more and inequalities in access to the tools of research would maintain and enhance local and global economic divides. This two-edged potential is typical of the possibilities tied to advances in technology in general.

Our edited collection focuses on how e-research is reshaping and will continue to reshape not only how research is done but, more important, its outcomes. These results emerge as a consequence of the way the tools are used to "reconfigure access" to research-related people, information, services, and technologies (chapter 1). Our aim is to create an understanding of this process in a way that enables researchers and an array of other relevant actors to generate a "virtuous cycle." This cycle would facilitate major advances in RCN innovations across the sciences and humanities, fostering advances in research that would then feed back to support further innovation in computational networks.

By anchoring our discussion in specific research settings, the book identifies and analyzes a promising set of practical developments and outcomes tied to e-research innovations. All actors involved in research should consider these outcomes carefully to identify how the latter can enable new approaches to the conduct of work in the actors' own fields.

The Social and Technical Underpinnings of Change in Research

The themes of this book's critical examination of e-research innovations are interwoven around the two interrelated but inseparable forces and constraints affecting the developments it highlights: the technical and social shapers of change. The expectations raised by new technological capabilities underpinning e-research are not based simply on a blind faith in technology, but on a developing consensus that advances in ICTs enable many new choices for researchers regarding how they can conduct their work as well as on the observation that parallel changes are occurring in other sectors of society. The social dimension includes the institutional infrastructures as well as the legal and ethical issues that shape, facilitate, and constrain the development and application of ICTs (e.g., see part III and chapter 12).

The ways these and other factors shape emerging opportunities and challenges are illustrated throughout the book—for example, to highlight the way that some data are shared, but some need to be kept private and secure. Technology can similarly enable more open access to research, but privacy, confidentiality, or other ethical considerations will sometimes preclude that access. Although new collaborative software and systems promise to support virtual teams, cooperation can be hampered by disciplinary demarcations or institutional concerns about issues such as intellectual property rights and liability.

RCNs can be used to transform both how researchers do their work and the quality and scope of the outcomes produced. Investigations across the disciplines rely increasingly on powerful computational and networking tools through nearly all stages: observation; distributed collaboration and data sharing; modeling and simulation; and dissemination and publishing. These tools also open a window on the possible future of communication more generally, just as the development of the Internet and Web helped to generate new tools for research collaboration (see box I.2).

Types of Research-Centered Computational Networks

The pattern of innovations in computation and networking that support research defy any simple trajectory. They have sometimes moved from initial specialized areas

Box I.2

Inventing the Internet and the World Wide Web

The Internet was itself a product of efforts to support research, in that it was triggered by the ARPANET network developed by the U.S. Department of Defense's Advanced Research Projects Agency, beginning in about 1969. The aim was to support the sharing of computing facilities among computer scientists and engineers. From the 1970s, a variety of academic network initiatives began to evolve, including the National Science Foundation's (NSF) NSFNET[a] in the United States (c. 1984) and GÉANT[b] across Europe (c. 2000). ARPANET was moved beyond academia in 1974 under the Internet name, but has continued to support all phases of research.

The Internet's success was limited until a team at the European Organization for Nuclear Research (CERN)—including a computer scientist trained in physics, Tim Berners-Lee, and colleagues in particle physics—invented the World Wide Web (c. 1989) as a means of sharing documents within a collaborative science project. In this way, the Web was invented by domain researchers, users, working with computer scientists, within a "big science" project, requiring large-scale, computationally demanding ICT resources (e.g., CERN's high-energy physics research).

Many other innovations in graphical user interfaces and browsers, such as Mosaic, contributed to the eventual success of the Internet and the Web through a series of top-down processes, but also more bottom-up processes of invention and diffusion.

Notes:
a. See http://www.nsf.gov/about/history/nsf0050/internet/launch.htm.
b. See http://www.geant.net/.
Sources: Adapted from Abbate 1999, Reid 2000, and Leiner, Cerf, Clark, et al. 2003.

---

requiring enormous computational power to other hard sciences before moving into the social sciences, law, and the humanities. However, there are many pathways to innovation, including user-led innovations. As David de Roure explains in essay 2.2, social networking and other Web applications that support a growing range of collaborations and interactions are increasingly moving from the world of everyday Internet use to the research arena, not just vice versa.

Despite many pathways to diffusion, similar advanced computing and data center capabilities are forming critical aspects of the infrastructure that enables e-research, the Internet, and the Web to offer what have become routine online uses in everyday life, such as Web searches, email, and other utility computing services (Carr 2008). In such ways, the boundaries between the RCNs that support research and the ICTs of everyday life increasingly intersect. This book explores this trend, while focusing primarily on RCNs, such as research applications of Grid computing. For simplicity, we generally use the term *e-research* to refer to the wide array of research activities encompassed because it is not tied to a particular disciplinary area and is therefore suited to encompassing the broader potential of the application of ICTs to research. However, we occasionally refer to related terms, many of which are equally general, but which have become tied to particular areas of application, such as:

• *e-science*   Used by the United Kingdom's e-Science Programme to denote "the systematic development of research methods that exploit advanced computational thinking."[5] Associated with worldwide collaboration in key areas of science, e-science moves to build "e-infrastructures" that can sustain the long-term growth of e-research (chapters 11 and 12 focus specifically on e-science).
• *Cyberinfrastructure*   Used in the United States to refer to RCNs in an equivalent way to e-infrastructure in the U.K. e-Science Programme (U.S. NSF 2007; essay 1.1).
• *e–social science*   Application and adaptation within the social sciences of many of the technologies and tools developed in e-Science (see chapter 6).
• *e-humanities*   Adapts technical innovation based on e-Infrastructures to the humanities, such as in libraries and rare collections (U.S. NSF 2003; chapter 3).

Despite the similarity of these broad conceptions, each has become tied to particular communities of researchers and periods of time in the development of this emerging field. This is one reason why the terminology chosen in this book, such as *research-centered computational networks*, is not tied to a particular community—however, a particular terminology is used when it is significant to the contributor or to the disciplinary or historical context.

The Multidisciplinary Range of e-Research: Changing How Researchers Work

Examples of e-Research Benefits
This volume aims to capture the potential significance of e-research in changing the nature of research processes and practices, such as in increasing collaborative opportunities. It does so by offering a concrete sense of how these capabilities are being applied across the disciplines, with illustrations of the many interrelated facets of the subject. Table I.1 gives a flavor of the new opportunities opened by applying human intelligence creatively to emerging RCNs.

Cross-cutting Themes
The examples in table I.1 illustrate some key themes in the book that apply across disciplines, such as:

• RCNs applied to outer space and microscopic observation demonstrate that researchers can change how they visualize objects of study and what they can see, thereby shaping the quality and impact of their own work and that of their colleagues involved in collaborations.

• E-research applied to environmental and biological sciences points to the potential transformation of the way information is collected, analyzed, and viewed.

• The use of embedded submarine sensor networks illustrates that e-research does not necessarily substitute for direct observation of events or other phenomena, but can be used to assist researchers to be where they need to be in order to observe rare or critical events or processes.

• The Hubble telescope project is based on "softer" social and institutional infrastructures of international and interinstitutional collaboration, financed by many government agencies, indicating the centrality of such institutional arrangements as joint-funding models in the support of worldwide research.

• New forms of data visualization can help researchers better communicate their theories and research to a broader public—for example, in the social sciences, humanities, and biology.

• The biological stream of e-science work highlights major ethical issues, such as questions about patients' privacy and confidentiality (essay 8.2) or other research subjects (chapter 8). These issues might constrain some e-research activities despite the activities' potentially beneficial outcomes (e.g., in gene research to enable physicians to identify and select out embryos carrying the genes associated with breast or prostate cancer).

Fostering e-Research and Innovation

New Environments for Researchers

Separate e-research developments have been brought together to create environments offering easy access to a wide range of relevant hardware and software digital resources. Such environments have generally become known as a "collaboratories" in the United States and as "virtual research laboratories" or "virtual research environments" (VRE) in Europe (chapter 10). These environments are designed to support the effective operation of collaborations and as much of the research process as appropriate for any given activity or role by providing a framework into which selected existing and new tools, services, data sets, and other resources can be plugged.

A feature of this kind of environment is the ability to underpin the workflow requirements of a particular research community (box I.3). However, the importing of engineering approaches into other disciplines has raised some concerns about the possibly unwelcome "industrialization" of the "art" of research as a creative process (see chapter 6).

There is a further sense in which e-Research is opening out. Many ICT innovations developed initially for scientific research have also been opened to broader user bases, as shown by the way in which the Internet evolved and grew from the U.S. Defense

Table I.1
Examples of the Multidisciplinary Range of e-Research Applications

Research Area	Examples
Observation of outer space	The U.S. National Aeronautics and Space Administration's orbiting Hubble telescope[a] integrates advances in satellites, optics, and computational science to enable scientists to see planets, stars, and galaxies that would otherwise be invisible. The images obtained can be accessed from anywhere in the world through the Internet.
Exploration of microscopic worlds	"Telescience" centers use advanced electron microscopes to view matter so small it could not be seen previously.[b] A Web portal offers remote control of such microscopes to scientists without access to similar local capabilities.[c]
Physics experiments	The European Organization for Nuclear Research (CERN) Grid is shared by particle physics researchers around the world, including thousands of scientists involved in high-energy physics experiments (Tuertscher 2008). Core aspects of collaboration across the world are managed using email, listservs,[d] and Web-based documents.
Social sciences	Research models to visualize social processes, computer modeling, and simulation of social and political networking (essay 2.1) are used in studying large-scale urban environments (Borning, Friedman, Davis, et al. 2005), such as in showing how rising water levels linked to climate change might affect London.[e]
Data visualization	New ways of visualizing information help to transform researchers' ability to model and display objects of research (e.g., to improve analysis of underlying patterns critical to reaching and explaining findings in many fields, from biological and environmental systems to social and economic trends).
Environmental and marine sciences	Embedded networked sensors (essay 4.1) enable the study of movements related to earthquakes in order to create powerful models to assist with early warnings. Placed under water, such sensors mean that marine biologists can respond to detections of actual events rather than having to plan expeditions in the hope of seeing such events occur.
Biological sciences	Complex, realistic, ICT-enabled models aid understanding of the working of the body, such as the heart (Noble 2002). E-research capabilities are also central to progress in genomics (e.g., the freely available International HapMap Project).[f]
Humanities and the arts	The arts and humanities can benefit from e-research, as in the virtual "haptic museum" (which enables visitors to manipulate three-dimensional models of objects)[g] or online access to high-quality digital facsimiles of valued historical documents and the tools to interpret and analyze them (essay 3.2) or in the rendering of a two-dimensional painting in three dimensions.[h]

Notes:

a. For information about the Hubble telescope, see http://hubble.nasa.gov/.

b. For example, the United States has supported the National Center for Microscopy and Imaging Research (NCMIR, http://www.ncrr.nih.gov/), and Japan has created a similar program in Osaka.

c. For a description of major telescience projects, including the NCMIR, see http://www.super computingonline.com/nl.php?sid=5183. More details of the U.K. Research Councils' e-Science Programme are at http://www.rcuk.ac.uk/escience/default.htm.

Table I.1

(continued)

d. A listserv facilitates the distribution of messages to members through an electronic mailing list, which can support discussion groups based on common interests.

e. This illustration is drawn from the work of the Geographic Virtual Urban Environments project at the University College London's Centre for Advanced Spatial Analysis (see http://www.casa.ucl .ac.uk/projects/projectDetail.asp?ID=57).

f. HapMap supports research into genetics associated with human disease (see http://www .hapmap.org/).

g. This project, conducted by the Integrated Media Systems Center of the University of Southern California, generated links with a wide variety of projects that were experimenting with touch in virtual environments in many fields (McLaughlin, Hespanha, and Sukhatme 2002).

h. Martin Kemp (2006) is a pioneer in new ways to apply computation to the visualization of art.

Department's Advanced Research Projects Agency Network (ARPANET). The global positioning system (GPS), which uses Earth-orbiting satellites to transmit signals, is a widely used development that followed a similar trajectory. It was initially developed for military applications (e.g., tracking movements of soldiers and equipment) but has become generally available as navigation guides for motorists. GPS can also be used in e–social science applications, such as in research that tracks the travel patterns of members of households enrolled in transportation studies, illustrating the diffusion of e-research innovations across disciplines.

Implications of Innovations in Research for Social and Economic Well-Being

The opening out of e-research means it increasingly intersects with general Web capabilities that offer parallel types of collaboration. Table I.2 highlights the key stages in the ongoing evolution of Internet and Web capabilities and applications toward these kinds of intersections.

A number of groups (e.g., OpenScience[6] and Science Commons[7]) have been set up to promote more open e-research technologies and applications (see essay 11.2). Neuro-commons[8] is such an initiative, providing an open platform that offers free powerful tools to allow scientists to improve the efficiency and effectiveness of searching for particular information. De Roure (essay 2.2) highlights the prospects for further broadening of e-research through more open forms.

The consequences of enhancing the value of research can be immense in many fields affecting everyday life and health. For instance, the use of e-research in biomedical disciplines is bringing more insight into the human genome and related tools that may enhance individual and social well-being. Business and industry also depend heavily on ICTs, which are increasingly including e-research capabilities. For instance, commercial enterprises are employing the Grid for the search and mining of massive

Box I.3

Workflow Requirements: The Diffusion of Engineering Techniques

The processes through which work is expected to flow to produce a desired outcome can be described or modeled as a sequence of operations (i.e., as a process in a chart that depicts the flow of operations required to conduct a survey). Workflow tools can coordinate elements of calculation or analysis processes by enabling researchers to select, edit, or add components easily. This general process originated in operations research and engineering, where parts of the workflow and links between steps can be completed by the supporting ICT services. It can be more widely adapted through e-research—for example, to assist the organization, analysis, and graphical presentation of data.

Table I.2

Types of Collaborative Networking and the Evolving Web

Phase	Type	Description
Collaboration 1.0	Sharing	The Web's original design, aimed essentially at finding and sharing electronic documents and information.
Collaboration 2.0	Contributing	Moving to a greater focus on interactions between people and groups, and blurring the distinction between producers and users of information on the Web. Typified by social networking and user-generated content services such as YouTube, Second Life, and the wider "blogosphere" of individuals' comments and reporting.
Collaboration 3.0	Cocreating	Developing and applying collaborative software to support cooperative working between groups and individuals, including networked research collaborations and other activities involving the cocreation or coproduction of reports, software, and other outputs.

Source: Adapted from Dutton 2008.

amounts of data to identify shifting consumer preferences or borrowers' credit worthiness—with some well-recognized limitations. And pharmaceutical companies are increasingly developing new medicinal drugs by searching through research results as a complement to clinical trials of newly developed drugs.

These kinds of developments demonstrate that e-research infrastructures are not simply strategies for better research, but key to everyday life and to global competition and collaboration. It is for this reason that many governments are supporting e-research and e-infrastructure initiatives, seeing them as critical to national industrial strategies in a networked society. The social and technological infrastructures and capabilities of e-research are particularly significant elements because they can underpin or undermine the quality of research and therefore of any potential benefits arising from these innovations.

Risks Tied to e-Research

Although we identify the numerous and often astonishing possible benefits of e-research, we also take a critical perspective on these innovations. This balanced approach helps us to assess both the potential prizes and risks at stake, which determine whether investment in the promise of RCNs is realized or not. For instance, e-research might privilege some researchers over others, such as those with less funding or from less-prestigious centers.

A core area of concern is to understand where and how e-research might boost or undermine the nature, quality, and agenda of research. For example, choices made about the use of e-research might lead some researchers to substitute virtual observation for more grounded experience in the field (see chapter 6). Many social scientists use ethnographic methods to study work, social and cultural processes, and behavior through detailed observation, documenting and analyzing how people behave and feel in particular contexts (e.g., see Hine 2008, an insightful study of e-science based on observing discussions and forums among scientists). Such study has usually been carried out by researchers who participate in the environments they are observing. If online approaches to ethnographic research become more common, how should researchers balance virtual online research with real experience? Or is this distinction perhaps becoming too blurred to be useful anymore?

E-research also raises new legal, institutional, and ethical issues, such as over privacy and data protection. Digital trails left by the use of networked services challenge efforts to protect personal privacy and the confidentiality of personal information vis-à-vis not only governments, but also researchers. For example, concern would be raised if social scientists tracked individuals through GPS or video recordings of public spaces without their consent. Collaboration in open-science medical trials may be put at risk if sharing data openly across jurisdictions proves to be intractable for institutional rather than technical reasons, such as conflicts over the ownership or confidentiality of data (see essay 7.1).

Outline of the Book

We employed three complementary strategies to achieve the book's objectives, as outlined earlier in this introductory chapter:

• Reaching out to contributors from a wide range of relevant disciplines. This task was assisted by contacts established by the editors during their careers within different disciplinary backgrounds, spanning the social and natural sciences.
• Extending a core foundation of work developed from a related set of projects in e-research based at the University of Oxford through contributions from research associates across the university and the United Kingdom, as well as colleagues from North America, the rest of Europe, and Asia.

• Including a range of short essays from world-leading experts in specialized areas of e-research, wherever a specific need was identified to deepen the coverage of that chapter.

The Structure

The book's guiding framework aims to inform a critical understanding of the ways in which the new technologies and processes can reconfigure the processes and outcomes of research. To achieve this goal, the book offers many tangible examples and case studies of the social and institutional shaping and implications of e-research across different disciplines and institutions. It is organized into four main parts:

• Part I, "Foundations" (chapter 1 and 2), sets out the basic themes and issues addressed, including an historical perspective, an outline of the book's conceptual frame, identification of key technological landmarks, and an overview of developments and implications more widely, beyond research arenas.
• Part II, "State of the Practice" (chapters 3–5), looks at how the emphasis placed on the social and institutional shaping of e-research does not diminish the role played by the underlying pace of technological innovation in giving momentum to the rapid advance of the research potential explored. This section exemplifies key underpinning technologies and application exemplars, including how the technology can be made more usable.
• Part III, "Social Shaping of Infrastructures and Practices" (chapters 6–8), provides a more detailed examination of some of the broader research and of the institutional and ethical dimensions being affected by the take-up of new processes and practices made possible by e-infrastructures.
• Part IV, "Implications for Research" (chapters 9–12), focuses on what the innovations analyzed earlier mean for research policy and practices, including the nature and politics of moving toward a more open science environment and the global implications for developing counties and regions.

A short summary coda after part IV is followed by a glossary and a list of abbreviations and acronyms used in this book.

Chapter Outlines

Foundations of e-Research   Chapter 1 (Dutton) explains why the concept of reconfiguring access to information, people, services, and technologies through e-research offers a coherent thematic structure within which contributions to this book can illuminate different aspects. Tied to this chapter are three essays: Geoffrey Bowker and his colleagues identify shared patterns, processes, and emergent lessons learned from examining the history of cyberinfrastructure developments; Mike Thelwall discusses how e-research might reconfigure research "winners and losers"; and Robert Ackland examines possible impacts on the rise of research "superstars."

Chapter 2 (Jeffreys) gives an introductory perspective on the history and future of e-research and the technologies it encompasses, distinguishing between the applications and the technologies underpinning them. The associated essays cover the emergence of the "Cloud" to complement the Grid's distributed-computing capabilities (Hey, Barga, and Parastatidis) and the wide promises and threats of the opening out of RCNs to general publics (De Roure) and to business and nations (Taylor).

Illustrations of e-Research Practices   Starting part II's exploration of the state of e-research practice, chapter 3 (Meyer, Madsen, and Fry) focuses on the future of libraries in an era where digital resources and collections rise in importance. Related essays move into the requirements for facilitating access to specific types of resources associated with libraries and digital collections: image repositories (Shotton) and ancient manuscripts (Bowman).

Chapter 4 (Wilks and den Besten) describes in depth some key technologies for selecting, gathering, analyzing, organizing, and displaying information to help researchers cope with the digital data flood being generated by e-research capabilities. The essays that follow this chapter provide further illustrations of related issues and solutions, such as embedded sensor networks (Borgman); methods of efficiently identifying digital objects (Fraser); and the emergence of the Semantic Web as a more effective way of sharing information than traditional document-based Web methods (O'Hara, Berners-Lee, Hall, and Shadbolt).

In chapter 5, Grace de la Flor, Marina Jirotka, Sharon Lloyd, and Andrew Warr examine, with examples and recommendations, how difficulties in using e-research systems can be overcome by adopting appropriate requirements analysis and usability design principles. Essays on this theme discuss examples of the ways in which designers and developers have addressed these issues (Martin on building trust in ICT systems and Thelwall on affordances provided by Web 2.0's social-networking innovations).

Social Shaping of e-Research   Part III's attention to the social dimensions of e-research starts with William Dutton and Eric Meyer's review of how e-research can transform the work of social scientists and how social scientists can help to shape e-research capabilities and outcomes (chapter 6). The risks they identify underscore the importance of research on the social factors shaping e-research. An essay by Rob Procter further explores how e-infrastructures can best support the social sciences. Jonathan Zhu and Xiaoming Li's essay illustrates the degree to which computational innovations take the availability of much data for granted, which is not always the case in the social sciences in some contexts, such as in rapidly developing nations—China, for example.

In chapter 7, Paul David and Michael Spence consider the institutional infrastructures for global research networks in the public sector. Building on the findings of a survey and case studies of e-science projects, the authors argue that "soft" institutional infrastructures are required to facilitate the formation and conduct of collaborative public-sector research projects, especially those that aim to be truly global in scope. Connected essays investigate two key aspects of such infrastructures that need special attention: ownership of research data or processes (Piper and Vaver) and the role of authorship in protecting the integrity of scientific collaboration (Pila).

Bill Dutton and Tina Piper address in chapter 8 the politics of privacy, confidentiality, and ethics relating to e-research, including the main directions in which existing research practices are challenged (e.g., how more open collaborative methods might lead to changes in institutional arrangements that better protect ethical standards). Michael Parker then examines such ethical and moral dimensions in detail, and Jane Kaye examines their implications specifically in genomics. Julia Lane directs her related essay to the technical and institutional issues involved in protecting personal data.

Broader Implications for Research   Part IV draws together the key dimensions of the developments discussed in the book. It starts in chapter 9 with an analysis by Jenny Fry and Ralph Schroeder of how e-research might reconfigure the boundaries within research landscapes. They describe key dimensions of the variation across disciplines and how these dimensions influence the use and impact of e-research. In the only essay tied to this chapter, Paul Wouters focuses on the implications of these developments for research agendas more generally.

In chapter 10, Annamaria Carusi and Marina Jirotka discuss the potential of new virtual forms of organizing research through concepts such as VREs and collaboratories. They assess to what extent these concepts may foster new forms of collaboration. They identify different types of VREs and evaluate their implications for research practices across the disciplines. Matthew Dovey contributes an essay on the future of VREs.

Paul David, Matthijs den Besten, and Ralph Schroeder investigate in chapter 11 the scope and limits of ICT-enabled support for more open forms of research. Using findings from e-science projects, they propose a framework for helping to understand where, when, and to what extent openness in research may be expected to advance in harmony with the growing deployment of wider e-research capabilities. In their related essay, Gustavo Cardoso, João Caraça, Rita Espanha, and Sandro Mendonça provide a broad perspective on the international politics of open access. A specific example of this issue is the basis of John Wilbanks and Hal Abelson's essay on the differences between open access and open viewing.

The main book chapters conclude with Marcus Ynalvez, Ricardo Duque, and Wesley Shrum's explanation in chapter 12 of why e-research outcomes will depend on how researchers' choices in specific localized contexts reconfigure the nature and dynamics of the social interactions involved in knowledge production using digital technologies. Based on their studies of the shaping of research in developing nations, their conclusions reinforce this book's overarching theme of the significance of the ways in which RCNs are being used to reconfigure access to information, expertise, and experience in worldwide research.

A final coda summarizes briefly some of the major issues and themes raised by the contributions to this collection, emphasizing the need to focus on the ends of research in the design and use of RCNs, such as the quality of research, rather than on technically defined outcomes derived from features enabled by the technologies, such as collaboration or data sharing.

Notes

1. Major overviews of research-centered innovations in the sciences and humanities include Hey and Trefethen 2003, Atkins 2005, and Olsen, Zimmerman, and Bos 2008.

2. Treatments of the role of e-research on the practices of scholars include Hine 2006 and Borgman 2007.

3. For instance, *Knowledge Lost in Information* is the title of a major report on digital libraries sponsored by the U.S. National Science Foundation (2003).

4. We use the term *research-centered computational network* to indicate the high computational element of the "big science" projects that gave e-research its strong momentum in the early twenty-first century and that continue to play a significant role in e-infrastructure developments.

5. This definition has been attributed to Professor Malcolm Atkinson, the United Kingdom's e-Science envoy. See http://www.rcuk.ac.uk/escience/default.htm.

6. See http://www.openscience.org.

7. See http://sciencecommons.org.

8. See http://sciencecommons.org/projects/data/.

References

Abbate, J. 1999. *Inventing the Internet.* Cambridge, MA: MIT Press.

Atkins, D. 2005. "Transformation through cyberinfrastructure-based knowledge environments." In *Transforming enterprise*, ed. W. H. Dutton, B. Kahin, R. O'Callaghan, and A. W. Wyckoff. Cambridge, MA: MIT Press, 155–176.

Berman, F., G. Fox, and A. J. G. Hey, eds. 2003. *Grid computing: Making the global infrastructure a reality.* Chichester, UK: Wiley.

Borgman, C. 2007. *Scholarship in the digital age: Information, infrastructure, and the Internet*. Cambridge, MA: MIT Press. See: http://mitpress.mit.edu/catalog/item/default.asp?ttype=2&tid=11333.

Borning, A., B. Friedman, J. Davis, and P. Lin. 2005. "Informing public deliberation: Value sensitive design of indicators for a large-scale urban simulation." In *ECSW 2005: Proceedings of the Ninth European Conference on Computer-Supported Cooperative Work, 18–22 September 2005*, ed. H. Gellersen et al. The Hague: Springer, 449–468.

Cairncross, F. 1997. *The death of distance: How the communication revolution will change our lives*. Boston: Harvard Business School Press.

Carr, N. 2008. *The big switch: Rewiring the world, from Edison to Google*. New York: W. W. Norton.

Dutton, W. H. 2008. "The wisdom of collaborative network organizations: Capturing the value of networked individuals." *Prometheus 26* (3):211–230.

Ellul, J. 1964. *The technological society*. New York: Alfred A. Knopf.

Foster, I. 2003. "The Grid: Computing without bounds." *Scientific American 288* (4):78–85.

Foster, I., and C. Kesselman. 2004. *The Grid: Blueprint for a new computing infrastructure*. 2d ed. San Francisco: Morgan Kaufmann.

Friedman, T. L. 2005. *The world is flat: A brief history of the twenty-first century*. New York: Farrar, Straus, and Giroux.

Hey, T., and A. Trefethen. 2003. "The data deluge: An e-science perspective." In *Grid computing: Making the global infrastructure a reality*, ed. F. Berman, G. Fox, and A. J. G. Hey. Chichester, UK: Wiley, 809–824.

Hine, C. M. 2006. *New infrastructures for knowledge production: Understanding e-science*. Hershey, PA: Information Science. See: http://www.amazon.com/New-Infrastructures-Knowledge-Production-Understanding/dp/1591407176#citing.

Hine, C. M. 2008. *Systematics as cyberscience: Computers, change, and continuity in science*. Cambridge, MA: MIT Press.

Kemp, M. 2006. *Seen, unseen: Art, science, and intuition from Leonardo to the Hubble Telescope*. Oxford, UK: Oxford University Press.

Leiner, B. M., V. G. Cerf, D. D. Clark, R. E. Kahn, L. Kleinrock, D. C. Lynch, J. Postel, L. G. Roberts, and S. Wolff. 2003. *A brief history of the Internet*. Reston, VA: Internet Society. See: http://www.isoc.org/internet/history/brief.shtml.

McLaughlin, M. L., J. Hespanha, and G. Sukhatme, eds. 2002. *Touch in virtual environments*. New York: Prentice Hall.

Noble, D. 2002. "Modeling the heart—from genes to cells to the whole organ." *Science 295* (5560):1678–1682.

Olsen, G., A. Zimmerman, and N. Bos, eds. 2008. *Scientific collaboration on the Internet*. Cambridge, MA: MIT Press. See: http://mitpress.mit.edu/catalog/item/default.asp?ttype=2&tid=11603.

Reid, R. H. 2000. *Architects of the Web.* New York: Wiley.

Tuertscher, P. 2008. *The ATLAS collaboration: A distributed problem-solving network in big science.* Working Paper. Oxford, UK: Oxford Internet Institute, Oxford University.

U.S. National Science Foundation (NSF). 2003. *Knowledge lost in information.* Report of the NSF Workshop on Research Directions for Digital Libraries. Mechanisburg, PA: School of Information Science, University of Pittsburgh. Available at: http://www.sis.pitt.edu/~dlwkshop/report.pdf.

U.S. National Science Foundation (NSF). 2007. *Cyberinfrastructure vision for 21st century discovery.* North Arlington, VA: Cyberinfrastructure Council, NSF. Available at: http://www.nsf.gov/pubs/2007/nsf0728/index.jsp.

I Foundations

This opening part has two chapters that provide the foundations for the remainder of the book. The first develops our central theme: that technical change in research is enabling the reconfiguration of access to information, expertise, and experience across the disciplines. The second describes the main technological capabilities underpinning e-research as well as the economic and policy forces that have shaped related development around the world. Although each author in this volume brings a unique perspective, these two chapters help provide a framework for integrating and understanding the broader significance of all contributions. This part also identifies and defines key terms that are used throughout the book.

In chapter 1, Bill Dutton explains how choices about the design and use of information and communication technologies (ICTs), from the telegraph to the Internet, have changed or "reconfigured" access to the vital resources of information, people, services, and technologies. He shows how this reconfiguration applies to research as much as to everyday life and describes why a perspective on it offers a coherent analytical framework to encompass the central themes emerging from contributions to this book. Many brief examples are provided, which are supplemented by more detailed cases in the chapters that follow. These examples indicate the multitude of ways in which emerging research-centered computational networks (e.g., Grid computing) can enable actors in the research process to reconfigure access to information, expertise, and experience—critical resources underpinning the quality of research across all disciplines.

Three essays are tied to this chapter. In the first, Geof Bowker, Paul Edwards, Steven Jackson, and Cory Knobel describe shared patterns, processes, and lessons learned from studies of cyberinfrastructures, in particular the social processes shaping technologies and their implications. Michael Thelwall's essay for this chapter examines techniques of Webmetrics (also known as "Webometrics") that can be used to identify the winners and losers in different research arenas, including how they can shed light on the dynamics of the growth of disciplines and specialisms. Rob Ackland focuses his essay on how e-research might reconfigure the research landscape by looking at the emergence of research "superstars," suggesting that worldwide research networks might facilitate a greater concentration of scientific authority or impact in some fields.

To complement chapter 1's analysis of the fundamental changes in research processes made possible using network-enabled collaborations, Paul Jeffreys explores in chapter 2 the history and potential directions of developments in this new kind of research activity. He highlights the spectrum of advanced ICT capabilities encompassed, such as very large data sets and high-speed computational capabilities, and distinguishes e-research applications from the technologies underpinning them (i.e., e-infrastructures). He also identifies important initiatives that have given momentum to e-research progress.

The essays associated with chapter 2 examine in more detail the key technological developments that Jeffreys explores. Tony Hey, Roger Barga, and Savas Parastatidis examine the emergence of "Cloud computing," a development that is likely to provide valuable access for researchers to very large computing and data-handling capabilities. These new capabilities will complement the researchers' existing capabilities while raising new issues, such as those regarding mechanisms to control access to their data. David De Roure emphasizes the promises and threats that arise from opening out research-centered computational networks to a much wider range of practitioners, which he believes may eventually represent a "new" form of e-research built on the foundations of Web 2.0 technologies. In the final essay of chapter 2, John Taylor, a key policymaker in the early years of e-science, extends the chapter's scope by focusing on the implications envisioned for such networks in business and industry as well as for nations as a whole.

1 Reconfiguring Access in Research: Information, Expertise, and Experience

William H. Dutton

The Scope of Research-Centered Computational Networks

The technological landscape of research is becoming increasingly distinctive. Until the late twentieth century, computer centers, research institutes, field interviews, lab notebooks, tape recorders, and filing cabinets characterized key aspects of the infrastructures for research. As highlighted in the introduction to this book, that infrastructure is now being replaced by cyberinfrastructures involving capabilities such as Web sites, networked data centers, Grids, Clouds, "collaboratories," video archives, blogs, embedded sensor networks, and many online digital collections with extensive content.

These e-infrastructures, which we call *research-centered computational networks* (RCNs), are the key innovations driving "e-research" (see also the introduction). This book explores the nature and significance of this shift. Across the globe, specialists in these technologies and researchers based in particular domains of application are creating and promoting new cyberinfrastructures to support research (see essay 1.1 and chapter 2). The collaborative nature of this effort increases the likelihood that such innovations will be anchored in concrete research objectives, which vary widely. Innovations in one domain can also have consequences across others. For example, the invention of the Web to support collaboration in physics research at the European Organization for Nuclear Research (CERN) has reshaped the way information is shared online across nearly every other discipline. What impact will follow from the many RCN initiatives designed to support e-research?

In many respects, e-research is a "vision" as well as a set of concrete practices. It is leading many researchers to think differently about how they will approach their work. If well implemented, these innovations will enable research to be conducted more quickly, better, and in more powerful ways. To paraphrase one scholar of science and technology, the use of technological innovations is enlarging the human footprint as they create a growing ecoskeleton (Schroeder 2007). In this sense, e-research can be seen to be enhancing the impacts of individual researchers and their teams, extending their potential to collaborate and reengineer the process of inquiry by overcoming previous technological limitations.

Transforming Research by Reconfiguring Access

Even this description of e-research might understate the diversity of ways in which the application of any information and communication technology (ICT) to the research process, from the book to the Internet to the Grid, can transform these practices and outcomes by reconfiguring access. In order to investigate the underlying dynamics of these changes, it is necessary to increase the attention paid to the actual role of advanced digital technologies in scholarship—how researchers do what they do and with what effect on the quality and productivity of the research enterprise (Nentwich 2003; Hine 2006; Borgman 2007; Olson, Zimmerman, and Bos 2008). E-research is not simply an assembly of new technical artifacts—a cyberinfrastructure fixed in a particular point in time and isolated from the people who influence its evolution and are affected by it. Instead, those involved in the new e-infrastructures are making "digital choices" about its development, use, and governance.

Acting on these choices continuously changes the role of individual researchers, teams, and their institutions as they reconfigure physical and electronic access to collaborative partners, the objects of their research, information of all kinds, services, and technologies that encompass all disciplines.[1] The reconfiguration illustrated in figure 1.1 can then lead to real consequences for the outcomes of research and to the centrality—or marginalization—of different actors in the research process. RCNs do not in themselves convey real power to e-researchers, but they do enable people and organizations to reconfigure their access to resources in ways that can empower or undermine different roles in the research process.[2]

The process of reconfiguring access depicted in figure 1.1 is not only shaped by new technologies, but entwined with the coevolution of a variety of organizational and disciplinary structures and practices. Digital choices about using or not using these capabilities are made in separate but interrelated social processes by research assistants, project teams, coders, ethics committees, research administrators, and many others. Substantially different outcomes can result from applications of the same technology in different research contexts.

A focus on how "digital choices" shape the outcomes of ICT-enabled research moves away from conceiving the potential for collaboration as being built into the technology and broadens concern over the implications of technology to encompass all the elements of research. It frames technical capabilities as bound up with a wide range of personal, social, and institutional dynamics that affect—and are affected by—innovations in RCNs. In addition, it indicates how an understanding of the relationship between e-infrastructures and the research they support needs to be based on more than just projections derived from technical capabilities. Instead, this understanding should also build an appreciation of how the creation, use, and governance of the

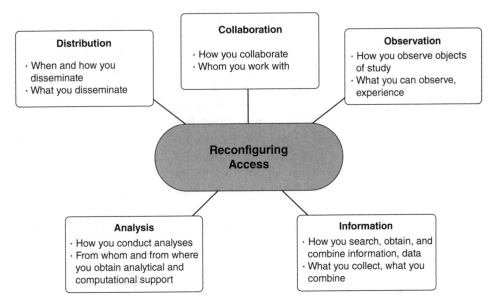

Figure 1.1
Reconfiguring access to key resources in research.

relevant technologies can be reshaped by the skills, know-how, and motivation of the wide range of actors involved in e-research.

Why a New Perspective on the Impacts of ICTs Is Needed

Many social scientists who have attempted to identify the practical implications of advanced ICTs on research are critical of overly simplistic perspectives on predicted "impacts" (e.g., Hine 2006; Borgman 2007; Olson, Zimmerman, and Bos 2008). The thrust of the more conventional impact perspective focuses on the potential contribution of well-implemented technological innovations to particular patterns of use and outcome, suggesting that predicted benefits will progress with an inherent logic after the successful adoption of a new technology. In e-research, that logic would point to the use of cyberinfrastructures, leading inevitably to better-connected researchers across institutional and national boundaries, with wider access to information resources (e.g., search engines). This result would be seen as flowing from the great and growing capacities brought about by the Grid and the Web's global footprint.

This traditional impact perspective has dominated discussion of technology and society from its emergence in studies of computers in the 1950s. However, empirical research routinely finds that this thesis is misleading because it ignores the degree to which these innovations can lead to a diversity of impacts (Dutton 1996, 1999). For example, the same technologies can be used in ways that isolate or connect researchers by enabling an individual to work either independently or collaboratively. More articles are becoming accessible online, but that does not mean that researchers are relying on more sources. In fact, they are citing proportionately fewer sources, possibly due to a "herd" or "winner-take-all" effect (Evans 2008; see also essay 1.3).

The expectations derived from the impact perspective can therefore be problematic. Its frequent focus on long-term impacts, such as the supporting of collaboration, can be shaped by many factors that are difficult to predict. A fuller range of implications can be anticipated by looking closely at the more immediate role of ICTs in reshaping access (i.e., in making strategic choices to change researchers' proximity to information, expertise, and experience critical to their work). This reconfiguring might have profound implications for the nature and quality of scholarship—for example, by exacerbating a winner-take-all effect to create "superstar" researchers (essay 1.3). Outcomes can be for better or worse, depending on the contexts of development and use.

Reconfiguring Access to Research Resources

The discussion so far explains how the development and application of RCNs are socially shaped. RCNs are the product of many actors' pursuing diverse objectives, including ICT specialists, domain researchers, administrators, and public and private sponsors. The interplay of multiple actors pursuing diverse objectives on a broad variety of projects shapes the outcomes tied to ICTs used for research.

A key insight from the reconfiguring-access perspective is to help understand how power is derived not from information as such, but from the ability to control access to resources critical to research, such as information. Institutional and other social arrangements that participate in the shaping of e-research outcomes include intellectual property rights (IPRs) policies in universities, public legislation (e.g., restrictions on personal data), the public funding of e-infrastructures, and geographical distance (e.g., in gaining tacit knowledge from direct observation).

Information is only one of a number of resources at stake in reshaping access. Social and technical choices about ICTs also contribute to reconfiguring electronic and physical access to five distinct but interrelated resources central to research:

1. *Expertise* how and with whom researchers collaborate. Will they isolate themselves or increase collaboration with more widely distributed teams?
2. *Observation* how researchers observe their objects of research, whether people or things—and what they can observe or experience. Will researchers be more distant from their objects of study or closer to them? Will they have more direct or more mediated experiences in observing their subjects of study?

3. *Information* how researchers get information or collect data, as well as what information they collect. Will researchers collect more data or be more dependent on data collected by others?

4. *Analysis* how researchers analyze data and from whom and where they will obtain analytical support. Will researchers design their analytical strategies or be more dependent on services provided by others (e.g., from within the academic sector or in a more proprietary Cloud)?

5. *Distribution* how and when research is distributed, as well as what is distributed, by whom, to whom. How much of the data underlying research will be distributed? How open will research become, and what will be the nature of such openness at different stages of the research process?

There are many ways in which e-Research can reduce, reinforce, or otherwise alter access, such as shaping information content and flow by accident or design. The use of ICTs also changes patterns of interaction between people, information, communities, and organizations. Likewise, it can change the interactions between researchers, disciplines, and organizations. Table 1.1 provides examples of how such changes are achieved.

The reconfiguring access perspective exemplified in table 1.1 provides a focus on how researchers can use the technologies for the many countervailing purposes outlined earlier, such as whether to remain autonomous or to build distributed collaborative teams (see box 1.1).

The Strategic Interplay of Multiple Actors

The interactions of different actors seeking to control and influence the design and use of e-infrastructures takes place in a variety of arenas at the same time. All actors are not involved in the same decisions: individuals and groups pursue different goals within their own domains (Dutton 1992). The complexity and significance of the choices made by a multiplicity of actors pursing diverse goals can be illustrated by looking at some of these choices related to the many stakeholders involved in e-research activities. The scenario may involve the many stakeholders shown in box 1.2. These stakeholders' behavior and decisions affect other actors' behavior and decisions. The outcomes of choices unfold as the products of countless strategic and everyday decisions made by many actors pursing different objectives in different social and institutional arenas.

How Digital Choices Reconfigure Access

ICTs can reconfigure access in multiple ways, including their role in changing cost structures, expanding or contracting the proximity of access, restructuring the architecture

Table 1.1

How Digital Choices Reconfigure Access

ICTs provide access to:	Kind of e-research activity	Examples
Expertise: Reconfigures how, where, and when colleagues interact with coauthors and coinvestigators, as well as with whom they communicate and collaborate	Collaboration within and between individuals and research teams; other one-to-one, one-to-many, many-to-many communications	Collaborative software, collaboratories, virtual research environments, multipoint video conferencing
Observation: Reconfigures the researcher's proximity to the object of study, whether a person or an object	Use of ICTs to bring a researcher closer to an object of study or to enable mediated observation of the phenomenon of study, replacing or complementing more direct methods	Web-based surveys that enable a researcher to collect information worldwide; networked instruments (e.g., telescopes) that allow researchers to see through the same lens from anywhere in the world
Information: Affects how and what researchers can collect, read, hear, see, archive—and know	Searching, retrieving, analyzing, and transmitting images, video, sounds, and statistics from one to many or many to one	The exchange of large amounts of multimedia research or statistical data; Web searches for a huge variety of information sources; Web "crawls" for link data and structures
Analysis: Identifies the services and their providers that influence how and from whom researchers obtain computing and data services; where and when they use in-house as opposed to external sources	Obtaining electronic services from distant or nearby sources, such as satellite images, maps, data archives; storing and analyzing data locally (e.g., over a federated database or in the Cloud)	Fast online delivery of multimedia products and services to any location, involving large amounts of data; digital art collections; access to medical images; remote sensors (e.g., via the Grid or Cloud computing)
Distribution: Shapes how and when one distributes information, what is distributed by whom, what is viewed by whom	Using the e-infrastructure so that it effectively becomes the researcher's virtual networking and computational resource	Institutional repositories, online data collections, blogs and Web sites, disciplinary and other digital archives

of networks, creating or eliminating gatekeepers, redistributing advantages between senders and receivers, and enabling more or less user control.

Changing Cost Structures

ICT innovations have contributed substantially to lowering the costs of accessing and distributing information and networked services. For instance, marginal costs of the

Box 1.1

Virtual Meetings over the Access Grid

The Access Grid is a multisite conferencing system composed of an ensemble of resources that includes multimedia displays, presentation, and interactive environments. These elements interface to the Grid to support group-to-group interactions and collaboration.

Source: See http://www.accessgrid.org/.

Box 1.2

Stakeholders Involved in e-Research Activities

Computer scientists engaged in software, middleware, and hardware design and development

Domain scientists and scholars who wish to apply e-research tools across a range of disciplines

E-researchers who work at the interface between ICT experts and domain specialists

Scholars opposed to investment in e-research initiatives

Research units with grants to develop e-infrastructures

Businesses and industries developing tools for RCNs (e.g., Cloud computing)

Companies or agencies with major expertise and information resources, such as in satellite imaging, maps, or the ability to combine Google Earth maps with national census data

Academics with entrepreneurial visions for creating a new business around their innovations

Research service organizations at universities

online transport and delivery of purely digital services and products are negligible (e.g., in the preparation and publication of an academic paper) once a researcher has a broadband Internet link. However, not every region, institution, or researcher has such access, as is the case in many developing counties (chapter 12).

Nevertheless, costs remain high in some contexts, such as in producing, reviewing, and promoting a major research database or report. For instance, the value of e–social science applications in China is limited by the lack of major social science data sets (essay 6.2). This example indicates that those institutions or nations that are "data rich" will have an advantage over those that are "data poor" (Sawyer 2008). At the same time, the free downloading of content (e.g., creative content such as professional journal articles) has posed a serious challenge to cost structures for academic publishers. It has also encouraged researchers, universities, and research councils to support the electronic distribution of papers, including supporting—even sometimes mandating—the development of institutional repositories.[3]

Many widely available Internet-based services are of great value to researchers, such as search engines or the Cloud (essay 2.1). However, most academic institutions are unable to compete because of the huge development costs of commercial data centers, such as those built by major service providers (e.g., Google, Amazon.com, Microsoft, and Yahoo!) that are anchored in substantial economies of scale in establishing and running the centers. As a result, the cost to each user is very low, but very high to providers. A key impetus behind Grid computing has been this reduction in the number of major players across the world who can provide capacities to compete with the major providers of computational services (Carr 2008).

Large-scale shared computational resources enable academic researchers to increase the power of RCNs by linking resources across institutional, geographic, and other boundaries in ways that make more efficient use of limited local ICT resources. However, it is often difficult to resolve the "soft" infrastructural issues of such interinstitutional collaboration (allocation of costs, ownership, liability, and more), as discussed, for example, in chapter 11.

Expanding or Contracting the Proximity of Access

ICTs can reconfigure distance, time, and control (Innis 1972 [1950]), which can transform the structure, size, location, and competitiveness of research activities by changing the ease, speed, and costs of gaining access to people, services, information, and technologies wherever they are located. The Internet and the Grid enable researchers to keep in regular, informal touch with people at distant locations and allow the delivery of files from around the world to desk, lab, and laptop personal computer as easily as if they were stored on the researcher's own computer.

This ability to enable distributed collaboration across locations or to observe remote objects can paradoxically lead to a distancing of researchers from one another and from the objects of their study (see chapter 6). Educators have also raised alarms over students' being "educated by Google," as they see surfing the Web being substituted for more structured readings, lectures, and experience (Brabazon 2007). Balancing face-to-face and virtual communication and observation therefore becomes a critical issue for RCNs. At one extreme, some traditional researchers reject new ICTs; at the other, some have stopped reading books and going into the field to do studies as they become glued to their computer screens.

Restructuring the Architecture of Networks

The architecture of a technical network often reflects the social and institutional forces shaping it. Vertical communication structures, such as those used by traditional publishers and mass media, allow a small group to broadcast to millions, following a more centralized distribution of information. Likewise, research projects have traditionally often imposed a hierarchical management and communication structure, with organizational charts and reporting relationships being an essential element of major project proposals.

One of the basic features of the Internet is its ease in supporting many forms of non-hierarchical structure, such as those based on horizontal "peer networks" of communication (e.g., one to one, many to many). This distributed pattern of communication underpins much of the recent push for open access to science, such as the Open Science project[4] (see also chapter 11 and essay 11.1). It has also enabled individual researchers to choose whether to participate in emerging collaborative network organizations, which often span the formal boundaries of organizations (Dutton 2008).

Creating or Eliminating Gatekeepers

Technological change can also alter the role of gatekeepers in the dissemination of information. Research Web sites, institutional archives, and a variety of electronic repositories enable the researcher to bypass journal editors, peer reviews, and even their own colleagues in getting research into the public domain. A clear example of this ability is researchers' increasing use of blogs to connect directly with their audiences (box 1.3).

Gatekeepers are relevant in communication beyond the publishing field. Secretaries were once the prime gatekeepers in research establishments, as elsewhere. Their screening and prioritizing of access to research teams (by answering telephone calls to an office) became less common as email and social networking Web sites grew in popularity. Academics are increasingly in direct contact with students, the press (not the press office), their colleagues, and even strangers in the blogosphere without the intervention of intermediaries.

Redistributing Power between Senders and Receivers

With electromechanical switching technology, telephone calls became anonymous, which shifted power to the person calling. The called party would not know who

Box 1.3
Research Blogs

The advent of blogging emerged as a form of entertainment and amateur "citizen journalism," but it has become a significant element of an array of research cultures. For example, the CombeChem chemistry laboratory project (see chapter 11) has substituted a blog for the lab journal. Even with initial restrictions on access limited to the project team, the blog opened up electronic access to the lab's day-to-day decisions, enabling CombeChem's community of researchers to have more oversight of decisions and the status of experiments.

Likewise, blogs have become part of many academics' routine work practices. The range of blogging activities include recording researchers' projects, distributing their work, explaining the rationale for decisions, offering new ideas, and comments on others' work.

was calling, so might be more inclined to answer a call in case it was important. With answering machines and caller identity capabilities, information about who is on the line has become increasingly available to the receiver, which has shifted the advantage to the receiver, who can now more easily screen out unwanted calls.

Although the Internet grew from a culture that promotes openness and freedom of expression, it can take away the anonymity that made automatic telephone switching so attractive. For example, email was originally designed to use an agreed standard that requires every message to identify the person sending it, the recipient, the date sent, and the subject. Recipients can use this standard to prioritize and screen messages in order to better manage their communications.

Other e-research technologies can similarly redistribute the relative communicative power of senders and receivers as well as change the pool of individuals who are accessible to a researcher. They thus can shift more communicative power to the centers and research groups that have access to the appropriate technology to communicate with key partners for collaboration.

User Control over Digital Content and Access

The proliferation of global communications channels opened by the Internet and other ICTs has added an important new dimension to traditional concerns about who controls the content and the access to communications and information. National governments can relatively easily ban or restrict traditional printed information or terrestrial broadcast channels, but not the Internet or the Web. In addition, academic norms promote freedom of inquiry without censorship. In many respects, RCNs have allowed academics greater unfettered access to more sources of information and other research resources. For example, an increasing number of free, open-source tools are available for conducting Web-based online surveys of local or global populations.

In the past, a field survey required significant financial and human resources for sampling and for undertaking interviews. Even mail surveys required the resources for generating mailing lists and for posting and returning questionnaires. Today, though, it has become increasingly possible for anyone to survey people around the world without a significant cost, while conducting the survey from his or her household or office. This ability has led to a flood of surveys, many of which yield little data of value because they are poorly designed and are not based on systematic sampling strategies, but are under the control of the end user. This downside of user control illustrates how RNCs can improve or undermine the quality of research.

There are also concerns about the loss of quality controls over academic, student, and public access to scientific and research content. The elimination of the "expert" gatekeeper has been made possible by the escalation of online communication channels. In this wider Internet space, experienced researchers compete for readers with a worldwide array of information providers. This equality of status has fueled debate over the assessment of the quality of research, which has traditionally been based on peer

Box 1.4
Examples of Visualization Technologies

Global maps to display social, environmental, health, and other quantitative trends (http://www.worldmapper.org/)

Dynamic visualizations of trends in areas such as population, economic, and health patterns, such as Gapminder (http://www.gapminder.org/)

Tools for visualizing the networks resulting from Webmetric and associated analyses (essay 1.2), such as the Virtual Observatory for the Study of Online Networks (http://voson.anu.edu.au/)

Tools that enable knowledge domains to be mapped, such as the Information Visualization Cyberinfrastructure (http://www.asis.org/Publications/ARIST/Vol37/BornerFigures.html).

review, citation analysis, or online readership. Will search engines become the new arbiters of academic quality through their use to identify the most central academics and content (see essays 1.2 and 1.3)?

An important area of user control is in visualizing research results. The value of visualizing data has been long recognized, as in Edward Tufte's (1990, 1997) seminal contributions, which highlight the scientific misjudgments that can stem from not seeing relationships in data if they are poorly presented. Incentives for developing technologies to support visualization have been generated by efforts to enhance analytical capabilities and to reach wide audiences, including other researchers, relevant policymakers, and members of the public.

The visualization tools that have been created can transform the way data are used for social research, such as with studies of demographic trends related to the aging of populations, global patterns of migration, and income inequalities. The challenge is to combine the collection and analysis of high-quality data sets with systems that can visualize the complex trends identified. This combination may help researchers to draw more powerful conclusions and to communicate them in attractive ways to research colleagues, policymakers, and the public. Such a highly interdisciplinary science lends itself especially to linking social science data sets with geospatial information and to connecting this information with environmental or health indicators and other types of information. For instance, the powerful and versatile "visual analytics" approach can help to discover patterns within massive and dynamically changing information spaces.[5] Box 1.4 highlights other examples of visualization technologies.

Social Factors Shaping Digital Choices

Choices concerning the use of RCNs and their implications are not random or unstructured. They are shaped by technical, economic, and other social factors, and are constrained by the

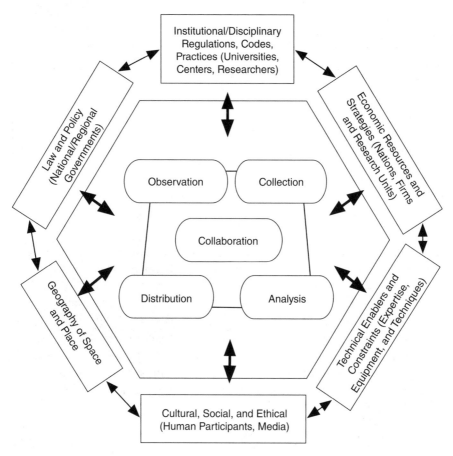

Figure 1.2
The social shaping of e-research: Choices and strategies.

choices of other actors in the research context. The main factors affecting these digital choices can be categorized along six dimensions: economic, technological, social and ethical, geographical, legal and public political, and institutional (see figure 1.2).

Economic Resources and Strategies

Major constraints on the development and use of e-research can arise from the size, wealth, and vitality of different research communities, including universities and national and regional environments. The tools open to a prestigious American university department can dwarf those available in a distressed area of the global South (chapter 12). Major initiatives in the United States, China, Japan, and Europe seek to place particular nations and regions in advantageous positions in the global research community (chapter 2).

Economic resources are a constraint not only in developing regions. For example, proposed cuts in funding for astronomy in the United Kingdom, including cancellation of membership in the Gemini telescopic telescience tool, led to a major disruption in access to images from these internationally shared telescopic resources that enabled U.K. astronomers to see the Northern Hemisphere through two of the best range of telescopes. Funding was eventually restored, but not before a number of academics left the United Kingdom to protect their academic careers (Pounds 2007; Rincon 2008).

Technological Enablers and Constraints
Technologies matter to the concept of reconfiguring access, which attaches much importance to the design of RCNs as platforms that make some activities easier or more rational to accomplish and others more difficult. This view also broadens understanding of the role of technology beyond the "hard" infrastructures and tools to include the ideas and cultures that support or constrain them.

Ideas about the technological underpinning of e-research have become the foundation of powerful belief systems, or paradigms, in this field. These paradigms create a way of interpreting reality that is very different from the way that people embedded in another paradigm interpret it. The core e-research vision is built around such notions as virtual collaboration, an arena that offers the means to shape choices about the potential pool of collaborative partners. Experience and knowledge about ICTs can influence or even create a paradigm change. At a meeting of e–social science researchers, for instance, a proposal for a seminar series led some to imagine that the series would be held on the Access Grid rather than at a single physical location. They had become embedded in a paradigm that took distributed virtual meetings for granted. It is in these ways that alternative perspectives on the role of the ICTs in e-research can be influential in shaping decisions about research practices and outcomes.

Cultural, Social, and Ethical Norms and Practices
Ideas shaped by cultural, social, and ethical norms and practices also matter in influencing choices in e-research. For instance, the underlying philosophy that shaped the emergence of the Internet in the 1970s was based on open access to information, communication, and collaboration between people. This framework reflected the noncommercial and academic culture that infused the perceptions and motivations of those people most influential in determining Internet capabilities at the time. A similar noncommercial culture at CERN shaped the sharing and collaborative capabilities that have helped to fuel the Web's global popularity (Reid 2000).

It was only in the 1990s that a strong push toward the commercialization of the Internet and the development of e-commerce introduced more competitive and proprietary values into shaping aspects of the Internet. However, the original culture of Internet pioneers had already created and embedded capabilities in Internet standards and infrastructure that were based on notions of trust and sharing more appropriate to an academic community. Commercial interactions require higher priority to confidentiality, security, pricing, IPRs, and related factors.

More generally, approaches to e-research can be shaped by users' values, norms, and practices. These values, norms, and practices are often anchored in disciplinary codes and practices and occur in very different ways from what would be expected by a simple extrapolation from the perceived potential of the technology (as in the "impact" view of technologically enabled change). For instance, many innovative technological and market failures can be understood as a consequence of having a weak conception of users (Woolgar 1996)—for example, perceiving them to be either more or less technically proficient that they actually are.

Users can be under- or overestimated. For example, early notions of a "paperless" office failed to take account of the many attractive features of paper for users. It took far more time than initially predicted for electronic media to begin to reduce the volume of paper clogging research offices by becoming a widely used substitute for paper in many activities (e.g. through growth of electronic archives and digital repositories). In contrast, few predicted that texting using mobile phones would be as popular as it has become, given the perceived difficulties of entering text on a small keypad.

A lack of good usability has been seen as a major constraint on the diffusion of e-research (see chapter 5). Users are not passive recipients of whatever is designed for them. Much of the push to develop ICTs has come from users with the skills and motivation to design and build their own systems. Personal computers were first known as "home brew" computers because they were developed by their users; a similar e-research phenomenon is the pattern of "bottom-up" innovation found in e–social sciences (see chapter 6).

Geography of Space and Place

One of the most prominent attributes of e-research is the relative ease with which it can be used to overcome constraints of time and distance. Nevertheless, there is also evidence that ICTs make geography matter even more (Goddard and Richardson 1996). They might actually bring new significance to locations—for example, by enabling researchers to be where they need to be for face-to-face communication through teleconferencing or by facilitating the making of appointments and travel arrangements for researchers to meet among the wider groups of contacts made through electronic networks. Researchers can be in the field more often and at the most optimal times if they are able to work remotely using effective network-enabled support. Mediated research might alternatively be used in place of field research work (see chapter 6).

E-research also offers new choices about how to configure where different kinds of research are conducted. For example, Web-based survey tools enable anyone with access to the Web to complete the same survey. This ability means that researchers' location may no longer be as relevant as it is in an offline world. It is also now possible to undertake truly global surveys.

Law and Public Policy

Public policy at all levels can constrain or promote RCNs (e.g., through the various e-science initiatives highlighted in this book, which have been led by national policymakers with the advice of leading academics). Many public-policy initiatives have promoted open-access approaches that are driving investment in e-research (see chapter 11). However, choices about access are also constrained by a variety of laws and public policies (chapter 8).

Rules related to copyright and IPRs can facilitate or restrict access to material in any form. Liability laws differ cross-nationally, and liability concerns can slow efforts to collaborate on scientific projects that cross national and institutional boundaries. Privacy and data-protection laws and policies vary, often dramatically, between jurisdictions (e.g., among the states of the European Union and across regions of the world). Research administrators are developing approaches that can overcome these issues. However, such cross-jurisdictional differences can pose a potential barrier to the free flow of information in many research domains, such as in the social and medial sciences.

Institutional and Disciplinary Regulations, Codes, and Practices

Digital choices in universities and other research establishments are affected by institutional arrangements and policies in areas such as IPRs, copyright, and liability (see chapter 11). They can also be a driving force behind innovations—for better or worse. An example is the way Harvard University's Faculty of Arts and Sciences and the U.S. National Institutes of Health (NIH) have mandated public access to research, such as requiring "peer-reviewed journal manuscripts that arise from NIH funds to be submitted to the NIH digital archive, PubMed Central."[6]

Powerful norms and practices in academia can stem from disciplinary codes. Most disciplines socialize their students by instilling norms, such as how to protect personal data, when to keep what confidential, how to maintain records, and how to publish their work (see chapter 9). Researchers can ignore even mandates from public authorities if they believe these mandates violate their disciplinary codes of practice— for instance, in protecting the anonymity of the participants in their research (see chapter 8).

Understanding the Intrinsic Social Nature of e-Research

This chapter has focused on how e-research technologies enable the reconfiguration of access to the objects of study, the colleagues one works with, the analytical tools of research, and the audiences being targeted. Choices aimed at reconfiguring access are constrained by an ecology of multiple actors, each with different objectives and in his or her turn constrained by a variety of other factors, as depicted in figure 1.2. This interaction of social and technical choices over time and across domains produces unpredictable outcomes, but the analysis here shows that actors can have an impact on outcomes through the choices they make on the way research is conducted.

Those scholars and administrators who understand the centrality of the ways in which e-infrastructures can be used to reconfigure access to local and global research resources may be in a better position to decide whether and how to use the technologies. This viewpoint contrasts with the traditional impact perspective on the social and economic outcomes of ICT innovation, which broadly suggests that using e-research will automatically lead to outcomes determined largely by the available technology, such as greater collaboration and productivity. In contrast, the view proposed here emphasizes the strong influence that researchers and others can have in determining the specific course taken in each environment in which e-research approaches are developed and used. Whether this influence leads to better-quality research outcomes depends on the choices made by individuals and groups about how to design and use (or not use) ICTs to reconfigure access strategically in ways that open up or close off networks of collaboration, calculation, and communication.

No single researcher or research team can be master of his, her, or their own fate. All operate in the context of multiple players within complex institutional settings that might not adapt to changing research practices (see chapter 7). Therefore, the success of e-research will depend on a widespread understanding of the nature of changing practices and their outcomes, as well as on individual actors' strategic choices. Legal, policy, institutional, and disciplinary contexts must adapt—not just individual scholars.

This approach provides an analytical and thematic framework for the remainder of this book. It points to the need for strategies and policies toward e-research that

1. Prioritize access, rather than information, as the prime focus in using e-infrastructures.
2. Move from a deterministic paradigm in which outcomes can be expected to follow from the adoption of an RCN to a paradigm anchored in a view of outcomes shaped through the strategic use of the technologies in ways that respond to the choices made by others who are shaping a field of research.
3. Understand better how the use of RCNs can be employed to address key related questions (e.g., creating a stronger research community or isolating researchers; restricting or expanding access to data resources).
4. Focus on ICT innovations that can enhance the quality of research by complementing and improving on traditional ways of doing things (e.g., field research), as well as by offering substitutions for old technologies and methods such as keeping a paper-based log of experiments.

5. Identify, where appropriate, the limits placed on individual researchers and the need for reshaping the rules and practices governed by disciplines, institutions, and law and policy. This strategy implies the need also to identify inappropriate adaptations, such as actions that undermine the interests of the subjects of research.

Researchers can use e-infrastructures strategically to reconfigure access to their objects of study, information, colleagues, analytical and communication services, and related ICTs. Nevertheless, these changes might not represent a revolution in underlying processes, institutions, and outcomes. There are many constraints on the choices and actions of other actors in the research process (e.g., research policymakers, universities, competing—as well as collaborating—researchers, and the beneficiaries of research). E-research cannot autonomously overturn entrenched and deeply rooted legal norms, institutional arrangements, or cultural and social influences, particularly because people often use RCNs to reinforce their existing practices. Nevertheless, shifts in various actors' research power enabled by the technology may open up possibilities for significant transformations in many traditional ways of conducting research, with far-reaching consequences for the outcomes of research.

Notes

1. The concept of reconfiguring access originated in my synthesis of research within the U.K. Programme on Information and Communication Technologies around the concept of "tele-access" in the 1990s (Dutton 1999). I have since moved to the concept of "reconfiguring access" to avoid associations with any particular technology (Dutton 2005).

2. The role of ICTs in shaping access to information, whether in a research community or in society as a whole, might be called "information politics" (Danziger, Dutton, Kling, et al. 1982:133–135; Garnham 1999). For instance, a researcher using ICTs to produce important results can apply them to gain status and influence.

3. For example, the University of Southampton has mandated the archiving of published papers in its institutional repository. Other universities have tended to leave archiving up to individual academics as one aspect of academic freedom—the right to control their own research.

4. See http://www.openscience.org/.

5. Visual analytics is a specialized field emerging out of e-research communities. It uses visualization techniques to enhance the analysis of data and its communication to wider audiences. Just as both an art and a science are involved in the traditional presentation of statistical data, such as rules governing the construction of tables, there are developing guidelines on visual representations that are anchored in both scientific principles on reporting and the art of presentation.

6. An overview of and relevant documents on the NIH public-access policy are at http://public access.nih.gov/.

References

Borgman, C. L. 2007. *Scholarship in the digital age*. Oxford, UK: Oxford University Press.

Brabazon, T. 2007. *The University of Google: Education in the (post) information age*. Burlington, VT: Ashgate.

Carr, N. 2008. *The big switch: Rewiring the world, from Edison to Google*. New York: W. W. Norton.

Danziger, J. N., W. H. Dutton, R. Kling, and K. L. Kraemer. 1982. *Computers and politics*. New York: Columbia University Press.

Dutton, W. H. 1992. "The ecology of games shaping communication policy." Communication Theory 2 (4):303–328.

Dutton, W. H., ed. 1996. *Information and communication technologies—Visions and realities*. Oxford, UK: Oxford University Press.

Dutton, W. H. 1999. *Society on the line: Information politics in the digital age*. Oxford, UK: Oxford University Press.

Dutton, W. H. 2005. "The Internet and social transformation." In *Transforming enterprise: The economic and social implications of information technology*, ed. W. H. Dutton, B. Kahin, R. O'Callaghan, and A. W. Wyckoff. Cambridge, MA: MIT Press, 375–398.

Dutton, W. H. 2008. "The wisdom of collaborative network organizations: Capturing the value of networked individuals." *Prometheus 26* (3):211–230.

Evans, J. A. 2008. "Electronic publication and the narrowing of science and scholarship." Science 321 (5887):395–399. doi:10.1126/science.1150473.

Garnham, N. 1999. "Information politics: The study of communicative power." In *Society on the line: Information politics in the digital age*, ed. W. H. Dutton. Oxford, UK: Oxford University Press, 77–78.

Goddard, J., and R. Richardson. 1996. "Why geography will still matter." In *Information and communication technologies—visions and realities*, ed. W. H. Dutton. Oxford, UK: Oxford University Press, 197–214.

Hine, C. M. 2006. *New infrastructures for knowledge production: Understanding e-science*. Hershey, PA: Information Science.

Innis, H. 1972 [1950]. *Empire and communications*. Toronto: University of Toronto Press.

Nentwich, M. 2003. *Cyberscience: Research in the age of the Internet*. Vienna: Austrian Academy of Sciences.

Olson, G. M., A. Zimmerman, and N. Bos, eds. 2008. *Scientific collaboration on the Internet*. Cambridge, MA: MIT Press.

Pounds, K. 2007. "Funding changes defy the workings of physics." *Times Higher Education*, 21 December. Available at: http://www.timeshighereducation.co.uk/story.asp?storyCode=310138&section code=26.

Reid, R. H. 2000. *Architects of the Web*. New York: Wiley.

Rincon, P. 2008. "Astronomers given Gemini reprieve." *BBC News*, 12 February. Available at: http://news.bbc.co.uk/1/hi/sci/tech/7240840.stm.

Sawyer, S. 2008. "Data wealth, data poverty, science, and cyberinfrastructure." *Prometheus 26* (4):355–371.

Schroeder, R. 2007. *Rethinking science, technology, and social change*. Stanford, CA: Stanford University Press.

Tufte, E. R. 1990. *Envisioning information*. Cheshire, CT: Graphics Press.

Tufte, E. R. 1997. *Visual explanations*. Cheshire, CT: Graphics Press.

Woolgar, S. 1996. "Technologies as cultural artefacts." In *Information and communication technologies—visions and realities*, ed. W. H. Dutton. Oxford, UK: Oxford University Press, 87–102.

1.1 The Long Now of Cyberinfrastructure

Geoffrey C. Bowker, Paul N. Edwards, Steven J. Jackson, and Cory P. Knobel

Academic scientists and funding agencies throughout the advanced industrialized world have recently embarked on major efforts to imagine, develop, and build new forms of "cyberinfrastructure" or "e-science."[1] Separately and for several decades, historians and social scientists have studied the development of other kinds of infrastructure such as railroads, waterworks, highways, telephony, business communication systems, the Internet, and so on (Edwards, Jackson, Bowker, et al., 2007). Reading across the body of this work produces two striking general results: first, a great deal of contingency, uncertainty, and historical specificity attends any process of infrastructural development; second, despite these variations, shared patterns, processes, and emergent lessons hold widely true across the comparative history and social study of infrastructure.

The "Long Now" of Infrastructure

The Long Now Foundation has built a "clock of the long now" that will chime once every millennium, when a cuckoo will pop out (Brand 1999). The aim is for the idea of the long now to act as a "counterpoint to today's 'faster/cheaper' mind set and promote 'slower/better' thinking" that will "creatively foster responsibility in the framework of the next 10,000 years."[2]

Accustomed as we are now to the "information revolution," the accelerating pace of the "24/7" lifestyle, and the multiconnectivity provided by the World Wide Web, we rarely step back and ask what changes have been occurring at a slower pace in the background. For the development of cyberinfrastructure, the long now is about two hundred years. This period is when two suites of changes began to occur in the organization of knowledge and the academy. These changes have accompanied—slowly—the rise of an information infrastructure to support them: an exponential increase in information-gathering activities by the state (statistics) and knowledge workers (the encyclopedists); and the accompanying development of technologies and organizational practices to sort, sift, and store information.

When dealing with infrastructures, we need to look to the whole array of organizational forms, practices, and institutions that accompany, make possible, and inflect the development of new technology. JoAnne Yates (1989) makes this point beautifully in describing the first commercial use of punch card data tabulators, which occurred in the insurance industry. That use became possible because of organizational changes within the industry. There would have been no niche for punch card readers to occupy if there had not been new forms of information management, heralded by such low-status technologies as the manila folder and carbon paper, and accompanied by new organizational forms. Similarly, Manuel Castells (1996) argues that the roots of the contemporary "network society" are new organizational forms created in support of large corporate organizations, which long predate the arrival of computerization. James Beniger (1986) describes the entire period from the first Industrial Revolution to the present as an ongoing "control revolution" in which societies have responded to mass production, distribution, and consumption with both technological and organizational changes, designed to manage ever-increasing flows of goods, services, and information. In general, there is more continuity than cleavage in the relationship of the contemporary "information society" to the past (Chandler and Cortada 2003).

The lesson of all these studies is that organizations are (in part) information processors. People, routines, forms, and classification systems are as integral to information handling as computers, Ethernet cables, and Web protocols. The boundary between technological and organizational means of information processing is constantly moving. It can be shifted in either direction, and technological mechanisms can substitute for human and organizational ones only when the latter are prepared to support the substitution.

Organizational, Technical, and Social Dimensions of Cyberinfrastructures

In this essay, we regard *cyberinfrastructure* as the set of organizational practices, technical infrastructures, and social norms that collectively provide for the smooth operation of scientific work at a distance. All three are objects of design and engineering; a cyberinfrastructure will fail if any one is ignored.

In the "long now," two key facets of scientific information infrastructures stand out. One clusters around the nature of work in the social and natural sciences. Scientific disciplines were formed in the early 1800s, a time Michel Serres (1990) felicitously describes as the "era of x-ology," where *x* was *geo*, *socio*, *bio*, and so forth. Auguste Comte (1975 [1830–1845]) produced a classification of the sciences entailing a division of labor between them, placing mathematics and physics as the most developed and best models, and sociology as the most complex and least developed—more or less where Norbert Wiener (1951) placed them 130 years later in his book *Cybernetics and Society*. During this period, the object we now call the "database" also came to be the lynchpin of the natural and social sciences. The term *statistics* etymologically refers to "state-istics," or the quantitative study of societies (states); the field arose along with censuses, medical records, climatology, and other increasingly powerful techniques for monitoring population composition and health (Porter 1996). The natural sciences—moved by the spirit of the encyclopedists—equally began creating vast repositories of data. Such repositories were housed in individual institutions, such as botanical gardens and museums of natural history. Today they are increasingly held in electronic form, which is fast becoming the norm rather than the exception. For example, the Ecological Society of America publishes digital supplements, including databases and source code for simulation models, for all articles published in its journals;[3] and a researcher publishing a protein sequence must also publish her data in the (now worldwide) Protein Data Bank.

The second outstanding facet of scientific information infrastructures clusters around scientists' communication patterns. In the seventeenth and eighteenth centuries, scientists were largely "men of letters" who exchanged both public and private correspondence, as in the Leibniz/Clarke exchange.[4] From the early nineteenth century, a complex structure of national and international conferences and publishing practices developed, including especially the peer-reviewed scientific journal. Communication within an ever-broader scientific community was no longer two way, but *n* way. New forms of transportation underpinned the development of a truly international scientific community, aided also by linguae francae, principally English and French.

Conclusion: Continuities and Discontinuities

Definitions of cyberinfrastructure in this essay can be ordered along two axes, the social/technical and the local/global.

In building cyberinfrastructure, the key question is not whether the problem is "social" or "technical." That is putting it the wrong way around. The question is whether we choose, for any given problem, a social or a technical solution—or some combination. The distribution of solutions is the object of study. An everyday example comes from the problem of email security. How do I distribute my trust? I can delegate it to my machine and use Pretty Good Encryption[5] for all my email messages. Or I can work socially and organizationally to make certain that system operations, the government, and others who might have access to my email internalize a value that protects my right to privacy. Or I can change my own beliefs about the need for privacy, which is arguably a necessity with the new infrastructure.

New scientific cyberinfrastructures can be understood as an outgrowth of the developments in the long now of cyberinfrastructures outlined in this essay. Databases and *n*-way communication among scientists have developed while embedded in organizational and institutional practices and norms. There is far more continuity than many recognize. However, as scientific infrastructure goes cyber, there is also genuine discontinuity. The social and natural sciences grew up together with communication and data-processing technology. Changes in the latter will have ripple effects throughout the complex web of relations that constitutes scientific activity. It is through the information managers that much of the eventual design work is done. As Steward Brand (1994) argues so well about buildings, the design process has only just begun when the building is completed.

Acknowledgments

This essay is based on work supported by the U.S. National Science Foundation under Grant no. 0630263.

Notes

1. Although this essay for the most part sticks with the term *cyberinfrastructure* used by the U.S. National Science Foundation in its related program (see http://nsf.gov/dir/index.jsp?org=OCI), we recognize that very similar arguments can be made for the use of *e-science* in the United Kingdom's e-Science Programme (http://www.rcuk.ac.uk/escience) and in similar efforts to develop new computational infrastructures to support the practice of innovative and collaborative science. See the introduction to this volume for a discussion on related terminology.

2. See http://www.longnow.org/about/.

3. See http://www.esapubs.org/archive/.

4. This correspondence centered philosophically around Leibnitz's relational, as opposed to Clarke's (and Newton's) absolute, theory of space. This distinction had implications for the understanding of calculus—for which both Leibnitz and Newton had good grounds to claim priority. Because Leibnitz did not write large treatises, much of his philosophy is known only through his correspondence.

5. Pretty Good Encryption is a technique used in the popular Pretty Good Privacy (PGP) program for encrypting and decrypting email over the Internet, based on the nonproprietary OpenPGP standard of the Internet Engineering Task Force (see, for example, the OpenPGP Alliance at http://www.openpgp.org).

References

Beniger, J. R. 1986. *The control revolution: Technological and economic origins of the information society.* Cambridge, MA: Harvard University Press.

Brand, S. 1994. *How buildings learn: What happens after they're built.* New York: Viking Press.

Brand, S. 1999. *The clock of the long now: Time and responsibility.* 1st ed. New York: Basic Books.

Castells, M. 1996. *The rise of the network society*. Cambridge, MA: Blackwell.

Chandler, A. D., and J. W. Cortada. 2003. *A nation transformed by information: How information has shaped the United States from colonial times to the present*. Oxford, UK: Oxford University Press.

Comte, A. 1975 [1830–1845]. *Philosophie première; Cours de philosophie positive, leçons 1 à 45*. Paris: Hermann.

Edwards, P. N., S. J. Jackson, G. C. Bowker, and C. P. Knobel. 2007. *Understanding infrastructure: Dynamics, tensions, and design*. Report of the workshop "History and Theory of Infrastructure: Lessons for New Scientific Cyberinfrastructures." Retrieved 15 November 2008 from: http://hdl.handle.net/2027.42/49353.

Porter, T. M. 1996. *Trust in numbers: The pursuit of objectivity in science and public life*. Princeton, NJ: Princeton University Press.

Serres, M. 1990. *Le contrat naturel*. Paris: F. Bourin.

Wiener, N. 1951. *Cybernetics and society*. New York: Executive Techniques.

Yates, J. 1989. *Control through communication: The rise of system in American management*. Baltimore: Johns Hopkins University Press.

1.2 Identifying Winners and Losers: The Role of Webometrics

Mike Thelwall

Evaluating Scientists and Their Outputs

Since the 1960s, the research field of scientometrics has been concerned with measuring the outputs of science to evaluate scientists and to shed light on the dynamics of the growth of disciplines and specialisms. The results help government bodies in some countries to allocate research funding, both in terms of individual research groups and broad initiatives. Scientometrics is also used to benchmark entire countries' research outputs to identify areas of strength and weakness as well as to reveal a pattern of overall improvement or decline (Moed 2005). Hence, when one is seeking quantitative evidence of winners and losers in e-science, scientometrics is a logical starting point.

The primary source of evidence for most scientometric investigations is citations within the Thomson Reuters database of the top journals of science and social science. The rationale for the choice of citations as a data source derives from Robert Merton's (1973 [1942]) sociology of science, which proposes essentially that good science tends to be cited often because many researchers find it sufficiently interesting, credible, and useful to underpin their own research. Thus, a crude way to evaluate the work of an individual scientist, research group, university, or country would be to count the citations to that work.

Although such a simple counting exercise would be poor scientometrics, more sophisticated versions (e.g., taking into account field differences in citation norms) can provide credible evidence in many cases. Scientometrics often incorporates multiple sources of evidence—for instance, peer review, funding, and patent awards—which helps to create a more rounded picture of research activities, especially for applied research. It can also be of value in the social sciences, arts, and humanities, where journal citations may not be central to the construction of knowledge within a field. The World Wide Web has also become an important new source of data, spawning "Webometrics."

Webometric Advantages and Methods

The key idea behind Webometrics is that hyperlinks can behave like citations in two respects. First, a successful research group can expect to attract many links to its Web site; counting these links can therefore provide some (admittedly limited) evidence of success, even for disciplines outside the hard sciences. Second, links between research groups can help to reveal patterns of collaboration and information use, which may further understanding of the dynamics of science. In both cases, citations are often a more reliable source of evidence, but the big advantage of Web links is their timeliness. For instance, a new research collaboration may well be first signaled by the creation of a joint Web site, which may begin to create and attract links several years before the first research result is accepted by a journal and published. Hence, at least in theory, Webometric link analysis can describe current research trends, whereas scientometric analyses are inevitably retrospective.

Webometric methods usually rely heavily on commercial search engines, which are able to report the number of pages that link to any given Web site. For example, a study of life science researcher mobility in Europe (Robinson, Mentrup, Barjak, et al. 2007) for the European Union's Institute for Prospective Technological Studies used Google to identify life science research groups in seven European countries. It then used Windows Live Search to count the number of pages linking to each research group's home page. These data were employed for two purposes. First, a breakdown of country sources of links revealed international partnerships in the social sciences and individual countries that did not use the Web to publicize their research effectively. Second, the link counts were used to help select the most active and successful research groups (and a percentage of the rest) for a more complete scientometric analysis.

A second useful application of Webometric link analysis is for self-evaluation. Any research group can count links to its Web site using an appropriate commercial search engine and compare the result to a search for links to the sites of similar research groups. This simple exercise can either provide confirmation that the group and its site are recognized and seen as valuable or offer evidence of a potential problem.

A third application is to investigate factors about researchers that influence their online visibility. One study investigated whether factors such as gender and industry connections influenced the visibility of life science researchers' Web sites, but found little evidence of any important factors other than research group size and Web presence (Barjak and Thelwall 2008). However, this study showed the difficulty in using Webometric data to identify anything except the most significant online trends.

Simple link counts can reveal crude but useful indicators of the impact of a Web site and its owners, but Webometric methods can provide improved data in terms of more data or more useful counting methods. The process of collecting data can be automated through the use of free software that interfaces with the search engines via their "Web search service" or similar facility. For example, this software may automatically retrieve, list, and summarize by domain name all of the pages linking to a Web site, even if there are more than one thousand (the normal maximum for search engines).

Webometric processing can produce improved link counts by counting linking domains or Web sites rather than pages. This is an improvement because it cancels out the impact of sites that contain large numbers of links—for example, in collections of standard links that sometimes appear on every page of a Web site (Thelwall 2004). Nevertheless, the wide range of reasons why links are created means that links are a relatively weak source of information. As a result, Webometric data tends to be "indicative" of trends rather than robust evidence for hypotheses.

Conclusion

Webometric link analysis methods provide a relatively fast method of accessing indicative quantitative information about the impact of research groups' Web sites and, on a larger scale, the interrelationships between the groups. Repeated over time, this analysis can give early warning of the winners and losers within research fields or disciplines.

References

Barjak, F., and M. Thelwall. 2008. "A statistical analysis of the Web presences of European life sciences research teams." *Journal of the American Society for Information Science and Technology 59* (4):628–643.

Merton, R. K. 1973 [1942]. *The sociology of science: Theoretical and empirical investigations.* Chicago: University of Chicago Press.

Moed, H. F. 2005. *Citation analysis in research evaluation.* New York: Springer.

Robinson, S., A. Mentrup, F. Barjak, and M. Thelwall. 2007. *Collection and analysis of existing data on RESearchers CAReers (RESCAR) and implementation of new data collection activities—the researchtTeam survey, final report.* EU Contract no. 150176–2005-FISC-BE. Brussels: ERAWATCH Network Asbl.

Thelwall, M. 2004. *Link analysis: An information science approach.* San Diego: Academic Press.

1.3 "Superstar" Concentrations of Scientific Output and Recognition

Robert Ackland

"Power Laws" on the Web

Research characterizing the structure of large-scale networks such as the World Wide Web has provided substantial evidence that the distribution of hyperlinks follows a "power law": a relatively small number of sites have a large number of hyperlinks directed toward them (called "in-links"), whereas the vast majority of sites have very few in-links. Albert-László Barabási and Réka Albert's (1999) preferential attachment model proposes that power laws can emerge in a growing network where new nodes have a tendency to link to existing popular nodes that have a high number of in-links. Within the social sciences, the implications of power laws on the Web have been assessed in the context of the prominence of political information (Hindman, Tsioutsiouliklis, and Johnson 2003) and the availability of scientific information and expertise (Caldas, Schroeder, Mesch, et al. 2008).

The "economics of superstars" (Rosen 1981) has been used to explain why in certain fields, such as the arts and sport, there is a concentration of output among a few individuals, accompanied by an associated marked skewness in the distribution of income, with very large rewards at the top.[1] This essay argues that the economics of superstars can explain the emergence of power laws on the Web and other digital networks, and can provide important insights into how cyberinfrastructure may change the practice of scientific research.

The Economics of Superstar Scientists

Sherwin Rosen (1981) observes that the distribution of the income of artists can be "stretched out" in the right-hand tail, compared with the distribution of talent, indicating that the differences in success (measured by income) can be far greater than the differences in talent. He proposes two explanations for this distinction. First, consumer preferences lead to small differences in talent being magnified into larger earnings differences (with greater magnification at the top of the scale), which is a result of the imperfect substitution among different sellers. Rosen gives the following example: if a surgeon is 10 percent more successful in saving lives, most people will pay more than a 10 percent premium for his services. Second, the existence of "joint consumption technology" such as the Web means that the cost of production does not rise in proportion to the size of a seller's market, allowing a concentration of output on the few sellers who have the most talent.

The economics of superstars is highly relevant here because cyberinfrastructure (and the Internet on which it sits) is a prime example of a joint consumption technology: via cyberinfrastructure, a scientist can make available her or his data or methods (e.g., simulation code), and there will be no difference (in terms of cost) whether these research resources are accessed by only a few or thousands of researchers.

For Moshe Adler (1985), an interesting puzzle about stardom is that stars are often not more talented than many artists who are less successful, and he presents a model where large differences in earnings can exist with no differences in talent. Adler argues that consumers accumulate "consumption capital" in art and that the more consumption capital they possess, the greater the enjoyment from each encounter with the art. Thus, stardom is not due to the stars' superior talent, but to the fact that people are inherently social and find value in consuming the same art that others do.

The formal model has dynamics that are similar to preferential attachment (but based on economic theory). Consumers initially select an artist at random, and, by chance, one artist ends up with more patrons than the rest. This initial advantage leads to new consumers preferring that artist and to existing consumers switching to him or her.

One can envisage a similar phenomenon in e-science: researchers use cyberinfrastructure to access the articles, data, or methods of a particular researcher not because of quality, but because this particular researcher is already popular or prominent. This process already happens in citations where authors may be cited on a topic just because they are recognized "names" in a particular field, even if another author's work may be more relevant to the topic.

Cyberinfrastructure and the Creation of Superstar Scientists

Cyberinfrastructure may therefore facilitate the emergence of superstar scientists, leading to a concentration of scientific authority or impact. For economists, the existence of concentration always leads to questions about efficiency. Drawing from Adler 2006, if cyberinfrastructure leads to superstar scientists, the e-science "market" will be inefficient (from an economist's perspective) if barriers to entry exist, and such barriers will in turn depend on exactly how superstars emerge.

If superstar scientists emerge because of differences in talent, no matter how small these differences may be (as per Rosen's model), and there are no barriers to entry, then the e-science market will be efficient. In contrast, if superstars emerge because other researchers preferentially use Grid-enabled research resources that are the most "popular" (and not necessarily the "best"), as per Adler's model, then barriers to entry will exist, and the e-science market will be inefficient. In such a case, there would be an argument for government regulation to lower the barriers to entry, perhaps via appropriate allocation of public funding of Grid-enabled research resources such as data and methods.

Notes

1. The "winner-takes-all" phenomenon described in Frank and Cook 1995 is an elaboration of Sherwin Rosen's earlier work.

References

Adler, M. 1985. "Stardom and talent." *American Economic Review 75* (1):208–212.

Adler, M. 2006. "Stardom and talent." In *Handbook of the economics of art and culture*, vol. 1, ed. D. Throsby and V. Ginsburgh. St. Louis: Elsevier, 895–906.

Barabási, A-L., and R. Albert. 1999. "Emergence of scaling in random networks." *Science 286*:509–512.

Caldas, A., R. Schroeder, G. Mesch, and W. Dutton. 2008. "Patterns of information search and access on the World Wide Web: Democratizing expertise or creating new hierarchies?" *Journal of Computer-Mediated Communication 13* (4):769–793.

Frank, R., and P. Cook. 1995. *The winner-take-all society*. New York: Free Press.

Hindman, M., K. Tsioutsiouliklis, and J. Johnson. 2003. "'Googlearchy': How a few heavily-linked sites dominate politics on the Web." Mimeograph, Princeton University, 2003.

Rosen, S. 1981. "The economics of superstars." *American Economic Review 71* (5):845–858.

2 The Developing Conception of e-Research

Paul W. Jeffreys

Early Steps toward Computing in a Networked World

Scientific research has a long history, but it has only been since the mid–twentieth century that scientific challenges have been able to draw on the resources offered by computational science—defined in this volume as the application of information and communication technologies (ICTs) to information processing, simulation, and modeling of complex phenomena. Research data have increasingly been captured by instruments, generated by simulations, and gathered from the modeling of systems and from sensor networks as well as by researchers themselves. As discussed throughout this book, the increasing scale of the data sources and computational resources involved may create a data deluge (Hey and Trefethen 2003), which poses a growing challenge for society. This challenge requires the ability to search for and find specific data sets or samples from a selection of independent repositories, to combine selections, and to undertake new types of intensive analysis using computer-processing power. Meeting this need often involves looking for correlations across different large data sets, visualizing the output, and thereby extracting information and knowledge in innovative ways.

Research within the sciences is embracing more and more a combination of empirical science, theory, and simulation. There has also been a growth in the amount of scientific research that is based on collaboration as a means of pooling expertise and resources; in many cases, cooperation between research groups is required to undertake increasingly complex investigations and analyses (chapter 10). Similar unification and cooperation across disciplines is also expanding across many areas of research outside science. The ambition to build a shared, unified, and collaborative computing environment to meet this challenge dates back to the earliest days of computing.

From the 1960s, scenarios were anticipated that saw the coming together of computational and communications technologies (e.g., Licklider and Taylor 1968). In the 1980s, the development of parallel computing, which runs applications across a number of separate processors at the same time, focused on the development of algorithms, programs, and architectures for enhancing processing power. The computer programs were designed to undertake ever more challenging tasks, which resulted in their becoming larger in scale. This drive eventually pushed against the resource limits of even the fastest parallel computers in individual computer installations. The building of networks of computers therefore became of increasing importance, rather than the enhancement of the processing capacity of stand-alone computers.

As a result of these trends, software developments increasingly focused on the provision of communication between processors as well as on tools to develop and execute single applications to run across different computers. The concept of linking computers to combine resources also created additional advantages, such as networking geographically separated but interconnected facilities and resources. Improvements in network performance, relative to computer speed, began to double every year, thus outpacing the continuing enhancement of processing speed that had been computer hardware engineers' prevailing prime target.

Once this position was reached, the creation of new types of distributed computing infrastructure not only became possible, but also became a strategic direction for the industry. This infrastructure included the streaming of large amounts of information from databases or instruments to remote computers in order to link sensors with each other and with computers, curate the data collected, connect people to build new forms of collaboration, store output in collaborative environments, and pool computational resources and research skills.

The Importance of Grid Computing

The term *Grid computing* originated in the early 1990s as a metaphor for making computer power as easy to access by the user as electricity from an electric power grid. A combination of technology trends and research advances came together and enabled innovations that resulted in the new class of computing infrastructure. According to Fran Berman, Geoffrey Fox, and Anthony Hey, "the Grid" is "the infrastructure which will provide us with the ability to dynamically link together resources as an ensemble to support the execution of large-scale, resource-intensive, and distributed applications" (2004:9). It has also been described as "a type of parallel and distributed system that enables the sharing, selection, and aggregation of resources distributed across multiple administrative domains based on their (resources) availability, capacity, performance, cost, and users' quality-of-service requirements."[1]

The experimental demonstration project I-WAY is generally considered to be the first modern Grid (see box 2.1).

I-Way heralded the start of sustained activity to develop a coherent set of software components for distributed computing. The subject at this time was known as "metacomputing," which took various computing resources, heterogeneous in many respects, and attempted to turn them into a single, uniformly accessible, computing

Box 2.1

I-WAY: A Pioneering Experimental Grid Demonstration

I-WAY was presented at the Super-Computing 95 conference[a] as a project linking eleven experimental networks together for a period of one week, creating an international high-speed network infrastructure across seventeen sites in the United States and Canada. A total of sixty application demonstrations were run, using a rudimentary unified software infrastructure (I-Soft). Provision was made for unified scheduling and a single sign-on procedure that offered access, which enforced security and coordinated the resources available. I-WAY was led by Tom DeFanti of the University of Illinois at Chicago and Rick Stevens of the Argonne National Laboratory (for more details, see DeFanti, Foster, Papka, et al. 1996).

Note:
a. The formal title of Super-Computing 95 was the International Conference for High Performance Computing (see http://www.supercomp.org).

---

environment. The fundamental research issues were associated with load sharing and balancing, task migration, and remote access. Grid computing was born as the set of capabilities required to achieve the dynamic linking of resources securely and in a controlled manner emerged and as the networks acquired suitable bandwidths.

Ian Foster, Carl Kesselman, and Steve Tuecke—widely regarded as the "fathers of the Grid" for drawing together the fruits of a decade of research and development (see Foster and Kesselman 1999)—created the Globus Toolkit (box 2.2). Other toolkits have been created, some offered commercially, such as the Condor project (which developed high-throughput scheduling) and the Storage Resource Broker (a facilitator of uniform access to heterogeneous data resources).[2] These kits offer complementary capabilities to those identified in box 2.2.

In summary, the key features supplied within a Grid environment are:

- *Resource sharing* enabling collaboration across groups on a global scale
- *Secure access* requiring a high level of trust between resource providers and the collaborating groups because individual users must be authenticated in order to access the shared resources
- *Effective and equitable resource use* meeting the demand for Grid resources across the Grid to be balanced
- *Decreased effects of distance* allowing geographically separated groups to operate with a shared infrastructure
- *Open standards* ensuring that Grids are interoperable and that everyone can contribute constructively to Grid development

Box 2.2
Globus and the Globus Toolkit

The open-source Globus Toolkit is a fundamental enabling technology for the Grid.[a] It allows its users to share computing power, databases, and other tools securely online in ways that cross corporate, institutional, and geographic boundaries without sacrificing local autonomy. It includes software services and libraries for resource monitoring, discovery, and management; security and file management; information infrastructure; data management; communication; fault detection; and portability. Its core services, interfaces, and protocols allow users to access remote resources as if they were located within their own machine room, while simultaneously preserving local control over who can use resources and when. The Globus Toolkit has grown through an open-source strategy, similar to that used to develop the Linux operating system.

Note:
a. See http://www.globus.org/ for more details about Globus.

Development and Deployment of the Grid

As understanding of Grid requirements has matured, standard technologies have emerged for basic Grid operations, such as those based on the Open Grid Services Architecture (OGSA). The OGSA aims to define a common, standard, and open architecture for Grid-based applications covering all the services in a Grid application, such as job management, resource management, and security (Foster and Kesselman 1999).

Such standards reflect the trend toward developing service-oriented Grid computing environments that are based on Web service technologies. A Web service is a software system that supports interoperable machine-to-machine interaction over a network, enabling computers to communicate with each other, just as humans communicate with computers through Web pages.[3]

Grids have been developed around a number of major science projects across the world (see box 2.3).

A wide range and variety of collaborative research that uses the kinds of shared computational resources illustrated in box 2.3 can be created by deploying components within a Grid toolkit, rather than by attempting to tailor new bespoke solutions for each application. The Grid also enables researchers to undertake new investigations and to make new discoveries using software known as "middleware" (box 2.4). To accomplish these tasks, agreed sets of standards have become essential, such as those specified by OGSA. A key challenge has been to create middleware that is easy to integrate and does not require developers and support staff with a high degree of specialized expertise. The role of middleware is further examined later in the chapter.

Box 2.3

Grid Implementations from around the World

Two major Grid projects at CERN are the Large Hadron Collider Computing Grid, which is dedicated to providing the processing power and storage capacity necessary for CERN's Large Hadron Collider, and the Enabling Grids for E-sciencE, funded by the European Commission.[a]

The U.S. National Aeronautics and Space Administration's (NASA) Information Power Grid is a high-performance computing and data Grid built primarily for use by NASA scientists and engineers.[b]

The U.S. Department of Energy's Science Grid infrastructure supports widely distributed computing, data, and instrument resources for large-scale science activities.[c]

The U.S. National Science Foundation's TeraGrid is an open scientific infrastructure combining advanced resources at eleven U.S. partner sites to help create an integrated, persistent computational resource.[d]

The U.K. e-Science Programme's National Grid Service provides coherent, reliable, and trusted electronic access for U.K. researchers to all computational and data-based resources and facilities required to carry out their research independent of resource or researcher location.[e] It is a full-production service, delivering a Grid infrastructure together with computing and storage resources on which researchers can build their applications.

Notes:

a. CERN's Grid activities are detailed at http://public.web.cern.ch/public/en/Spotlight/SpotlightGrid-en.html.

b. Information about NASA's Information Power Grid is at http://www.gloriad.org/gloriad/projects/project000053.html.

c. For more on the Science Grid, see http://www.doescienceGrid.org/.

d. Details of the TeraGrid project are at http://www.teraGrid.org/.

e. For information on the United Kingdom's National Grid Service, see http://www.Grid-support.ac.uk/.

A number of approaches, such as virtual research environments (VREs) (chapter 10), have been developed to enable the domain researcher to participate more directly and to use the new functionality without being a computer expert. In parallel, there has been a move toward combining Grid, Semantic Web (essay 4.3), and Web 2.0 approaches to offer "do-it-yourself" Grid application development (essay 2.2).

The Growth and Broad Vision of e-Research

Widespread deployment of Grids, the use of middleware to bridge some of the complexity, and improvements to the storage and computational resources of networks have opened new avenues for research and created challenging new demands. This vision has

Box 2.4

Middleware Grid Software

> Middleware is computer software that is "in the middle" between application software and the underlying operating systems, with the aim of hiding the complexity of the underlying systems from the researcher. For the Grid, this software consists of a set of enabling services that allow multiple processes to run on one or more machines that interact across a network. The distinction between operating system and middleware functionality is to some extent arbitrary. Although core kernel functionality can be provided only by the operating system itself, some functionality previously provided by separately sold middleware is now integrated into operating systems.

been encompassed by new national activities, such as e-science[4] and e-infrastructure programs in the United Kingdom[5] and cyberinfrastructure[6] in the United States. Such terms broadly encompass scientific research that is generally large scale and conducted via distributed collaborations, often leveraging access to large-scale data and powerful computing capabilities.

A major aim of the growing e-research community is to apply the benefits from advances in ICT to research activities in ways that move beyond science and engineering disciplines to include the humanities (e.g., U.K. Office of Science and Innovation 2007). Accordingly, the generic term used to describe the new field of activity is *e-research*. Expertise from various research domains and a range of computational resources can be collected globally and brought to bear on the area under study, which can deliver a secure infrastructure that delivers good performance to the user. New ICT capabilities have the potential to "flatten" the research world in some respects by lowering the barriers that researchers must overcome in order to access rich new information and communication resources.

Therefore, e-research is more than just an extension of e-science to cover all areas of research: it is a generalization beyond a Grid-centric world to one that encapsulates research activities that use a spectrum of advanced ICT capabilities.[7] The Australian government's vision of e-research includes research activities that use a spectrum of advanced ICT capabilities to cover new research methodologies emerging from increasing access to e-infrastructures.[8]

Thus, e-research can be seen as encompassing much more than the Grid. In the broadest sense, it incorporates a new culture that embraces the opportunities provided by the growing wealth of digital information and resources and by the facilitating of global collaboration. Computation has become a fundamental tool for modern research that often overlaps a number of disciplines, which requires assembling and managing large data collections as well as exploiting these collections through computer models and simulations.

Box 2.5
The DAME and BROADEN Projects

The Distributed Aircraft Maintenance Environment (DAME) project exploited a Grid service architecture based on the Open Grid Services Infrastructure (OGSI) and Open Grid
Services Architecture (OGSA).[a] DAME demonstrated how the data-management aspects of
maintenance support systems can be handled within a unified knowledge broker model
that delivers the right knowledge at the right time, using disparate services within a distributed environment. A proof-of-concept demonstrator was built around the business scenario
of a distributed aircraft engine–maintenance environment, motivated by the needs of Rolls
Royce and its information system partner Data Systems and Solutions. DAME was followed
by the BROADEN project, which has been funded by the United Kingdom's Technology
Programme with the aims of putting in place the necessary hardware, evaluating software
options, offering an opportunity to demonstrate the benefits of Grid computing within
industry and business, and thus ensuring that the United Kingdom gains from the more
effective, flexible, and cost-efficient usage of expensive ICT resources that it enables. The
project was a success, and all the partners are looking to exploit the capability further. The
technology has been taken into neuroscience in the Carmen project.[b]

Notes:
a. See more on the DAME project at http://www.cs.york.ac.uk/dame/ and the BROADEN
project at http://www.nesc.ac.uk/talks/ahm2006/657.pdf.
b. For more on the Carmen project, see http://www.carmen.org.uk/.

Key research challenges that can be addressed using the new resources include real-
time intelligent feature extraction (which identifies a reduced set of features from a very
large data set that may contain a significant amount of redundant data), intelligent data
mining (sorting and picking out relevant information from a very large data sample),
and the application of decision-support techniques (using applications to validate the
human interpretation of data, notably in the field of medicine). In each case, the expertise and software tools are within a distributed infrastructure. These challenges often
require going beyond the resources available within academic research to encompass
distributed collaboration in many industrial contexts, as exemplified by the Distributed
Aircraft Maintenance Environment (DAME) and BROADEN projects (box 2.5).

Cyberinfrastructure and e-Infrastructure Developments

The Push from Government Initiatives
Governments around the world have sought to exploit the potential that e-research
offers to advance research and improve social and economic well-being (essay 2.3).[9]
Many bodies that make public policy have recommended the creation of a national

infrastructure to underpin e-research activities for the benefit of academia, industry, and society. Some of the major public initiatives across the world seeking to promote Grid applications in science and industry are highlighted in box 2.6.

What Is an e-Infrastructure?

Box 2.6 shows examples of national Grid initiatives, but such initiatives compose only one component within an e-infrastructure. A report by the U.K. Office of Science and Innovation (2007) on proposals for a national e-infrastructure states that the targeted capabilities will "support the entire data and information life cycle, accelerating the research process itself," and "allow for the re-use and re-purposing of digital data in all their forms." Its plans include developments in the visualization of data; the data deluge; data analysis preservation and curation; the data and information life cycle; high-performance computing; virtual research communities and collaboration; interoperability; standards; and "better, faster, different" research. In this sense, e-infrastructure is at the very core of e-research.

The physical components of an e-infrastructure need to provide a secure, robust, and resilient environment for the researcher. In addition to the networks, computational resources are required for a wide range of simulations, data analyses, and control of instruments and experiments. In many cases, such as the United Kingdom's National Grid Service, the computational resource embraces large supercomputers, national Grids, and local Grids—all of which use spare cycles from local computers. Researchers' applications should not use the relatively scarce high-performance computational resources unless they are specifically required, and Grid facilities offer the less-expensive alternative.

The e-infrastructure should also provide data services that offer full life-cycle data curation created from instruments, models, and digital libraries, and should manage the operations for these collections of data. It must offer interconnection and interoperability provision for continued use of legacy systems, with diversity to cover multiple needs, particularly where primary data is located close to the high-volume data generators. The e-infrastructure that integrates geographically distributed resources inevitably presents researchers with more of a challenge to use them effectively than centralized systems do. VREs (chapter 10) address the complexity of e-infrastructure by offering relatively easy access to the breadth of resources and facilities available to researchers. Each component of e-infrastructure discussed so far depends on software—software that often has to deal with demanding loads in distributed and persistent contexts. Coordinated software development and maintenance are therefore essential.

This description of e-infrastructure is not complete because it focuses on the creation, management, and preservation of researcher data, but does not address the overall management of digital content. A number of models of cyberinfrastructure[10] have been proposed, often suggesting a type of layering, as illustrated in figure 2.1. These models suggest that scientific databases, digital libraries, and other collections of digital content

Box 2.6
National and Transnational e-Research Initiatives

The U.S. NSF's (2007) Cyberinfrastructure Vision[a] aims to develop a cultural community that supports peer-to-peer collaboration and new modes of education, based on broad and open access to advanced computing, data and information resources, online instruments and observatories, and visualization and collaboration services.

The U.K. e-Science Programme[b] began in 2001 as a coordinated initiative involving all the Research Councils and the government. Its Core Programme supports the creation of computing Grids and the development of generic technologies, including middleware, needed to enable different resources to work together across networks. Each Research Council funds its own e-science activities across a broad range of research and applications.

The Australian Research Collaboration Service (ARCS)[c] aims to provide long-term e-research support services for the Australian research community with a particular focus on interoperability and collaboration infrastructure, tools, services, and support. It offers a set of services that include data fabric, remote computing, remote instrumentation and sensor network services, Web-based collaboration, and video collaboration.[d]

The German Grid Initiative (D-Grid)[e] is a joint initiative involving German research and industry, with the Federal Ministry of Education and Research funding its development and applications that started in 2005. The initiative has moved from offering initial ICT services for scientists, designed and developed by the computer science and scientific computing communities, to proving services for scientists, industry, and business.

There are three major Grid middleware efforts in China: the China National Grid (CNGrid),[f] supported by the key "863 program" project of the National High-tech R&D Programme; the China R&D Over Wide Area Network, supported by the China NSF key research program; and the China Grid Supporting Platform, supported by the Ministry of Education.

The European e-Infrastructure Reflection Group,[g] sponsored by the European Commission, supports the creation of a political, technological, and administrative framework for sharing the use of distributed e-resources across Europe, particularly for Grid computing, storage, and networking.

Notes:
a. For more on the U.S. NSF cyberinfrastructure vision, see http://www.nsf.gov/pubs/2007/nsf0728/index.jsp.
b. For more on the UK e-Science Programme, see http://www.rcuk.ac.uk/escience/default.htm.
c. For more on ARCS, see http://www.unisa.edu.au/eresearch/nationalactivity.asp.
d. The ARCS services are described at http://www.arcs.org.au/.
e. For more on D-Grid, see http://www.d-grid.de/index.php?id=1&L=1.
f. For more on CNGrid, see http://ieeexplore.ieee.org/stamp/stamp.jsp?arnumber=01316605.
g. For more on the European e-Infrastructure Reflection Group, see http://www.e-irg.eu/.

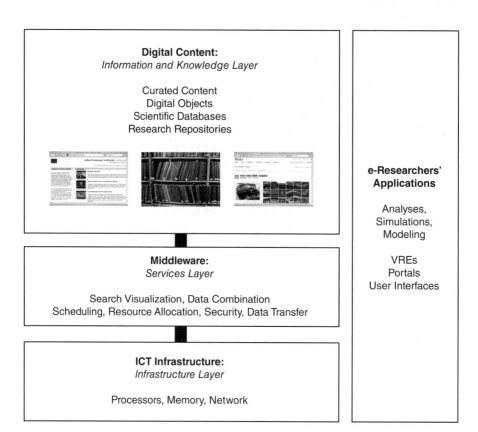

Figure 2.1
Cyberinfrastructure: Layered model.

can be seen to form an "information and knowledge layer": the middleware enables the services in the higher layer to use the underpinning computing infrastructure (computer systems, processors, memory, and networks).

The model depicted in figure 2.1 demonstrates powerfully that the technology represents much more than the computing infrastructure alone, and that the digital content should be considered as important a part of the infrastructure as the ICT services supported. The "Applications Space" box to the right in figure 2.1 conveys the idea that e-research applications cut vertically across the three layers and are dependent on each of the layers to deliver services effectively, interoperating with each other. Achieving success in this interoperation is a fundamental challenge for e-infrastructure. Each of the layers is operated by different organizations, with different agendas and different funding models. Yet the overall resource should be managed and developed coherently in order for it to deliver a satisfactory service to the researcher.

In summary, box 2.7 indicates a minimum set of requirements for an e-infrastructure.

Box 2.7
Typical e-Infrastructure Capabilities

An e-infrastructure is usually multipurpose. It also has to be sustainable and dependable so that researchers can plan to use it for the duration of their work. Growing researcher expectations and ongoing innovations in digital technologies and information systems are generating requirements for incremental enhancements. To meet these requirements, the key components of such an integrated network-enabled research infrastructure should therefore include the following elements:

1. An ICT infrastructure that delivers the necessary broadband and networking capabilities, physical connections, computer systems, large data-storage facilities, sensor networks, and other underpinning e-research resources.

2. Middleware and organization environments to enable secure connectivity and interoperability for collaborative working, through the deep integration of individual components across the network, including access controls (security, authentication, authorization), tools for finding resources (search engines), tools for collaboration (video conferencing, shared VREs), and convenient software toolkits (e.g., Globus).

3. Digital content and application tools that encompass discipline-specific and interaction needs, such as well-curated collections of research data (national and scientific databases, individual and project data), digital libraries (bibliographies, text, images, sound), online experimental equipment (telescopes, satellites, special physics equipment, spectrometers), and large data collections (e.g., from social science surveys).

Sources: Based on material from the Australian government's description of e-research and the European e–Infrastructure Reflection Group Roadmap on e-Infrastructure (see box 2.6).

The major Grid projects listed in box 2.3 were produced, operated, and managed under the responsibility of specific authorities. They were initially driven by disciplines (e.g., particle physics at the European Organization for Nuclear Research [CERN]) because the disciplines were easier to mobilize and coordinate. Large organizations (such as the U.S. National Science Foundation [NSF]) and nations have developed programs to create e-infrastructures, generally encompassing significant Grid services.

This procedure, however, may be changing. It is increasingly likely that e-infrastructure will be provided through a "Cloud": an ecosystem of technologies that enable the hosting of an organization's major ICT infrastructure components (hardware and software) in large data centers managed by external company providers (essay 2.1).

The Importance of Social Dimensions to e-Research

The concept of e-infrastructure as developed and explored in this chapter and as summarized in figure 2.1 misses an essential ingredient of e-research—the social dimension.

Addressing this dimension is essential to ensuring that researchers can exploit the potential of an e-infrastructure fully. Joseph Licklider and Robert Taylor recognized the importance of social aspects of computing in 1968 when they made bold predictions that foresaw two of the challenges faced today: "In a few years, men will be able to communicate more effectively through a machine than face to face," and "For the society, the impact will be good or bad, depending mainly on the question 'Will, to be on line, be a privilege or a right?'" (52).

The American Council of Learned Societies (ACLS) Commission on Cyberinfrastructure for the Humanities and Social Sciences recognized the broad scope of opportunities offered by e-infrastructure when it concluded: "We should place the world's cultural heritage—its historical documentation, its literary and artistic achievements, its languages, beliefs, and practices—within the reach of every citizen. The value of building an infrastructure that gives all citizens access to the human record and the opportunity to participate in its creation and use is enormous, exceeding even the significant investment that will be required to build that infrastructure' (ACLS 2006:40). Cyberinfrastructure created initially for researchers within a scientific organization therefore offers a crucially important platform for society and across all disciplines.

More than a set of computing resources made available to researchers, e-research is a collaborative working environment with shared resources, where computer scientists research new capabilities, and technologists implement developments to the e-infrastructure to meet evolving needs. An increasing number of computer scientists are suggesting the need to consider the social dimensions of technological change, arguing that e-research has three inseparable elements: the e-infrastructure; researchers who recognize new opportunities and place new user demands on the e-infrastructure; and social science analyses (e.g., Schroeder and Fry 2007) that acknowledge, as explored throughout this book, the ways in which modern research can result in important new cultural, legal, and social issues. Figure 2.2 depicts the relationships between the technical, user, and social aspects of network-enabled research.

Social Science and e-Research

An NSF Workshop on Cyberinfrastructure and the Social Sciences concluded that cyberinfrastructure is "just as critical for the advancement of the social, behavioral, and economic (SBE) sciences as it is for engineering and the physical, natural, biological, and computer sciences," and that "the SBE sciences can also help assess the effects of Cyberinfrastructure on science, engineering, technology, and society so that its potential can be realized and its benefits maximized" (Berman and Brady 2005:4).

An interesting case highlighting the way social dimensions can influence outcomes of even technically excellent e-research projects is the United Kingdom's flagship Diagnostic Mammography National Database (e-DiaMoND) (essay 7.1; Jirotka, Procter, Rodden, et al. 2005). This £4.25 million interdisciplinary U.K. collaborative e-science

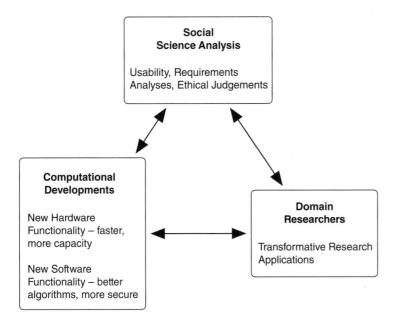

The three dimensions are inseparable and rely and feed on each other.

Figure 2.2
Intrinsic technical, user, and social dimensions of e-research.

project sought to use Grid technology to manage a series of services throughout the United Kingdom to create a federated database in which X-ray images for breast cancer screening could be stored and annotated digitally. The reading of these images could be undertaken in distributed mode, thereby reducing the need for expert readers at each site. As a proof of principle, e-DiaMoND was a technical and computational success. However, as Tina Piper and David Vaver explain in essay 7.1 in this volume, for nontechnical reasons, such as legal aspects, it failed to be incorporated into the national breast-screening program.

This kind of interplay between e-research and the social sciences is explored in a number of chapters in this volume.

Virtual Collaborative Organizations

E-infrastructures underpin the resources and services shared by researchers working in different disciplines and in different locations, which is helping to establish virtual collaborative organizations (VCOs), also known as virtual organizations (VOs), in which researchers with common interests function as coherent units while being distributed geographically or temporally or both. Such VOs are an important component within e-infrastructures, drawing membership from distributed legal entities to pursue a common research goal and bound by memoranda of understanding, policies, federations, and so on.

As the number of digital resources, databases, computational algorithms, and collaborative technology grows, a wide variety of tools is emerging that facilitates and supports the research process within VCOs, thus further flattening the research landscape and holding the potential to change significantly the conduct of research (see also U.K. Office of Science and Innovation e-Infrastructure Steering Group 2006). VREs encompass a broad range of online tools, content, and middleware within a coherent framework that includes facilities for all disciplines and all types of research. They therefore help to broaden the popular definition of e-research beyond Grid-based distributed computing used by scientists with large amounts of data to manage.

Ensuring That e-Research Systems Are Easy to Use

Increasing emphasis is being given to the importance of ease of use within e-research, inspired by initiatives such as Web 2.0 social networking (see the introduction and essay 2.2). Finding complex middleware solutions is too large a hurdle for many communities, such as chemists, biologists, and engineers, as well as professionals in the social sciences and humanities. Researchers need to be able to create with little effort or special expertise and with varying degrees of security the kinds of loosely coupled VCO that fit their needs—just as Web users can easily create "mash-ups" of information from different Web sites. For instance, users of an e-infrastructure should to be able to access services through a simple browser interface rather than having to wrestle with complex middleware to ensure compatibility with other libraries and system software.

Researchers in very large disciplines, such as particle physicists, have the resources to manage the creation of a complex and effective world-spanning environment;[11] researchers in other fields cannot. The e-research vision must be much broader than that which can be provided by such specialist services; it must also embrace opportunities for researchers to experiment with and build VOs with very little overhead and with simple interactions. Ease of access, shaped by knowledge of the social and psychological sciences, is essential to making the riches of the digital age widely accessible.

The Way Ahead

This chapter has presented a historical perspective for e-research, appraised its growth, considered Grid deployment in large-scale national and international projects, demonstrated that the Grid is but one component within an e-infrastructure, emphasized the importance of social dimensions within e-research, and shown that e-research is increasingly moving toward an outsourcing of technology and a new form of research for a networked world where any researcher can and should participate.

Essay 2.2 glimpses ahead to the future by exploring the increasing scale and diversity of participation in the "new e-research"—where anyone can participate and there are incentives to do so. Such participation would bring increasing scale, diversity, and complexity of digital content, and may require an expansion of existing tools and some further development of new tools to discover, visualize, combine, and share resources. If this vision is translated into reality, it may create a new form of "open research" where data, collections, methods, work flows, and outputs are increasingly shared and reusable, with the tools and services and the software that provide them being equally shared.

As Tony Hey, Roger Barga, and Savas Parastatidis explain in essay 2.1, this kind of environment will shift the emphasis from complex middleware to simple services. In addition to software installed on servers and desktops, there will be an increase in the provision of e-research services delivered from the Cloud. The remainder of this book explores the implications of this next step along the road ahead.

Notes

1. See "IBM Solutions Grid for Business Partners: Helping IBM Business Partners to Grid-Enable Applications for the Next Phase of e-Business on Demand," at http://www-304.ibm.com/jct09002c/isv/marketing/emerging/Grid_wp.pdf.

2. For the Condor project, see http://www.cs.wisc.edu/condor, and for Storage Resource Broker, see http://www.npaci.edu/DICE/SRB/.

3. See http://www.w3.org/2002/ws/ regarding Web service technologies.

4. Definitions of e-science are offered at http://www.nesc.ac.uk/nesc/define.html.

5. See the U.K. Research Councils' e-Science Programme at http://www.rcuk.ac.uk/escience/default.htm.

6. See the U.S. NSF Office of Cyberinfrastructure at http://www.nsf.gov/dir/index.jsp?org=OCI.

7. A similar approach has been adopted by many initiatives, such as the Oxford e-Research Centre (http://www.oerc.ox.ac.uk/), which aims to offer "innovative technology for multi-disciplinary research."

8. The Australian government's description of e-research is at http://www.dest.gov.au/sectors/research_sector/policies_issues_reviews/key_issues/e_research_consult/.

9. For instance, the U.K. Office of Science and Innovation (2007) has recognized that the growth of the United Kingdom's knowledge-based economy depends significantly on the continued support of the research community and, in particular, on research activities that engage with industry to apply its world-leading innovations to commercial use.

10. For further details of the model, see http://www.dlib.org/dlib/july05/griffin/07griffin.html.

11. For example, GridPP, the U.K. Grid for particle physicists (http://www.Gridpp.ac.uk/).

References

American Council of Learned Societies (ACLS). 2006. *Our cultural commonwealth: The report of the American Council of Learned Societies Commission on Cyberinfrastructure for the Humanities and Social Sciences.* New York: ACLS. Available at: http://www.acls.org/Cyberinfrastructure/OurCulturalCommon wealth.pdf.

Berman, F., and H. Brady. 2005. *Final Report: NSF SBE-CISE Workshop on Cyberinfrastructure and the Social Sciences, Cyberinfrastructure Council, National Science Foundation, North Arlington, VA, 12 May 2005.* Available at: http://vis.sdsc.edu/sbe/reports/SBE-CISE-FINAL.pdf.

Berman, F., G. C. Fox, and A. J. G. Hey, eds. 2004. *Grid computing—making the global infrastructure a reality.* Chichester, UK: Wiley.

DeFanti, T. A., I. Foster, M. E. Papka, R. Stevens, and T. Kuhfuss. 1996. "Overview of the I-Way: Wide-area visual supercomputing." *International Journal of High Performance Computing Applications 10* (2–3):123–130.

Foster, I., and C. Kesselman, eds. 1999. *The Grid: Blueprint for a new computing infrastructure.* San Francisco: Morgan Kaufmann.

Hey, A. J. G., and A. E. Trefethen. 2003. "The data deluge: An e-science perspective." In *Grid computing—making the global infrastructure a reality*, ed. F. Berman, G. C. Fox, and A. J. G. Hey. Chichester, UK: Wiley, 809–824.

Jirotka, M., R. Procter, T. Rodden, and G. C. Bowker. 2005. "Collaboration and trust in healthcare innovation: The eDiaMoND case study." *Computer Supported Cooperative Work 14* (4):369–398.

Licklider, J. C. R., and R. W. Taylor. 1968. "The computer as a communications device." Science and Technology (April):21–31. Available at: ftp://gatekeeper.dec.com/pub/DEC/SRC/publications/taylor/licklider-taylor.pdf.

Schroeder, R., and J. Fry. 2007. "Social science perspectives on e-science: Framing an agenda." *Journal of Computer-Mediated Communication 12* (2). Available at: http://jcmc.indiana.edu/vol12/issue2/schroeder.html.

U.K. Office of Science and Innovation. 2007. *Developing the UK's e-infrastructure for science and innovation.* Report of the Office of Science and Innovation (OSI) e-Infrastructure Working Group. London: Department for Innovation, Universities and Skills. Available at: http://www.nesc.ac.uk/documents/OSI/index.html.

U.K. Office of Science and Innovation (OSI) e-Infrastructure Steering Group. 2006. *Report of the Working Group on Virtual Research Communities.* London: Department for Innovation, Universities and Skills. Available at: http://www.nesc.ac.uk/documents/OSI/vrc.pdf.

U.S. National Science Foundation (NSF). 2007. *Cyberinfrastructure vision for 21st century discovery.* North Arlington, VA: Cyberinfrastructure Council, NSF. Available at: http://www.nsf.gov/pubs/2007/nsf0728/index.jsp.

2.1 Research Platforms in the Cloud

Tony Hey, Roger Barga, and Savas Parastatidis

Challenges and Opportunities for e-Research

One can look at the challenges facing researchers today through a number of dimensions. Here we focus on three: the increasingly data-intensive computing nature of research; the rise of distributed collaborations; and researchers as "extreme information workers."

Many advances in science are being achieved not by spending hours in a laboratory or by examining the skies through a telescope, but rather through analyses conducted on large volumes of data. Researchers struggle to keep up with the continuing data deluge and the overhead required to address it (Hey and Trefethen 2003) in terms of the time, people, funding, and coordination required to manage the growing information and communication technology (ICT) infrastructure. What is needed in much of the global research community is technology to reduce the time to new insights, enabling researchers to spend more time on investigation and discovery instead of fighting ICT-related issues. Computer-based technologies are increasingly used as the tools for managing, processing, and visualizing the mountains of information.

Requirements to support research are more complex than simply providing easy access to cheap storage and fast processors. As researchers address increasingly complex problems, collaboration across disciplines is becoming essential, and interdisciplinary work is being pursued more enthusiastically than ever. At the same time, domain-specific communities of experts are being formed to attack grand research challenges, such as through the major e-science and cyberinfrastructure projects in the United Kingdom and the United States, as discussed earlier in this book.

However, despite the increasing demand for software to support virtual research teams and collaborations, it is proving difficult to build such platforms from scratch, as most research groups have chosen to do. Meanwhile, social networking (e.g., through Web sites such as Facebook and YouTube) is enabling millions of people to communicate, share files, and keep in touch. There is no reason why researchers cannot leverage the same principles and technologies underlying social networking, as ongoing projects are trying to demonstrate.[1]

Finally, we consider the role of an individual researcher who typically both consumes and creates information and knowledge. Researchers daily search and browse the Web, exchange emails, use instant messaging, read and write blogs, navigate paper citations, participate in social networks, produce papers, go to conferences, and so on. The extreme information-management needs of a modern research environment require expertise in a plethora of general-purpose productivity tools and highly sophisticated, domain-specific applications. A new generation of software and services can help researchers deal with the modern information overload.

Doing Research in the "Cloud"

The name "Cloud" is used to describe the ecosystem of technologies that enable the hosting of an organization's or individual's ICT infrastructure (hardware and software) in large data centers managed by service providers. It is the equivalent of "outsourcing," but this time technology rather than people is hosted elsewhere.

Data and Computational Services

The data-intensive nature of modern research makes it increasingly difficult for research institutions to manage the required data-storage and computational infrastructure. In the future, it may well be less expensive and faster for research projects to outsource their computing and data-storage needs rather than building and maintaining their own infrastructure. This is especially true for projects that can't efficiently utilize dedicated infrastructure over long periods of time, so a potential investment in peak hardware, software, and ICT support requirements can't easily be justified. Furthermore, by utilizing such Cloud services, the researchers can take advantage of features that would be impossible to implement and deploy on their own, such as geodistribution of data for fast access by collaborating researchers around the world, replication for fault tolerance, and so on.

Domain-Specific Services

Many research projects take advantage of common functionality or "tools of the trade," such as data-analysis routines, visualization tools for interpretation and understanding, and data cleaning and transformations. Such projects often incorporate similar algorithms in what are effectively their own specific work flows. These algorithms are executed many times on different data-analysis pipelines. Researchers are not interested in having to deploy and manage the associated codes in their computational services; rather, they are likely to expect them simply to be present and will thus demand appropriate tools and services that support their particular version of the research life cycle.

Scientific and Technical Services

In the future, following the model of "software as a service," software tool providers may choose to offer the functionality of their products as services. In order to avoid the huge costs of having to maintain a global infrastructure network, such enterprises can leverage the capabilities of those offering services-hosting platforms for use by others. Their products can then be accessed by researchers around the world on a pay-per-use basis and incorporated into work flows and research project portals. A plethora of scientific services are already being offered on the Web (e.g., BLAST,[2] GenBank,[3] ClustalW2,[4] and PubMed[5]).

Scholarly Communication

Once the data-processing and analysis phase of a project has been completed, researchers are typically interested in publishing their findings. An ecosystem of services and tools, integrated with project portals and productivity tools, can be provided to researchers to support their dissemination processes. Metrics to assess the impact of the research work, making use of social networks, researchers' reputations, citations, and so on, are natural extensions to existing techniques of peer review.

Software Plus Services

Researchers usually work within the context of a particular project; they collaborate with other researchers, exchange documents and emails, chat, wish to be notified of interesting things that might have happened, go to conferences, publish papers, search the Web, and so on. Services have already begun to appear on the Web to help with the continuously increasing information-management requirements of research (e.g., see Yang and Allan 2006; Barga, Andrews, and Parastatidis 2007). Portals can be envisaged for the aggregation and integration of all the Cloud services and functionality that researchers use on a daily basis (e.g., see figure 2.3). Furthermore, the same functionality can surface through the use of familiar productivity tools, such as word processors, to implement the "software plus services" vision.

Building the e-Research Platform

Available software and services can already be employed as the basis for building a collection of Web tools (e.g., project-management portals), Web-based interfaces to aggregated functionality (e.g., literature search tools across a variety of online services and clipboards), integration with desktop-based productivity applications (e.g., a Research Ribbon interface for Microsoft Office), and other relevant capabilities.

More advanced services can be incorporated into the ecosystem—for example, to address the move toward data-intensive computing and the need for utility computing and data-storage services. The demand for tools to perform scientific data analysis is

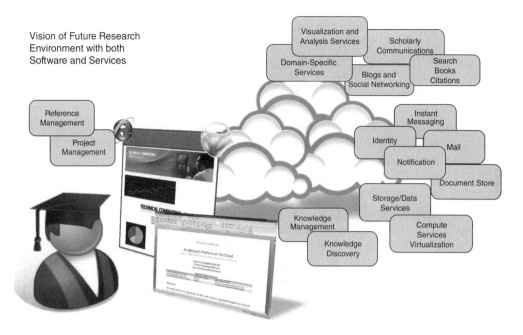

Figure 2.3
Software plus services to support all aspects of e-research.

rising even faster than data volumes (Gray, Liu, Szalay, et al. 2005). Researchers would also benefit from services such as data indexing (both spatial and temporal), metadata extraction and tagging services, support for hosted work flows to perform automatic data cleaning and analysis, and very high-powered petascale data-mining and analysis services. A rich list of useful tools for data-intensive research is being established to meet these needs (e.g., see Gray et al. 2005; Bell, Gray, and Szalay 2006).

In addition, researchers would benefit from the availability of high-level programming and orchestration tools that seamlessly integrate with services such as data storage and computation, data visualization and streaming, scholarly communication–related services, research-oriented social networks, virtual lab notebooks, and so on. Such capabilities can be built as part of the ecosystem of services on e-research platforms.

Conclusion

In the future, the rapidity with which any given discipline advances is likely to depend on how well the community acquires the necessary expertise in database, work-flow management, visualization, and Cloud computing technologies. These technical trends will also raise social, legal, and ethical issues, however, such as over the privacy and protection of personal data. The eventual success of these shifts in e-research will therefore depend on social and computer scientists' ability to anticipate and address these issues collaboratively.

Notes

1. See, for example, Connotea by Nature Publishing at http://www.connotea.org and SciLink at http://www.scilink.com.

2. BLAST finds regions of similarity between biological sequences (http://www.ncbi.nlm.nih.gov/blast/Blast.cgi).

3. GenBank is the U.S. National Institutes of Health's genetic sequence database, an annotated collection of all publicly available DNA sequences (http://www.ncbi.nlm.nih.gov/Genbank/).

4. ClustalW2 is a general-purpose, multiple-sequence alignment program for DNA or proteins (http://www.ebi.ac.uk/Tools/clustalw2/index.html).

5. PubMed is a service of the U.S. National Library of Medicine that includes more than 17 million citations from MEDLINE and other life science journals for biomedical articles dating back to the 1950s (http://www.ncbi.nlm.nih.gov/sites/entrez).

References

Barga, R., S. Andrews, and S. Parastatidis. 2007. "The British Library Research Information Centre (RIC)." In *Proceedings of the UK e-Science All Hands Conference 2007*, ed. S. J. Cox. Edinburgh: National e-Science Centre. Available at: http://www.allhands.org.uk/2007/proceedings/proceedings/proceedings.pdf.

Bell, G., J. Gray, and A. Szalay. 2006. "Petascale computational systems: Balanced cyberInfrastructure in a data-centric world. Letter to NSF Cyberinfrastructure Directorate." IEEE Computer 39 (1):110–112. Available at: http://research.microsoft.com/~Gray/papers/Petascale%20computational%20systems.pdf.

Gray, J., D. Liu, A. Szalay, D. DeWitt, and G. Heber. 2005. "Scientific data management in the coming decade." SIGMOD Record 34 (4):35–41. Available at: ftp://ftp.research.microsoft.com/pub/tr/tr-2005-10.pdf.

Hey, A. J. G., and A. E. Trefethen. 2003. "The data deluge: An eScience perspective." In *Grid computing—making the global infrastructure a reality*, ed. F. Berman, G. Fox and A. J. G. Hey. Chichester, UK: Wiley, 809–824. Available at: http://eprints.ecs.soton.ac.uk/7648/.

Yang, X., and R. Allan. 2006. *Web-based virtual research environments (VRE): Support collaboration in e-science*. Warrington, UK: CCLRC e-Science Centre, Daresbury Laboratory. Available at: http://epubs.cclrc.ac.uk/bitstream/1413/paper06H.pdf.

2.2 The New e-Research

David De Roure

The success stories of e-science have emerged in so-called big science, where researchers harness large-scale computational and data resources to cope with the huge volumes of data arising from new experimental techniques and data-capture technologies. But what about all the other researchers in our universities and research and development departments—the everyday researchers, working on their Ph.D.s or assisting other researchers in and across the diversity of disciplines? Although e-science provides a case study of advanced techniques in early-adopter communities, other researchers have not been standing still. Here I define the "new e-research" as a set of observations on the key trends that frame our future research environment.

Increasing Scale and Diversity of Participation and Digital Content

The single most influential driver for the "new e-research" is the increasing scale and diversity of participation. The decreasing cost of entry into digital research means more people, data, tools, and methods. Anyone can participate: researchers in labs, archaeologists at digs, or schoolchildren designing drug molecules in Web browsers; they may be professionals or amateur enthusiasts. This claim leads to talk of "citizen science" and "crowd sourcing." Everyone becomes a first-class citizen: each can be a publisher as well as a consumer. It isn't enough that people *can* participate—they are also incentivized to do so by the benefits of working digitally and by the opportunity to play a role. Elitists may disapprove of this state of affairs.

The scale of participation, together with spectacular data volumes from new research instruments, also brings increasing scale, diversity, and complexity of digital content. Research increasingly involves discovering and combining sources, so we now have more to find and more to combine. Furthermore, digital research is generating new digital artifacts: work flows, data-provenance records, ontologies, electronic lab books, and interactive papers. Associated with research content are attribution and licensing to support rights flow as well as technical challenges in versioning, aggregation, and security.

Context and provenance information is essential for data reuse, quality, and trust. Not only are there more data of more kinds, but policy and practice are moving to make all these data more available: we are seeing open data, open-access journals, and increasing adoption of Creative Commons licenses and Science Commons recommendations (see chapter 11). The technologies of linked data (analogous to the Web's linked documents) are now gaining traction to assist with discovery, integration, reuse, and trust. With all this comes a very substantial challenge to digital curation.

Supporting Wider and More Efficient Sharing

Our next defining characteristic is sharing—anyone can play, and they can play together. Research has always been a social process in which researchers collaborate in order to compete, but now we're using new social tools such as wikis, blogs, instant messaging, and social Web sites. In comparison with traditional scholarly communications, the new knowledge life cycle accelerates research and reduces time to experiment. Some of our new digital artifacts are not just pieces of data. Instead, they capture pieces of the research process itself—such as the details of a method, a work flow, an experimental plan or script. These digital representations of methods make research repeatable, reproducible, and reusable. They facilitate automation, and sharing them is particularly powerful because it enables practice to propagate and reputations to grow.

Empowering Researchers

Increased participation, content, and sharing are building a social network of people and things. We see the network effects through "community intelligence": tagging, reviewing, discussing, and recommending based on usage. This intelligence is a powerful new force with which to tackle discovery of data and methods, and to rise to the curation challenge. We also see more and more services being made available for researchers to access remotely, which in itself is a mechanism for sharing capability and know-how—a form of distributed global collaboration.

Researchers are crucially being empowered: increasing fluency with new tools and resources puts them in control of their supporting tools, techniques, and methods. Empowerment enables creativity and encourages bottom-up innovation in the practice of research, giving rise to new and potentially sharable methods. The techniques for automated processing, one of the great successes of e-research, are empowering when they enable researchers to do what they're good at and let the digital machinery deal with the drudgery, but not when they take away control or challenge autonomy. Researchers favor tools that make their work better or easier, rather than complex solutions that demand disproportionate effort to adopt or that constrain desired practice. This de facto principle of "better not perfect" is sometimes at odds with software and service providers' established mindset. A traditional software-engineering approach of requirements capture and top-down design fails in this bottom-up world, where requirements can be elicited only by sharing the journey with the researchers (De Roure and Goble 2009).

The Future: Pervasive Deployment?

The computing infrastructure that supports research is also evolving. The 1990s instinct to harness remote computing resources is giving way to a new problem, which can be called "pervasive deployment": making full use of the resources we have around us on an everyday basis. There is an increasingly rich intersection between the physical and digital worlds as we interact with the devices around us, from phones to laboratory equipment to sensor networks. Researchers at the desktop favor interaction through familiar Web-based interfaces as opposed to software supported by the enterprise.

This evolution of infrastructure and access is consistent with the shift toward Cloud computing (see essay 2.1) and virtualization, whereby remote computers can trivially be summoned on demand. Whereas big science attracts highly engineered infrastructure solutions delivered by specialists, the Web provides a highly adequate distributed computing infrastructure for the work most of us do.

The future research environment has great potential because it can enable us to do things that were not possible before. This development isn't just about acceleration; it's about entirely new research outcomes. Lines can be redrawn as *in silico* practice evolves and entirely new methods and even disciplines can be created. The emerging pattern is an "open-science" world where data, methods, and outputs are shareable and reusable, where tools and services and the software that provides them are shared. Though the pioneers of e-science intended this development, it may come about through the emergence of a bottom-up paradigm where the simplicity of assembly of the pieces can enable the new e-research to flourish.

References

De Roure, D., and C. Goble. 2009. "Software Design for Empowering Scientists." *IEEE Software 26* (1):88–95.

2.3 The Promises and Threats of e-Research in the Strategies of Firms and Nations

John Taylor

Implications for Organizations as Well as Researchers

The global information and communication technology (ICT) infrastructure—based on the Internet, the World Wide Web, Grids, and broadband wireless— has attained a critical mass of connectivity and capability through exponential growth. It provides access to unprecedented amounts of information, expertise, and tools as well as new opportunities for communities of interest to form and cooperate. And there is no indication that we are near a plateau of capability yet, with clear expectations that the underlying technology infrastructure will continue to evolve rapidly for the foreseeable future.

This book explores in detail the implications of using this infrastructure for researchers across all disciplines. One of the most powerful innovations of all in this space has been the emergence of "search" as a key organizing paradigm, making it feasible and efficient to search for and find almost any required data very quickly and inexpensively, wherever it exists on the Web and whoever owns it. Even more powerfully, search has revolutionized our ability to find other people and groups who are interested or involved in almost any activity. This ability is enabling a move into a richly connected mesh of millions of self-discovering, self-organizing communities within which no one is in overall control or ownership.

Although most of the media focus is on the public Internet and the Web, it is important to remember that there is an equally rapid deployment of these technologies inside public and private organizations around the world, as intranets and intrawebs. This deployment is having very profound effects on the way companies and organizations of all kinds do their business and organize their operations.

In many respects, the Internet and Web technologies have started to dissolve national and organizational boundaries, becoming major enablers of the accelerated globalization of business and industry that has been happening since the late 1990s. These technologies have increased the ability and scope of companies everywhere to service global markets and to work with other companies in global supply chains. But it has also more subtly spurred many disruptive new businesses and business models.

Implications for Research

Research in science has traditionally been an international enterprise, with intense competition between national academic champions set against very open publication and sharing of results in the interests of advancing the sum of human knowledge. In contrast, research in engineering and technology has usually been highly proprietary between the various companies and countries involved in order to advance national and company prosperity. There has also always been tension in the gray areas where open and proprietary modes overlap and one becomes the other.

Globalization of research of all kinds has been greatly facilitated by the Internet and the Web, and, indeed, it has enabled whole new classes and scales of collaboration that would have been impossible without it, such as the sequencing of the human genome. The ICT infrastructure is also proving to be invaluable in researching, monitoring, and managing the worldwide processes for mitigating global warming and understanding how to deal with increased problems such as floods and droughts.

Firms' Strategies

Companies' basic aims remain to survive and thrive, provide an adequate return to their owners, and meet the needs of their customers, employees, suppliers, and partners. In order to stay in position, some companies also feel the pressure to serve the perceived national interests of their country of origin. In this context, key implications of e-research for companies are that

1. Companies are finding it increasingly hard to determine their nationality because globalization means that they can service markets worldwide, with suppliers worldwide, and backed by shareholders worldwide, so they can locate their operations and facilities wherever is most cost effective and tax efficient. This development is fast running ahead of national governments and international bodies' ability to regulate, legislate, and police. In areas ranging from intellectual property (IP) law to tax and contractual jurisdictions to product liability law, the international business environment is struggling to keep pace. In whose jurisdiction is a bank in an orbiting satellite operated by an international consortium of companies? Who owns the IP of a "musical utterance" compiled by sampling the work of twenty artists around the world obtained by Web search? Who should pay whom for its consumption?

2. Easier access to global IP means that competitive advantage is increasingly dependent on exploiting technology, IP, and innovation from any appropriate source around the world. This means a company needs excellent awareness of what is available, fast access to what is relevant, and rapid exploitation of it in the company's products and services. Companies have to become expert at "inward technology transfer" and

"research by shopping around" because both are much easier with a powerful e-research infrastructure.

3. New markets, businesses, and business models can emerge quickly based on innovations happening in the e-research space. A new dimension of business and competitive risk for many companies is that they may not even notice what developments are occurring if they are not "players" adequately tuned in to what is going on.

Countries' Strategies

Nation-states continue to pursue a number of basic objectives. These objectives range from surviving and maintaining national identity and values to expanding or entering into alliances and partnerships with other countries to providing their citizens with acceptable levels of security and prosperity—which involves the provision of various public goods, including education, health care, defense, and the rule of law—and exerting some influence in international affairs. For nations, some key implications of e-research arising from this development in objectives include:

1. Almost every aspect of national infrastructure has become heavily dependent on ICT in general and on Internet, Web, and wireless technologies in particular. Safeguarding national capabilities against threats to this infrastructure will become increasingly important. The ICT infrastructure also greatly changes the environment that a state must monitor if it is to fulfill its duty of providing security and maintaining rule of law for its citizens. Security, intelligence, and police services will need to become expert in their own versions of e-research. The new infrastructure also greatly changes the threats to which its citizens are subject from crime and illegal surveillance.

2. For those managing public-sector undertakings such as health care, education, public administration, security, and defense, digital technologies are enabling radically new ways of delivering their services to the public and for delivering quite new services to quite new communities of users.

3. The ICT infrastructure makes it easier for individuals and organizations of all kinds to move information and ideas easily and rapidly across national boundaries in huge volumes that are difficult to monitor, much less supervise. This ability will significantly complicate a state's ability to enforce commercial and legal jurisdictions, collect taxes and duties, and so forth, making it much more difficult to identify companies and other organizations as belonging to a particular nation. It also greatly increases the opportunities for international organized crime and terrorism. Nations will therefore increasingly need to participate in international treaties, agreements, and organizations to deal with these issues.

4. Some national governments are starting to question whether basic science research should continue to be funded wholly on a competitive national basis, with all the re-

sultant duplication and competition. This issue is compounded by the insatiable appe-
tite of much science research for ever larger and more expensive facilities. As e-research
makes international collaboration easier and more essential, national governments
may discern a reason for reducing their national expenditures on science research,
relying more on international cooperation instead, and sharing to move the global
science base forward. These adjustments will work only if the nation invests enough
in its e-research infrastructure so that the nation continues to be attractive to the best
research people and the best high-tech businesses. Even then, there might well be serious unintended consequences for education and training capacities if an advanced
nation decides to reduce its spending on basic research.

5. The increasingly rapid diffusion of high technology to "less-developed" countries
around the world will mean that all nations will be striving to move their domestic economic activity "up the value chain." Doing so will be essential if they are to maintain
their competitive position in adding value in the global economy, which they must do
in order to fund the ever-increasing levels of less-expensive manufactures and energy
that they will require. Thus, a first-class e-research infrastructure will become a prime
need for economic competitiveness for more and more countries.

II State of the Practice

The social and institutional shaping of e-research is a key perspective characterizing this volume. At the same time, all contributors recognize the crucial importance of the new opportunities being opened by rapid advances in the technologies underpinning research-centered computational networks. This part has three chapters and seven essays that explore some of the most influential technologies, complemented by illustrations of the varied ways in which they are being applied (e.g., library-oriented developments in chapter 3 and data-handling technologies in chapter 4). The need to ensure that technologies not only have the required capabilities, but are also designed to be as easy to use as possible rounds out this part of the book in chapter 5.

One of the key issues highlighted in part I is the way e-research approaches across all disciplines are increasingly producing more information more rapidly. However, the traditional storehouses of scholarly information—academic libraries and archives—are still negotiating the new roles they must fulfill if they are to have influence in the new scholarly information paradigm represented by e-research. In chapter 3, Eric Meyer, Christine Madsen, and Jenny Fry look at the challenges these roles pose at this crucial time of change for modern libraries. Among the topics they discuss are the tensions between open access and intellectual property rights, the way informal scholarly communications are increasingly being made public on the Internet, and the movements toward decentralized production and storage of data. The chapter examines how the current position has been arrived at and possible future paths.

Two essays after this chapter examine important examples of the types of digital resources that libraries should consider to assist research in the sciences and humanities. David Shotton describes how data webs can be used to integrate image and other data distributed across several heterogeneous repositories or databases. Alan Bowman looks at the ways information and communication technologies (ICTs) are assisting scholars who work on ancient documents and explores how these changes are improving techniques of digital image capture for research purposes as well as what opportunities and constraints are related to these technological developments.

One of the most visible and urgent impacts of the take-up of e-research is what many contributors refer to as the "data deluge": the huge volumes of data being gathered, generated, organized, analyzed, and otherwise handled across e-infrastructures. In chapter 4, Yorick Wilks and Matthijs den Besten describe in some depth the key technologies and data-management approaches that can help researchers cope with this flood. They explain why the processing of data—taken in a very broad sense—is central to researchers' ability to understand the world they are investigating, which includes the important ability to distinguish facts from less-grounded "factoids." Key challenges for e-research include the escalating quantity of data and the level of human intervention needed to deal with them. These authors also show how available and emerging technologies can help to address the deluge, while also pointing to the underlying complexities that are likely to keep the pursuit of improvements in dealing with data as a continuing priority in e-research (e.g., in efforts to support resource sharing among researchers and other users).

Further illustrations of key issues and solutions related to chapter 4 are provided in three essays. The embedded sensor networks examined by Christine Borgman are based on electronic sensors and devices in the environment that are linked by wireless networks to collect vast amounts of data. She argues that the way these networks enable the environmental sciences, biosciences, and other fields to ask new research questions in new ways makes them a particularly good arena in which to study the transformations made possible by e-research advances. Michael Fraser's essay looks at significant techniques being developed for identifying and managing digital objects of all types, moving toward a long-term prospect of an "Internet of Things," comprising anything from books and images to clothing, flora, and fauna. The emergence of the Semantic Web—described by Kieron O'Hara, Tim Berners-Lee (a key inventor of the World Wide Web), Wendy Hall, and Nigel Shadbolt—offers a potentially more effective way of sharing information than traditional document-based Web methods. Their essay discusses how Semantic Web technologies are proving to be important in automating scientific and social scientific research, and points to efforts being made to take research forward to underpin the potential of this approach.

Chapter 5 steps back to view key technical artifacts of e-research, such as e-infrastructures and application software tools, from the point of view of the researchers who are trying to achieve their research goals using these capabilities. Grace de la Flor, Marina Jirotka, Sharon Lloyd, and Andrew Warr explore how traditional approaches to improving the usability of ICT-based systems can be reconceptualized to become of greater value in e-research projects' software-development process, where a prime consideration is to support cooperative work arrangements in network-enabled research. They provide examples and recommendations on how the design of e-research systems can facilitate their easy and effective use.

Essays on this usability theme present examples of two approaches that can help to address the issues raised in chapter 5. One of the most important and frustrating areas of difficulty faced by researchers is the serious security weaknesses underlying Internet-enabled technologies and devices. Andrew Martin looks beyond flawed security approaches implemented in the past, such as firewalls to keep out unwanted intruders, toward sustainable ways of building trust in e-research systems. Michael Thelwall explores the implications for e-research of the popular social-networking approaches that typify Web 2.0. He identifies both the advantages of designing social networking into some e-research applications and reasons why social networking will probably be inappropriate for other applications.

3 Digital Resources and the Future of Libraries

Eric T. Meyer, Christine Madsen, and Jenny Fry

The New Roles Emerging for Libraries and Archives

As e-research and digital scholarship mature, academic libraries and archives are re-assessing their roles in relation to scholarship. Although the traditional responsibilities of academic libraries have not ceased, evolving research practices across all disciplines have changed library users' expectations. Researchers depend on desktop access to a wide range of information in multiple formats and across diverse resources, and they increasingly do not expect for this access to come via their libraries (Lynch and Smith 2001; ARL Joint Task Force 2007). In addition, the proliferation of informal channels of scholarly communication and data sharing now include repositories of working papers, data repositories, blogs, wikis, and a growing list of other nontraditional outlets of scholarly activity beyond the journal article and scholarly monograph.

New media and means of storing and accessing information put pressure on academic libraries and archives, but something new and different appears to be arising as a result of the current shift toward e-research. The scale of data produced across all disciplines is larger than ever before, and this growth appears to be accelerating. Online production of and access to formal and informal communications have blurred the lines between the two, creating new challenges in information literacy and management. There is also growing evidence that work practices are changing across the disciplines—with collaborations increasing in the sciences and access to digitized primary and secondary sources revolutionizing how scholars in the humanities access and use these materials.

Lying just below the surface of all of this is the little talked about issue of digital preservation, which is placing further stress on libraries and archives. Will the historians of the future studying this era be able to access the materials they require to reconstruct their subjects' activities? When today's equivalent of Louis Pasteur is studied, will his digital lab notes have been as carefully preserved as Pasteur's one hundred plus volumes of notes at the Bibliothèque Nationale in Paris? Will the future scholar who proves to be as influential as Richard Feynman leave a store of letters that will serve as inspirations to others, or will all communications have been emailed, instant messaged, or twittered[1] to their recipients and never preserved?

It is also important to take into consideration the data that researchers are collecting and generating. In 2007, the Association of Research Libraries in the United States issued a report arguing that e-science presents a major opportunity for research libraries to become involved in the management and preservation of scientific data, but that so far "libraries have had little immediate engagement with these processes . . . [even though] e-science has the potential to be transformational within research libraries by impacting their operations, functions, and possibly even mission" (ARL Joint Task Force 2007:13). In the face of these changes, it is important to get beyond hype and assumptions to ask: What is really different for libraries and archives as they continue to support research processes that include an increasingly hybridized mix of electronic and physical materials? And what does this difference mean for the future of libraries?

We do not have space in this chapter to summarize fully how the increasing dependence on digital resources in academia is affecting libraries. There is not only huge variation across the social sciences, humanities, and natural sciences, but significant differences among disciplines and subdisciplines. Thus, rather than attempt a comprehensive review, this chapter highlights what we feel are some of the most pressing issues facing libraries in relation to networked-enabled research and looks at how these issues might be influencing the direction that academic libraries and archives will take in the future.

The Push for Open Access

The Faculty of Arts and Sciences in Harvard University voted in 2008 to create a repository "to give the University a worldwide license to make each faculty member's scholarly articles available. . . . Harvard will take advantage of the license by hosting FAS faculty members' scholarly articles in an open-access repository, making them available worldwide for free" (Mitchell 2008). That open-access repository will be built and maintained by the Harvard University Library. Similar mandates for openness have been seen elsewhere, particularly in the sciences, and have come not just from faculties, but from funding bodies. For example, beginning in 2008, recipients of funding from the U.S. National Institutes of Health were required to make all publications freely available to the public by depositing them in PubMedCentral.[2] Developments in the United States followed earlier similar mandates in the United Kingdom, such as the 2006 directives from the Wellcome Trust (2006), a large medical research funder, and from Research Councils UK (2006), the umbrella organization for the various U.K. domain-specific research councils.

These kinds of moves signify a number of considerable changes for the academic research library at large, not just for individual institutions, including a shift toward libraries as publishers, opportunities for new forms of informal communication engagements, changes in the scope and scale of intended audiences and collections, and a general "disintermediation" of the scholarship process, with publishers perhaps no longer playing as pivotal a role as they have up to now in mediating between researchers and the audiences they are trying to reach. These aspects are discussed in the next four subsections.

The Library as Publisher

Although many academic libraries and archives have long been open to readers from other institutions and the general public, opening up the amount of material on the scale made possible by e-research developments is unprecedented. The motivation for scholars to participate in open access initiatives is reasonably clear—the promise of enhanced visibility (Borgman 2007:101)—but the repercussions are not. Growing support for open access[3] is calling into question both the need for commercial publishers and the existence of a viable model for sustaining open academic resources (Nicholas, Huntington, and Jamali 2007). Libraries in many ways are caught between these two forces. They have long existed in a symbiotic relationship with the commercial publishers who assemble the materials that libraries wish to access and distribute. The relationship is often strained, however, because of the need to negotiate journal subscriptions and bundled licenses. When looked at purely in terms of the output of these decisions—the production of large accessible databases of academic writings—the trend toward open access, as exemplified by the Harvard University Library example, can be seen as a move toward the academic library's acting as publisher.

A 2008 Association of Research Libraries report indicates that this move has already been happening: "By late 2007, 44% of the 80 responding ARL member libraries reported they were delivering publishing services and another 21% were in the process of planning publishing service development. Only 36% of responding institutions were not active in this arena" (Hahn 2008: 5). Because libraries are in a logical place to host a faculty's data and intellectual property, the increasing demand for access to that work might be met through the creation of new models for scholarly publication within academic libraries. Andrew Abbott (2008) argues that the university presses will continue to meet scholars' most significant needs in terms of publishing monographs, particularly in the humanities and social sciences. But will libraries be able to fulfill the demand for journal materials? The alternatives are either that commercial publishers will successfully realign themselves and create revenue models that generate income from open-access journal publication or that completely new players will step in and assume these roles.

Informal Communications

The question of how libraries can or should become involved in the system of informal communication of scholarly activity is also of some significance. The emphasis that e-research places on sharing, collaboration, and data reuse means that the informal interactions that go into these collaborative efforts are also of potential interest to researchers interested in the scholarly process (Barjak 2006). Informal communications have conventionally been fairly invisible, but are becoming increasingly visible as their traces appear in digital records and on Web sites (Wilkinson, Harries, Thelwall, et al. 2003). For example, domain-based institutional repositories and specialist Digital Curation Centres in the United Kingdom[4] are examples of initiatives to harness unpublished scholarly communication produced not only as part of programmatic e-research, but also as more broadly defined research involving digital innovation.

Informal communications, such as correspondence, once were collected by archives through the acquisition of a scholar's papers either posthumously or at the end of his or her career. Such an acquisition system contains at least two points of selection that are now commonly missing from the acquisition of electronic communications. The first is the initial selection of the archive itself—with traditional collections, libraries and archives select whose papers they want. The second happens when the archive is processed: in a document-by-document selection process, archivists weed out what they do not want to keep. With the increasingly heavy use of email, wikis, and blogs, informal communications are now becoming immediately available for collection and study, but this immediacy often belies the ephemeral nature of these mediums. Web sites are taken offline, blogs are deleted, and email accounts are discontinued as researchers move to new organizations or email systems are upgraded. The imperative to archive these materials is clear, but how and whether to separate personal communications from professional content is murky.

The Growing Audience of the Academic Research Library
Making materials freely available to the public on the scale made possible by network-enabled research also calls into question the intended audience of the library itself. Most large academic libraries have some notion embedded in their mission statement of serving academia at large and may also extend to serve the general public, but the general public usually comes last in the hierarchy of institutional priorities. A shift toward making the intellectual output of an entire faculty available to the world seems to put a much greater emphasis on the broader audience of academia, if not of the world at large. This change in emphasis raises important questions about the strategy libraries adopt in serving different audiences, such as either focusing on faculty and students above all else—the traditional top priority—or moving toward becoming a distribution point to the wider public. Box 3.1 summarizes the approach being taken by the Harvard College Library.

The Disintermediation of the Scholarship Process

The mandates for open access expand not only the scale of the users of academic libraries, but the scope of the materials that these libraries are being asked to archive

Box 3.1

Audiences Served by the Harvard College Library

The mission statement of the Harvard College Library makes a direct reference to serving "the larger scholarly community" while still stating that the teaching and research activities of the Faculty of Arts and Sciences and the university remains its first priority (Harvard College Library 2009). The mandate to open the scholarly output of its faculty freely to the world, however, indicates an increasing emphasis on the world outside of the university: "At Harvard, where so much of our research is of global significance, we have an essential responsibility to distribute the fruits of our scholarship as widely as possible" (Mitchell 2008).

Box 3.2

Strategy for Preprints and Drafts in Cornell University's arXiv

The arXiv.org e-print archive came into operation in August 1991; by the mid-1990s, essentially the whole of the high-energy physics community was thought to be participating in the archive. It is based on the concept of a "unified global archive," where authors are responsible for "self-archiving" preprints (Ginsparg 2006). There is no formal process of peer review in arXiv, which enables it to continue on a long-standing tradition in the field of the informal exchange of preprints. What is new about arXiv is:

- the scale with which this exchange can now take place;
- the exposure of this informal communication to the public at large; and
- the involvement of the library in storing and providing access to preprints.

and deliver. Although archives have long dealt with unpublished materials and manuscripts, libraries traditionally have worked almost exclusively with "finished" content. The line between published and unpublished used to be much more clearly defined. For example, PubMedCentral serves as an open-access publisher, whereas projects such as arXiv from the Cornell University Library[5] are blurring the line between published and unpublished materials by accepting and delivering preprints and drafts (see box 3.2).

Large public repositories such as arXiv highlight one of the biggest shifts for libraries brought about by open-access mandates—the general disintermediation of the scholarship process. The relationship between academic libraries and journal publishers and distributors has been increasingly tense in the past few decades. As the prices for journal subscriptions continue to rise rapidly,[6] libraries realize that they have been paying very large amounts for electronic journals that contain their own faculty's intellectual property. In the sciences, where a pay-to-publish model is more common, universities have in fact been paying twice for this material. Thus, if the shift to open access signifies a shift from the prevailing model, the relationship between libraries and authors may no longer be mediated by publishers. Whether seen as a shift toward library as publisher or as a blurring of the lines between the published and the unpublished, the result is that libraries are becoming involved at an earlier point in more facets of the knowledge creation life cycle.

Of Data, Tools, and Mash-ups

Data-centric e-Research

Many (e.g., Hey and Trefethen 2003) have seen the physical sciences as leading the way in data-centric e-research, but the field of digital humanities also has a long history in this area. This movement is not a sudden shift, but an acceleration in electronic resources that began many decades ago. It has been accompanied by increasing collaboration across disciplines; although disciplinary differences in scale remain, the general trend has been toward greater collaboration (Wuchty, Jones, and Uzzi 2007). With a critical mass of materials now available, research practices are changing, and academic research libraries and archives must change accordingly (Gold 2008).

The marked changes in research processes that are necessitating an equivalent change in libraries come not only from the quantity of data now being produced, but also from the means and location of their production and intended uses. The ease with which data can now be recorded does not necessarily match the ease with which they can be preserved. Furthermore, the ease with which data capture can be automated is pressing libraries to question the costly and time-consuming process of selection. Libraries have traditionally paid considerable attention to selection issues, deciding whether particular materials are appropriate expenditures in light of limited resources. This attention makes sense in the context of deciding whether to purchase a book or journal, both of which cost money and take up shelf space. In the area of data, however, the notion of selectivity is quite different.

From a data-management point of view, selectivity is relatively expensive. Raw data are cheaper to produce than carefully cleaned data, and complete data sets are cheaper to produce than a carefully selected subset of data. Why is this so? In order for data to be reusable by researchers not involved with the original data collection, representations of the data (such as metadata, data dictionaries, or ontologies) need to be created. This process can be expensive in terms of the person power required to clean and annotate the data, even in the research areas where data curation is semiautomated. The intermediate data that have been cleaned and managed are often of more value to other researchers than either the raw data that were originally collected or the aggregated and summarized data that were later reported in publications. However, if *all* data in a domain can be captured more easily and cheaply than a selection of *some* data in a domain, does the library have the obligation to collect and subsequently manage *all* possible data?

Data Archiving and Reuse

Should the department that produced complicated data sets with bespoke tools be obligated to archive its data? In addition, for those data that reside in nonstandard formats, will the tools needed to access these data also be archived and maintained, or will the data be converted to standardized formats and documented with metadata (Lynch 2008)? Archiving of raw data is quickly becoming the norm in some fields, which leads to the need to archive the tools with which the data can be read or reinterpreted. The question of whether centralized library-based or decentralized department-based data storage is better in the long run will play itself out in the coming decade as disciplines redefine what it means to use and reuse data. Although libraries may be the most logical place for the long-term preservation of data—if only because decentralized departments may be a poor choice to ensure the long-term survival of this material—the tools and software needed to create, interpret, and reinterpret the data reside in those disciplinary-based departments and with those domain experts.

The issue of data reuse becomes even more complex when researchers recombine data they control with other data from sources they do not control. For example, data "mash-ups" using tools such as Google Earth combined with researcher-generated data will cause particular difficulties with regard to establishing provenance, authenticity, and quality, as well as raise the additional issue of determining who holds the intellectual property rights for these outputs. With a Google Maps mash-up, the components are inseparable and further complicated by the intellectual property issues that arise from archiving components belonging to a commercial company. Does the library have the right to archive and provide long-term public access to a part of Google? What are the technical issues involved in archiving something that includes the continued presence of a commercial product? Reuse of data in novel ways is now easy. Checking up on all of the related legal and ethical issues before one reuses data is not.

Dealing with Information Overload

Information overload is not a new issue. There are records of scholars complaining of it as far back as the sixteenth century (Blair 2003). What is new, however, is the speed and ease with which data are being collected and recorded. Data points from the Large Hadron Collider (LHC) of the European Organization for Nuclear Research (CERN), for instance, will be collected 40 million times per second. In one year, the combined output of data from four experiments will be fifteen petabytes, corresponding to a stack of CDs about twenty kilometers tall (CERN Communication Group 2008). Compare this output to more than a hundred years of data gathering at the Harvard–Smithsonian

Center for Astrophysics, which produced five hundred thousand glass photographic plates between 1885 and 1993 (Harvard–Smithsonian Center for Astrophysics 2008).

Prior to the introduction of continuous (or nearly continuous) recording devices in sciences such as physics, decisions had to be made beforehand about data capture. In essence, the scientists were enforcing a selection policy upfront. Large-scale projects like the LHC, in contrast, gather data almost constantly, both for the immediate use of those who designed the experiments and for future uses that are currently unknown. There was never an expectation that everything that could be seen from a land-based telescope would be recorded and archived, but now there is an expectation that all scientific data capable of being captured will be kept indefinitely. Beyond the CERN example, continuous or near-continuous data collection and storage are becoming commonplace, using tools such as remote sensor arrays and automated data-collection tools (Borgman, Wallis, Mayernik, et al. 2007). It is not clear whether continuous collection is always done in anticipation of future research uses of these data (as with the LHC) or because relatively inexpensive storage makes it easier and less expensive from the start to save everything rather than to spend considerable time and effort deciding what to save.

Strategies for Long-Term Data Curation

Libraries and archives responsible for the long-term curation of data are thus faced with essentially two main choices. The first is to accept a new, often unspoken mandate to keep and archive "everything." The second is to become the first point of selection and decide what to keep and what to cull. The selection process has always been an integral part of the library's function. In the decision of what to keep, there is always the implicit expectation that some things are not appropriate for long-term preservation. The e-research data flood is manifest in libraries not solely through a crisis over quantity, but through a shift of practice away from selection and toward an expectation of wholesale archiving.

We are not arguing that one of these options is clearly a more defensible position than the other. Each has considerable costs and benefits. Wholesale archiving, on the one hand, greatly reduces the intake costs for data, particularly if the institution responsible for maintaining the archive is not responsible for time-consuming and expensive steps such as data cleaning, documentation, and validation. The data will also potentially be available for future uses, some of which may be wholly unforeseen at the time of deposit. The costs of wholesale archiving, on the other hand, include contributing to information overload—not with quantity, but by the taking in of data without appropriate metadata. The upfront costs associated with selection often come under fire as being unnecessary, particularly as storage costs decrease. But well-described, organized data selected by domain experts may be of greater use to scholars in the long run.

Underlying this discussion about use and reuse of data lies an increasingly complex relationship among libraries, data, and users. A side effect of the maturation of e-research has been a significant—yet implicit—redefinition of what it means to use and reuse data. This effect stems both from the seemingly endless array of tools at the disposal of anyone with access to the Internet and the increasingly tight relationship between data and the tools with which they are produced. Clifford Lynch, director of the Coalition for Networked Information, raises questions about the implications of this relationship on current disciplinary norms in scholarship: "to what extent should articles *incorporate* the data they present and analyze, and to what extent should they simply *reference* that data?" (2007:2, emphasis added). Seeking to take advantage of the Web's basic abilities to link to referenced data may seem to be logical. However, this answer is complicated by issues such as the current lack of persistent identifiers and the moves being made in digital preservation toward maximizing copies (both of which would favor incorporation of data).[7] Similar to the way the lines between formal and informal communication have increasingly become blurred, changes in practice with regard to reference data may blur the line between raw and published data.

The intertwining of digital objects of research and the research tools required to access, analyze, and manipulate those data also raises new archival issues. As for the case of mash-ups and data reuse discussed earlier, is it sufficient to archive the article or journal alone if a data model is published in a journal or an overlay journal[8] (Ginsparg 1996) linked to a data archive, or do the underlying data also need to be archived? And what of the tool(s) used to create, access, and analyze those data? The answers to these questions will vary from discipline to discipline as practices and conventions emerge. The British Atmospheric Data Centre (BADC 2007), for example, now has an archiving policy for simulated data, based on algorithmic models and statistical analyses or composites of either simulations or real data or both.

Although not an example of a library repository, BADC (like arXiv) represents a new move toward large, centralized repositories. Yet there is still significant disagreement over whether centralized data archives or decentralized methods for data preservation are preferable. Microsoft Research's report on science in 2020, for instance, argues that "large, centralized, archival repositories are both dangerous and unworkable. They are dangerous because the construction of a data collection or the survival of one's data is at the mercy of a specific administrative or financial structure; unworkable because of scale, and also because scientists naturally favor autonomy and wish to keep control over their information" (2020 Science Group 2006:19). Large archives are not unique in facing this danger: small, decentralized departments producing data may similarly be at the mercy of a specific administrative or financial structure; and the autonomy that scientists naturally favor may encourage them to keep their data closed. However, data requiring complicated tools for reading and reuse may be best left to those who have

Box 3.3
The Perseus Digital Library

The Perseus Digital Library is a set of mostly textual digital collections with a particular focus on the Greco-Roman world. Embedded within these collections is a set of linguistic and geographic tools enabling users to interact with the collections in novel ways. It was built in the classics department of Tufts University and has been heavily used, expanded, and developed by classicists there and elsewhere since its inception in the late 1980s. Although built on the kinds of textual collections familiar to libraries, in the Perseus Digital Library it is no longer clear where the data end and the tools begin—they are inseparable.

---

created it, precisely because of the issue of tools mentioned earlier. Removing data from the context in which they were created may render them unusable.

Although libraries have always faced the risk of removing information from the context needed for interpretation and analysis, the scale of the problem is greater than ever before. The raw materials of our scholarly outputs are requiring more and more complicated hardware and software just to be readable. Providing access to nontraditional materials is no longer as simple as archiving the proper audio equipment along with a wax phonograph cylinder—and is not just a problem for the sciences, as shown by the widely used Perseus Digital Library[9] (see box 3.3).

How Libraries Can Meet the e-Research Challenge

Academic research libraries and archives are implementing, using, and storing more electronic technologies than ever before. These activities, in turn, are changing the way librarians and archivists do their jobs. Various studies have reported the increasing demands in job advertisements requiring that librarians possess new computer technology skills (Lynch and Smith 2001). In addition, the trend in library and information science education is toward an increasing focus on information science and technology. This trend constitutes either a crisis (Gorman 2004) or an opportunity to embrace changes that will ensure libraries remain relevant in an increasingly technological world (Dillon 2005). These changes arguably represent a technological elaboration on the kinds of roles that librarians and archivists have always played.

Libraries have always been collectors, aggregators, repositories, and disseminators of scholarly information, and these roles will continue for the foreseeable future. Abbott argues that libraries have been engaged in continuous processes of indexing, dating back to the 1920s, to address the issues of the "rapid expansion of the academic population . . . and their aim has been to make the library a universal identification, location, and access machine' (2008:10–11). As he points out, these same issues are at stake today, and they long predate the Internet and digital libraries. In fact, he argues that the basic structure of scholarly communication, somewhat surprisingly in his estimation, remains essentially unchanged from its beginnings in the 1920s.

Focusing on Libraries' and Archives' Core Purposes

Libraries and archives must address the changes discussed in this chapter regardless of whether the changes are revolutionary alterations of existing practices or more evolutionary extensions of long-established practices. They can do so best by recognizing that their essential core purpose remains unchanged: they are dynamic spaces (physical or virtual) for the creation and preservation of knowledge. The architecture of a library is not defined by geographic boundaries, but by the collection of services it offers in support of scholarship.

In terms of the act of information retrieval, libraries face numerous questions imposed by the changing nature of e-research and may risk becoming irrelevant in the future. If they are understood as spaces to support the creation of new knowledge, however, they can revisit and reconstruct their basic services in ways that meet the needs of scholars across all disciplines. A possible cause for optimism was indicated in 2008 when a number of major academic library stakeholders in the United Kingdom announced a two-year initiative "to develop a transformative agenda that will help ensure the continuing relevance of libraries to the communities of information creators and users they serve" (Research Information Network 2008:1).

ArXiv and other library projects that involve the collection and dissemination of preprints and forms of informal communications represent not a shift from libraries' basic responsibility to support the knowledge-creation life cycle, but a recognition that e-research practices necessitate libraries' involvement at an earlier point in the cycle. Taking a broader perspective—across disciplines, formats, and time—will show us that although our libraries are amassing huge digital collections, they are not turning into purely digital libraries. All of the issues raised here need to be considered within the context of already large and still growing analog collections. Once again, librarians and archivists can take advantage of many years of experience with selection, preservation, and use of physical collections in order to expand these same services to the digital domain.

Possible Future Roles for Libraries

Libraries of the future clearly have roles to fulfill in serving researchers, but this message has been increasingly difficult for libraries to convey, particularly to the new generation of graduate students and researchers. The "Google Generation" project and report argues that "many young people do not find library-sponsored resources intuitive and therefore prefer to use Google or Yahoo instead." "Tools like Google Scholar," they say, "will be increasingly a real and present threat to the library as an institution" (as "students usually prefer the global searching of Google to more sophisticated but more time-consuming searching provided by the library" (Centre for Information Behaviour and the Evaluation of Research 2008:12, 13, 31).

However, although these so-called digital natives may tend to prefer electronic resources, the authors of this report reject the notion that the Google Generation is composed of "expert searchers" (Centre for Information Behaviour and the Evaluation of Research 2008:20). Instead, they suggest, libraries must work harder to show these younger researchers the value that libraries and library resources can have for their research and teach them the skills needed to assess the quality of information resources. This issue is still in flux: Bradley Hemminger and his colleagues, for instance, report that although "researchers still primarily use library and bibliographic database searches . . . the use of Web search engines such as Google Scholar is almost as common" (2007:2215). The issue will also grow over time as older generations of academics retire and younger scholars with new work habits that favor online resources take their places. Libraries' arguments in favor of their continuing relevance may fall on deaf ears unless they find ways to engage with these younger scholars beyond simply being the organization tasked with negotiating site licenses for access to subscription-only resources—for example, by providing access to the knowledge resources these new scholars need.

Summary

In this chapter, we have discussed libraries' changing roles in the expanding e-research landscape in terms of open-access publishing of scholarship; their increasing role as publishers; the disintermediation of the scholarly process; and their involvement (or lack thereof) in dealing with the data used and generated as part of the scholarly process. None of these issues is simple, but failing to deal with them will mean that libraries risk relinquishing their central position in the production, dissemination, and preservation of scholarly communication. Loss of this position will increase the risk that the researchers of the future will find that they have lost essential access to the resources they need to advance human knowledge.

Notes

1. *Twittering* is the term used for electronic communication through the quick exchange of brief messages via, for example, a short message service or instant messaging. The term is derived from the free Twitter service: http://twitter.com/.

2. Consolidated Appropriations Act, 2008, Public Law no. 110–161, Division G, Title II 218 (2008). See http://www.pubmedcentral.nih.gov/ for more on PubMedCentral.

3. For example, nearly three thousand journals are listed in the Directory of Open Access Journals (see http://www.doaj.org/).

4. See, for example, the Digital Curation Centre, which provides a national focus for research and development in curation issues and promotes expertise and good practice (http://www.dcc .ac.uk/).

5. ArXiv.org was originally hosted at the Los Alamos National Laboratory but moved to Cornell University when its founder, Paul Ginsparg, relocated there. See Gunnarsdottir 2005 for the history of arXiv.org, originally known as xxx.lanl.gov.

6. In 2007, the Association of Research Libraries reported that the annual cumulative cost for journal subscriptions for their 123 member libraries in the United States and Canada was $750 million (Johnson and Luther 2007:viii).

7. See essay 4.2 in this volume and the Lots of Copies Keep Stuff Safe program for more on key issues concerning digital preservation (http://www.lockss.org/).

8. An open-access journal that takes submissions from the preprints deposited at an archive (perhaps at the author's initiative) and subjects them to peer review (http://www.earlham.edu/~peters/ fos/guide.htm).

9. For more on Perseus, see http://www.perseus.tufts.edu/hopper/.

References

2020 Science Group. 2006. *Towards 2020 science*. Cambridge, UK: Microsoft Research. Retrieved 9 July 2008 from: http://research.microsoft.com/towards2020science/downloads.htm.

Abbott, A. 2008. "Publication and the future of knowledge." Keynote address to the Association of American University Presses (electronic version). Retrieved 4 August 2008 from: http://home .uchicago.edu/~aabbott/Papers/aaup.pdf.

Association of Research Libraries (ARL) Joint Task Force on Library Support for E-Science. 2007. *Agenda for developing e-science in research libraries: Final report and recommendations to the Scholarly Communication Steering Committee, the Public Policies Affecting Research Libraries Steering Committee, and the Research, Teaching, and Learning Steering Committee*. Washington, DC: ARL. Retrieved 3 January 2008 from: http://www.arl.org/bm~doc/ARL_EScience_final.pdf.

Barjak, F. 2006. "The role of the Internet in informal scholarly communication." *Journal of the American Society for Information and Science Technology 57* (10):1350–1367.

Blair, A. 2003. "Reading strategies for coping with information overload ca. 1550–1700." *Journal of the History of Ideas 64* (1):11–28.

Borgman, C. L. 2007. *Scholarship in the digital age: Information, infrastructure, and the Internet*. Cambridge, MA: MIT Press.

Borgman, C. L., J. C. Wallis, M. S. Mayernik, and A. Pepe. 2007. "Drowning in data: Digital library architecture to support scientific use of embedded sensor networks." Paper presented at the seventh Association for Computing Machinery/Institute of Electrical and Electronics Engineers–Computer Society joint conference on digital libraries, Vancouver, BC.

British Atmospheric Data Centre (BADC). 2007. *Archiving of simulations within the NERC data management framework: BADC policy and guidelines*. Chilton, UK: BADC. Retrieved 6 November 2008 from: badc.nerc.ac.uk/data/BADC_Model_Data_Policy.pdf.

Centre for Information Behaviour and the Evaluation of Research. 2008. "Information behaviour of the researcher of the future" (electronic version). Retrieved 16 January 2008 from: http://www.bl.uk/news/pdf/googlegen.pdf.

CERN Communication Group. 2008. *CERN FAQ: LHC: The Guide*. Geneva: CERN. Retrieved 6 November 2008 from: http://cdsmedia.cern.ch/img/CERN-Brochure-2008-001-Eng.pdf.

Dillon, A. 2005. "Crying wolf: An examination and reconsideration of the perception of crisis in LIS education." Journal of Education for Library and Information Science 46 (4):280–298.

Ginsparg, P. 1996. "Winners and losers in the global research village." Invited contribution for the conference held at UNESCO headquarters, Paris, 19–23 February 1996, during the session "Scientist's View of Electronic Publishing and Issues Raised," 21 February. Retrieved 17 June 2001 from: http://arxiv.org/blurb/pg96unesco.html.

Ginsparg, P. 2006. "As we may read." *Journal of Neuroscience 26* (38):9606–9608.

Gold, A. 2008. "Cyberinfrastructure, data, and libraries. Part 2: Libraries and the data challenge: Roles and actions for libraries." D-Lib 13 (9–0). Available at: http://www.dlib.org/dlib/september07/gold/09gold-pt2.html.

Gorman, M. 2004. "Special feature: Whither library education?" *New Library World 105* (1204–1205):376–380.

Gunnarsdottir, K. 2005. "Scientific journal publications: On the role of electronic preprint exchange in the distribution of scientific literature." *Social Studies of Science 35* (4):549–579.

Hahn, K. L. 2008. *Research library publishing services: New options for university publishing*. Washington, DC: Association of Research Libraries.

Harvard College Library. 2009. *HCL Mission Statement*. Cambridge, MA: Harvard College Library. Retrieved 15 September 2009 from: http://hcl.harvard.edu/about_hcl/mission_statement.cfm.

Harvard–Smithsonian Center for Astrophysics. 2008. *The Harvard College Observatory astronomical plate stacks*. Cambridge, MA: Harvard-Smithsonian Center for Astrophysics. Retrieved 10 December 2008 from: http://tdc-www.harvard.edu/plates/.

Hemminger, B. M., D. Lu, K. T. L. Vaughan, and S. J. Adams. 2007. "Information seeking behavior of academic scientists." *Journal of the American Society for Information Science and Technology 58* (14):2205–2225.

Hey, T., and A. Trefethen. 2003. "The data deluge: An e-science perspective." In *Grid computing—making the global infrastructure a reality*, ed. F. Berman, G. Fox, and T. Hey. Chichester, UK: Wiley, 809–824.

Johnson, R. K., and J. Luther. 2007. *The e-only tipping point for journals: What's ahead in the print-to-electronic transition zone.* Washington, DC: Association of Research Libraries.

Lynch, B. P., and K. R. Smith. 2001. "The changing nature of work in academic libraries." *College and Research Libraries 62* (5):407–420.

Lynch, C. 2007. "The shape of the scientific article in the developing cyberinfrastructure." CTWatch Quarterly 3 (3). Available at: http://www.ctwatch.org/quarterly/articles/2007/08/the-shape-of-the-scientific-article-in-the-developing-cyberinfrastructure/.

Lynch, C. 2008. "How do your data grow?" *Nature 455*:28–29.

Mitchell, R. 2008. "Harvard to collect, disseminate scholarly articles for faculty: Legislation designed to allow greater worldwide access." Harvard University Faculty of Arts and Sciences Communications 13 (February). Retrieved 9 December 2008 from: http://www.news.harvard.edu/gazette/2008/02.14/99-fasvote.html.

Nicholas, D., P. Huntington, and H. R. Jamali. 2007. "The impact of open access publishing (and other access initiatives) on use and users of digital scholarly journals." *Learned Publishing 20* (1):11–15.

Research Councils UK. 2006. *RCUK position on issue of improved access to research outputs.* Swindon, UK: Research Councils UK. Retrieved 9 December 2008 from: http://www.rcuk.ac.uk/research/outputs/access/default.htm.

Research Information Network. 2008. *Towards the academic library of the future.* London: Research Information Network. Retrieved 12 December 2008 from: http://www.rin.ac.uk/library-future/.

Wellcome Trust. 2006. *Position statement in support of open and unrestricted access to published research.* London: Wellcome Trust. Retrieved 9 December 2008 from: http://www.wellcome.ac.uk/About-us/Policy/Spotlight-issues/Open-access/Policy/index.htm.

Wilkinson, D., G. Harries, M. Thelwall, and L. Price. 2003. "Motivations for academic website interlinking: Evidence for the Web as a novel source of information on informal scholarly communication." *Journal of Information Science 29* (1):49–56.

Wuchty, S., B. F. Jones, and B. Uzzi. 2007. "The increasing dominance of teams in production of knowledge." *Science 316*:1036–1039.

3.1 Data Webs for Image Repositories

David Shotton

The Need for Descriptive Metadata for Digital Images

Images play vital roles in academic research and teaching, and their acquisition is often costly and time consuming. Furthermore, the storage requirement for such images is large, particularly if they are multidimensional. However, despite popular misconception, the central problem with images is not their size or dimensional complexity, but that, unlike text documents and certain forms of scientific data (e.g., gene sequences), they are generally not self-describing. Although images may be easily interpreted by humans, their internal semantics have not been easily extractable by available computing technologies. Descriptive metadata about the images are therefore essential to bridge this "semantic gap"; without them, digital image repositories become little more than meaningless and costly data graveyards.

However, even with good metadata, finding images is not easy. Despite some commonality of the mechanisms of basic metadata exposure (e.g., use of the Open Archives Initiative Protocol for Metadata Harvesting[1]), data repositories exhibit varying degrees of syntactic and semantic incompatibility. These make it impossible to find relevant images scattered across several repositories reliably without searching each source individually. As a solution to this problem, this essay describes subject-specific data webs.[2]

What Is a Data Web?

Sir Timothy Berners-Lee, the inventor of the World Wide Web, has long argued for a distributed "web of data" in which all Web-accessible information carries its own machine-readable semantics (Berners-Lee 1999; Berners-Lee, Hendler, and Lasilla 2001). A subject-specific data web is a step toward Berners-Lee's "Semantic Web" vision.[3] The data web concept rests on the fundamental observation that distributed metadata related to a particular subject can be integrated, both syntactically and semantically, if they can first be mapped to a common core data model and represented as a Resource Description Framework (RDF) graph.[4] Such a data web uses the Web as the platform, employs lightweight simple hypertext transfer protocol in the representational state transfer style (Fielding 2000), and uses loosely coupled robust open-source software components.

The fundamental components of a data web are shown in figure 3.1. Data webs do not require all the data provided by third-party resources to be semantically coordinated or constrained to conform to a single externally imposed model of information management. Rather, they permit third parties to maintain their unique characters and continue independent publication of information describing their holdings. Using the premise that a little semantics goes a long way, interoperability is instead enabled by creating a semantically integrated view over the heterogeneous data within the distributed data repositories. This integrated view is achieved by bespoke mapping of their independent database schemas to a common representation.

The data-integration process illustrated in figure 3.1 is carried out separately for each data web serving a particular knowledge domain. It occurs in three stages:

1. A core schema specific to the domain of interest is created, giving the basic vocabulary that defines the domain. This schema will be used to search the data web.

2. In a separate act of "subscription" to the data web, the independent metadata schema of each subscribing data source is mapped to the data web's core schema. This mapping is recorded within the schema alignment service.

3. Any known coreferences to data objects identified by elements of the data web are recorded within the data web's coreference service.

These initial activities require hand crafting by either the data source or the data web personnel. Key metadata elements describing particular digital objects ("instances") within the data sources can subsequently be accessed via the data web and integrated in an entirely automated process.

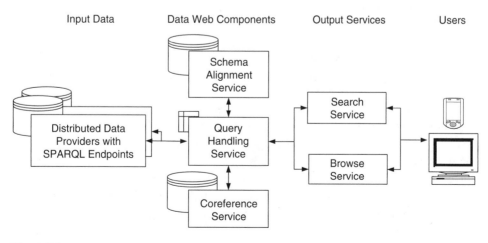

Figure 3.1
The fundamental components of a data web.

Depending on the technical nature of the data source, a software "adapter" may need to be installed, enabling metadata elements describing particular digital objects (instances) within the data source to be obtained by the data web's central query handling service. This adaptor should ideally provide a Simple Protocol and RDF Query Language (SPARQL) endpoint[5] so that a SPARQL query from the data web can retrieve an RDF description of data-source holdings, thus enabling resource discovery.

Advantages of Data Webs over Conventional Web Searches

Data webs of the type described here will have all the advantages of the World Wide Web itself—namely, distributed data, freedom and decentralization of publication, a "missing isn't broken" open-world philosophy, lack of centralized control, evolvability, and scalability. However, unlike the Web as a whole, each particular data web will provide tailored access to just one bespoke information market, with the following potential advantages over Web search engines such as Google:

• It will enable access to the "deep Web" of database content that search engines conventionally cannot access.
• By being specifically targeted to a particular knowledge domain, it will achieve a significantly higher signal-to-noise ratio within search returns.
• It will involve integration of information with ontological underpinning, semantic coherence, and truth maintenance, so that anything that was true or logically consistent before data web integration will remain so afterward.
• Perhaps most important, it will permit programmatic access (i.e., automated metadata access from another software service on the Web), enabling added-value services to be built on top of one or more data webs.

Conclusions

This essay has described a lightweight data web approach, involving initial SPARQL searches to acquire core metadata, followed by linking to the sources to obtain selected data objects. This approach will prove to be a fast, scalable, and generic method of access to data held in multiple content repositories, as demonstrated in the integration of *Drosophila* gene expression data.[6] In principal, different data webs might access the same data sources for quite distinct purposes—for example, accessing cellular images either to compare microscopy techniques or to study disease progression. The technology is generic and can be applied to a variety of disciplines, such as creating a data web to integrate images of classical art objects from distributed research archives.[7]

Data webs for image repositories will benefit the primary data holders by making their holdings cross-searchable and by bringing additional users to their sites, without in any way controlling or constraining access to the primary data. The latter remain under the full copyright and access control of their source repositories, whereas their metadata remain available on the Web for use by other presently unforeseen applications, including novel data-mining and analysis services. In this way, the image holdings of academic publishers, museums, and institutional repositories will become more integral components of the day-to-day information environment of academic researchers, teachers, students, and even the general public.

Notes

1. See http://www.openarchives.org/OAI/openarchivesprotocol.html.

2. For more on the topics raised in this essay, see http://rin.ac.uk/data-webs and http://imageweb .zoo.ox.ac.uk/wiki/index.php/Main_Page.

3. See http://www.w3.org/2001/sw/.

4. RDF (http://www.w3.org/RDF/) is a simple knowledge-representation language for making statements about things in machine-readable form. RDF conceptually defines a Web-wide graph of nodes (subjects and objects) connected by links (their predicates).

5. SPARQL (http://www.w3.org/TR/rdf-sparql-query/) is the standard query language and protocol for querying RDF data. It stands to the Semantic Web as standard query language does to relational databases, but has the additional advantage that it can also be used to query "legacy" relational databases, other data sources, and RDF triple stores by the expedient of creating a SPARQL endpoint (http://semanticweb.org/wiki/SPARQL_endpoint) over each non-RDF resource. The SPARQL endpoint acts either by translating the incoming SPARQL query into the native query language of the particular resource (e.g., into standard query language) and then translating the query results back into RDF, or by rewriting some of the metadata from the resource into RDF, which is cached in a local triple store, where it can be interrogated directly by an incoming SPARQL query. The importance of this cannot be overemphasized because it permits Semantic Web applications to work over the non-RDF "legacy" data that forms the bulk of the world's digital information.

6. See the FlyData Project at http://imageweb.zoo.ox.ac.uk/wiki/index.php/FlyWeb_project and http://www.openflydata.org.

7. See the CLAROS Project (Classical Art Research Online Services) at http://www.clarosnet.org.

References

Berners-Lee, T. 1999. *Weaving the Web: The original design and ultimate destiny of the World Wide Web by its inventor*. San Francisco: Harper Collins.

Berners-Lee, T., J. Hendler, and O. Lasilla. 2001. "The Semantic Web." *Scientific American 284* (5):35–43.

Fielding, R. T. 2000. "Representational state transfer (REST)." In "Architectural styles and the design of network-based software architectures," chap. 5. Ph.D. diss., University of California, Irvine. Available at: http://www.ics.uci.edu/~fielding/pubs/dissertation/abstract.htm.

3.2 Digital Technology and Ancient Manuscripts

Alan Bowman

Exciting developments in digital technology since the late twentieth century have transformed the research environment and the access to resources available to scholars who work on ancient documents. This essay outlines four key aspects of these changes: the ways in which improved techniques of digital image capture benefit the research process; the development of access to resources in an information and communication technology (ICT) environment; possible directions of future research on the applications of digital technology to the interpretation of damaged documents; and the opportunities and constraints relating to digital research.

Benefits of Digital Image Capture for Research on Ancient Manuscripts

Scholars studying ancient manuscripts have long recognized the importance of image capture and the potential of using ICTs for digital imaging. High-profile documents, such as the Dead Sea Scrolls and the carbonized papyri from Herculaneum, have tended to grab the headlines. They are the tip of an iceberg of work, however, that essentially has exploited multispectral imaging techniques in the infrared spectrum as applied to texts written in carbon-based ink on a variety of different materials, such as papyri[1] from Oxyrhynchus and elsewhere, wooden writing tablets from Vindolanda,[2] parchments, and skins (e.g., see Bagnall 1997; Obbink 1997).

The benefits of the techniques used, of course, are not confined to ancient manuscripts. Fruitful dialogs have taken place with scholars working on other kinds of texts, such as the *Canterbury Tales*,[3] early music manuscripts,[4] and virtual vellum,[5] among many others. The problems addressed are common ones: mainly damaged or lacunose[6] manuscripts, abrasion, dirt, palimpsest[7] writing, and so on.

Despite some sensational journalistic claims, the resulting improvements in reading and interpretation have always tended to be gradual and incremental—it is rare that whole new passages of previously invisible writing of a text leap from the page with unimagined clarity. Nevertheless, the new approaches have demonstrably produced large numbers of new and important readings whose cumulative significance is considerable. Despite the many scholars who are persuaded of the benefits of this technology, and despite significant improvements in the technology itself (including better portability and reduced exposure times), it is notable that the wheel is continually reinvented, and there is a lack of commonly adopted and agreed standards for image capture and the recording of metadata.

Among the problems to be addressed by future research, palimpsests offer particularly significant challenges, but these challenges are likely to be met effectively. Another significant development is the ability to produce flat images of texts written on scrolls without unrolling the scrolls.[8] Imaging ink-written manuscripts in two dimensions presents one set of challenges that has been partly met.

A different and more difficult set of challenges is presented by incised or inscribed documents, which require imaging in three dimensions and offer analogous obstacles, such as abrasion, damage, wood-grain overlaid texts, and so on. Working closely in collaboration with experts in medical imaging, those who deal with ancient manuscripts have made significant progress in developing new techniques of image capture, such as through variable angles of illumination and signal processing. The principal development, called "shadow stereo," has been applied with success to wooden stylus tablets and to curse tablets incised on lead from Roman Britain (e.g., see Bowman and Tomlin 2004; Brady, Pan, Terras, et al. 2004). The next step is to address the rather different challenges offered by the stone inscriptions for which the stonecutter's chisel marks on the original surface have disappeared. Can we re-create them by measuring changes in the crystalline structure of the subsurface?

Improving ICT Access to Document Images

Most ancient documents have been removed from their original context and now lie dispersed in museum collections (with fragments of the same documents not infrequently thousands of miles apart) or are immovable for other reasons. The ability to create high-quality digital facsimiles and make them available in an ICT environment therefore offers the opportunity for scholars in remote locations to gain direct access not only to manuscripts and documents, but also to the tools and scholarly aids they need to decipher and interpret them. This access would involve not only images, viewing tools, and image-processing software, but also the ability to call up (for example, via the Access Grid) images of multiple documents for comparison and collation, lexical and other reference works, and collaborative discussion, annotation and on-screen editing in real time with colleagues. Such access should offer large-format audio- and video-based collaboration between groups of people in different locations.[9] An example of such a potentially long-lasting and adaptable environment is that provided in the U.K. research project A Virtual Workspace for the Study of Documents and Manuscripts.[10]

Research Directions

Future research can continue to build on the results achieved so far by better understanding how to apply emerging computing technologies (including digital imaging) to support textual research in the humanities. This understanding is characterized by the frequently collaborative deployment of complex, expert, and often tacit knowledge that is both dynamic and adaptable. It also seeks to elucidate the best possible fit of the textual evidence to prior understanding while minimizing uncertainty in interpretation.

These developments build on an earlier aspect of the collaborative research between palaeography and medical imaging that explored developments in the representation of semantics, recent developments in theories of reading, and ideas about knowledge representation and constraint propagation from artificial intelligence in order to develop a preliminary prototype version of a system that can "reason" about texts (Terras 2006). Analysis of the expert "reading" process shows how that knowledge enables us to use ICT tools that will recognize shapes of letter strokes without in any way supposing the possibility of an automated reading technique. It also offers the expert a degree of probability in assessing what the signal being looked at is more likely to be (e.g., whether it is an *a* rather than an *r*).

Semantic analysis is crucial to this process because it deals with the cognitive relationships between visual recognition of "signs" and the generation of hypotheses about their meanings in the "symbols" by which they are represented. This analysis is based on expert knowledge in fields such as palaeography, language, and historical context, and it attempts to describe explicitly and transparently the processes of reasoning under uncertainty—where the data to be interpreted will be wholly or partly unknown either to the individual reader or more generally in the canon of scholarship.

Another important research challenge is to demonstrate, for a number of different kinds of texts and media, ways in which explicit description of the reasoning processes can help develop ICT tools that enable the expert reader to make better-informed choices and hypotheses in interpreting a damaged document. This is of crucial importance in helping to determine the future direction of major ICT developments, such as the creation and configuration of digital repositories of research resources. For example, in order to make collections of images useful, we need to know what the researcher can or should be doing with them.[11]

Research Opportunities and Constraints

Digital technology offers the researcher in this field many exciting opportunities, but also some significant constraints. The editing of ancient manuscripts and inscriptions has always demanded acquaintance with a wide range of subdisciplines and techniques in which the editor frequently has to call upon the superior expertise of collaborators in particular specialisms. The abilities to move among specialisms and to build networks in which the problems can be addressed with virtually simultaneous access to a larger universe of researchers and resources is crucial.

It remains important to determine how best to gain these abilities—technically, cognitively, and managerially—and how best to preserve the research outputs. The result should be not merely that we can perform the same editing functions more quickly and efficiently, but that we can reassemble the dispersed fragments of past societies in ways that have previously been impossible, following the growth of museum and collection culture. Ancient texts are no longer words simply transcribed on a page, but can and should also be seen as objects in a landscape or as artifacts deriving from a specific physical context.

The constraints placed on the development of such research are largely managerial and institutional. The availability of financial and human resources is an obvious potential limitation. Another important issue is the difficulties involved in bringing into the network a range of digital resources and collaborators operating in very different environments and with different technical capabilities. Potential significant obstacles are also inherent in matters relating to copyright, intellectual property, and the rights (or the lack of rights) to publish or make available original manuscripts or documents originating in countries and institutions that have different conventions and laws regulating the acquisition of, movement of, access to, and dissemination of antiquities.

Notes

1. See http://www.papyrology.ox.ac.uk/.

2. See http://vindolanda.ox.ac.uk/.

3. For example, see http://www.canterburytalesproject.org/CTPresources.html.

4. For example, see http://www.diamm.ac.uk/.

5. For example, see http://www.shef.ac.uk/french/research/froissart/vvellum.htm.

6. Manuscripts with a gap or missing element.

7. A manuscript that has been reused—for example, by scraping off the original text and writing over it.

8. See http://www.research.uky.edu:80/odyssey/fall04/seales.html.

9. See http://www.accessgrid.org/.

10. This project is sponsored by the Joint Information Systems Committee Virtual Research Environment Phase 2 program (see http://bvreh.humanities.ox.ac.uk/VRE-SDM/ for details).

11. For a summary presentation, see http://www.oerc.ox.ac.uk/activities/presentations.xml.

References

Bagnall, R. S. 1997. "Imaging of papyri: A strategic view." *Literary and Linguistic Computing 12* (3):153–154.

Bowman, A. K., and R. S. O. Tomlin. 2004. "Wooden stylus tablets from Roman Britain." In *Artefacts and images of the ancient world*, ed. A. K. Bowman and J. M. Brady. Oxford, UK: Oxford University Press for the British Academy, 7–14.

Brady, J. M., X. Pan, M. Terras, and V. Schenk. 2004. "Shadow stereo, image filtering, and constraint propagation." In *Artefacts and images of the ancient world*, ed. A. K. Bowman and J. M. Brady. Oxford, UK: Oxford University Press for the British Academy, 15–30.

Obbink, D. 1997. "Imaging the carbonized papyri from Herculaneum." *Literary and Linguistic Computing 12* (3):159–162.

Terras, M. 2006. *Image to interpretation*. Oxford, UK: Oxford University Press.

4 Key Digital Technologies to Deal with Data

Yorick Wilks and Matthijs den Besten

Data, Information, and Knowledge

It is commonly accepted that data is not the same as information, let alone knowledge. For instance, the numbering and photographing of the fins of thousands of dolphins would certainly be data, but doubtfully information or knowledge; a city's large phone directory is undoubtedly information, but hardly knowledge—and certainly not permanent or reliable knowledge. These distinctions preoccupy philosophers (e.g., Dretske 1981) but few ordinary folk. Yet in science all these forms are of crucial importance—for example, when the data on dolphin fins turned out to be identifying information about individual dolphins and their behavior (Wilson, Black, Curran, et al. 1995).

Data are often quantified by the amount of computer storage they require. In contrast, information is more likely to be counted by the word and knowledge by the time needed to acquire it. A Joint Information Systems Committee (2004) study has described the specific volumes of data encountered by people every day in terms of the computer storage that would be required to store such data outside human brains (e.g., one megabyte for a novel).[1] These numbers may have been very large throughout human history, but it is only now, with the existence of such storage, that such figures have gained any real meaning. It has become possible for the first time to quantify the data and information to which human sense organs are exposed. For our purposes, we can discuss how much of that putative stored data people can retrieve and try to structure and use.

It is another commonplace that each of us can control and retrieve many megabytes of data an hour through the Internet, even though these amounts are much smaller than the putative terabytes we encounter daily in our environments—retrieving at the touch of a search button all the documents on a topic, for example. But we are then quite incapable of reading or understanding all those retrieved documents in any finite time. And so, also in everyday life, we are likely to encounter the "information overload" that is at the heart of the so-called data deluge in e-research (Hey and Trefethen 2003). How, then, can we—not only as individuals, but also collectively as research group, discipline, or society—cope with, understand, or process for any real purpose the sheer quantities of data and information that modern hardware technologies allow us to access?

The term *data deluge* suggests that we have no choice but to deal with the data. However, it is important to remember that the data are there only because we want to assemble them in the first place. We can just ignore the data if they are of no interest to us. Or we can set them aside and wait for the moment when we are able to cope with them. What makes the data deluge urgent is that we want to make sense of the data, and we want to do that now.

This chapter reviews a number of technologies for searching and processing information content in order to make it tractable for some defined purpose. It is important to understand that this issue is not wholly modern and that some of the technologies described to deal with the data deluge have strong relationships to the ways in which earlier data deluges were dealt with before the emergence of computer technology.

For example, the worldwide shipping insurers Lloyds Register employed, until the 1990s, thousands of people to read daily newspapers in every known language to extract reports of ship sinkings, all of which were of interest to Lloyds. Many readers knew little of the languages they were skimming—just enough to recognize and extract the facts of a sinking: time, place, tonnage, country of registry, lives lost, and so on. This approach was a traditional response to the deluge of data in the world's newspapers and worked well for more than a century. It has now been replaced by an information-extraction (IE) technology we describe later, which can do all this work in seconds and at virtually no cost because the Web texts of nearly all newspapers are now available.

Although technologies that should be able to deal adequately with the data deluge are becoming available, the deluge is likely to remain a problem for some time because it is much easier and cheaper to collect and store data than it is to acquire the skills and organization to curate and survey them effectively. Dealing with the deluge might therefore involve more than technological breakthroughs.

The Data Deluge

Characteristics of the Flood

The data deluge is the result of many positive developments arising from factors such as people's willingness to share, the low cost of digital storage, and how easy it is becoming to measure both physical events ranging from the movements of tagged objects to the detection of molecular structures and virtual events such as mouse clicks and bank transactions. The instruments required for such measurements are increasingly becoming widely available at exceedingly low cost.

The term *data deluge* describes a situation in which there are many more data coming toward us than we are currently able to process. It is the result of a world in which the collection and storage of data are becoming less and less expensive, and the potential benefits from processing the data are growing. Behind the deluge is the choice to invest disproportionately in collection with the hope that, once the data are collected, there will be more funds to do the processing and realize the benefits from those data.

Of course, to a great extent, the data deluge is the result of technical trends. Storage capacity increases as computer disks contain more megabytes per square inch and because computers start to appear everywhere. These developments may be leading to an era of "ubiquitous computing": the trend for people no longer to interact with one computer at a time, but rather with a dynamic set of small, networked computers, often invisible and embodied in everyday objects in the environment.[2]

In the meantime, collection capacity increases because devices that record observations are also becoming more ubiquitous. In addition, there is also the social trend that people and organizations' willingness to share data also seems to be growing (see the discussion on open science in essay 11.2). Moreover, it is important to keep in mind that the deluge is of our own making: without a reason to collect data, sensor networks would not be deployed, additional disks would not be bought, and our capacity to process the data would remain unchallenged.

Forces Driving the Deluge

There can be many reasons why we would want to gather data. The amount of processing that is needed afterward to reap the intended benefits from that act depends on our ambitions as consumers. For instance, although it is relatively straightforward to store and browse through the photos we make with our digital cameras, having them represent our life stories requires more organization. Similarly, the project to sequence the human genome, complex as it was, would have been relatively straightforward in terms of data processing if it were just about the detection and description of every gene. The need for more data-processing capabilities arose from the ambition to do something more with the sequence information (such as connecting it with other pieces of information in order to find a cure for cancer), in combination with the rapid rise in the rate at which sequence information could be obtained (den Besten 2003).

Just as it has become increasingly affordable to gather data, three particular trends in society and science are also encouraging such data gathering:

1. *Transience* The world as we know it seems to be disappearing at a faster and faster rate, which is an incentive to try to capture it while we can. Biodiversity research, for instance, has turned to digitization to capture the diversity that can still be found and is fueled by fears among many experts about the decrease in biodiversity (Bowker 2000).
2. *Threats* In order to assess the impact of climate change, data about the past and current climate need to be analyzed and used to calibrate climate models. Terrorism is another threat whose treatment depends on gathering, sharing, and processing data, this time to profile people and identify risks.

3. *Dreams*   From a more optimist perspective, opportunities continue to be identified. There are visions of important advances, such as the use of automated drug discovery—a dream that has been only partially realized. Also, a great deal of the data gathering by supermarkets regarding our purchases seems to have started while the directors had only a vague idea of how exactly these data could be used for direct marketing and other means. The lower costs of data gathering have meant that the decision to start collecting data can be taken more lightly because figuring out what to do with them can more safely be left to later.

Making Sense of the Data

The developments described so far have led us to a world of closed-circuit TV in public places, global positioning system (GPS) devices, and radio frequency identity (RFID) tags. Cameras are everywhere, networks of sensors record the state of the ocean, and every other object under the sun has been tagged. GPS tells us where we are; RFID tells others who we are. What's more, in the course of analysis, it is common practice to add even more data to the data being processed.

First of all, there are efforts to attach meaning to data and to make the logical structure of the data explicit, as is represented by the Semantic Web (essay 4.3). A second class of practices is less rigorous, but more fun and not necessarily less useful: *mash-ups* that enable people to make connections between disparate sets of data, *tagging* to allow people to associate labels with the data in structured and unstructured ways, and *discussion forums* and *blogs* for an even richer kind of annotation.

Experience is also growing with ways to induce people to provide increasingly detailed information not only about themselves and their relations to others, but also about their understanding and interpretation of the world at large. The ideas of Luis von Ahn (2006) illuminate this trend to enlist humans in areas, such as image interpretation, that are notoriously difficult for computers on their own. For this purpose, von Ahn devised a game in which players are presented with a postcard picture of, say, the glass pyramid at the Louvre in Paris. The player's task is to come up with a term that best describes the picture, but that another player has not yet chosen. Thus, a more accurate description of the picture is obtained each time the picture is presented to another player.

Spammers have developed a similar innovation. In order to get access to the blogs they would like to spam, spammers needed to solve "captchas" (completely automated public Turing tests), which aim to distinguish between computers and humans (von Ahn, Blum, and Langford 2004). A common captcha presents a user with difficult-to-interpret characters that need to be entered as a password. Because humans are better than machines at interpreting such degraded graphical representations, it is therefore more difficult for automated systems to read and interpret captchas accurately. To counteract this barrier, some spammers sought to make access to certain pornographic sites conditional on the user's revealing the captchas on the sites to which the spammer wants access (Zittrain 2008).

Nevertheless, photo-sharing sites such as Flickr show that many people are perfectly happy to provide metadata simply for the sake of sharing. On Facebook and other social-networking sites, many people's identities are also disclosed on a remarkable proportion of photos, both as an aide memoir and as a way to notify "friends" that a picture of them has just been put up. It should also be noted that the complexity of the contributions that people volunteer to provide goes well beyond the annotation of images. Witness, for instance, the emergence of *Wikipedia* or of the open-source software on which much of the Internet depends (Mateos-Garcia and Steinmueller 2003).

Technologies to Help Users Manage Their Data Needs

Technologies are being developed to deal with the deluge in several ways. What we cover here is more applicable to data in symbolic forms and less to the representation of image content and search. Applications for the latter are now available for certain specific image types, especially faces (e.g., Riya,[3] an image search engine that determines similarity of image content through analysis of color, shape, and texture). However, these applications are less developed and understood than the symbolic content and search that we focus on here.

Our discussion is also oriented to search and representation as the basis of subsequent search; we are not discussing the data deluge present in sciences such as astronomy, where a vast quantity of numerical data must be transformed, sometimes graphically, so that it can be understood and modeled. Rather, we focus on the type of large data flows present in the life sciences, among other sciences, where the relatively limited quantity of data compared to astronomical data is counterbalanced by a greater complexity that requires more meticulous techniques of annotation and aggregation to enable sets of data to be modeled and understood.

There are two basic approaches toward the data deluge as described here. One is to try and contain the on-flow of information; the other is to promote it. On one side are the "guardians of content," whose aim is to develop nonambiguous and noise-free representations of the data. At the other side are "examiners of content," who rely on the sheer quantity of the data to do their statistical disambiguation. Whereas the examiners have developed technologies to acquire and explore more and more detailed data, the guardians have put their energies into more and more sophisticated means to describe these data. This tension, or complementarity, between examiners and guardians plays out at different levels with regard to the acquisition of data and creation of content and in the extraction of information and the search of content.

Information Search and Content

Information Retrieval and Artificial Intelligence

The notion of information search is not always easy to separate from that of the content searched for; it depends to some extent on one's intellectual tradition. Consider the relationship of information retrieval (IR), the original search technology (box 4.1), and artificial intelligence (AI), whose researchers see themselves as "the guardians of content" according to a remarkable paper by Karen Spärck Jones (1999). Spärck Jones argues against what she sees as the mainstream of AI research based on a long tradition of work on the representation of knowledge in a computer, which has led to developments such as the Semantic Web. Her view can be taken as the core view regarding IR: "One of these [simple, revolutionary IR] ideas is taking words as they stand" (2003:21). This argument opposes the view generally taken in AI, which is committed to representations, their computational tractability, and their explanatory power—over and above the surface words of documents.[4]

Natural-language processing (NLP) is a widely applied AI engineering technique; the most obvious use is for the machine-translation (MT) facilities available on most search engines. However, there remains a lively debate among researchers over whether, in the end, NLP techniques can do anything that cannot be done by sufficiently sophisticated statistical techniques. That is the force of the Spärck Jones quotation: she remains committed to the core IR notion that statistical methods are ultimately sufficient for good retrieval of information, whereas those in favor of NLP (and other AI approaches she criticizes) remain equally convinced that some notion of linguistic processing or "understanding of content" is essential for effective information search.

IR's original search methodology was simply to look in the document for the terms in the query. This approach was not very successful. The basic strategy was to index every document (before search time) with its key or most relevant terms, using the "inverse

Box 4.1
Information Retrieval

Since the 1950s, information retrieval (IR) has been a basic search technology for information (Cowie and Wilks 2000). It was designed to enable the selection of the most relevant set of documents from a wider set in response to a user's query, normally stated as a string of key terms. In principle, this idea is not far from the everyday democratic use of the Internet, where a user types words into a search engine to locate information (on average two and a half terms per query). But that everyday procedure is very different from traditional IR, which was originally developed as a technique for library and science professionals, where strings of key terms can be up to two hundred terms long. Search engines such as Google now make substantial use of natural language–processing techniques of which the user is unaware. These techniques vary enormously in type and scale, but what distinguishes them from IR is that they make some use of linguistic knowledge—the actual disposition of words in a text. It may involve something as simple as finding only those documents containing the name "Tony Blair," before finding all those with just "Tony" and all those with just "Blair" in a much larger—and probably less useful—set.

document frequency" measure of the relevance of terms (Salton 1972). This strategy is based on the notion that a document is relevant not only because key terms are frequent in it, but because those terms are not frequent in other, nonrelevant documents. All this rests on collecting corpora of nonrelevant documents so as to do the indexing. Additional techniques required the use of thesauri, either hand made by experts or created automatically from corpora of related documents. These expanded the sets of relevant terms so that documents were retrieved that did not exactly match index terms but were closely related to ones in a thesaurus.

Four further developments rescued IR from a somewhat static condition in the 1980s:

1. Systems can be improved by means of "relevance feed back": information from users about which documents found by a system were relevant and which were not. This was the first clear use in IR of machine learning, a technique that became essential to IE and text mining, as discussed later.
2. The spread of hyperlink algorithms, most famously in the method Sergey Brin and Larry Page used as the basis of Google, came with the growth of the Web. Here, relevance is based not on text terms in documents, but on pointers to documents. This has led to a culture of Web search where queries are normally about two and a half words long rather than hundreds; because the ambiguity of terms in short queries is more significant, the relevance of NLP therefore seems to return.
3. The Web revived Gerald Salton's (1972) idea of "cross-language IR"—retrieving documents in one language by means of a query in another. Salton showed that this method can surprisingly be as successful as standard (monolingual) IR.
4. A new mode of analysis emerged in terms of "language models" or "translation models" (Berger and Laferty 1999). In 1988, Frederick Jelinek, Peter Brown, and others at IBM New York began to implement a plan of research to import into NLP and into MT in particular the statistical techniques that had been successful in automatic speech recognition. Although this project never achieved an MT success rate of more than 50 percent of sentences correctly translated, it began an empiricist wave in NLP that has continued to be its core methodology, as discussed later. An extended metaphor is at work here, where IR is described as MT because it involves the retrieval of one string by means of another. IR classically meant the retrieval of documents by queries, but IR researchers have extended the string-to-string notion to question-answering (QA) applications, where an answer is described as a "translation" of its question (Berger and Laferty 1999).

Information Extraction

The newer search technology, IE, is quite different. The key notion in IE (see box 4.2) is that of a "template": a linguistic pattern of text, usually a set of attribute–value pairs, with the values being text strings. The templates are normally created manually by

Box 4.2

Information Extraction

> Information extraction (IE) (see van Rijsbergen 1979) is an automatic method for locating facts in electronic documents (e.g., newspaper articles, news feeds, Web pages, transcripts of broadcasts, etc.) and for storing them in a database for processing—using techniques such as data mining or off-the-shelf products such as spreadsheets, summarizers, and report generators. A typical application for IE is illustrated by a company such as Lloyds of London, which wanted to extract information (in its case, all ship sinkings) from public news sources in any language worldwide and to collect that information into a single database (for Lloyds, showing sunken ships' names, tonnage, etc.) rather than perform this task with many human readers of newspapers.

experts in order to capture the structure of the facts sought in a given domain. The IE system then applies the templates to text corpora, assisted by extraction rules that seek "fillers" in the corpus—pieces of text that give specific kinds of information such as tonnage, as discussed in box 4.2.

IE achieved a similar level of success as IR and MT in attaining commercial viability (on differing measures, of course). The main barrier to IE's wider use and commercialization is the relative inflexibility of its basic template concept. Classic IE relies on the user's having an already developed set of templates, as was the case when intelligence analysts in U.S. military agencies were seeking information from newspapers on "terrorist events." It was another U.S. agency, the Defense Advanced Research Projects Agency, that largely developed the technology before it was taken up more widely around the world (Gaizauskas and Wilks 1998). The intellectual and practical challenge for IE is how to develop new domains and genres rapidly: templates, their filler subparts (such as named entities), the rules for filling them, and associated knowledge structures.

IE is now widely deployed on the Web and elsewhere to locate names of certain classes of entity (e.g., air crashes) in news wires and other sources. It has also become the basis of NLP developments such as QA, where the goal is to retrieve not only relevant facts, but the correct answer. IE and QA are quite different from IR in that they rest on linguistic techniques for finding structure in the text in which it ceases to be a mere "bag of words," as is traditional in IR; most important, higher categories are introduced in the processing—such as capturing all names that refer to people or places. These techniques are inherently semantic and involve categories outside the text (such as "SHIPS NAME"). Words then no longer "stand only for themselves," but are grouped into classes with meanings.

AI, or at least nonconnectionist, nonstatistical AI, remains committed to the representation of propositions in some more or less logical form. Mainstream IR may not be dogmatically antirepresentational (as are some statistical and other areas of AI and language processing), but at least it is not committed to any notion of representation beyond what is given by a set of index terms or strings of index terms along with numbers computed from text that may specify clusters, vectors, or other derived structures. However, it is known that many modern search engine companies, such as Google, employ large numbers of people with NLP training and backgrounds, and proprietary engines embody techniques going far beyond documents indexed as "bags of words." This augmented search capacity is in part due to the ability to search the full text of documents rather than just the indexing terms. At the simplest level, this ability allows a search engine to distinguish the same terms in different orders—for example, in such cases as the undoubted difference of interpretation between a search on MEASURE-MENTS OF MODELS and a search on MODELS OF MEASUREMENT. Each search might well be expected to access different literatures, even though any retrieval based only on those (unordered) words should be the same. In fact, these two collections of words get 363 and 326 hits respectively in Netscape, but the first 20 items have no common members.

An extension to syntactic notions in search is that of the use of proposition-like objects as part of document indexing, which can be seen as an attempt to index documents by IE template relations. For example, this approach may involve extracting and filling binary relation templates (X manufactures Y; X employs Y; X is located in Y) so that documents can be indexed by these facts in the hope that much more interesting searches can in principle be conducted (e.g., find all documents that talk about any company that manufactures drug X, where this set would be much more restricted than all those sets that mention drug X).

Applying semantic analysis to IR goes back to IR's earliest days, as in the complex structures derived from MT developments in the 1960s by researchers such as Maurice Gross (1964) and Jean Claude Gardin (1965). There was no hardware or software then to perform searches based on these approaches. The notion of what we would now call a full-text search by such patterns also goes back to the mid-1960s (e.g. Wilks 1964, 1965), even though no real experiments could be carried out with the computers of that time. Within IR, Michael Mauldin (1991) implemented document search based on case-frame structures applied to queries (ones that cannot be formally distinguished from IE templates). Indexing of texts by full, or scenario, templates appeared later (e.g., Pietrosanti and Graziadio 1997).

This indexing-by-template idea is one of the approaches being explored as an aid to retrieval, and its fulfillment may require advances in hardware, architectures, and techniques. What seems clear is that in the Web world there is an urge to revive something along the lines of "get me what I mean, not what I say" (see Jeffrey 1999).

In mainstream IE developments, fuller AI techniques—using ontologies, knowledge representations, and inference—are likely to play a stronger role as basic pattern matching and template-element finding become subject to more efficient machine learning. There is also a good opportunity for IE to become the technology vehicle by means of which the old AI goals of adaptive, tuned lexicons and knowledge bases can be pursued. IE may also be the only technique that will ever provide a substantial and consistent knowledge base from texts, which the AI project Cyc (Lenat, Prakash, and Shepherd 1986) has failed to do by hand coding over a period of more than twenty years. The traditional AI/QA task may yield to a combination of IR and IE as researchers mix and match what were once the quite separate task-defined technologies of IR and IE, on the one hand, and MT and QA, on the other.

Text Mining

Text mining is a technique that shares with IR a statistical methodology, but, being linked directly to the structure of databases (Kao and Poteet 2006), it does not have the ability to develop in the way IR has in creating hybrid techniques with NLP aspects. Text mining can be seen as a fusion of two techniques: first, the gathering of information from text by some form of statistical pattern learning; second, the insertion of such structured data into a database to carry out a search for patterns within the structured data—the best results being novel patterns not intuitively observable.

The first covers more or less similar ground to the IE task, and the second is a more specific form of data mining. Users of the term *text mining* often cite tasks such as "text categorization, text clustering, concept/entity extraction, production of granular taxonomies, sentiment analysis, document summarization" (Kao and Poteet 2006:38). These tasks are standard and long-standing NLP, IR, or IE tasks. Hence, the distinctive feature of text mining is the statistical search for novel, interesting, or relevant relations in such data once it has been extracted and which can involve associations with other time-series information, such as stock movements (if the texts are from news sources).

Conclusion: Toward a Toolkit for Data Management

This chapter has provided an overview of technologies to deal with the data forest known as the "deluge." We have seen how technologies such as ubiquitous computing and sensor networks will exacerbate the influx of data and how technologies such as the Semantic Web promise to funnel it into different channels. In addition, it has described a number of ad hoc methods for annotation and linkage of data. However, a continuing underlying debate involves whether "understanding of content" is essential for effective information search or whether statistical methods will do. Practitioners of IR and IE would traditionally believe the latter, whereas practitioners of NLP would opt for the former.

A convergence of both traditions—the statistical tradition of IR and the semilinguistic tradition of IE—has meant statistical techniques are being adopted in NLP and MT, and search engines now embody techniques that go far beyond indexing documents as "bags of words." Moreover, artificial companions,[5] games, and other applications will allow us to improve the quality and quantity of the data, even through the engagement of human brains. It is such technologies that will ultimately turn the challenge of the data deluge into an unprecedented opportunity.

The data deluge was brought about by a relative underinvestment in the capacity to survey and curate data being gathered. Over time, this gulf will be bridged, where necessary by powerful techniques that deal with the data. Most spectacularly, but still in the realm of speculation, advances in data gathering and data processing have already enabled us to "upload our mind," in the sense that—for many people—so much personal data are available that computer programs are able to mimic personal traits. Much like the way some machine-learning programs can produce new music scores as variations on old ones, such programs should also be able to construct stylistically congruent emails or patents on the basis of old ones, or even write articles for the American Chemistry Society.[6]

Notes

1. Other examples include one gigabyte for the information in the human genome and one terabyte for the annual world literature production (adapted from table 1 in JISC 2004).

2. For more background on ubiquitous computing, see, for example, Weiser 1991, Greenfield 2006, Bell and Dourish 2007, and http://nano.xerox.com/hypertext/weiser/UbiHome.html.

3. See http://www.riya.com/.

4. The word *knowledge* is used conventionally here and is not intended to be rigorously analyzed by contrast with *data* or *information*. AI researchers, like scientists in general, often refer to attested and generally believed material as "knowledge," even though the history of science is full of surprises in this regard.

5. An artificial companion is an intelligent program (e.g., using advanced graphics to look and act like a person) or physical embodiment (e.g., a robot) that can become a companion to its user-owner by learning about and remembering the user-owner's preferences, habits, and wishes (see Peltu and Wilks 2009). It can help with the data deluge by acting as a filtering agent familiar with its user-owner's preferences.

6. At a seminar at the Oxford e-Research Centre in October 2008, Peter Murray Rust remarked on how stable and stylized the language of chemistry has been in the past century. NLP is employed to extract chemical formulae from articles. It is not a huge leap to try the same in the reverse direction.

References

Bell, G., and P. Dourish. 2007. "Yesterday's tomorrows: Notes on ubiquitous computing's dominant vision." *Personal and Ubiquitous Computing 11* (2):133–143.

Berger, A., and J. Lafferty. 1999. "Information retrieval as statistical translation." In *Proceedings of the 22nd Annual International ACM SIGIR Conference on Research and Development in Information Retrieval*. Berkeley, CA: SIGIR.

Bowker, G. 2000. "Biodiversity, data diversity." *Social Studies Science 30* (5):643–683.

Cowie, J., and Y. Wilks. 2000. "Information extraction." In *Handbook of natural language processing*, ed. R. Dale, H. Moisl and H. Somers. New York: Marcel Dekker, 241–260.

Den Besten, M. 2003. "The rise of bioinformatics: An historical approach to the emergence of a new scientific discipline." Master's thesis, University of Oxford, Oxford, UK.

Dretske, F. 1981. *Knowledge and the flow of information*. Cambridge, MA: MIT Press.

Gaizauskas, R., and Y. Wilks. 1998. "Information extraction: Beyond document retrieval." *Journal of Documentation 54* (1):70–105.

Gardin, J. 1965. *Syntol*. New Brunswick, NJ: Rutgers Graduate School of Library Science.

Greenfield, A. 2006. *Everyware: The dawning age of ubiquitous computing*. Berkeley, CA: New Riders.

Gross, M. 1964. "On the equivalence of models of language used in the fields of mechanical translation and information retrieval." *Information Storage and Retrieval 2* (1):43–57.

Hey, A. J. G., and A. E. Trefethen. 2003. "The data deluge: An e-science perspective." In *Grid computing—making the global infrastructure a reality*, ed. F. Berman, G. C. Fox, and A. J. G. Hey. Chichester, UK: Wiley, 809–824. Available at: http://eprints.ecs.soton.ac.uk/7648/.

Jeffrey, K. 1999. "What's next in databases?" *ERCIM News 39*. Available at: http://www.ercim.org/.

Joint Information Systems Committee (JISC). 2004. *The data deluge*. Bristol, UK: JISC. Available at: http://www.jisc.ac.uk/publications/publications/pub_datadeluge.aspx.

Kao, A., and S. R. Poteet, eds. 2006. *Natural language processing and text mining*. New York: Springer.

Lenat, D., M. Prakash, and M. Shepherd. 1986. "CYC: Using common sense knowledge to overcome brittleness and knowledge acquisition bottlenecks." *AI Magazine 6* (4):65–85.

Mateos Garcia, J., and W. E. Steinmueller. 2003. *Applying the open source development model to knowledge work*. INK Open Source Research Working Paper no. 2. Brighton, UK: Science and Technology Policy Research, University of Sussex.

Mauldin, M. 1991. "Retrieval performance in FERRET: A conceptual information retrieval system." In *Proceedings of the 14th Annual International ACM SIGIR Conference on Research and Development in Information Retrieval, Chicago*. Berkeley, CA: SIGIR, 347–355.

Peltu, M., and Y. Wilks. 2009. "Engaging with artificial companions: Key social, psychological, ethical, and design Issues." In *Artificial companions: Social, technical, and philosophical perspectives*, ed. Y. Wilks. Amsterdam: John Benjamins.

Pietrosanti, E., and B. Graziadio. 1997. "Extracting information for business needs." Paper presented at the Unicom Seminar on Information Extraction, London, March.

Salton, G. 1972. "A new comparison between conventional indexing (MEDLARS) and automatic text processing (SMART)." *Journal of the American Society for Information Science and Technology 23* (2):75–84.

Spärck Jones, K. 1999. "Information retrieval and artificial intelligence." *Artificial Intelligence Journal 114* (1–2):257–281.

Spärck Jones, K. 2003. "Document retrieval: Shallow data, deep theories, historical reflections, and future directions." In *Proceedings of the 25th European IR Conference (ECIR03)*. Lecture Notes in Computer Science. Berlin: Springer, 21–23.

Van Rijsbergen, K. 1979. *Information retrieval*. 2d ed. London: Butterworths.

Von Ahn, L. 2006. "Games with a purpose." *Computer 39* (6):92–94.

Von Ahn, L., M. Blum, and J. Langford. 2004. "Telling humans and computers apart automatically." *Communications of the ACM 47* (2):56–60.

Weiser, M. 1991. "The computer for the twenty-first century." *Scientific American* (September): 94–104.

Wilks, Y. 1964. *Text searching with templates*. Cambridge Language Research Unit Memo, ML.156. Cambridge, UK: Cambridge Language Research Unit.

Wilks, Y. 1965. *The application of CLRU's method of semantic analysis to information retrieval*. Cambridge Language Research Unit Memo, ML.173. Cambridge, UK: Cambridge Language Research Unit.

Wilson, B., A. Black, S. Curran, K. Grellier, P. M. Thompson, and P. S. Hammond. 1995. "The movements, behaviour, and characteristics of individually recognisable bottlenose dolphins in the Moray Firth." Unpublished contract report to Scottish Natural Heritage.

Zittrain, J. 2008. *The future of the Internet—and how to stop it*. New Haven, CT: Yale University Press.

4.1 Embedded Networked Sensing

Christine L. Borgman

Innovations in embedded and wireless sensor networks are enabling the environmental sciences, biosciences, and other fields to ask new research questions in new ways. These technologies are also substantial contributors to the data deluge that typifies e-research and cyberinfrastructure activities (Atkins, Droegemeier, Feldman, et al. 2003; Hey and Trefethen 2005; see also chapter 4 in this volume). Sensor networks are shaping the ways in which many fields conduct their research and in how they capture, manage, disseminate, and preserve their research products. Embedded networked sensing research is a microcosm of e-science and thus a fruitful arena in which to study the transformation of scientific work, collaborative research, and the emergence of communities of practice associated with new forms of data production (Borgman 2007).

Sensor networks per se are not a new technology. Large manufacturing operations and chemical-processing plants, for example, rely heavily on sensor technology to manage operations. The monitoring of water flow and water quality similarly relies heavily on in situ sensor networks. In the United States alone, public regulatory agencies monitor several hundred million individual sensors in streams, lakes, and rivers. The density and granularity of data collection enabled by embedded sensor networks—what the Center for Embedded Networked Sensing (CENS) refers to as "robust distributed systems of thousands of physically embedded, unattended and often untethered devices"[1]—promise to transform the environmental sciences and many areas of biology, medicine, engineering, and other fields.

Range of Embedded Sensor Networks

The physically embedded nature of wireless sensing technologies is expected to reveal previously unobservable phenomena, leading to better understanding and management of our complex physical environment. Technology research fronts in embedded sensor networks include distributed system design, robotics, wireless communications, signal processing, and low-power, multimodal sensor-technology design. Engineering, computer science, and domain science researchers are conducting experiments and field deployments to identify the challenges and opportunities for advancing e-science, thus breaking new ground in collaborative research.

Static Observatory Networks

Observatory networks that are deploying embedded sensor networks to collect longitudinal and comparative data include the Long Term Ecological Reserve System;[2] WATERS Network,[3] a merger of the CUAHSI and the CLEANER initiatives;[4] the GEON;[5] and NEON.[6] Most of these applications of sensor networks are static deployments in which sensors are placed in appropriate positions to report data continuously on local conditions. Sensors are monitored by both humans and computers to determine changes in conditions. Autonomous networks can rely on machine actuation to capture scientifically relevant data, to alter data collection (e.g., capture data more frequently if excessive pollution is suspected), or to report emergencies that require intervention (e.g., faults in dams, water contamination). Data repositories can capture real-time data from autonomous networks—for instance, in the Real-time Observatories, Applications, and Data Management Network.[7]

Exploratory Field Research with in Situ Sensing

Autonomous sensor networks are effective for capturing data on phenomena that can be specified explicitly and whose location is static. They are less effective for exploratory research in which field requirements cannot be specified sufficiently in advance to operate systems remotely. The alternative, pioneered by CENS, uses dynamic "human in the loop" deployments, where investigators can adjust monitoring conditions in real time. Teams from CENS conduct data collection "campaigns" in which they deploy an embedded sensor network in the field for a few hours or a few days. They may return repeatedly to the same site or to a similar site, each time with slightly different equipment or research questions. These discrete field deployments offer several advantages to scientific researchers. The scientists can deploy prototype equipment that is much more sophisticated than the robust equipment required for autonomous networks. Engineering researchers often participate in deployments to test, evaluate, and adjust their equipment in the field. CENS teams also conduct longer-term field deployments to study phenomena that change slowly (e.g., plant roots) or suddenly (e.g., seismology).

Brief deployment campaigns also enable researchers to use equipment that is too delicate, too expensive, too premature, or with too short a life span to leave unattended in the field. For example, some chemical sensors are sufficiently volatile that they lose sensitivity within a few days. Scientists can finalize the precise positioning of equipment in the field based on current conditions (e.g., moisture, temperature, light, shade). Hand-collected samples of water and soil are often required to calibrate sensors. While in the field, scientists can also alter the position of their sensors and the frequency of sampling. For example, if the water depth chosen is not yielding interesting data, field researchers may raise, lower, or move their sensors. Dynamic deployments also benefit computer science and engineering research because equipment may be tested sooner and more iteratively than with autonomous networks. By collaborating in the field, researchers and students from all the participating disciplines learn very quickly about each others' problems and needs.

Although dynamic, human-in-the-loop sensor deployments yield better science for exploratory research, the data they generate are much harder to manage by traditional methods. Each deployment may have different research questions, methods, equipment, and data. In research areas whose methods are being transformed by sensing technologies, participants have yet to agree on common semantics, data structures, services, ontologies, and preservation policies necessary for robust data repositories (Borgman, Wallis, and Enyedy 2007; Borgman, Wallis, Mayernik, et al. 2007).

Big Science and Little Science

Not surprisingly, "big science" domains such as physics and astronomy were among the first to build distributed data and document repositories in support of collaborative research (Ginsparg 2001).[8] These endeavors are the large, complex scientific ones in which society makes major investments (Weinberg 1961). They are characterized by expensive equipment that must be shared among many collaborators, such as particle accelerators or space stations, and by agreements on data sources and structures.

"Little science" is the three hundred years of independent, smaller-scale work to develop theory and method for understanding research problems (Price 1963; Taper and Lele 2004). It is little-science fields such as habitat ecology that are experiencing the most profound transformations through the use of embedded and wireless sensing technologies (Zimmerman 2003; Borgman, Wallis, and Enyedy 2007). Differences between little and big science are more qualitative than quantitative. Big science encourages standardization of processes and products, and thus the growth of data repositories; metadata standards are predictable outcomes of the trajectory from little to big.

Digital Libraries

Digital libraries for scientific documents and data can facilitate collaboration and promote the progress of science. They also can hinder progress, however, by forcing standardization prematurely (Bishop, Van House, and Buttenfield 2003; Bowker 2005). Many scientific research areas continue to be productive without the use of shared instrumentation, shared repositories, or agreements on standards for data description. As research areas such as habitat ecology become more instrumented, especially through the deployment of embedded sensor networks, they are facing many challenges associated with the transition from little science to big science, including what to standardize, when, and for what purposes. Each style of sensor network deployment has its own data life-cycle characteristics, which in turn influence the architecture of digital library services (Mayernik, Wallis, and Borgman 2007).

Conclusions

Modern science is distinguished by the extent to which its practices rely on the generation, dissemination, and analysis of data. These practices are themselves distinguished both by the massive scale of data production and by the global dispersion of data resources. The rates of data generation in most fields are expected to increase much more quickly with new forms of instrumentation such as embedded sensor networks. Networked sensing technologies will be harbingers of change for e-science and cyberinfrastructure as research methods and data practices evolve.

Notes

1. See http://www.cens.ucla.edu/.

2. For the U.S. Long Term Ecological Research Network, see http://lternet.edu/.

3. See http://www.watersnet.org/.

4. CUAHSI is the Collaborative Large-Scale Engineering Analysis Network for Environmental Research (http://www.cuahsi.org/). CLEANER is the Consortium of Universities for Advancement of Hydrologic Science (http://cleaner.ncsa.uiuc.edu/home/).

5. See http://www.geongrid.org/.

6. See http://neoninc.org/.

7. See http://roadnet.ucsd.edu/.

8. See, for example, the International Virtual Observatory Alliance (http://www.ivoa.net/) and the arXiv.org e-Print archive in disciplines such as physics, mathematics, computer science, and quantitative biology (http://arxiv.org/).

References

Atkins, D. E., K. K. Droegemeier, S. I. Feldman, H. Garcia-Molina, M. L. Klein, P. Messina, D. G. Messerschmitt, J. P. Ostriker, and M. H. Wright. 2003. *Revolutionizing science and engineering through cyberinfrastructure: Report of the National Science Foundation Blue-Ribbon Panel on Cyberinfrastructure.* Arlington, VA: National Science Foundation. Available at: http://www.nsf.gov/cise/sci/reports/atkins.pdf.

Bishop, A. P., N. Van House, and B. P. Buttenfield, eds. 2003. *Digital library use: Social practice in design and evaluation.* Cambridge, MA: MIT Press.

Borgman, C. L. 2007. *Scholarship in the digital age: Information, infrastructure, and the Internet.* Cambridge, MA: MIT Press.

Borgman, C. L., J. C. Wallis, and N. Enyedy. 2007. "Little science confronts the data deluge: Habitat ecology, embedded sensor networks, and digital libraries." International Journal on Digital Libraries 7 (1–2):17–30. Available at: http://www.springerlink.com/content/f7580437800m367m/.

Borgman, C. L., J. C. Wallis, M. Mayernik, and A. Pepe. 2007. "Drowning in data: Digital library architecture to support scientists' use of embedded sensor networks." In *JCDL '07: Proceedings of the 7th ACM/IEEE-CS Joint Conference on Digital Libraries.* Vancouver, BC: Association for Computing Machinery, 269–277.

Bowker, G. C. 2005. *Memory practices in the sciences.* Cambridge, MA: MIT Press.

Ginsparg, P. 2001. "Creating a global knowledge network." In *Second Joint ICSU Press–UNESCO Expert Conference on Electronic Publishing in Science.* Paris: UNESCO. Available at: http://people.ccmr.cornell.edu/~ginsparg/blurb/pg01unesco.html.

Hey, T., and A. Trefethen. 2005. "Cyberinfrastructure and e-science." *Science 308*:818–821.

Mayernik, M. S., J. C. Wallis, and C. L. Borgman. 2007. *Adding context to content: The CENS Deployment Center. Information today.* Milwaukee: American Society for Information Science & Technology.

Price, D. J. D. S. 1963. *Little science, big science.* New York: Columbia University Press.

Taper, M. L., and S. R. Lele, eds. 2004. *The nature of scientific evidence: Statistical, philosophical, and empirical considerations.* Chicago: University of Chicago Press.

Weinberg, A. M. 1961. "Impact of large-scale science on the United States." *Science 134* (3473): 161–164.

Zimmerman, A. S. 2003. *Data sharing and secondary use of scientific data: Experiences of ecologists.* School of Information PhD Thesis. Ann Arbor: University of Michigan.

4.2 Identifying Digital Objects

Michael A. Fraser

Defining and Managing Digital Objects

Establishing the policies, infrastructure, and tools to create long-term persistent, accessible, and reusable digital data is one of the great challenges for the research and library communities today. This challenge applies to the petabytes of data generated from large-scale scientific instrumentation as much as it does to individual journal articles and is as relevant to the humanities and social sciences as it is to the physical and biosciences.

In this essay, a "digital object" is defined as a combination of one or more files with metadata (including identifiers) that can be stored in and retrieved from a file system (Lagoze, Payette, Shin, et al. 2005; Kahn and Wilensky 2006). However, any concise definition risks hiding the complexity inherent to digital objects.[1]

The raison d'être for a digital repository is the management of digital objects, and most repository systems have well-defined processes for ingesting, storing, exposing, and accessing them. Other systems, whether managed within an institution or by third-party "community" services, are increasingly providing de facto repository services. For example, a virtual learning environment (see chapter 10) is unlikely to have been designed as a digital repository, in any sense of the term as understood within the library and information science community, but at least it is a managed system.

The multitude of disks in offices, laboratories, computer rooms, and dangling from key rings also contain myriad tangled digital objects, clearly not managed within a repository system.

For the majority of digital objects created in the course of employment, an institution clearly has a vested interest in their management. A proportion of these objects, probably a small proportion overall, will find their way in some version or another to formal digital repository systems, but most will not. It is imperative that the relevant parties (researchers, information scientists, institutional managers) collaborate on supporting the life cycle of an institution's digital asset. This support must start when a device (desktop, mobile phone, camera, sensor, scientific instrument, etc.) brings the object into being, rather than only when the object is offered to a digital repository in a one-off event (Hockx-Yu 2006).

Assurance through Digital Object Identification and Authentication

At the heart of the challenge in creating persistent, accessible, and reusable data lies the identification of digital objects. This identification is fundamentally about assurance (Renear and Dubin 2003)—a match between the data and a set of assertions about those data—and is essential for:

• *Discovery and access*   People and systems need to be able to discover and retrieve digital objects within a networked environment to match predefined criteria.
• *Provenance and assurance*   Levels of assurance are required to determine what the digital object is, from where it originates, how it has evolved, and the relationships beyond itself.
• *Reusability*   Digital objects are increasingly reused and repurposed, with new objects derived from aggregation, enhancement, or subtraction.
• *Preservation*   The unpredictability of when any of the previous elements might be desirable and the increasing complexity of the process of identification as software, data formats, and hardware technologies advance must be dealt with.

The identity of a digital object comprises attributes related to its name (identifier), intellectual content, format(s) in which it is represented, and internal and external relationships (including how the object might be processed and any earlier or later versions, revisions, and derivatives).

The authentication of digital objects is problematic. There are various robust schemes for authenticating people within the digital sphere (the most secure of which depend on authentication outside of the digital world—for example, using some combination of birth certificate, passport, and affiliated institution). There is no requirement, however, to register the birth of a digital object, no universally acknowledged passport and visa system that permits a digital object to move from one domain to another. Moreover, existing systems for the authentication of digital objects have been bound up with digital rights management, placing greater emphasis on the license or authorization that sits between the user and the object.

Examples of Digital Object Identifiers

The most basic identifier is the file name. However, many file-naming conventions are arbitrary, specific to a system or application, or based on parochial practice. They also have no defined process for change, tend not to make explicit any relationships with other digital artifacts, and are therefore hardly mobile once the object leaves its immediate local context.

There have been various attempts to create persistent naming schemes for digital objects. One of the best known is the digital object identifier (DOI),[2] comprising an address, resolver, and set of policies governed by an international foundation (Vitiello 2004). The business model for maintaining the DOI system is aimed at publishers—for example, with DOIs often being assigned to digital journal articles, which are a reasonably simple type of digital object. The granularity at which persistent identifiers are applied is an issue for composite digital objects. The relationship between identifiers must maintain the integrity of a digital object in its immediate context (Arnab and Hutchison 2006).

Establishing the Provenance of Digital Objects

In the study and trade of artworks and antiquities, provenance is the process by which the history, context, and ownership of an object is established, and its realization is in effect a very rich set of metadata. The issues are very similar with respect to the identification of digital objects within the scholarly environment.

The provenance of a digital object is required to establish the process by which the object and its constituent parts were created (e.g., work flows, subsequent additions or subtractions) as well as its ownership—which can be complex when data arise from large-scale consortium projects. Documenting the provenance of a digital object must not only capture the most useful information for establishing identity and trust, but also ensure that the often extensive provenance metadata, or a reference to them, are carried with the digital object.[3] There must also be a trusted means by which provenance data are created or added, such as digital signatures (Arnab and Hutchison 2006).

Future Bridges between the Digital and the Physical

Although this essay has focused on the attributes necessary for the persistent identifying of digital objects, similar digital attributes assist in identifying nondigital objects. In the world of increasingly pervasive computing, various bridges exist between digital and physical objects. For instance, the combination of radio frequency identity electronic tags, microsensors, embedded networked systems, global positioning systems, and corresponding receivers blurs the boundaries between the physical and the digital realms. Location and context-aware relationships between such objects can be defined and recorded for history. Bruce Sterling (2004) has coined the term *spime* to describe objects that can be "precisely located in space and time. They have histories. They are recorded, tracked, inventoried, and always associated with a story."

The resolution of issues around the identification of digital objects has barely begun. Imagine, however, the emergence of an "Internet of Things" (ITU 2005), composed of anything from books to clothing to flora and fauna, each streaming metadata about what it is, whom it's with, and where it's been. Welcome to the metadata deluge.

Notes

1. This essay follows the digital object approach of the Functional Requirements for Bibliographic Records in making a distinction between the abstract "work" and one or more "expressions" of work manifested digitally. See Renear and Dubin 2003; Bide, Fraser, Kahn, et al. 2006; IFLA 2007 [1997].

2. See http://www.doi.org/.

3. Software applications increasingly embed metadata within files. However, open standards and tools for managing embedded metadata are also required.

References

Arnab, A., and A. Hutchison. 2006. "Verifiable digital object identity system." In *Proceedings of the ACM Workshop on Digital Rights Management 2006, Alexandria, VA, 30 October 2006*. New York: Association for Computing Machinery, 19–26. Available at: http://doi.acm.org/10.1145/1179509 .1179514.

Bide, M., M. Fraser, D. Kahn, H. Look, H. Noble, S. Rumsey, and F. Shipsey. 2006. *Scoping study on repository version identification (RIVER): Final report*. Joint Information Systems Committee (JISC) Working Group on Scholarly Communication. Bristol, UK: JISC. Available at: http://www.jisc.ac .uk/uploaded_documents/RIVER%20Final%20Report.pdf.

Hockx-Yu, H. 2006. "Digital preservation in the context of institutional repositories." *Program: Electronic Library and Information Systems 40* (3): 232–243.

International Federation of Library Associations (IFLA). 2007 [1997]. *Functional requirements for bibliographic records: Final report*. The Hague: IFLA. Available at: http://www.ifla.org/VII/s13/frbr/.

International Telecommunication Union (ITU). 2005. *The Internet of things: ITU Internet report*. Geneva: ITU. Available at: http://www.itu.int/publ/S-POL-IR.IT-2005/e.

Kahn, R., and R. Wilensky. 2006. "A framework for distributed digital object services." *International Journal of Digital Libraries 6* (2):115–123.

Lagoze, C., S. Payette, E. Shin, and C. Wilper. 2005. "Fedora: An architecture for complex objects and relationships." Draft of submission to Journal of Digital Libraries, special issue on complex objects, version 6, 23 August. Available at: http://arxiv.org/abs/cs/0501012v6.

Renear, A., and D. Dubin. 2003. "Towards identity conditions for digital documents." In *Proceedings of the 2003 Dublin Core Conference, Seattle, WA, October 2003*, ed. S. Sutton. Seattle: University of Washington. Available at: http://www.siderean.com/dc2003/503_Paper71.pdf

Sterling, B. 2004. *When blobjects rule the earth*. Los Angeles: SIGGRAPH, August. Available at: http://www.viridiandesign.org/notes/401-450/00422_the_spime.html.

Vitiello, G. 2004. "Identifiers and identification systems: An informational look at policies and roles from a library perspective." D-Lib 10 (1). Available at: http://www.dlib.org/dlib/january04/vitiello/01vitiello.html.

4.3 Use of the Semantic Web in e-Research

Kieron O'Hara, Tim Berners-Lee, Wendy Hall, and Nigel Shadbolt

A New Way of Finding Information: Basic Technologies of the Semantic Web

A key factor in the way the World Wide Web has revolutionized research has been its radical decentralization: any page can link to any other. This decentralization is scalable and removes bottlenecks in supply. Navigation can be via associational links, maintaining relevance, or key-word search, which allows the user a measure of control that makes a suitably connected computer a virtual, near-universal library.

Yet automation of research has farther to go. Information embedded in a document may still not be easy to find, a problem exacerbated when it is distributed over several documents. For these reasons, research continues to evolve the Web from a "Web of Documents" to a "Web of Data." "Semantic Web" is the name given to a conception of a Web of linked data, underpinned by a series of technologies and standards developed under the auspices of the World Wide Web Consortium[1] since the late 1990s. Here we briefly summarize four key components of the Semantic Web (for more detail on its various layers, see, for example, Shadbolt, Hall, and Berners-Lee 2006).

1. The basis for a Web of linked data is the system of uniform resource identifiers (URIs).[2] The URIs allow widespread and consistent reference by providing a global convention for naming resources, interpreted consistently across contexts. Associating a URI with a resource allows anyone to refer to it; retrieve a representation of it if it is a document; retrieve a document about it if it is not a document; or—crucially—link to it.

2. The Resource Description Framework (RDF)[3] is a simple knowledge representation language for the Semantic Web based on the "subject-predicate-object" form. A statement in RDF, called a "triple," links two objects (individuals, kinds of things, attribute values) and a property, relation, or two-placed predicate. Each member of the triple is assigned a specific URI. Using RDF therefore involves the use of URIs to ground reference to objects and relations, which opens the door to automatic processing not only of documents, as in the current Web, but also directly of data. Linked RDF statements form a directed, labeled graphical representation.

3. "Ontologies" are common conceptualizations pinning down the vocabularies of domains. They support interoperability, information integration, and knowledge sharing by aligning vocabularies and underpinning translations between terms. We can distinguish two types of ontology. *Deep* ontologies are detailed presentations of the scientific vocabulary where great effort is put into the conceptualization of the domain and the maintenance of the ontology relative to ongoing scientific discovery; this type of ontology is often encountered in scientific or engineering contexts. *Shallow* ontologies, by contrast, are composed of a relatively small number of commonly used terms describing basic relations that tend not to change very much in the short to medium term; such shallow ontologies, though relatively simple, can be used to organize very large quantities of data.

4. Simple Protocol and RDF Query Language (SPARQL)[4] is a protocol and query language designed for Semantic Web resources. In particular, it can be used to express queries across diverse data sources, if the data is either stored in RDF or can be viewed as an RDF graph via middleware. SPARQL supports a number of querying functions, including the querying of an RDF graph for required or optional graph patterns, as well as for conjunctions and disjunctions of patterns.

These four technologies allow a research community to develop heterogeneous data repositories as a common resource—grounded out by URIs and linked and integrated by ontologies. Ontologies themselves have become important resources in science and e-science (e.g., Shadbolt, Hall, and Berners-Lee 2006:96), which is particularly evident in interdisciplinary studies such as climate change or epidemiology, where several different sets of terms are employed, and data stores are particularly diverse and large scale.

The Semantic Web's Value to Researchers

Enthusiastic early adopters of the Semantic Web approach were typically communities needing to integrate and share information. Such communities have a degree of cohesion and a perceived need for shared semantics. For example, researchers often need to query large numbers of databases. Without Semantic Web technology, this task would require either complex scripts to overcome incompatibilities or a laborious manual process of cutting and pasting between Web interfaces. Semantic Web technologies, including ontologies and annotation, have been shown to be very useful in preserving information quality (Preece et al. 2006), and SPARQL provides a network protocol that allows effective querying.

One fruitful approach is the idea of a "Semantic Grid," whereby the data, computing resources, and services characteristic of the Grid computing model are given semantics using Semantic Web ideas and technologies (De Roure and Hendler 2004). The myGrid project,[5] for example, supports data-intensive querying in the life sciences, linking together diverse resources using Web service protocols and providing support for managing scientific work flow, sharing and reusing information, and understanding provenance.

Such "*in silico* experimentation" using a computer simulation has also been used outside the life sciences. In chemistry, the synthesis of new compounds requires the assembly, integration, and querying of large quantities of primary data. The CombeChem project[6] has employed a similar large, service-based infrastructure to create a knowledge-sharing environment, using pervasive devices to capture live metadata in the laboratory and linking data using shared URIs. This approach allows knowledge sharing across data sets created by different stakeholders, with provenance traceable back to the source.

Semantic Web technologies have also been used to support research in social science. The UK's National Centre for e–Social Science has been set up to apply e-science techniques to social science data, both quantitative and qualitative (Procter, Batty, Birkin, et al. 2006). For instance, the PolicyGrid project[7] brought social scientists and Semantic Web technologists together to create a metadata infrastructure to support annotation, data sharing, and social simulation.

The sharing of raw data in social science raises privacy concerns. Releasing someone's zip or postal code is not a problem, but releasing his or her medical history is, and Semantic Web technology allows this distinction to be made. Contrast this capability with the traditional document Web, wherein a document containing both pieces of information has to be either released or withheld as a whole or laboriously anonymized. Research on a "policy-aware Web" (Weitzner, Hendler, Berners-Lee, et al. 2005) will enable more automated reasoning to be carried out on privacy policies in the Web's open environment.

Building on the Semantic Web Approach

Semantic technologies have proved important in automating scientific and social scientific research, enabling it to cope with the much larger quantities of data available through advanced computing techniques and better-founded data-sharing practices. The automation of information processing will have many effects on research and other aspects of Web use. These effects are hard to predict in detail without study of the two-way relation between microlevel protocol development and macrolevel social change. The Web Science Trust[8] was set up to explore precisely this interrelationship in order to ensure that developments such as the Semantic Web have benign effects on society, knowledge sharing, and the performance of scientific research (Berners-Lee, Hall, Hendler, et al. 2006). The future of science *on* the Web will depend on the development of the science *of* the Web.

Notes

1. For progress on the consortium's work, see http://www.w3.org/2001/sw/.

2. See http://tools.ietf.org/html/rfc3986.

3. See http://www.w3.org/TR/rdf-concepts/.

4. See http://www.w3.org/TR/rdf-sparql-query/.

5. See http://www.mygrid.org.uk/.

6. See http://www.combechem.org/.

7. See http://www.policygrid.org/.

8. See http://webscience.org/.

References

Berners-Lee, T., W. Hall, J. A. Hendler, N. Shadbolt, and D. J. Weitzner. 2006. "Creating a science of the Web." Science 313 (5788):769–771. Available at http://eprints.ecs.soton.ac.uk/12615/.

De Roure, D., and J. A. Hendler. 2004. "E-science: The Grid and the Semantic Web." *IEEE Intelligent Systems 19* (1):65–71.

Preece, A., B. Jin, E. Pignotti, P. Missier, S. Embury, D. Stead, and A. Brown. 2006. "Managing information quality in e-science using Semantic Web technology." In *Proceedings of 3rd European Semantic Web Conference*. Berlin: Springer, 472–486. Available at: http://www.csd.abdn.ac.uk/~apreece/qurator/resources/qurator_eswc2006.pdf.

Procter, R., M. Batty, M. Birkin, R. Crouchley, W. H. Dutton, P. Edwards, M. Fraser, P. Halfpenny, Y. Lin, and T. Rodden. 2006. "The National Centre for e–Social Science." In Proceedings of the 2006 e-Science All-Hands Meeting. Edinburgh: National e-Science Centre, 542–549. Available at: http://www.allhands.org.uk/2006/proceedings/proceedings/proceedings.pdf.

Shadbolt, N., W. Hall, and T. Berners-Lee. 2006. "The Semantic Web revisited." IEEE Intelligent Systems 21 (3):96–101. Available at http://eprints.ecs.soton.ac.uk/12614/.

Weitzner, D. J., J. Hendler, T. Berners-Lee, and D. Connolly. 2005. "Creating a policy-aware Web: Discretionary, rule-based access for the World Wide Web." In *Web and information security*, ed. E. Ferrari and B. Thuraisingham. Hershey, PA: Idea Group. Available at: http://www.w3.org/2004/09/Policy-Aware-Web-acl.pdf.

5 Embedding e-Research Applications: Designing for Usability

Grace de la Flor, Marina Jirotka, Sharon Lloyd, and Andrew Warr

Sir John Taylor well encapsulates the vision of e-research : "e-Science is about global collaboration in key areas of science, and the next generation of infrastructure that will enable it" (quoted in Hey and Trefethen 2002:1017; see also essay 2.3).

To achieve this vision, e-research projects initially focused on developing technical solutions to generic technical requirements. These solutions include: large federated databases, data-compression and transfer techniques, and the design of security mechanisms within distributed architectures (Hey and Trefethen 2003:1817). Even when these technical successes are achieved, some e-research applications have not been adopted by their intended user communities because they challenge researchers' conventions and work practices (Jirotka, Procter, Hartswood, et al. 2005; Bos, Zimmerman, Olson, et al. 2007). There are many barriers to the uptake and adoption of the new information and communication technologies (ICTs). One of the key barriers is the difficulty involved in the required large-scale distributed project management (Lloyd and Simpson 2005), and this chapter's focus is therefore on designing systems for usability.

The chapter begins by discussing the concept of usability as it has traditionally been defined. We then attempt to reconceptualize its definition and scope in order to make it a relevant feature in the software-development process of e-research. The e-research vision of supporting distributed collaborative research requires building a better understanding of usability so that it is no longer seen as fundamentally a matter of evaluating software interfaces. Rather, usability practices need to be viewed as a means through which support can be given to the requirements of cooperative work arrangements (Schmidt and Bannon 1992). We present examples of how this reconceptualization of usability has been put into practice, drawing on our experiences within e-research projects. We also offer a sample of novel techniques used in social science research that may be adapted to support the design of usable technologies. We conclude with recommendations for future e-research projects.

Reconceptualizing Usability

Although there is no unified agreement on a definition of usability, various activities relating to the evaluation of software systems and the application of these activities to the design process have emerged from fields within computer science and computer-related studies, such as requirements engineering, human–computer interaction, and computer-supported cooperative work (CSCW).

Requirements Engineering

In the domain of requirements engineering, usability is traditionally seen as a distinct activity undertaken in order to specify a series of characteristics that a software system should posses in order to be usable. From the International Standards Organization (ISO), ISO 92491 defines usability as "the extent to which a product can be used by specified users to achieve specified goals with effectiveness, efficiency and satisfaction in a specified context of use." It is often viewed as a nonfunctional requirement that is an emergent property of the system as a whole. Due to its emergent characteristic, it is thought that the properties of usability can be discovered only after all of a system's individual subsystems have been integrated. Thus, usability evaluation has traditionally been conducted as part of the assessment phase, after design has been completed.

Human–Computer Interaction

This view of usability resonates with early approaches to human–computer interaction that developed design guidelines for the interface design in an attempt to circumscribe measurable characteristics of a usable system (Shackel 1981). However, simple generic guidelines were very hard to define, particularly when applied to users' interactions with technology as they conducted typical workplace activities. In an attempt to go beyond the level of the interface and develop more complex understandings of users and their interactions with systems (Grudin 1990), approaches began to focus on developing cognitive models of the user, such as Goals, Operators, Methods, and Selection rules (Card, Moran, and Newell 1983); interacting cognitive subsystems (Barnard and May 1993); and task action grammars (Payne and Green 1986). Through modeling users' intentions, goals, and plans, these approaches claimed that it may be possible to predict the actions of users. Techniques were developed that included complex models and grammars that were found to be particularly useful for designing simple and routine tasks (Gray, John, and Atwood 1993). However, these were found to be less effective for predicting user actions when conducting flexible, open-ended activities perhaps because such models did not take sufficient account of the contexts in which work is achieved.

Usability Approaches

Similar to requirements engineering, usability evaluation has traditionally been conducted as a postdesign and postdevelopment activity, with various usability goals considered through usability testing (Nielsen 1993). However, modeling approaches required the designer to consider the characteristics of the system much earlier in the design process and to present ongoing challenges for designers regarding the positioning of usability activities within the system-development process.

A feature of the user-modeling approach was in part a refocusing of the software-development process in terms of placing greater emphasis on understanding users and their behavior in relation to technology design. User needs and how to design systems to make them appropriate to their context was a fundamental concern of the user-centered system design approach (Norman and Draper 1986). This approach reoriented the activities of design around the user and thus strongly countered the conventional practice of conducting user testing after a system had been developed. However, as such approaches began to take users and their needs seriously, critiques emerged particularly with respect to the notion of user's plans and goals.

Workplace Studies

In response to the cognitive-modeling approaches, researchers such as Lucy Suchman (1987) and Terry Winograd and Fernando Flores (1987) argued that it was unclear how the notion of goals and plans characterized in the cognitive-modeling perspective actually reflected how people behave. In contrast, they claimed that activities were situated and matched the contingencies and local context of action. Drawing on contemporary developments in the social sciences, these researchers, and others, developed a situated understanding of human behavior and considered its implications for design.

Research in this area, known collectively as *workplace studies*, examine technologies in use. Some of the most influential papers in this area include the naturalistic studies of air-traffic controllers (Hughes, King, Rodden, et al. 1994), the organization and management of documents in a civil engineering group (Trigg, Blomberg, and Suchman 1999), and the support of interaction in hybrid, physical/digital spaces (Luff, Heath, Kuzuoka, et al. 2006). Collaborative activity became a new focus for research, which was made increasingly relevant due to developments in high-speed distributed networked systems, shared applications, and groupware. Within the field of CSCW, studies investigated groups of people engaged in similar activities in organizations that seemed to have "common objectives."

Research in this area is known collectively as "workplace studies." Examples of this approach to examining technologies-in-use can be found in the naturalistic studies of air-traffic controllers (Hughes, King, Rodden, et al. 1994), the organization and management of documents in a civil engineering group (Trigg, Blomberg, and Suchman 1999), and the support of interaction in hybrid, physical/digital spaces (Luff, Heath,

Kuzuoka, et al. 2006). In these studies, the ways in which technologies are used and how new technologies might be employed to support cooperative work are examined within the contexts of workplace settings. One goal of workplace studies is to provide an analysis of the ways in which technologies may constrain or support work practices. These studies often unpack various key concepts of collaboration, such as awareness (Suchman 1993; Goodwin and Goodwin 1996; Luff, Heath, and Jirotka 2000).

Despite some initial concerns regarding the tensions between providing explanatory accounts and developing usable design recommendations (Plowman, Rogers, and Ramage 1995), it is now not uncommon—either within the design processes of large organizations such as Xerox, Hewlett Packard, Microsoft, or Intel, or in smaller organizations—to undertake ethnographic fieldwork. Researchers in these contexts investigate workplaces, domestic environments, and public spaces to understand how they use existing technologies and their practical requirements for future work. Although numerous case studies have been conducted, there are as yet relatively few handbooks on the topic (Beyer and Holtzblatt 1999, Crabtree 2003, and Randall, Harper, and Roucefield 2007 being the exceptions).

Computer-Supported Cooperative Work

CSCW has focused primarily on small-group interactions. However, the challenge of designing for usability is made more complex as systems are developed to support large-scale, distributed, multidisciplinary, and multiinstitutional e-research. There are many challenges to managing an e-research project. For instance, communication across distributed teams and locations may be difficult. This problem of communication may impact the coordination of stakeholders' activities (Finholt 2003; Cummings and Kiesler 2005). Furthermore, scientists' unique knowledge, experiences, and vocabularies may present challenges for effective communication with software developers. These added well-known complexities are exacerbated due to the number of multidisciplinary stakeholders involved in e-research projects.

An e-research project is itself a multidisciplinary endeavor in which software engineers, project managers, requirements engineers, and domain researchers collaborate to design a system. In addition, e-research users do not belong to a single domain. Rather, they may belong to different disciplines and institutions, each with its own work practices and organizational concerns that may conflict in some circumstances with other disciplines and institutions that share the system (Welsh, Jirotka, and Gavaghan 2006).

It may be possible to draw upon the key concepts of collaboration identified in CSCW, such as support for mutual awareness within e-research systems. People will still need to be aware of and support each other when collaborating though e-research technologies. Yet it is not clear how far this requirement may apply across disciplines and organizations; such concepts may need to be rethought in light of the more complex interactions and collaborations envisioned by network-enabled research approaches.

Design for a Variety of User Requirements

Designing e-research systems for researchers requires the ability to understand vastly different end-user populations. In order to achieve this, design teams must coordinate investigations at the multiple research sites of those who will initially use the system. Additionally, the software must be usable among large and distributed groups while simultaneously negotiating transformative changes in a research community's practice (Zimmerman and Nardi 2006). Furthermore, the users of e-research tools do not just perform a set of predefined tasks. Rather, they conduct research that is directed by the priorites within their scientific communities. These priorities often change and can have implications for the types of software tools that will become relevant to them. In the next section we consider various approaches that can be used to elicit requirements for e-research.

Usability Practices for Network-Enabled Research

A research discipline typically shares within its community similar research goals and interests, which naturally results in research collaborations that may evolve in many ways, from formal approaches organized through research institutes to casual conversations with other researchers (Katz and Martin 1997). Whichever way a collaboration is initiated, its goals are most likely to advance the discipline(s), share knowledge, increase funding opportunities, and encourage mutual learning (Katz and Martin 1997:4). Aligned with these purposes, e-research projects aim to develop technologies that enable long-distance collaborations, from running simultaneous distributed experiments to collaborative data analysis and data sharing. As briefly examined in the previous section, successfully embedding usable systems may require that e-research project teams understand researchers' cooperative activities and the ways in which researchers communicate and collaborate. This understanding may be achieved by engaging in an iterative design process informed by requirements elicitation practices that will be presented here.

In the next section, we present five approaches suitable for eliciting requirements for e-research systems. Each has challenged traditional notions of usability that have focused exclusively on interface design. The five approaches include in situ fieldwork, analogy experiments, situated evaluation studies, end-user development, and multi-sited ethnography.

Using Fieldwork to Support Design

One approach that has helped to reveal the existing practices within a user community is ethnographically informed design (Randall, Harper, and Rouncefield 2007; see box 5.1 for an example).

Box 5.1

Requirements Engineering for the Integrative Biology Virtual Research Environment Project

In the Integrative Biology Virtual Research Environment project, requirements engineers carried out interviews, focus groups, and fieldwork studies to understand the ways in which both heart and cancer modelers collaborate with workbench experimentalists, mathematicians, and each other in designing simulations of biological systems.[a] The aim of these exercises was to understand the scientific work flow and research processes of *in silico* experimentalists. To do this, the requirements engineers asked researchers to provide accounts of their everyday life showing how communication and collaboration might typically occur, while also observing this behavior.

Note:
a. For more on this project, see http://www.vre.ox.ac.uk/ibvre/.

Findings from an ethnographic study conducted within the Integrative Biology Virtual Research Environment requirements engineering study revealed that

• Researchers engage in informal collaborations initiated among fellow colleagues, where even cold calling can occur to establish contacts.

• Research ideas and data are kept private (for a discussion of data security, see essay 5.1). This occurs because researchers compete as well as collaborate with each other. This can make data sharing a complex issue (Jirotka, Procter, Rodden, et al. 2006; Welsh, Jirotka, and Gavaghan 2006).

• Mathematical modelers do extensive reading of biology journals and engage in face-to-face meetings with biologists to inform the design of computational models.

• Models are also discussed in face-to-face meetings where equations and algorithms are annotated and revised using whiteboards before being coded into computational programs.

Box 5.2 summarizes how an e-research project has used video-based observations within an ethnographic fieldwork study to inform software design (Crabtree, O'Brien, Nichols, et al. 2000; Heath, Knoblauch, and Luff 2000).

Fieldwork findings for the Building a Virtual Research Environment for the Humanities project included the following:

• The processes of collaboratively deciphering ancient manuscripts requires researchers to discuss and defend line by line their interpretations of letter-forms, words, and sentences. However, deciphering is not a sequential process; researchers place their attention on different areas of the document depending on how easy or difficult it is to recognize characters. One researcher on the project commented that it is similar to

Box 5.2
Requirements Engineering for the Building a Virtual Research Environment for the Humanities
Project

Requirements engineering for the Building a Virtual Research Environment for the Humanities project[a] involved project members' conducting observational fieldwork during four
sessions in which three classicists engaged in the collaborative deciphering of ancient texts.
Video recording these sessions aimed to reveal the ways in which the classicists organized
their activities and the types of resources they used both to communicate with each other
and to accomplish the work of deciphering ancient texts.

Note:
a. For more on the this project, see http://www.vre.ox.ac.uk/ibvre/more.

"putting a crossword puzzle together" because they continually reference letters and
words occurring throughout the manuscript to make sense of adjacent text.
• Researchers moved between viewing a digital image of the ancient text and viewing
a photocopied image. The digital image is manipulated by adjusting its contrast and
brightness so that characters and words can be made more recognizable.
• In some cases, characters and words are written out on blank sheets of paper to provide researchers a workspace in which to discuss their interpretations.

Each of these e-research projects provide examples of how fieldwork has been used
to understand the work practices of researchers across a variety of academic settings.
Through these activities, each project team was able to make informed decisions
about the types of functionality that would best support the research processes of each
research community.

Using Analogy to Identify Requirements

A contrasting approach (illustrated in box 5.3) seeks to explore work practices within
a research community through the use of analogy to facilitate the understanding of
complex domain-specific activities (Schraefel and Dix 2007).

Analogy-based approaches such as those outlined in box 5.3 have been useful for
making transparent to requirements and software engineers the tasks and activities of
domain experts. The approach can be applied to other scientific domains by considering what analogies may help software developers better understand the work that
researchers are performing. In the case of bioinformatics, for example, a jigsaw puzzle
analogy was used to understand the work practices of that particular domain (Schraefel
and Dix 2007).

Box 5.3
The Making Tea Requirements Elicitation Approach

Making Tea is a requirements-elicitation approach developed to understand experimental practices in the synthetic chemistry domain.[a] It relies on mapping analogies to the real tasks end users conduct in any given domain. In this instance, requirements engineers asked chemists to make tea as if it were a chemical experiment. Both software engineers and requirements engineers observed and videotaped the Making Tea exercise to understand how paper laboratory books were used as experiments were conducted. Observational data and subsequent interviews with chemists were then used to inform the design of digital lab book prototypes. The use of analogy experiments informed the design of interfaces (taken from paper forms) and functionality (derived from work processes).

Note:
a. For more on the Making Tea requirements-elicitation method, see http://mytea.org.uk/.

Situated Evaluation Studies

Usability evaluations of technology have been conducted within actual work settings through two approaches: "use experiment" field studies and "situated evaluations."

Büscher, Christensen, Hansen, et al. (2008) performed use experiments to evaluate infrastructures that enable the execution of software applications. In their case study, visible and flexible infrastructures have been shown to be essential so that domain experts have the ability to adapt technology for their particular purposes as their work practices evolve. The use experiment approach evaluates three aspects of a system: "architecture design, application design, and experience of use" (Büscher, Christensen, Hansen, et al. 2008). In combination, evaluating these three attributes provided a more comprehensive approach to usability evaluation than focusing exclusively on the look and feel of software interfaces.

In a situated evaluation, activities that originate as computing activities are studied using digital log files that serve as representations of the actions taken by end users. In addition to log data, activities originating in the physical world can be studied using video data recordings to analyze physical activities. Using a combination of video observation and tracking of users' activities within a system using log-file data may provide researchers with a greater understanding of how actions in the physical world are supported through digital technologies. Box 5.4 summarizes one such case.

Log-file data has been used for many years by website developers to understand the activities of end users—for example, by tracking the number of visits and most frequently visited areas of a Web site (see essay 1.2). What is new here is the repositioning of log-file data as ethnographic accounts within a situated evaluation. Such

Box 5.4

Example of a Situated Evaluation

In one situated evaluation of usability in action, researchers conducted studies to derive requirements for a pervasive computing game. The game involved the use of hybrid spaces where both physical and virtual activities unfold simultaneously. In the study, participants' movements in a city street game were tracked using a combination of digital log-file analysis and video data from the field. The study was concerned with how participants made sense of and used technology across a city environment. Combining material and digital data sources within the situated evaluation helped to produce ethnographic accounts that provided a rich picture of how virtual and physical activities interleaved to support simultaneous activities within the game's hybrid environment.

Source: Crabtree, French, Greenhalgh, et al. 2006.

repositioning provides researchers with the opportunity to combine log-file data and video-recorded fieldwork in the evaluation of systems. The approach can be modified to evaluate e-research systems where participants engage in typical work processes across distributed locations using the software developed specifically for this type of analysis, called the Digital Replay System.[1] This type of study can offer a more complete view of a situated evaluation (using multilocal views through video recordings) as well as a networked view (through log-file data).

Both use experiments and situated evaluations can be used to discover and document not only how users adapt technology but also the ways in which new practices emerge through technology use. These types of studies may also make explicit the relationship between infrastructure and software applications and how their dependencies may have implications for the end-user experience.

Software Design and Work Practice in End-User Development

We have described how fieldwork, analogy experiments, and situated evaluation studies can be used to understand researchers' work practices. End users, however, are increasingly participating in the development of tools primarily through Web 2.0 technologies and the use of agile methods (Cockburn 2007). Both of these approaches are blurring the distinction between software design practice and work practice. Henry Lieberman and his colleagues have defined end-user development as "a set of methods, techniques, and tools that allow users of software systems, who are acting as nonprofessional software developers, at some point to create, modify or extend a software artifact" (Lieberman, Paternó, and V. Wulf 2006:2).

The use of computer models and simulations that process large data sets have become central activities in some areas of scientific research. End-user programming thus has become an increasingly important activity to support because scientists need to retain a significant amount of control over the code that is used to develop work flows and simulations. However, their primary objective is to conduct domain-specific research. In such circumstances, the challenge for researchers is to maintain an appropriate balance between the time they spend coding and the time they spend conducting research. Bringing software engineers in to work alongside researchers within a scientific research area may provide a solution to this challenge.

Some have suggested that Web 2.0 technologies can facilitate scientists as end-user developers of e-research applications (Pierce, Fox, Yuan, et al. 2006). National e-research initiatives in the United States and the United kingdom initially drew on an industry enterprise model in which heavyweight server-side middleware and applications were designed by highly skilled software engineers. Such a top-down software-development approach often creates situations in which domain scientists are reliant on software engineers to modify their applications. However, the Web 2.0 model focuses on lightweight community-driven application development that makes it possible for end users themselves to make modifications to applications for specific local purposes. For Web 2.0 to be taken up successfully as a modifiable resource, domain researchers need to have programming skills to create or modify applications for use within their local environments. This approach has its foundations in the open-source model (Pierce, Fox, Yuan, et al. 2006), where code and applications are shared within a community of interested developers, users, and end-user developers.

The myExperiment project provides a Web 2.0 model for researchers to share and execute scientific work flows (see box 5.5).

A further example of end-user development may be found in the use of agile methods (see box 5.6).

Box 5.5
myExperiment Using a Web 2.0 Model

A virtual research environment, myExperiment promotes the sharing of tools, in this case the sharing of work flows for *in silico* experiments.[a] It focuses on providing mechanisms for researchers to build social networks based on the free exchange of work flows among themselves. It also enables discussion of experiments and work flows with others who take part in the myExperiment community. One of the project's aims is to provide an avenue of communication where none previously existed.

Note:
a. See http://www.myexperiment.org/.

Box 5.6
The Agile Approach to End-User Development

> Agile approaches provide a link between software engineers and end users through the deployment of specific practices that can be incorporated into a software-development process, such as short coding iterations, continuous code testing, refactoring and integration, daily stand-up meetings, and pair programming (Cockburn 2007). Using pair programming, for instance, these activities enable the exchange and execution of design ideas through sessions where domain researchers work closely with software engineers to enhance the speed and performance of code.

The Cancer, Heart, and Soft Tissue Environment (CHASTE) is an e-research initiative that has been developing scientific software for computational biology (Pitt-Francis, Bernabeu, Cooper, et al. 2008). One of its original purposes was to assess the use of agile methods as a new approach for the development of scientific software. To do this, CHASTE fostered a close collaboration between heart and cancer modelers, who have expertise in the research domain, and software engineers, who have expertise in the optimization of code. The team has reported (Pitt-Francis, Bernabeu, Cooper, et al. 2008) that an Agile approach is far more useful than plan-driven software development methods because

• it is responsive to the high workforce turnover typical in academic projects, allowing for quick integration of new team members;
• it increases the quality of the code through the sharing of different types of expertise;
• it encourages rapid code development using short timeframe iterative cycles based on user stories; and
• it enables the development of adaptable and extensible code that can be modified as requirements change based on scientific discoveries in the field.

Using an agile approach encourages all members of the project to develop the code base together, whether in pair programming sessions or in the peer review of code developed by individuals. It also enables researchers to improve their understanding of the code and to extend its capabilities for their specific research purposes.

Multisited Ethnography

Finally, we present the multisited fieldwork approach, which has great potential as a requirements elicitation technique for systems that are designed to support distributed research. This method arose in response to empirical changes that are tied to the ways in which culture is produced (Marcus 1995). More specifically, the locations of cultural production are no longer limited to the boundaries of a single location. Instead, qualitative social science researchers are also experiencing firsthand the effects

Box 5.7
Multisited Ethnography

Multisited ethnography can be used to examine network-enabled research as:

A *transnational activity* in that it seeks to support scientific collaboration beyond national borders through the implementation of ICTs that connect worldwide research communities using large-scale, distributed systems designed to support cooperative research, data sharing, and the publication of findings.

A *multilocal activity* wherein both regional and global networks are enabled through local collaborators who create linked activities with other researchers across distributed locations.

A *wide-ranging activity* that encompasses diverse actors, including domain researchers, global research disciplines, computer scientists, local institutions, virtual organizations, funding councils, schools, and the general public.

---

of globalization and transnationalism when conducting fieldwork (Green 1999; Freidberg 2001; Hannerz 2003). In this new landscape, social science researchers are frequently introduced to a reconfigured space where multiple locations both inform and shape the shared meanings of distributed communities.

Multisited ethnography is an approach to fieldwork that takes into consideration the key concern with which e-research environments are also engaged: the composition of distributed activities (box 5.7). For this reason, multisited fieldwork can be incorporated into the requirements-elicitation process to inform both the design and the evaluation of virtual research environments.

Identifying system requirements can be challenging in the complex, heterogeneous environment outlined in box 5.7. In addition, e-research projects that focus on developing technologies for the sciences generally require their project members to cultivate a working knowledge of the research domain that can be considered "good enough" for the purposes of designing virtual research environments. Christine Hine (2007) notes that traditional studies of scientific practice, pioneered in science and technology studies, have produced single-site ethnographies of laboratory settings. She argues that such an approach may no longer be adequate.

According to Hine, placing too much emphasis on the laboratory as a field site for ethnography is an obstacle to developing approaches that engage with the experience of doing science because

• scientific practices are carried out between varyingly identified groups and institutions and individuals;

• science increasingly takes place not just in physically bounded laboratories, but also in computer-mediated locations;

• different media combine into complex communication ecologies;

• material and virtual culture overlap and are inextricable; and

• social scientists need to be agile, itinerant, and attentive to trace these connections (2007:669).

Hine suggests that the relevancies of a discipline may be overlooked when fieldwork is undertaken exclusively at a single location, especially when the realities of the domain are far more complex.

Along with the benefits of using a multisited approach, there are a number of challenges to implementing it in practice (Wogan 2004):

• The impression may be given that the researcher is conducting "walk-through research," as opposed to describing a setting in minute detail.

• A dilemma may arise as to which locations to observe, along with the recognition that all locations may not receive the same level of engagement.

• There may be a tendency toward comparative analysis of individual locations as opposed to developing an understanding of the whole system.

• There is a risk of spreading oneself too thinly, causing long-term fieldwork to be at risk.

• In software design, a team of requirements engineers may be needed rather than just one to ensure that fieldwork can be conducted within the timeframe of typical software-development projects.

• A comparative analysis of locations may lead to a situation in which the most technologically advanced site sets the standard for the types of technologies that should be implemented across sites. The development of such a standard may perhaps bias the project's intended goal of designing a usable system that is relevant to all its end users.

Conclusion and Recommendations

The goal of many e-research projects is to design and embed technical artifacts into research environments in the expectation that they will be integrated into the daily work practices of the communities for which they are developed. Designing for these communities requires project teams to take into account the variety of organizations and individuals associated with their e-research projects. In addition to the research community that will use the features of technical innovation, there are funding institutions, such as research councils; collaborating academic institutions that work as project partners to design and embed technologies; virtual organizations that exchange computational resources and data; researchers who collaborate in distributed research activities; application developers who develop tools with appropriate interfaces; and system administrators who provide technical support. As e-research projects mature, other stakeholders will become involved (e.g., schools and the general public).

The infrastructures and applications of e-research introduce changes that affect not only the research communities that are being asked to modify their working practices through the use of new technologies, but also technology partners who need to reconsider the ways in which projects are proposed, planned, designed, and evaluated.

In terms of technology development, e-research projects coordinate multidisciplinary design teams that include application developers and research domain experts working together to design useful and usable systems. It is therefore likely to be inevitable that the successful embedding of e-research applications requires a change in the way projects frame the software development process to make room for a shift away from traditional software design approaches and toward incorporating some of the more novel approaches described in this chapter.

Based on our case study work (de la Flor, Jirotka, Warr, et al. 2007), box 5.8 offers recommendations to help e-research project teams consider the usability concerns of research communities (how and whether such recommendations can best be employed will depend on each project's contingencies and constraints).

Box 5.8
Guidelines for Enhancing the Usability of e-Research Systems

Usability is more than interface and interaction design, so anyone who is evaluating it for an e-research system should

• Consider how research communities organize collaborative work arrangements and the work practices that will need to be supported in the new system
• Develop an understanding of how researchers communicate and collaborate within the organizational context in which they are working.

Because e-research is a unique technological domain, the evaluator should

• Take into account the large-scale, distributed, multidisciplinary, and multi-institutional nature of these projects.
• Focus in particular on acquiring an understanding of the research domain, including its research life cycle, work processes, and activities.
• Conduct ethnographic fieldwork. Include on-site observation, interviews, and focus groups to understand work practices, including scientific work flow. Also provide an account of and observe "the day in the life of" the research community.
• Consider incorporating agile practices. The project vision needs to be flexible enough to evolve to meet end users' needs and their research objectives.
• Evaluate the system. Consider a comprehensive assessment of three key aspects of a system: its architecture, applications, and its situated use.
• Conduct regular cross-disciplinary workshops to facilitate shared understandings between participants. Encourage project members to go beyond their normal sphere of activity by collaborating closely with others to facilitate mutual learning and knowledge transfer.
• Manage expectations of project partners. This activity can be facilitated by creating a "reflection" document that highlights the project's complexities, documenting lessons learned and possible requirements for the ongoing development of a system in further phases.

Source: de la Flor, Jirotka, Warr, et al. 2007.

Key Avenues for Future e-Research Usability Studies

Many areas offer opportunities for research into advancing the design and evaluation of usable e-research systems. For instance, investigations could include examining the use of multisited ethnography as a new approach for gathering requirements for distributed systems as well as revisiting key concepts of collaboration identified within CSCW. We are exploiting the creation of a systematic approach for the evaluation of collaborative systems in general and for e-research applications in particular.

Quasi-naturalistic prototype evaluations conducted since the late 1980s (e.g., Heath, Luff, and Sellen 1997) have usually been undertaken in an ad hoc manner by highly skilled researchers in academic settings who use the technique to gain insights into the design of experimental and novel technologies. These evaluations will benefit from more systematic procedures for those working in product-driven software-development projects to assist requirements engineers who are working within typical product-driven projects. The formulation of such an approach would result in a set of guidelines that e-research project teams could use to conduct quasi-naturalistic experiments with end users in the evaluation of prototypes. This, and the other approaches detailed here, provide an alternative orientation from which to consider usability evaluation for e-research systems.

Notes

1. See http://www.ncess.ac.uk/research/digital_records/drs/.

References

Barnard, P. J., and J. May. 1993. "Cognitive modelling for user requirements." In *Computers, communication, and usability: Design issues, research, and methods for integrated services*, ed. P. F. Byerley, P. J. Barnard, and J. May. North Holland Series in Telecommunication. Amsterdam: Elsevier, 101–145.

Beyer, H., and K. Holtzblatt. 1999. "Contextual design." *Interactions 6* (1):32–42.

Bos, N., A. Zimmerman, J. Olson, J. Yew, J. Yerkie, E. Dahl, and G. Olson. 2007. "From shared databases to communities of practice: A taxonomy of collaboratories." *Journal of Computer-Mediated Communication 12* (2).

Büscher, M., M. Christensen, K. M. Hansen, P. Mogensen, and D. Shapiro. 2008. "Bottom-up, top-down? Connecting software architecture design with use." In *Configuring user-designer relations: Interdisciplinary perspectives*, ed. A. Voss, M. Hartswood, K. Ho, R. Procter, M. Rouncefield, R. Slack, and M. Büscher. Berlin: Springer, 157–192.

Card, S., T. Moran, and A. Newell. 1983. *The psychology of human–computer interaction*. Hillsdale, NJ: Lawrence Erlbaum Associates.

Cockburn, A. 2007. *Agile software development: The cooperative game*. 2d ed. Boston: Addison-Wesley.

Crabtree, A. 2003. *Designing collaborative systems: A practical guide to ethnography.* Berlin: Springer.

Crabtree, A., A. French, C. Greenhalgh, S. Benford, K. Cheverst, D. Fitton, M. Rouncefield, and C. Graham. 2006. "Developing digital records: Early experiences of record and replay." *Journal of Computer Supported Cooperative Work 15* (4):281–319.

Crabtree, A., J. O'Brien, D. Nichols, M. Rouncefield, and M. Twidale. 2000. "Ethnomethodologically informed ethnography and information systems design." *Journal of the American Society for Information and Science Technology 51* (7):666–682.

Cummings, J. N., and S. Kiesler. 2005. "Collaborative research across disciplinary and organizational boundaries." *Social Studies of Science 35* (5):703–722.

De la Flor, G. 2010. *Contextual evaluation framework: A prototype evaluation technique for e-Research.* Unpublished doctoral dissertation, Oxford: University of Oxford.

De la Flor, G., M. Jirotka, A. Warr, and S. Lloyd. 2007. "Designing software in support of workplace activities—embedding e-science applications." Paper presented at the Third International Conference on e–Social Science, 7–9 October, Ann Arbor, MI.

Finholt, T. A. 2003. "Collaboratories as a new form of scientific organization." *Economics of Innovation and New Technology 12* (1):5–25.

Freidberg, S. 2001. "On the trail of the global green bean: Methodological considerations in multi-site ethnography." *Global Networks: A Journal of Transnational Affairs 1*(4): 353–368.

Goodwin, C., and M. H. Goodwin. 1996. "Seeing as a situated activity: Formulating planes." In *Cognition and communication at work,* ed. Y. Engeström and D. Middleton. Cambridge, UK: Cambridge University Press, 61–95.

Gray, W. D., B. E. John, and M. E. Atwood. 1993. "Project Ernestine: Validating a GOMS analysis for predicting and explaining real-world performance." *Human-Computer Interaction 8* (3):237–309.

Green, N. 1999. "Disrupting the field, virtual reality technologies, and 'multisited' ethnographic methods." *American Behavioral Scientist 43* (3):409–421.

Grudin, J. 1990. "The computer reaches out: The historical continuity of interface design." In *Proceedings of the SIGCHI Conference on Human Factors in Computing Systems, CHI'90, 1–5 April 1990, Seattle, WA.* New York: ACM Press, 261–268.

Hannerz, U. 2003. "Being there . . . and there . . . and there! Reflections on multi-site ethnography." *Ethnography 4* (2):201–216.

Heath, C. C., H. Knoblauch, and P. Luff. 2000. "Technology and social interaction: The emergence of 'workplace studies.'" *British Journal of Sociology 51* (2):299–320.

Heath, C., P. Luff, and A. J. Sellen. 1997. "Reconfiguring media space: supporting collaborative work." In *Video-mediated communication,* ed. K. Finn, A. Sellen, and S. Wilbur. Hillsdale, NJ: Lawrence Erlbaum Associates, 323–349.

Hey, T., and A. E. Trefethen. 2002. "The UK e-Science Core Program and the Grid." *Future Generation Computer Systems 18*:1017–1031.

Hey, T., and A. Trefethen. 2003. "E-science and its implications." *Philosophical Transactions of the Royal Society 361*:1809–1825.

Hine, C. 2007. "Multi-sited ethnography as a middle range methodology for contemporary STS [science and technology studies]." *Science, Technology, and Human Values 32* (6):652–671.

Hughes, J., V. King, T. Rodden, and H. Andersen. 1994. "Moving out from the control room: Ethnography in system design." In *Proceedings of the 1994 ACM Conference on Computer-Supported Cooperative Work*. New York: ACM, 429–439.

Jirotka, M., R. Procter, M. Hartswood, R. Slack, A. Simpson, C. Coopmans, and C. Hinds. 2005. "Collaboration and trust in healthcare innovation: The eDiaMoND case study." *Computer-Supported Cooperative Work 14* (4):369–398.

Jirotka, M., R. Procter, T. Rodden, and G. Bowker eds. 2006. "Collaboration in eResearch." *Journal of Computer Supported Cooperative Work* (special issue) *15* (4):251–255.

Katz, J. S., and B. R. Martin. 1997. "What is research collaboration?" *Research Policy 26*:1–18.

Lieberman, H., F. Paternó, and V. Wulf, eds. 2006. *End user development.* London: Springer.

Lloyd, S., and A. C. Simpson. 2005. "Project management in multi-disciplinary collaborative research." In *Proceedings of the Professional Communications Conference 2005*, ed. M. Davis. New York: IEEE Press, 602–611.

Luff, P., C. Heath, and M. Jirotka. 2000. "Surveying the scene: Technologies for everyday awareness and monitoring in control rooms." *Interacting with Computers 13* (2):193–228.

Luff, P., C. Heath, H. Kuzuoka, K. Yamazaki, and J. Yamashita. 2006. "Handling documents and discriminating objects in hybrid spaces." In *Proceedings of CHI 2006*. New York: ACM Press, 561–570.

Marcus, G. 1995. "Ethnography in/of the world system: The emergence of multi-sited ethnography." *Annual Review of Anthropology 24*:95–117.

Nielsen, J. 1993. "Usability engineering." In *User centred system design: New perspectives on human computer interaction*, ed. M. Kaufmann, D. Norman, and S. Draper. Boston: Academic Press.

Norman, D. A., and S. W. Draper, eds. 1986. *User centered system design: New perspectives on human-computer interaction.* Hillsdale, NJ: Lawrence Erlbaum Associates.

Payne, S., and T. Green. 1986. "Task-action grammars: A model of the mental representation of task languages." *Human–Computer Interaction Archive 2* (2):93–133.

Pierce, M., G. Fox, H. Yuan, and Y. Deng. 2006. "Cyberinfrastructure and Web 2.0." *Proceedings of HPC2006* (Cetraro, Italy) (July):4.

Pitt-Francis, J., M. O. Bernabeu, J. Cooper, A. Garny, L. Momtahan, J. Osborne, P. Pathmanathan, B. Rodriguez, J. P. Whiteley, and D. J. Gavaghan. 2008. "Chaste: Using agile programming techniques to develop computational biology software." *Philosophical Transactions of the Royal Society A 366*:3111–3136.

Plowman, L., Y. Rogers, and M. Ramage. 1995. "What are workplace studies for?" In *Proceedings of the Fourth European Conference on Computer-Supported Cooperative Work*. Dordrecht, The Netherlands: Kluwer, 309–324.

Randall, D., R. Harper, and M. Rouncefield. 2007. *Fieldwork for design*. London: Springer.

Schmidt, K., and L. Bannon. 1992. "Taking CSCW seriously: Supporting articulation work." *Journal of Computer Supported Cooperative Work 1* (1–2):7–40.

Schraefel, M. C., and A. Dix. 2007. "Within bounds and between domains: Reflecting on making tea within the context of design elicitation methods." International Journal of Human Computer Studies 67 (4) 313–323. Available at: http://eprints.ecs.soton.ac.uk/882.

Shackel, B., ed. 1981. *Man–computer interaction: Human factors aspects of computers and people*. The Hague: Sijthoff and Noordhoof.

Suchman, L. 1987. *Plans and situated actions: The problem of human–machine communication*. New York: Cambridge University Press.

Suchman, L. 1993. "Technologies of accountability: On lizards and aeroplanes." In *Technology in working order*, ed. G. Button. London: Routledge, 113–126.

Trigg, R. H., J. Blomberg, and L. Suchman. 1999. "Moving document collections online: The evolution of a shared repository. In *Proceedings of the Sixth European Conference on Computer Supported Cooperative Work*. The Hague: Kluwer, 331–350.

Welsh, E., M. Jirotka, and D. Gavaghan. 2006. "Post-genomic science: Multidisciplinary and large-scale collaborative research and its organizational and technological implications for the scientific research process." *Philosophical Transactions of the Royal Society A 364* (1843): 1533–1549.

Winograd, T., and F. Flores. 1987. *Understanding computers and cognition: A new foundation for design*. Boston: Addison-Wesley.

Wogan, P. 2004. "Deep hanging out: Reflections on fieldwork and multisited Andean ethnography." *Identities: Global Studies in Power and Culture 11*:129–139.

Zimmerman, A., and B. Nardi. 2006. "Whither or whether HCI: Requirements analysis for multi-sited multi-user cyberinfrastructures." In *Extended abstracts of the SIGCHI Conference on Human Factors in Computing Systems, CHI'06, 24–27 April 2006, Montreal, Canada*. New York: ACM Press, 1601–1606.

5.1   Trusted Computing Platforms

Andrew Martin

The Internet's Security Vulnerability

Serious security weaknesses in underlying Internet-enabled technologies and devices pose a major threat to the take-up of distributed computing technologies. The standard initial response to address these vulnerabilities was to build boundary protections, such as firewalls that filter and guard against unwarranted access to a system, to help form carefully managed local networks where all of those connected could be trusted to behave properly—or face the consequences. This approach has many flaws—for instance, in the way that the growing use of many mobile devices that shift promiscuously from one network to another has made the idea of such a "safe zone" almost untenable.

Nowhere is this question of a safe zone more evident than in the kind of interconnected e-research endeavor described in this book. Where should the zone of trust begin and end? How does one join? Who will be responsible when collections of scientific data span tens of servers and are processed on thousands of nodes under the care of dozens of different administrators? We may develop measures of trust based on past performance, but as the cautious advertiser always warns, the past is not a reliable predictor of future behavior. The highly connected resources themselves, the data being processed, and the programs being run are all of great interest to a would-be attacker.

To look at the problem from another perspective, more and more network participants will want to exercise their "digital rights." Previously the preserve only of the entertainment industry, an interest in protecting digital content has now arisen for nearly every form of highly mobile material—whether email texts, documents, research data and images, valuable software, personal data, or corporate secrets.

Meanwhile, Internet attacks have become ever more sophisticated. Suppliers have responded by plugging more and more gaps in their applications and operating systems. However, would-be virus writers and creators of "trojans" to infiltrate users' computers have shifted their attention from making a big noise on the network. Instead, they are often to be found in the pay of organized crime, undertaking potentially dev-astating targeted attacks against particular companies, groups, or individuals. Such con-cerns lead those with the most valuable assets to seek to keep these assets very far from public networks because they are fearful of genuine network-based work.

Building trust in the security of e-research systems requires finding a balance between the need to make some elements private, such as a research project dealing with confi-dential information, and the need to retain flexibility in enabling individuals, groups, and organizations to choose the level of public openness they prefer. This essay illus-trates one approach to trying to achieve this balance.

Developing a More Trustworthy Computing Architecture

The concerns described here are not new, but have previously been almost the sole pre-serve of high-integrity systems designed to protect national security. Specifications for such systems introduced the notion of a trusted computing base—that indivisible part of the computer you simply have to trust to be untainted. Computer science has long regarded these scenarios as a pair of related problems: "trusted host; untrusted code" (the owner of the Grid node should not inherently trust the software sent to be run on it) and "untrusted host; trusted code" (the owner of the job should not inherently trust the node where it is to be executed).

A number of theoretical solutions to the problem have been proposed, without no-table practical impacts. The development of service-oriented computing in the style of Grids and Clouds has prompted a resurgence in research in operating systems and net-work designs. The result is a collection of new emerging patterns of interaction based around medium-scale "trusted" components. A trusted platform module (TPM), for example, draws on precedents of a cryptographic coprocessor, but aims for minimal hardware and software costs while offering very strong assurance about the software running on a particular host and the safety of its cryptographic keys.

Related developments have brought into the mainstream strongly encrypted storage devices (with an option to "lock" them to a particular trusted platform) and encrypted, access-controlled networks (willing to offer connectivity only to trusted hosts). Net-works and hosts have become part of a virtual space as a way of managing and utilizing the immense amount of available power. The same technologies further allow separa-tion of trusted and untrusted components.

These capabilities enable the user (or the operating system's designer) to construct very strongly isolated compartments within a computer wherein data is available only to particular, nominated applications. Thus, one's personal data or corporate secrets might be incapable of being emailed to a third party, or one's scientific results might be bound inextricably to the software (and user) intended to analyze them. However, such capabilities have attracted a great deal of adverse publicity because they also have the potential to limit what a computer owner can do with his or her own computer and data. This potential raises, for example, the specter of software from which no migration can ever be possible (because it offers no "export" facility), and the TPM's cryptography prevents any other package from reading its files.

Application domains such as e-research are beginning to demonstrate that many of these fears are likely to be unfounded. This conclusion is shown, for instance, by the value of "rights management for all users" as a counterbalance to concerns that some approaches to trusted computing can use commercially based digital rights management to restrict users' flexibility in their choice of solutions (chapter 5). Here, network barriers such as firewalls (which were never part of the Internet's original design) become much less critical.

In such a context, encrypted data can flow freely around the network, with an overlaid system of keys and policy-management systems ensuring that the data are eventually available only to those for whom they were intended. Giving to the user such a reliable basis for the measurement of the trustworthiness of a remote system enables a whole new pattern of activity wherein we can decide in a rational way whom to trust. It also offers the opportunity to put in place an unobtrusive but very strong enforcement regime.

How Trusted Computing Technologies Might Work

Picture a world in which the systems within a research project dealing with sensitive personal information employ trusted computing technologies. Before the key to such data is transmitted to another system—inside or outside the project—the software can ensure that the recipient is authorized to view the data and that their software will not permit him or her to pass the data on to a third party or even to retain a copy longer than is necessary. The separation of generic middleware from application-specific code may even permit this management of access to be decoupled from the choice of final software application.

Another context to benefit would be massive public-participation projects, such as SETI@home[1] and climate*prediction*.net.[2] Conventional technology means that these kinds of project participants must simply be trusted not to interfere with the science in which they have volunteered to participate: whether to falsify results or just to complete work units more quickly than their rivals. A trusted platform will enable the project leaders to have a high degree of confidence that the results received at the center are indeed those that relate to the planned experiment.

Such protections do not entirely eliminate the need for network perimeter protection, but they can ensure that trusted applications communicate with each other over the Internet so that there can be confidence that they enjoy protection from hackers, malign administrators, and other kinds of users.

Notes

1. SETI@home (http://setiathome.berkeley.edu/) is a scientific experiment that uses Internet-connected computers in the search for extraterrestrial intelligence (SETI); it is based at the University of California at Berkeley's Open Infrastructure for Network Computing.

2. Climate*prediction*.net is the largest experiment to try and produce a forecast of the climate in the twenty-first century (http://www.climateprediction.net/). Its forecasting draws on the willingness of people around the world to give the project time on their computers when the computers are switched on but are not used to their full capacity.

5.2   Social Networking and e-Research

Mike Thelwall

The Rise of Social Networking

The rise of social networking points to a need to discuss whether it will have an impact on e-research.[1] At one level, it already has: as early as 2007, several social sciences conferences were dedicated to blogs or other Web 2.0 sites. In addition, e-science projects such as myTea[2] are relevant to Web 2.0 because of their focus on collaboration. But how widespread can or should the impact of Web 2.0 be?

Social-networking Web sites such as MySpace and Facebook have several common features. Members create their own profile page with a photograph and some personal information. They can agree with other members to become "friends," in which case they are pictured and listed on each other's home page (space permitting). Perhaps most important, it is always possible to navigate to a friend's friends via a list in their profile (Boyd and Ellison 2007).

Profile pages also often have spaces for friends' messages to be displayed. In addition, email-like personal messages are supported, and some sites allow users to keep blogs and to post and tag sets of pictures. More specialist Web 2.0 sites, such as CiteULike, Flickr, and Digg, have some or all of the these features. However, their primary goal is not to facilitate networking, but to share citations, pictures, news, stories, and so on.

Why are sites such as MySpace and Facebook so popular when they seem to offer relatively little valuable information? The answer seems to be that they are fun to use because they support maintaining relationships and making new friends[3] (see Thelwall 2009) and because they support gossiplike chat (Tufekci 2008), which is important for effective group relationships.

Typical users seem to have many more "friends" online than they do offline, so the system supports maintaining more casual friendship—perhaps better described as "acquaintanceship"—and reconnecting with old friends (Boyd and Ellison 2007). For example, Facebook offers graduates the chance to enter their college name and year of attendance, so that they can search for previous acquaintances and friends at college.

Implications for e-Research

From an e-research perspective, the rise of Web 2.0 social-networking environments is interesting for two reasons. First, the software is complex and based on huge databases of users' details, pictures, and other resources. The computer science engineering challenge of getting this software to work is significant, especially because the creation of home pages requires extracting friends and other complex information relationships from the databases in real time.

Second, the success of these complex systems defies accepted wisdom. A typical e-research application involves a significant quantity of "requirements engineering," such as engaging with users to identify needs and to test prototypes throughout all development stages. In contrast, sites such as last.fm and Flickr were created by two or three programmers, apparently without an extensive user-participation exercise during development—although user feedback and ongoing testing have presumably influenced system upgrades and can help to find unexpected uses for existing features (Boyd and Ellison 2007).

Social-networking systems seem to work because they are enjoyable enough to attract enthusiastic users from an early stage, perhaps even adopting them for new purposes. At the same time, as discussed in the conclusion to this essay, the limitations of social networking in e-research should be recognized.

The Role of Social Networking in e-Research

The previous commentary indicates that it is logical to ask whether this social-networking type of fun can play a role in ensuring the uptake of e-research software or even in deciding which kinds of e-research software should be built. Scientific communities include many friendship circles, and conferences are often pleasurable because of the opportunity to meet like-minded people and engage in, among other things, recreational activities. All of these elements are part of the "invisible college" of science.

Of course, the modern invisible college already includes email, discussion boards, and email lists, as well as more sophisticated services called "virtual research environments" or "collaboratories" (see chapter 10). Nevertheless, the success of social networking suggests that it can be even more pleasurable than these activities. Using social networking to create communities of friends rather than just groups of discussants may therefore be an incentive to use associated e-research software.

It is not clear, however, if such groups would need to be embedded in the system itself or whether they can operate remotely via an application such as Facebook (e.g., a special Facebook group for each e-research application). The group might be more engaging if it interfaced significantly with the science application in some way that gave at least one type of interesting extra functionality, such as high-quality video conferencing. Embedding social networks within new scientific applications is being made easier by developments that allow third-party Web sites to include functionality and interactions with existing popular social-networking sites, such as Facebook Connect[4] and Google Friend Connect,[5] both of which debuted in 2008.

Opportunities and Risks for Social Networking in e-Research

There is a case for designing social networking into at least some e-research applications if doing so might increase their uptake and the chance that they would be viable in the long term, although it might make them less powerful. There has been significant interest in the value of making interactions with computer systems enjoyable, so-called funology, which may assist such e-research developments.

Nevertheless, social networking will probably be inappropriate for some e-research applications, such as those with important security or privacy implications. There is also the risk that social networking might be counterproductive because it inevitably takes up researchers' time both to create the system and to participate in the networking. It is not clear whether it would be a significant draw on participants' time. However, this risk should be offset against the risk that expensive e-research applications may remain unused because potential users don't have "friends" to engage with them in ways that would encourage and support their use of the facilities.

Notes

1. For example, the MySpace and Facebook social-networking sites were apparently among the world's ten most popular Web sites in mid-2008 according to Alexa's Web traffic analysis (see the current rankings at http://www.alexa.com/site/ds/top_500).

2. See http://mytea.org.uk/.

3. See http://www.pewinternet.org/PPF/r/198/report_display.asp.

4. A working example of Facebook Connect is at http://www.somethingtoputhere.com/therun around/.

5. See http://www.google.com/friendconnect/.

References

Boyd, D., and N. Ellison. 2007. "Social network sites: Definition, history, and scholarship." *Journal of Computer-Mediated Communication 13* (1). Available at http://jcmc.indiana.edu/vol2013/issue2001/boyd.ellison.html.

Thelwall, M. 2009. "Social network sites: Users and uses." In *Advances in Computers*, ed. M. Zelkowitz. Amsterdam: Elsevier 76:19–73.

Tufekci, Z. 2008. "Grooming, gossip, Facebook, and MySpace: What can we learn about these sites from those who won't assimilate?" *Information, Communication, & Society 11* (4):544–564.

III   Social Shaping of Infrastructures and Practices

The social shaping of e-research and its implications are covered in this part. Chapter 6 examines how the use of information and communication technologies (ICTs) can transform the work of social scientists and the ways they are enabling e-research capabilities and outcomes with wider research as well as institutional and ethical implications. Chapter 7 focuses on the institutional infrastructures within which global research networks operate, and chapter 8 focuses on the politics of privacy, confidentiality, and ethics tied to the new capabilities and practices of e-research.

In chapter 6, Bill Dutton and Eric Meyer provide an overview of the nature and implications of the growing application of emerging ICTs in social science research. They address central questions for e–social science: Will the use of e-research capabilities support social scientists to be better artisans of their craft, or will the artisan model be eclipsed as scholars become specialists on research teams following an industrial model? Will failure to take up e-research methods place some on the wrong side of a digital skills and technology divide? To what extent will the choices that social scientists make about how to employ the new tools of e-research enable them to enhance the quality of the social sciences? How far will e–social science approaches based on the use of networked technology (e.g., in field research) replace more traditional methods of learning about social phenomena? The risks these authors identify in the new methods underscore the importance of research on the social factors shaping e–social science, as well as its broader research implications.

Two essays complement Dutton and Meyer's contribution. Rob Procter presents a strong case to show how e-infrastructures can support the social sciences, arguing that significant investment in research infrastructures is capable of achieving two key objectives: making data easier to discover, access, and analyze; and enabling increased collaboration across traditional disciplinary boundaries. Jonathan Zhu and Xiaoming Li's essay illustrates the degree to which innovations in research-centered computational networks may take the availability of a great deal of data too much for granted, which is not always the case in the social sciences in some contexts. They explain how this problem is being dealt with in developing nations such as China and describe the kinds of techniques being created to meet these needs.

In chapter 7, Paul David and Michael Spence argue that new and more appropriate "soft" institutional infrastructures are needed to facilitate the formation and conduct of collaborative public-sector research projects, especially those that are truly global in scope. They outline wider implications of the findings of a survey and case studies for the U.K. e-Science Programme. For example, they highlight how interinstitutional agreements become more difficult to negotiate when they involve multiple funding agencies belonging to different national jurisdictions, where the introduction of competing claims to intellectual property rights is just one of the major elements that may derail negotiations. The authors identify several respects in which standard forms of legal contract are ill suited to the needs of collaborations in areas such as basic science. Instead, they propose a modular approach to the design of necessary agreements, including the creation of a new public actor to construct consistent sets of contract subprovisions suitable for selection and assembly in various combinations.

Two related essays reinforce David and Spence's view that the "soft" infrastructure of e-research needs to be paid as much attention to as its "hard" physical counterpart if the promised benefits are to be fully realized. Tina Piper and David Vaver illuminate this point through their analysis of the results of a detailed study of how questions about the ownership of medical images had a strong impact on an e-research project. By analyzing the role of authorship in protecting the integrity of scientific collaboration, Justine Pila opens a window on the detailed legal issues that are bound up in the authorship and copyright of intellectual property developed in many e-research projects.

The reframing of ethical concerns relating to privacy, confidentiality, and consent within and between disciplines is occurring as a result of the changing legal and institutional boundaries and dynamics of research organizations, as discussed in chapter 7. It is also affected by the kinds of information observed, collected, analyzed, and distributed by researchers within these structures. In chapter 8, Dutton and Piper consider this reframing through the lens of the politics of research ethics in projects involving human subjects, which are often arenas for interplays between conflicting values and interests. In addition to looking at the ways e-research may question traditional research ethics and related legal and administrative frameworks, they examine the possibility that open, collaborative methods might be able to ensure institutional arrangements that offer better protection of ethical standards. They also propose a novel method to enhance the administration of research ethics.

The implications for established relationships, expectations, and practices of emerging distributed e-research collaborations is the basis of the ethical and moral dimensions examined in an essay by Michael Parker. He outlines key ethical issues that may become barriers to e-research, suggesting that such obstacles can be overcome through interdisciplinary research into the identification and analysis of such factors. Jane Kaye takes the case of sharing of genomics data as a public resource to highlight ethical issues in e-research. She looks particularly at the technical and institutional approaches involved in protecting personal data, including the framework set by the European Union's directive on data protection. Part III concludes with an essay by Julia Lane that asks how social scientists can protect the confidentiality of the people they study when deploying the tools of e-research to collect and analyze personal information about them. She describes what she sees as the social science research community's limited progress in taking account of emerging e-research applications in changing how data are accessed. She therefore calls for a more focused approach to demonstrating how the benefits of e-research can be obtained without compromising confidentiality.

6 Enabling or Mediating the Social Sciences? The Opportunities and Risks of Bottom-up Innovation

William H. Dutton and Eric T. Meyer

The social sciences have sought to apply developments in e-research to social, behavioral, and policy research. In addition, they have provided insights on the legal, ethical, and other social factors shaping the use and implications of e-infrastructures across the disciplines. However, advanced Internet and Grid technologies have experienced slower uptake and diffusion in the social sciences and humanities—including in some data-rich areas where information and communication technologies (ICTs) might seem particularly relevant—than in the natural and physical sciences.

Skeptics argue that most foreseeable communication and computational needs can be accommodated by the use of state-of-the-practice ICTs, such as software packages installed on personal computers linked to the Internet. Advocates of e–social science, in contrast, believe that advances in Internet and Grid technologies will enable innovations in the capacity and quality of research that would be impossible to contemplate using only the traditional tools of the field (essay 6.1). This vision has supported the emergence of what has become known as "e–social science": efforts by the social sciences to join with computer science and engineering to launch national initiatives that seek to employ many of the same innovations in e-research that have been fostered in the "hard" sciences as e-science initiatives (chapter 2).

Growing evidence of interest in e-research within the social sciences is tied to innovative applications across a range of quantitative and qualitative fields (Dutton and Meyer 2009). However, the emergence of e–social science as a distinctive area of research has raised concerns over the impact of network-enabled research on and in the social sciences. As discussed later in the chapter, social scientists' traditional roles are being drawn into question by e-research infrastructures that may lead to changes in the basic ways in which scholarly work is conducted (Borgman 2007).

This chapter begins by providing an overview of the use of ICTs within the social sciences, followed by a discussion on the nature and scope of e–social science. It distinguishes between research on the social shaping of technology and the application of emerging technologies, such as Grid-enabled data sets and tools. Early exploratory research on awareness and attitudes toward e-research in the social sciences suggests there is a growing base of support for its innovations, which is tied to a history of bottom-up processes shaping its uptake. The chapter then takes a critical look at the implications for social scientists of the wider diffusion of e-research tools, as well as at the potential and risk that use of these tools poses for the quality of research in this field. Our analysis highlights the need for research on how social, ethical, and institutional factors are shaping the ways in which e-research is applied across the disciplines.

Use of e-Research in the Social Sciences

Computing and telecommunications have long been central to the conduct of social science research. The first nonmilitary applications of computing in government after the Second World War were for the census as well as in finance and accountancy.[1] Initial use in the social sciences was anchored in mainframe computers. These computers supported statistical analyses, often using software written in house by statisticians and social scientists, but increasingly based on "packaged" programs (e.g., SPSS).[2] By the mid-1970s, interactive minicomputers enabled researchers to conduct more research online via telecommunications and to begin exploiting email and, occasionally, computer conferencing systems for collaboration.[3]

The personal computing revolution of the early 1980s led to new journals focused on the use of computers in the social sciences, such as the *Social Science Computer Review*, and a new perspective on the way the personal computer would empower individual social scientists to free themselves from queuing for the mainframe and conduct their research from their desktop at any time, writing many of their own programs.[4] During the 1990s, social scientists found that their personal computers and standard software packages became their own workplace equivalent of the spinning jenny and hand-loom,[5] bringing the ability to address from their local machine(s) nearly every phase of their research, from analysis to publication. Increasing digital computational and storage capacities meant that their computers enabled them to work with increasing versatility in dealing with larger and larger data sets, more complex analyses, more elegant approaches to the graphical representation of findings, and more effective ways of processing text and statistics.

The potential applications of ICTs in the social sciences were greatly enhanced and extended by the growing availability of academic and other networks, culminating in wide availability of the Internet and the World Wide Web (chapter 1). This availability brought to networked social scientists a set of increasingly powerful tools for exploring research questions. The technology supported all forms of traditional social research methods and new online approaches.[6]

The Reach of e-Research in the Social Sciences

The personal computer, the Internet, and related ICTs have become embedded in nearly every phase of social research. Although this process can be portrayed as linear, from problem formation through analysis to the archiving of final reports, in practice it is far more cyclical, spiraling, and iterative. Nevertheless, it has involved many separate, identifiable—but interrelated—stages. Table 6.1 illustrates such phases of social science research and their ties to the use of ICTs, including many advanced Internet and Grid applications.

The personal computer and the Internet have become indispensable tools for networked social scientists because they are increasingly tied to advances in search and social networking that enable researchers to be productive on their own or in collaboration with colleagues around the world. However, some shortcomings have been recognized.

First, social scientists in much of the less-developed world have not been able to exploit the same technologies—lacking access not only to computers and networks, but also to basic infrastructures, such as reliable supplies of electricity (chapter 12). Second, a number of basic potentials have remained largely unrealized, such as the prospects for collaboration. For example, many initiatives for supporting distributed collaboration have fallen far short of their developers' visions (Olson, Zimmerman, and Bos 2008; chapter 10).

As the field has sought to address these concerns, technological innovation has continued at an even faster pace, generating new visions of the potential for advanced Internet and Grid technology to support scientific research. This growth in technology has led to questions regarding whether the social sciences can apply emerging innovations, such as the Grid, to their own fields to overcome these shortcomings in order to realize more global collaboration and study of the social sciences.

What Is e–Social Science?

The term *e–social science* refers to the growing use of advanced Internet and Grid applications to support scientific research in the social sciences (e.g., see Procter, Batty, Birkin, et al. 2006). As social scientists became more aware of national initiatives to develop e-infrastructures within the hard sciences (see chapter 2), their respective funding bodies and government agencies saw the social sciences and humanities as natural extensions of efforts to maintain the international competitiveness of their research. Several funding bodies thus began to explore initiatives for the social sciences, including the U.S. National Science Foundation's Directorate for Social, Behavioral, and Economic Sciences program called "Next Generation Cyberinfrastructure Tools"[7] and the

Table 6.1

E-research across Phases of the Social Science[a]

Phase	Roles	e-Research Example(s)
Setting an agenda	Observing and establishing contacts in the field and with media and colleagues	Blogosphere; Web; listservs and discussion boards; email
Assembling collaborative team	Developing academic networks of collaboration	Email; social-networking sites; voice over the Internet; virtual research environments; distributed content generation (wikis; Basecamp); Access Grid
Defining the problem	Brainstorming, testing ideas	Web; Mind Maps; e–White Boards; groupware
Reviewing the literature	Searching and reading working papers and publications	Bibliographic tools and databases; search engines and agents; the Web; digital libraries; email notifications; Web alerts
Establishing research question(s) and designs	Writing; presenting; testing ideas	Word processing; Mind Maps; listservs; wikis
Conducting ethical review	Exposing methods and procedures to peers and the lay public	Greater openness to public scrutiny over collaborative networks (chapter 8)
Locating available data and funding	Searching and retrieving; communicating	Data registries; data archives; funding listservs; Web search; email
Developing a proposal	Writing; budgeting and doing work-flow analysis	Word processing; spreadsheets; project management
Collecting data	Conducting surveys, experiments, network analysis, direct observation; setting up focus groups, doing interviews, modeling, ethnographic fieldwork	Online and Web-based surveys; computer-based experimental labs; virtual experiments; Webometrics and log-file analysis; embedded sensor networks; online focus groups and interviews; digital recordings; electronic logs of fieldwork; simulated and manufactured data
Analyzing data	Doing quantitative and qualitative analyses	Statistical packages; data mining; concordances; distributed annotation; computer modeling and simulation
Reporting and visualizing	Doing presentations and reports	Simulation; visualization; Web files and Webcasts; blogs; posting of slides; email; listservs; grammar and spell checkers; bibliographic citation tools
Getting peer reviewed and published	Reviewing work; publishing in journals and books	Online submission forms; Web-based review systems; online journals; online search; citation analyses
Archiving	Archiving data; writing reports and publications	Institutional repositories; project Web sites; Internet archives; digital collections

a. The idea and early version of the processes illustrated in table 6.1 were developed through a workshop (Crouchley, Dutton, and Allan 2007).

Box 6.1

The National Centre for e–Social Science and Its Nodes

> The National Centre for e–Social Science (NCeSS) was established in 2004 as a means to
> support social science in the United Kingdom, including the development of new method-
> ological tools, and to contribute to the country's e-science mission (Halfpenny, Procter, Lin,
> et al. 2009; chapter 2). The Economic and Social Research Council initially commissioned
> scoping studies, which led to funding for a series of pilot projects and the specification of
> the NCeSS research program. The program's first phase, launched in 2004–2007, focused on
> two streams of research: applications of e-infrastructures to the social sciences and studies
> of the social shaping of e-science. Seven "nodes" of the NCeSS "hub" were funded during
> this first phase. Most were continued, and new nodes were added during the second phase
> (2008–2011).

United Kingdom's National Centre for e–Social Science (NCeSS) and its various nodes, funded by the Economic and Social Research Council (box 6.1).[8]

In the United Kingdom, advanced Internet and Grid technologies first emerged within the social sciences through leading-edge projects and "demos" that showcased the potential of e–social science (Procter, Batty, Birkin, et al. 2006). An early effort focused on the use of the Grid to support meetings for multipoint "group-to-group" collaborations through multimedia, large-screen formats such as the Access Grid.[9] In this case, an application developed for the e-science community was translated in a straightforward way for application within the social sciences because the demands of holding meetings are not radically different across fields. Tools focused on the collection and analysis of data, however, can require more translation to cross from the physical to the social sciences.

Table 6.2 describes a number of concrete types of applications in this arena. In many respects, e–social science applications enable more powerful approaches to standard methods, from statistical analysis to the study of group dynamics and the representation of findings. However, these tools might move social scientists to scale up their ambitions—for example (see essay 6.1), by working with more geographically distributed teams and with larger data sets (such as entire populations rather than samples), creating new sources of data (e.g., links on the Web), and representing statistical results in more visually meaningful ways for social scientists and larger public audiences, such as through Gapminder,[10] which visualizes worldwide statistical trends.

Since the launch of the kinds of programs and applications outlined here, e–social science studies have focused on understanding factors shaping the application and implications of e–social science, such as usability, law, and policy issues. Most early work in this field was focused on practice in a prescriptive manner because it was often

Table 6.2

Types and Examples of e–Social Science Applications

Area of Application	Focus of Development	Illustrative Projects
Quantitative analysis	Middleware to enable analysis of large-scale and geographically distributed data sets through standard desktop computer software	Collaboratory for Quantitative e–Social Science at Lancaster University and Daresbury Laboratory (United Kingdom)
Analysis and annotation of video records	Tools to support the distributed analysis and annotation of shared audiovisual records	Mixed Media Grid at Bristol University and King's College, London (see chapter 11)
Virtual research environments and collaboratories, for social research	Collaborative tools and virtual settings for social research	Access Grid for multipoint video conferencing; LifeGuide, a psychology virtual research environment at Southampton University; and efforts to develop virtual safe settings for quantitative analyses of sensitive personal data
Integration, management, and analysis of multiple forms of data	Tools to capture and integrate multiple sources of digital data (video, audio, and annotations)—for instance, along a timeline	Digital Records for e–Social Science at Nottingham University; and Data Management through e–Social Science at Glasgow and Stirling Universities
Modeling and simulation of social processes	Models and tools for visualizing and simulating social or environmental processes, such as urban development or social segregation	Geographic Virtual Urban Environments at University College, London, and the Modeling and Simulation for e–Social Science at Leeds University, UK
Visualization of data and processes	Visualization of cross-sectional or longitudinal trends for analysis and communication, such as in three-dimensional Internet environments	Generative e–Social Science for Socio-Spatial Simulation at University College London; the Obesity e-Lab at University of Manchester, UK
Definition, structuring, and retrieval of information	Semantic approaches for enabling better use of the Grid for social and policy research	Semantic Grid Tools for Rural Policy Development and Appraisal (PolicyGrid) at Aberdeen University, UK

initiated by proponents attempting to launch this field, but an increasing range of literature has taken a more critical perspective on its social shaping and implications (Schroeder and Fry 2007).

The Diffusion and Sustainability of e–Social Science Tools and Data Sets

In the early years of e–social science initiatives, from about 2003, its practitioners focused on stimulating uptake across the social sciences (Barjak, Wiegand, Lane, et al.

2007). Its diffusion had been limited (Barjak, Lane, Kertcher, et al. 2008), and the motivations for adoption within the social sciences were unclear (Woolgar 2003). Proponents were concerned about both a general lack of awareness of these innovations and the risk that overt advocacy could be seen as excessive and counterproductive (Halfpenny, Procter, Lin, et al. 2009).

Following Donald MacKenzie's (1999) concept of a "certainty trough"—the tendency for those least and most informed to exhibit more uncertainty—it is possible that the growing awareness of the potential of these innovations may in itself instill support for using them. To test this hypothesis, in 2008 we conducted an exploratory survey of a nonprobability sample of researchers, purposively targeted at individuals who might be aware of e-research, such as members of mailing lists for e-research centers.[11] The sample was purposive, not random, aimed at researchers with some involvement in e-research. More than five hundred researchers completed the questionnaire, which asked about their awareness of and attitudes toward e-research and their use of particular e-research tools and data sets.

Many of this exploratory survey's findings are suggestive of the emergence of an e-research community (Dutton and Meyer 2009):

• There was a sizeable core of researchers with an interest in e-research. Although the survey was more likely to be of interest to those engaged in e-research, there was variance in levels of interest. Moreover, those with greater levels of interest were not tied to particular methodological approaches, but were more likely to have been trained recently: interest was more prominent among more recent doctoral and postdoctoral students. The latter finding suggests that the coming cohort of researchers will be more likely to be engaged in e-research.

• Lone researchers were as interested in e-research as those who regularly participated in collaborative research teams. However, collaboration tended to be the norm among respondents. This finding is consistent with other studies' findings of increasing levels of coauthorship and collaboration in the social sciences (Wuchty, Jones, and Uzzi 2007). For example, most respondents said they coauthor at least half of their work.

• The more experience individuals had with the tools of e-research, the more supportive they were of e-infrastructures for social research. This finding supported the results of other research that suggest that the Internet and related ICTs were "experience" technologies (Dutton and Shepherd 2006). Respondents believed that e-research would enhance their personal productivity and research teams' productivity, but would not pose a threat to the quality of research. In fact, those most interested in e-research tended to view these tools as becoming indispensable for research.

• The greatest constraints on more uptake were the degree to which new e-research tools were too difficult to use (chapter 5), required more training (chapter 5), and raised ethical questions (chapter 8).

These findings run counter to the expectations of those who develop e–social science tools, such as Grid middleware and Grid-enabled data sets—namely, that there was both a lack of awareness and core of opposition to e–social science approaches. This difference can be reconciled by understanding that those who develop projects for adoption by the larger social science community have anticipated more interest in a top-down uptake of tools, as illustrated by the view that the computer science community would "develop powerful new software tools and assist in building a new research infrastructure" (Hey and Trefethen 2008:15).

In contrast, a clear pattern that emerged in the exploratory survey was the degree to which members of the research community are inventing tools for their own use (Meyer and Dutton 2009). For instance, the survey found:

1. A high proportion of each type of social science tool, from statistical to qualitative, was developed in-house (Meyer and Dutton 2009).
2. Researchers tended to use a wide variety of research tools and data sets within any particular functional area, from statistical analysis to visualization. It was found that most researchers rely on multiple tools and data sets rather than converging on any single centrally available tool or data set.

There is thus clearly a base of support for e-research that our research suggested was potentially strong among more recent doctoral graduates. Yet, like earlier generations of social scientists, these graduates have approached innovation in the development and use of ICTs in research through a more bottom-up than top-down process.[12] Similar patterns of research innovation were evident in earlier eras of computing, from the mainframe and personal computer to the Internet, both internationally (e.g., see essay 6.2) and more locally. The survey findings also reflect the degree to which advances in ICTs enable individual researchers to decide how to create links with information and people in ways that put themselves in the center of their network (chapter 1). This means that efforts to foster e-research might be most successful if focused on infrastructures, such as the Internet, that enable bottom-up innovation.

Implications for the Routines and Norms of Social Science Research

How will e-research impact the day-to-day work of social scientists? The following subsections highlight some key distinctive expectations.

Empowered Researchers

Optimists expect e-research to be transformative, empowering social scientists by providing resources for computation, communication, and control that will enable both more productivity and the pursuit of innovative research that would never have been done without e-research tools. The promotion of e–social science is anchored in a belief that e-research will enable social scientists to enhance their research—going where no social scientist has gone before—and will improve their ability to observe, collect, process, and visualize information.

Methodological, Commercial, and Global Divides

Skeptics see potential benefits, but expect the costs and benefits to be lopsided. There are three main variants of this redistribution of benefits:

• *Methodological*: Quantitative researchers may be the prime beneficiaries of investments in e-infrastructures, possibly to the detriment of qualitative researchers (Scott and Venters 2006).
• *Commercial*: Academic research continues to support the lone artisan researchers with their personal tool boxes, whereas commercial sectors move rapidly into "big" social science using tools and data sets that are not accessible to academics in the higher education sector (due to cost, licensing arrangements, and contractual demands for confidentiality).[13]
• *Research Capacity*: There is concern over global digital divides in research capacity, with the most-developed economies creating new e-infrastructures that will further distance them from the less-developed economies (chapter 12). However, these concerns assume that e-research will deliver for the "haves." Policy interventions should therefore be focused on more equitable distribution of the benefits—for example, by using e–social science as one strategy for catching up with or surpassing the capabilities of private commercial research units.

Industrialization of Knowledge Work: Social Science Craftsmen or e–Assembly Line Workers?

A more pessimistic vision is a fear that the next generation of e-infrastructures will usher in nothing less than the industrialization and routinization of academic work. For instance, Robert Holt and John Turner argued more than thirty years ago that the traditional academic scholar can be compared to the medieval artisan who "produces a commodity that is useful to the members of the society; he pays careful attention to the quality of the product; and he trains his protégés both in the techniques of his craft and in the values of the guild" (1974:257). The social science craftsman may become the assembly line worker of the information age as the Grid creates more centralized control over networked technologies and data resources while requiring more specialization across a wider range of experts, including the engagement of computer scientists and engineers in the conduct of the social sciences.

It is also possible, however, to see the development of Grid technologies as being analogous to changes in an earlier period of the Industrial Revolution, before the mass-production revolution introduced by Henry Ford in automobile manufacturing.

Charles Sabel and Jonathan Zeitlin note that "before the widespread use of electric motors . . . [networks of small artisan enterprises] might be grouped in large buildings housing a steam engine; a system of belts transmitted torque to workrooms which could be rented by the day" (1985:148).

Grid applications can enable scholars to operate in much the same fashion as these belt-driven production systems, which allowed small enterprises to share the central power of a large, expensive steam engine. By harnessing the power of large, distributed computing systems and allowing scholars to run applications on them depending on their needs, the Grid system might allow for the continuation of small enterprises within the context of big science. Social scientists rarely need the sustained power that physicists must harness to run a particle accelerator. However, they may be able to make use of small portions of that combined power to answer new research questions.

A similar scenario has been developed around Cloud computing over the Internet (essay 2.1), where data centers around the world provide information utilities, comparable to power plants of the industrial age, but turning users either into a "global pool of cut-rate labor" for the digital elite (Carr 2008) or into semi-independent artisans collaboratively sharing the power of centralized infrastructure. Will social scientists remain artisans in control of the entire research process from beginning to end? Or, alternatively, will the new infrastructures create an increasing number of social science specializations within more complex team-based research? Will individuals continue to play significant roles in specific aspects of the research process or become part of an industrialization of social science research or the new networked research organizations? Because of these networks, will social science jobs go to where the expertise already exists—to be pulled together by a small number of elite academic managers orchestrating the research process?

Types of e-Researcher: An Empirical Study

Each of these scenarios has some plausibility. There are high expectations of the ways e-research may empower social scientists, as outlined in essay 6.1, but the benefits are unlikely to be evenly distributed. Many aspects of industrial-age research are emerging, such as the growth of teams and the increasing need for expertise in computer science within the social sciences. Of course, these are early days in the development of e–social science, and any emerging patterns may be more indicative of a transitional period than of a final outcome.

That said, the exploratory survey of e-researchers described here suggests that the e-infrastructures being developed can support a multiplicity of research practices and collaborative arrangements (Dutton and Meyer 2009). For example, in this same study, a cluster analysis was conducted across a range of variables related to the ways in which researchers were involved with the development of research methods, the use of different research methods, the coding of applications, and the choice of being a member of a team or a sole researcher on projects. This analysis led to the empirical identification of four types of researcher (Dutton and Meyer 2009: table 3):

1. *The Lone Researcher*: Often the sole investigator, frequently or always coding or designing applications and employing a mix of quantitative and qualitative techniques.
2. *Team Players*: Those usually working as members of a team developing and using e-research and employing a mix of quantitative and qualitative methods.
3. *"Quals"*: Primarily users of e-research, who identify themselves as qualitative researchers, most often as a sole investigator.
4. *"Quants"*: Researchers who usually work as members of a team, often coding or designing their own applications and relying more on quantitative than qualitative research.

Among respondents, the cluster analysis identified nearly one-third (29.1 percent) of the respondents as quals, followed by team players (26.2 percent), lone e-researchers (23 percent), and, finally, quants (12 percent).

The Emergence of Collaborative Network Organizations

The exploratory survey findings outlined here, although far from definitive, reinforce a theme arising from related research on "collaborative network organizations" (Dutton 2008). Individual researchers can choose to employ e-research to support a variety of alternative research networks and practices. The Internet and related e-infrastructures increasingly enable individual researchers to work alone or be a part of a larger team, whether it is local or global. In line with being given this choice, a sizeable proportion of e-researchers in the survey were lone investigators. Institutions are not well positioned to impose team structures on researchers who can reconfigure their access to information, colleagues, and services in ways that meet their needs. Although more collaboration may be occurring in the social sciences than was the case traditionally, the infrastructures still appear to support a wide array of organizational arrangements.

There is also no clear evidence of a methodological bias toward quantitative research. Proportionately fewer quantitative social scientists responded to the survey than qualitative scientists, suggesting that these tools have a potentially more widespread value across methods. Moreover, methodological approaches were generally not related to a researcher's awareness of or interest in e-research (Dutton and Meyer 2009).

Global divides are apparent. E–social science initiatives are most prominent in the United States and Europe (Meyer, Park, and Schroeder 2009). Chinese initiatives in e-science have been significant, but initiatives in the social sciences have been limited (essay 6.2). Only a small proportion of respondents to the survey were from the global South (15 percent), reflecting global divides in awareness and interest in e-research. The benefits of e–social science are likely to enhance global divides, but as Marcus Ynalvez, Ricardo Duque, and Wesley Shrum show in chapter 12, the relationship between e-research and productivity is not straightforward in developing areas.

Implications for Social Science Research Quality, Creativity, and Excellence

The most significant issue as e-research moves forward is its role in shaping the quality of research carried out using these technologies—its creativity, excellence, and impact on policy and practice. To what degree are researchers likely to be more productive through the replacement of pen and paper by the personal computer and the Internet—and increasingly by more sophisticated and powerful Grid-enabled tools? Most significant for social scientists, is network-enabled research being applied to reconfigure access in ways that complement—or substitute for—direct observation of social processes in ways that mediate rather than amplify social science concerns?

The Dutton and Meyer (2009) survey of researchers found that relatively few believe that e-research poses a risk to the quality of research. Respondents were asked whether they agreed or disagreed with the following statement: "e-research undermines the quality of social science research." Less than 10 percent of the respondents who were disengaged, simply spectators or proponents of e-research, agreed with this statement. Only 21 percent of those identified as opponents of e-research also agreed. However, this study and other recent studies by the authors and their colleagues point to more general themes that may pose risks to the quality of the social sciences as a result of the growth of e–social science.

Three emerging patterns raise particular concerns, although longer-term outcomes will become clearer only when there has been greater experience with applying e-infrastructures in this field. These patterns are summarized in the next three subsections.

Implications for Observations of Social Phenomena

The most significant issue raised by e–social science is whether its tools may increasingly substitute for, rather than complement, direct observation of social phenomena. A range of key innovations in e–social science (see table 6.2) illustrate the degree to which new developments enable more researchers to conduct research in mediated ways. The concern here is that tools that mask the complexities of research and distance researchers from their objects of study will allow for nonexperts to conduct qualitatively inferior research more easily.

Of course, weak research has always been possible. However, consider the ease with which anyone with a vague idea and no training in instrument design can distribute a relatively professional-looking but fundamentally poorly designed online survey. Likewise, if pasting randomly acquired data onto a digital map requires no understanding of either geography or the data, will faulty conclusions flow from such easy exercises? The problem of easy access to digital data was mentioned in interviews with researchers;[14] for example, a humanities scholar noted how submissions to his scholarly society were increasingly computational text-analysis papers that seemed to have been done quickly and with little understanding of the underlying historiography.

Distancing Social Scientists from Their Objects of Study

E-research tends to broaden the scope of observation in ways that require social scientists to be further removed from the phenomena they are studying. For instance, increasingly powerful Webometric tools enable researchers to map the structure of the Web on a global scale. However, researchers would be unlikely to gain a personal sense of the meaning of the links they study, except for a small subset of their observations. Web-based online surveys similarly enable a single researcher to survey the world, but will the researcher have sufficient local, contextual knowledge to understand different cultures' and regions' interpretation of his or her questions?

The "Winner-Takes-All" Effect

Network-enabled research can support a winner-takes-all effect, in the sense of radically centralizing sources of expertise (essay 1.3). However, studies indicate that it is more likely to enable more niche networks of researchers, within which there is a winner-takes-all effect (Caldas, Schroeder, Mesch, et al. 2008). Networks of researchers are likely to be clustered around particular centers, such as those with control over powerful simulation models or around data sets that generate communities of researchers. Thus, smaller proportions of researchers will be building their own simulations or collecting their own data sets. They may thereby lose the tacit knowledge gained from building their own tools and collecting their own data. Not only will researchers then be steps removed from their instruments and data, but the multidisciplinary nature of e-research will mean that their work will probably be more fragmented across the social sciences. These outcomes are already evident in the proliferation of specialized journals.

Minimizing the Risks

These negative outcomes are not established impacts, but risks tied to the potential for e-research to reconfigure access to information and expertise in ways that distance researchers from their subjects rather than helping them to focus on directly observing the most pertinent social phenomena. As a consequence, emphasis should be given to the recruitment and training of social scientists who not only are skilled observers comfortable and gifted in conducting interviews or being participant-observers, but also are attuned to working with the new technologies of the social sciences.

It may seem obvious that well-rounded social scientists should be favored. Yet anec-dotal observations indicate that there is some tendency among e–social science projects to focus on the technology and to include the social science theory and method only as an offshoot of the developers' technological interests—for example, projects that include user engagement at the *end* of the project rather than as an integral aspect of the design process (see chapter 5).

The Social Shaping of Technology and the Social Sciences

The potential risks and opportunities we have outlined indicate the significance of research on the social shaping of technology. This school of research focuses on under-standing how social factors shape the development and impact of innovations in science and technology (Williams and Edge 1996). Efforts in e-infrastructures and e–social science provide focused arenas to explore the social shaping and implications of changes tied to ICTs.[15] From this perspective, the features of emerging technology do not determine the implications of e–social science. Instead, the technology will be shaped by the choices that social scientists and other critical actors, such as funding agencies and research institutions, make within the constraints of their particular con-texts. Increasingly powerful tools might enable researchers to change how they con-duct their research and with what impact on its quality. Nevertheless, the researchers' strategies will be facilitated or constrained by a variety of social, technical, ethical, and legal factors.

Although there have been strong arguments for investigations into the social shap-ing of e-research, it is difficult for social scientists to reflect on their own social roles in relation to technology. As the risks as well as the opportunities of e–social science become more widely understood, the priority placed on ICTs' role in the practices and outcomes of the social sciences should gain a higher priority.

Summary and Conclusion: e–Social Science in the Network Society

If e–social science is understood within the context of the field's use of computing and telecommunications over many years, there is ample evidence of continuity in pat-terns of innovation. Leading-edge innovations in e-research are moving into the social sciences, primarily through a process of "bottom-up" development that has charac-terized e-research innovation in this field over the decades. However, the benefits of e-research will not be fully realized within the social sciences without major efforts to demonstrate the new tools' potential to build infrastructures than enable bottom-up innovation and to facilitate use by nontechnical experts. Moreover, there are risks in the uneven up-take of e–social science—across methods, between academia and the commercial world, and between countries and regions around the globe.

Understanding the Limits and Potential of e–Social Science

Given its still early stages of development, e–social science has been applied in a limited number of ways, such as in analysis, simulation, and visualization. Understanding why these areas are being targeted more than others might contribute to understanding the limits on the use of these tools and the patterns of awareness of these applications across the social sciences as a whole. However, early use and interest in e–social science appears to span the methodological landscape, supported by innovation from individual social scientists.

E–social science has the potential not simply to gain access to global data, such as through Webometrics and online surveys, but also to extend worldwide access to locally developed Grid-enabled tools and data sets. For example, the availability of social data is a major limitation on e–social science in China (essay 6.2). Moreover, the constraints on global access to e-research are formidable in the less-developed nations and regions (chapter 12).

For all of these reasons tied to the diffusion of innovations, most social research on e-research has been focused on the factors constraining the adoption of the new tools that are being made available. However, there is much evidence to show that many social scientists have embedded the innovations of e-research tools into almost every phase of their social research processes. This holds for every subfield, including survey researchers, experimentalists, modelers, qualitative participant observation, and ethnographic and interpretative studies. Moreover, the exploratory surveys discussed in this chapter suggest that there is a core constituency of social scientists who are aware of and interested in applying new e-research tools—albeit a core that is focused among the cohorts of more recent graduates.

Key e–Social Science Directions

It is important to continue tracking the social shaping of emerging e–social science to help understand the frequent needless delays in innovation. However, the constraints on innovation might be less significant than the implications of its development for the role of social scientists and outcomes for social science research. More attention should also be given to the role of e–social science in reshaping the social scientist's work.[16] Will social scientists develop as networked artisans or specialist knowledge workers? Research in e–social science has most often focused on the role of ICTs in supporting collaboration (Olson, Zimmerman, and Bos 2008), but collaboration comes in many forms and sizes. The future might well accommodate many potential roles in the diverse ways that networked social scientists approach e-research, particularly if appropriate infrastructures are available to support bottom-up innovation and collaborative network organizations formed by the researchers.

Social scientists need to develop skills and experience in working with e-research tools, and product developers need to create more usable software and systems for e-research applications in general and for e–social science in particular. Not to make progress on both of these fronts will mean that social science users will be dependent on technology-oriented specialists as a gateway to these tools, and the specialists will be limited to collaborating with their counterparts elsewhere rather than with their users.

E-research is creating a greater multiplicity of general and specialized roles. It is networking true artisans of their craft, while also empowering a new set of specialists with the skills to use and exploit the new tools of e-research. However, social scientists' changing roles need to be tracked over time. The piecemeal use of ICTs within specific stages of research has limited the degree to which this process can be reconfigured to take full advantage of the new tools. As the longer-range implications for the nature of work—how social scientists do what they do—unfold in the coming years, it is important that trends in research practices and engagement with e-research be tracked over time.

In parallel, there is reason for concern about the potential for e–social science to virtualize research, moving researchers farther from the subjects of their inquiry. The most significant focus for research might be on the implications of e–social science for the excellence of research—its creativity, productivity, reliability, and validity. Therefore, it is equally important to place renewed emphasis on recruiting and training observers with the traditional skills of the interviewer or participant-observer. The more mediated e-research becomes, the more researchers may need to be grounded in real-life observation.[17]

This chapter has not and cannot forecast the long-term implications of e–social science. Rather, it has sought to identify critical choices facing social scientists in how they will use the capacities provided by networks. There are serious issues concerning the degree to which e-research will reinforce and enhance an increasing range of divides among social scientists. Most important, will social scientists increasingly substitute mediated for direct observation or use networks in ways that enable the better selection and direct observation of major social phenomena? The risk of e-research is not that social scientists will quit going to the library, but that they will quit going into the field.

Notes

1. The first Universal Automatic Computer (UNIVAC I) was delivered on 31 March 1951 to the U.S. Census Bureau (Ceruzzi, 2003:27).

2. SPSS, formally known as the Statistical Package for the Social Sciences, was itself the result of demand-driven, bottom-up innovation created by then Stanford University Ph.D. candidate Norman Nie and colleagues in response to the frustration of using tools built for biologists rather than social scientists (see http://www.spss.com/corpinfo/history.htm).

3. Computer-based teleconferencing systems were first developed to support hearing-impaired individuals, but were also aimed at distributed problem solving by experts in critical emergencies (Hiltz and Turoff 1978).

4. Journals such as the *Social Science Computer Review* published reviews of new software for social scientists, most often written by the researchers (see http://faculty.chass.ncsu.edu/garson/SSCORE//info.htm).

5. Prior to the Industrial Revolution, the spinning jenny and handloom allowed for the development of cottage industries centered on textile production. With these relatively small devices, a household could take wool from sheep raised on its property, turn it into yarn, and produce a finished product in house.

6. This support is illustrated by the publication of a handbook with this focus (Fielding, Lee, and Blank 2008).

7. See http://www.nsf.gov/funding/pgm_summ.jsp?pims_id=13553&org=SBE.

8. A number of "scoping studies" informed this initiative, including Anderson 2003; Cole, Schurer, Beedham, et al. 2003; Fielding 2003; and Woolgar 2003.

9. Information about the Access Grid is available at http://www.accessgrid.org/.

10. See http://www.gapminder.org/.

11. The survey and its methods and sampling strategy are provided in more detail in Dutton and Meyer 2009 and in Meyer and Dutton 2009.

12. Further support for this pattern of bottom-up versus top-down innovation in the social sciences is provided in Pearce 2008.

13. Roger Burrows posed this possibility while on an expert panel on social science in e-society at the Tenth Anniversary Symposium of Information, Communication & Society, University of York, UK, 21 September 2006.

14. Conducted as part of the Oxford e–Social Science (OeSS) Project, a node within NCeSS focused on the social shaping of e-sciences.

15. This was the focus of the OeSS Project within NCeSS. A number of other related projects also focused on this issue within NCeSS, such as one entitled "Entangled Data" conducted at Essex University, UK (Procter, Batty, Birkin, et al. 2006).

16. As social scientists simultaneously studying e-research and engaged in e-research initiatives, we are particularly sensitive to the need for social scientists to apply theory and research on the social shaping of technology in a reflexive way, considering their own practices.

17. In other social contexts, this theme was captured well by the U.K. Economic and Social Research Council program on virtual society, specifically in Steve Woolgar's (2002) "rules of virtuality." It is also reinforced by a history of empirical research on the degree to which online

communication tends to be positively associated with face-to-face, offline communication (Dutton 1999).

References

Anderson, A. 2003. "Human-centred design and grid technologies." Unpublished paper. Economic and Social Research Council, Swindon, UK.

Barjak, F., J. Lane, Z. Kertcher, M. Poschen, R. Procter, and S. Robinson. 2008. "Case studies of e-infrastructure adoption." Paper presented at the Fourth International Conference on e–Social Science, Manchester, UK, 19 June.

Barjak, F., G. Wiegand, J. Lane, M. Poschen, R. Procter, and S. Robinson. 2007. "Accelerating transition to virtual research organization in social science (AVROSS)." Paper presented at the Third International Conference on e–Social Science, University of Michigan, October. Available at: http://ess.si.umich.edu/papers/paper141.pdf.

Borgman, C. L. 2007. *Scholarship in the digital age: Information, infrastructure, and the Internet.* Cambridge, MA: MIT Press.

Caldas, A., R. Schroeder, G. S. Mesch, and W. H. Dutton. 2008. "Patterns of information search and access on the World Wide Web: Democratizing expertise or creating new hierarchies." *Journal of Computer-Mediated Communication 13*:769–793.

Carr, N. 2008. *The big switch: Rewiring the world, from Edison to Google.* New York: W. W. Norton.

Ceruzzi, P. E. 2003. *A history of modern computing.* 2d ed. Cambridge, MA: MIT Press.

Cole, K., K. Schurer, H. Beedham, and T. Hewitt. 2003. "Grid enabling quantitative social science datasets: A scoping study." Unpublished paper. Economic and Social Research Council, Swindon, UK.

Crouchley, R., B. Dutton, R. Allan, R. Procter, and M. Daw. 2007. "Missing e-infrastructure: Exploring scenarios, use cases, and reference models for shaping e-research." Paper presented at a workshop at the National Centre for e–Social Science, University of Manchester, UK, 15–16 January.

Dutton, W. H. 1999. *Society on the line.* Oxford, UK: Oxford University Press.

Dutton, W. H. 2008. "The wisdom of collaborative network organizations: Capturing the value of networked individuals." *Prometheus 26* (3):211–230.

Dutton, W. H., and E. Meyer. 2009. *Experience with new tools and infrastructures of research: An exploratory study of distance from and attitudes toward e-research. Prometheus 27* (3):223–238.

Dutton, W. H., and A. Shepherd. 2006. "Trust in the Internet as an experience technology." *Information, Communication, & Society 9* (4):433–451.

Fielding, N. 2003. "Qualitative research and e–social science: Appraising the potential." Unpublished paper, Economic and Social Research Council, Swindon, UK.

Fielding, N., R. M. Lee, and G. Blank, eds. 2008. *The Sage handbook of online research methods*. Thousand Oaks, CA: Sage.

Halfpenny, P., R. Procter, Y. Lin, and A. Voss. 2009. "Developing the UK e–Social Science Research Program." In *e-Research: Transformation in scholarly practice*, ed. N. Jankowski. New York: Routledge, 73–90.

Hey, T., and A. Trefethen. 2008. "E-science, cyberinfrastructure, and scholarly communication." In *Scientific collaboration on the Internet*, ed. G. M. Olson, A. Zimmerman, and N. Bos. Cambridge, MA: MIT Press, 15–31.

Hiltz, R. S., and M. Turoff. 1978. *The network nation*. Reading, MA: Addison-Wesley.

Holt, R. T., and J. E. Turner. 1974. "The scholar as artisan." *Policy Science 5* (3):257–270.

MacKenzie, D. 1999. "The certainty trough." In *Society on the line*, ed. W. H. Dutton. Oxford, UK: Oxford University Press, 43–46.

Meyer, E. T., and W. H. Dutton. 2009. *Top-down e-infrastructure meets bottom-up research innovation: The social shaping of e-research. Prometheus 27* (3):239–250.

Meyer, E. T., H. W. Park, and R. Schroeder. 2009. "Mapping global e-research: Scientometrics and webometrics." Paper presented at the 5th International Conference on e-Social Science, Cologne, June. Manchester: National Centre for e-Social Science.

Olson, G. M., A. Zimmerman, and N. Bos, eds. 2008. *Scientific collaboration on the Internet*. Cambridge, MA: MIT Press.

Pearce, N. 2008. "Report on ICT survey: The uptake and use of information and communication technologies by Lancaster University researchers." Unpublished manuscript for the Centre for e-Science, Lancaster University, UK.

Procter, R., M. Batty, M. Birkin, R. Crouchley, W. Dutton, P. Edwards, M. Fraser, P. Halfpenny, and T. Rodden. 2006. "The National Centre for e–Social Science." In *Proceedings of the UK e-Science All Hands Meeting, AHM'06, National e-Science Centre (NeSC), September 2006*. Edinburgh: National Centre for e-Social Science, 542–549.

Sabel, C., and J. Zeitlin. 1985. "Historical alternatives to mass production: Politics, markets, and technology in nineteenth century industrialization." *Past Present 108* (1):133–176.

Schroeder, R., and J. Fry. 2007. "Social science approaches to e-science: Framing an agenda." *Journal of Computer-Mediated Communication 12* (2). Available at http://jcmc.indiana.edu/vol12/issue2/schroeder.html.

Scott, S. V., and W. Venters. 2006. *The practice of e-science and e–social science: Method, theory, and matter*. Working Paper Series, Department of Management, Information Systems Group. London: London School of Economics and Political Science.

Williams, R., and D. Edge. 1996. "Social shaping of technology." In *Information and communication technologies—visions and realities*, ed. W. H. Dutton. Oxford, UK: Oxford University Press, 53–67.

Woolgar, S. 2002. "Five rules of virtuality." In *Virtual society? Technology, cyberbole, reality*, ed. S. Woolgar. Oxford, UK: Oxford University Press, 1–22.

Woolgar, S. 2003. *Social shaping perspectives on e-science and e–social science: The case for research support.* A consultative study for the Economic and Social Research Council. Available at: http://www.ncess.ac.uk/docs/social_shaping_perspectives.pdf.

Wuchty, S., B. F. Jones, and B. Uzzi. 2007. "The increasing dominance of teams in production of knowledge." Science 316:1036–1039.

6.1 An e-Infrastructure for the Social Sciences

Rob Procter

Realizing the Full Potential of Digital Social Science Data Resources

Since the 1960s, funding bodies in many parts of the world have invested heavily in research resources for the social sciences and, in particular, in the provision of a data infrastructure based on census and other survey-based collections. These resources collectively play a vital role in providing the evidence base for social science research. For some time, however, there have been concerns that they are not being used to their full potential. These concerns have been magnified with the proliferation of new sources of social data.

New sources of social data are distinctive in that they are "naturally occurring" and "born digital"—that is, captured at source in digital form and continuously updated by people's everyday activities. Examples include administrative data, such as employment and education records; transactional data, such as purchases; logs of mobile phone messages and emails; and online material from Web sites, blogs, and forums. The sheer volume and heterogeneity of these new sources of social data makes their harnessing for research a major challenge. The World Wide Web archive, for example, in 2007 contained more than 55 billion Web pages or 2 petabytes (2×10^{15}) of data and was growing at the rate of 20 terabytes (20×10^{12}) per month.

The social science research community has realized that improving the reuse of existing data and exploiting this deluge of new data will be impossible without significant investment in research infrastructure that is capable of making data easier to discover, access, and analyze.[1] At the same time, social science research priorities increasingly call for collaboration across traditional disciplinary boundaries; their complexity and scale therefore demands more powerful research tools. These are the kinds of challenges that e-infrastructure was created to address.

Overcoming Barriers to Efficient and Effective Explorations of the "Data Deluge"

A profusion of different user and technical interfaces has made it difficult to retrieve and combine data sets from multiple sources when seeking to undertake more complex forms of analysis. These multiple interfaces also act as a barrier to interdisciplinary working and to automating complex analyses that must be rerun periodically (e.g., whenever a particular data set is updated). Integration of data from different sources is hampered by lack of harmonization among data-collection instruments. As sources of social data grow and proliferate, the problem of resource description becomes more acute, and yet solving it remains critical to data discovery and use.

Powerful new computationally based analysis tools will be essential if researchers are to harness the mass of varied digital social data and analyze them in ways that provide a better understanding of complex and dynamic social and economic processes in finer detail and with greater precision. Statistical modeling and simulation is a well-established social science research tool, but models will need to be more complex and will need much more computing power. The application of data- and text-mining techniques to social and economic data will be critical in exploiting new large-scale data resources such as transactional data and the Web.

Solving complex problems often involves multiple steps and iterations, where the output of one step is used as the input in the next. Managing these steps manually is potentially difficult, and performing the data integration and modeling using desktop personal computer tools may be very time consuming.

E-research has the potential to provide ways for social scientists to overcome to these barriers. For instance, it can:

• Make available better tools for: describing data; discovering and accessing data; cleaning data; making access to sensitive personal data simpler and more convenient while maintaining confidentiality; combining data sets more easily; and facilitating secondary analysis.
• Enable researchers to access scalable computing power on demand for computational-intensive applications such as statistical modeling, simulation, and data mining.
• Provide tools that enable researchers to compose research work flows as sequences of multiple analytical steps using combinations of different data sources and tools, execute them (semi)automatically, save them for reuse, and share them with collaborators.
• Bring opportunities to use powerful, new analytical tools such as data mining, text mining, and social network analysis to extract knowledge from large-scale data sets.
• Create the potential to deliver integrated support for the complete research life cycle, beginning with literature searches and reviews, through analysis and discussion of results to the writing and publishing of papers.

Building an e-Infrastructure for the Social Sciences

Creating an e-infrastructure for the social sciences raises a wide range of technical and nontechnical problems that will need to be addressed. For instance, new tools

are required to expedite the process of creating the metadata necessary to ensure that data resources can be more easily discovered and reused. Work is needed to develop and refine both research environments and persistent and secure digital workspaces based on familiar, easy-to-use browser-style interfaces. These workspaces should provide a single authentication process through which users can discover and gain access to whatever resources (data, tools, and services) they need, create work flows to carry out their analyses, and work in collaboration with colleagues wherever they may be. Finally, institutional and cultural barriers to the adoption and future sustainability of e-infrastructure need to be understood and addressed.

An example of an attempt to establish such an e-infrastructure for the social sciences is the U.K. National Centre for e–Social Science (NCeSS).[2] Its aims are broadly similar to other initiatives in this field:

• Develop and make available new, powerful, easy-to-use research tools and services that will reduce the effort needed to discover, integrate, and reuse data sets; simplify the way in which current research is carried out; and stimulate the development of new kinds of research methods.
• Make available research demonstrators to illustrate the potential of e-infrastructure in the social sciences and promote its wider adoption through targeted outreach and awareness raising.
• Enhance understanding of issues around resource discovery, data access, security, and usability by providing a test bed for the development of metadata and service registries, tools for user authorization and authentication, and collaborative research environments.
• Help social researchers make informed choices from an increasing range of technical options in what is a rapidly changing e-research landscape.
• Increase capacity building within the social science research community by training researchers in new methods and developing technical expertise.
• Lay the foundations for an integrated strategy for the future development and sustainability of e-infrastructure, and produce a road map that identifies the human, technical, and financial resources required.

Notes

1. For instance, in 2006 the U.K. Economic and Social Research Council initiated a program of work to develop a national data strategy that aims to create a data infrastructure capable of delivering all the data necessary to address current and future research needs in the social sciences (see http://www.esrc.ac.uk/ESRCInfoCentre/NDS/).

2. See http://www.ncess.ac.uk/.

6.2 Chinese e–Social Science: A Low-End Approach

Jonathan J. H. Zhu and Xiaoming Li

The Chinese Social Science Data Bottleneck

Chinese scholars are relative latecomers to the arena of e–social science. As many research articles and other publications produced by pioneering teams have indicated, e–social science researchers in Europe and North America have focused on the use of Grid computing in this field, which is indeed a powerful tool for social scientists to test complex models or collaborate online. The underlying assumption is that the relevant data are already in place; Grid computing provides the necessary means to process these data.

This "high-end" approach may bring much excitement and promise, but what happens if there are simply no data available in the first place? In our view, lack of data is the biggest bottleneck for social scientists in China (and perhaps in other developing countries), where there is no tradition of archiving or sharing social science data. The rapid diffusion and widespread adoption of the Internet in China and elsewhere, however, has fortunately made it possible for social scientists in these developing regions to collect data from open and (mostly) free online sources, such as Web pages, discussion boards, blogs, and online surveys. What they most need, therefore, are simple and affordable tools to collect Web-based data, much of which can be accomplished by using technologies less expensive than Grid computing (Li and Zhu 2006).

Developing Lower-End e–Social Science Tools

Given this context, we have organized and run a Chinese e–social science program that has the aim of developing low-budget tools for use by Chinese social scientists to collect, process, and disseminate online data. The first tool under development is a simple and affordable content-analysis system for Web pages in the Chinese language, called the e–Content Analysis Tool (e-CAT). To make it affordable, a limited amount of manpower (about three months of a midlevel computer programmer's time) was invested in developing this simple "metasearch" engine.

E-CAT works in the following way (see also Zhu and Li 2007). The user enters a query (e.g., a key word, phrase, sentence, etc.) into the system. This query is forwarded to major search engines with Chinese-language capabilities, including Google, Baidu, and Soguo. Once the search results are returned, e-CAT filters (often many) duplicated pages. It extrapolates from the cleaned pages those words pertaining to the so-called five W questions (who, where, when, what, and why); these words include terms such as named entities (individuals, institutions, locations, etc.), time, and events.

The processed data are provided to the user in several formats in an increasingly sophisticated order: univariate lists of word frequency organized by each of the five Ws; bivariate cross-tabulations of the word frequencies; and raw data sets of all extrapolated words, with each relevant Web page as the unit of analysis. The research user, depending on his or her purposes and skills, can simply examine the lists or cross-tabulations or perform sophisticated analyses of the raw data using cluster analysis, correspondence analysis, network analysis, or other means.

Training for Use of Free Online Services

We are fully aware of the gap between limited resources in China and the soaring demands from Chinese social scientists. One solution is to help train them to make effective use of free online services provided by the commercial sector. In the Chinese context, two categories of free services are particularly relevant to and useful for social scientists:

1. Aggregated content/user data from search engines, including a count of query words that users input into search engines (which can be considered a "quasi–public opinion polling" series), ranking of "hot words" extrapolated from Web pages, and hyperlinks among Web pages.
2. Online questionnaires from Web hosting sites, which allow users to design fairly sophisticated questionnaires, deploy them online, and download the completed data for in-depth analysis.

Many Chinese social scientists are not aware of the free tools; others do not know how to make use of them. Since 2006, we have therefore organized annual workshops for scholars and graduate students to provide hands-on training on how to utilize online resources for research. In one workshop, students from thirty institutions across the country carried out six online surveys on a variety of research topics. Within a week, at virtually no cost, they were able to design, implement, and analyze surveys with sample sizes varying from two hundred to eight hundred. After taking another workshop, one young scholar applied the learned skills to a large-scale study of the formation process of opinion leaders in a popular online forum.

Platforms for Data Sharing

We are building on the foundations outlined here by focusing on moving forward with technological platforms for data sharing among Chinese social scientists and, in the long run, between Chinese social scientists and their counterparts abroad. Although lack of data has been a primary bottleneck for Chinese social science research, medium- or large-scale data have been becoming gradually more common, largely because of a rapid increase in government funding for social research. However, almost all the data have remained within the hands of the original collectors.

Of the various obstacles to data sharing we are addressing, a critical one is the absence of convenient and secure mechanisms to protect the integrity of the data and the interests of the data owner. This impediment can be minimized, if not completely removed, by thoughtfully designed technological platforms. These platforms should provide the owners with full control over how the data are shared (e.g., overall summary statistics, aggregated data at the group level, or data of original form at the individual level). In addition, they should allow both owners and users to operate with maximum ease and flexibility. Survey Documentation and Analysis,[1] a Web-based tool developed by researchers at the University of California at Berkeley, offers a good pointer in this direction. In order to foster greater data sharing, we are creating more general tools to accommodate a wide range of types of data and formats.

Acknowledgments

The project has been funded in part by Hong Kong Research Grants Council Competitive Earmarked Research Grant (CityU/1456–06H), City University of Hong Kong Strategic Research Grant (7001882), and National Science Foundation of China Grant no. 60773162.

Note

1. For more on Survey Documentation and Analysis, see http://cases.berkeley.edu/sda.html.

References

Li, X. M., and J. J. H. Zhu. 2006. "Let social sciences ride on the IT bullet train" (in Chinese). *Communications of the Chinese Computer Federation 2* (2):43–46.

Zhu, J. J. H., and X. M. Li. 2007. "An easy and affordable tool for e–social science research: e-CAT" (in Chinese). *Communications of the Chinese Computer Federation 3* (4):39–43.

7 Institutional Infrastructures for Global Research Networks in the Public Sector

Paul A. David and Michael Spence

e-Science Visions and the Promise of Worldwide Research

This book describes the potential of e-research to help form unprecedented connections among scientists as well as between researchers and the scientific information, data, computational services, and instruments that are being made accessible to them via a new generation of information and communication infrastructures supporting all stages of the research process (Foster and Kesselman 2001; see also chapter 2). This process was conceptually formulated and technologically implemented in the "collaboratory" and "virtual laboratory" demonstrations undertaken by U.S. scientists in the late 1980s and received further impetus and new nomenclature from the U.K.'s "e-science" initiative at the start of this century. It is now beginning to enable much greater direct and shared access to more widely distributed computing resources than previously was possible, stirring hopes of future scientific breakthroughs that will provide more powerful means of addressing pressing global problems.

The term *e-science* came into increasing application in British scientific circles after 2001, when the U.K. e-Science Programme was launched.[1] At the time, John Taylor, then the director of the U.K. Research Councils, said e-science is "about global collaboration in key areas of science and the next generation of infrastructure that will enable it" (Taylor 2001).[2] Future collaborative scientific enterprises were envisaged as requiring access to very extensive data collections, very large-scale computing resources, and high-performance visualization of research data and analysis of results by members of geographically distributed research teams.

This conceptualization resonated with an infrastructure-building program whose rationale stressed the connections between international efforts to provide Grid services for ubiquitous computing and the e-Science Programme's initial focus on developing generic Grid middleware platforms (e.g., Hey and Trefethen 2002).[3] A major driving force behind its Core Programme was the potential for these technological advances to support new and more fruitful levels of collaborative activity in science and engineering and, subsequently, other domains.[4]

After 2006, focused discussion and clear indicators of direction relating to public funding for electronic network infrastructure and tools for activating and enhancing global collaborations among researchers became less frequent in U.K. government publications. The scope of the existing e-Science Programme was broadened (e.g., see U.K. Office of Science and Innovation 2007) and became more loosely associated with "the systematic development of research methods that exploit advanced computational thinking," according to the government's e-science envoy Professor Malcolm Atkinson. The methods in question afforded researchers' access to resources held on widely dispersed computers "as though they were on their own desktops."[5] In contrast to Taylor's definition, Atkinson's view marks an evolution in Britain's e-science efforts away from its initial emphasis on direct collaboration toward more passive, asynchronous collaboration. The new formulation significantly shifted near-term attention toward connecting individual researchers with data and information resources, and away from the previous visions of "virtual laboratories" and "virtual research communities."[6]

Science and technology policy leaders acquainted with these technological developments continue to anticipate that deploying them will eventually have transformative effects on the organization and conduct of "knowledge work," thereby mobilizing global collaborations for scientific and engineering research. In the United States, a much larger and most likely more sustained initiative to realize that goal took up the torch as it was being relinquished by the U.K. government.[7]

A 2003 report by a distinguished advisory panel to the Directorate of Computer and Information System Engineering of the U.S. National Science Foundation (NSF) explained why the potential to revolutionize science and engineering provided the rationale for a major programmatic commitment by the foundation. This panel's report (Atkins, Koegemeier, Feldman, et al. 2003) envisaged that the enhanced computer and network technologies supporting such collaborative connections would form a vital infrastructure, dubbed the "cyberinfrastructure." Its effects were intended to be analogous to the historical impacts of superhighways, electric power grids, and other physical infrastructures in raising the productivity of conventional work. In response to this report, the NSF quickly established the Office of Cyberinfrastructure. It tasked multidisciplinary, cross-foundational teams to elaborate further a "vision" that would guide the NSF's projected billion-dollar program of cyberinfrastructure investments.

The Sociotechnical Nature of Research Transformations
During the period from 2005 to 2007, the NSF cyberinfrastructure vision was articulated and adopted, targeting four overlapping and complementary infrastructure-development domains for related projects: high-performance computing; data, data analysis, and visualization; cyber services and virtual organizations; and learning and workforce development. As had been the case when the U.K. e-Science Programme

was first launched, the germinal idea and animating expectation remained the conviction that the solution of essentially technical problems associated with the design and engineering of an advanced cyberinfrastructure would unleash new scientific capabilities—that it would eventually bear fruit in key discoveries, such as improved drug designs, deeper understanding of fundamental physical principles, and more detailed environmental models.

With the passage of time, however, has come increasingly explicit acknowledgment that such gains, were they to materialize, would most likely be produced by *the combined effects of social and technical transformations*. For example, in a preface to the 2007 NSF report on its cyberinfrastructure vision, NSF director Arhen L. Bement writes less of network engineering than of new cultural formations:

At the heart of the cyberinfrastructure vision is the development of a cultural community that supports peer-to-peer collaboration and new modes of education based upon broad and open access to leadership computing; data and information resources; online instruments and observatories; and visualization and collaboration services. Cyberinfrastructure enables distributed knowledge communities that collaborate and communicate across disciplines, distances and cultures . . . becoming virtual organizations that transcend geographic and institutional boundaries. (U.S. NSF Cyberinfrastructure Council 2007:i)

Yet, as one pursues the specifics of the cyberinfrastructure vision, even in the NSF document's chapter on "virtual organizations," the original, primarily technical conceptualization of the promise and the challenge resurfaces quite clearly.[8] The overriding theme is that these new social formations will be called forth more or less automatically by the empowering features of the new collaboration technologies and data resources that are being promised to geographically distributed researchers. One of the less technically detailed, but nonetheless emblematic, expressions of that promise is:

The convergence of information, Grid, and networking technologies with contemporary communications now enables science and engineering communities to pursue their research and learning goals in real-time and without regard to geography. . . . [T]he creation of end-to-end cyberinfrastructure [CI] systems—comprehensive networked resources—by groups of individuals with common interests is permitting the establishment of Virtual Organizations (VOs) that are revolutionizing the conduct of science and engineering research and education. . . . These CI systems provide shared access to centralized or distributed resources and services, often in real-time. Such virtual organizations supporting distributed communities go by numerous names: collaboratory, co-laboratory, Grid community, science gateway, science portal, and others. (U.S. NSF Cyberinfrastructure Council 2007:32)

One might be quite confident about the pace and scope of future technical advances in computing that will follow from the dynamics of "Moore's law,"[9] at least in the near future, and therefore in the continuing descent of the price–performance ratio of microprocessors and the consequent expansion of inexpensive digital memory and bandwidth. Novel and more powerful technological systems can be engineered on those foundations, and there is now a widely shared commitment to undertake the funding needed to create ubiquitously accessible computation facilities of a Grid-enabled cyberinfrastructure. Fortunately, however, even among the most enthusiastic advocates of public funding for this essentially technological enterprise, it is increasingly acknowledged that a profound gap may exist between the resulting "raw" performance of a system (e.g., bandwidth, storage capacity, processor speed, interconnection protocols) and the realized performance based on the "usability" properties of the constituent system designs.[10] Indeed, the usability gap is not the only reality gap that can significantly limit the transformational potential of cyberinfrastructure investments, as the following subsections endeavor to make clear.

Realities That Intervene between Promises and Their Fulfillment

Achieving the aims and aspirations of the foregoing e-science and cyberinfrastructure visions involves more than just a matter of breakthroughs in hardware or software engineering, or of system design improvements to provide readily usable tools to individual researchers and their organizations—however challenging such tasks may be. Providing an enhanced infrastructure to support scientific collaborations is not just about getting the computing science right; it is also about getting the social science right. If global research networks are to deliver the fruit that they promise, they need effective institutional infrastructures.

Take the example of the Grid-based collaborative U.K. e-Science Diagnostic Mammography National Database (eDiaMoND) pilot project to build a national database of mammographic images that would pool and distribute information on breast cancer treatment (see chapter 2 and essay 7.1). Key aims were to use this database to enable early screening and diagnosis, to provide medical professionals with tools and information to treat the disease, and to give patients, physicians, and hospitals fast access to a vast database of digital mammogram images. A key expectation was that it would help reduce the rate of false-positive diagnosis and overcome problems created by inconsistent mammogram image formats and lost X rays.[11]

This undertaking was managed by the University of Oxford Computing Laboratory and involved the University of Oxford Engineering Department, two commercial partners (IBM and Mirada Solutions), and four public hospitals and the universities to which they were attached (three in England and one in Scotland). It was funded by the U.K. Engineering and Physical Sciences Research Council, the U.K. Department of Trade and Industry, and an IBM Sur Grant. The project was based on a head contract between the University of Oxford, IBM, and Mirada Solutions, and a series of letters of agreement with partner universities. The legal agreements did not extend directly to the hospitals. Their involvement was covered by agreements with research and development departments within the relevant hospital trusts.

From an organizational viewpoint, this project can be deemed to have been relatively straightforward in three respects:

1. Many of the parties and regulatory bodies were willing to forego dispute over potentially contentious issues because the project was a two-year trial.
2. The project was national rather than international.
3. Because the project was to construct a database and the platform to support that database, it was seen to be one of the more institutionally simple of the categories of e-science project.

This proof-of-concept project may have been far from the most complex technological and organizational effort in building e-research infrastructure, but its designers faced an imposing assortment of challenges. For instance, it was not always clear as the project was put together that the institutional obstacles it faced would be overcome, and many crucial issues remained unresolved. It also had to cope with differences between England and Scotland in the policies related to government health and information technology services. Permission to use mammographic images had to be obtained from the ethics committees of each of the relevant hospitals and from the U.K. Medical Research Ethics Committee. Questions about the extent of patient consent for the use of images would need to be reexamined if more family information were to be linked to images in the future.

Attitudes varied among the partners with regard to the ownership of the images created and used in the project. The question of who owned the rights in the standardized images database as a whole was one of the main issues left unresolved.[12] Other issues concerned the impact of the norms of competition law on the development of the library and the liability for any aspect of the database that might give rise to misdiagnosis were it to be used clinically. Inappropriate institutional arrangements made in such areas might have as damaging consequences for e-research projects as any technical obstacles to progress.

The Critical Challenge of Designing Institutional Infrastructures

One of the many ways in which the experience of the eDiaMoND project is emblematic of wider e-research challenges is its important demonstration that the design of institutional infrastructures is so critical that it may be even more difficult than the engineering of technical infrastructures for the next generation of collaborative science. We would therefore argue that projects involving significant public-sector funding should set the standard for the supposedly "softer" institutional parts of cyberinfrastructures.

Public-funding bodies must ensure not only that good science is done, but that the institutional context in which it is carried out maximizes the social payoffs from the bodies' investments in the pursuit of reliable knowledge. Funding agencies that take seriously their role in the promotion of collaborative public science and the equipping of research communities for that purpose also need to accept that they have a role in the promotion of the best institutional designs and procedures if the activities they support are to perform effectively. Although this argument may sound like common sense, it is not at all easy to set a standard for effective institutional infrastructures in e-research. This task may seem to be so daunting that some funding agencies might well be tempted to leave it alone, trusting that the new technology itself will induce the emergence of the right institutional arrangements. This sort of technological determinist thinking, however, is mistaken (as chapter 1 emphasizes) in taking social and institutional arrangements to be passive, adapting to rather than actively shaping development and use of technological innovations. Instead, we should look at the threefold nature of the institutional design challenge:

1. There is considerable diversity in the types of e-research projects.
2. There is considerable variety in the social contexts in which these projects are undertaken.
3. Any appropriate infrastructure needs to be sufficiently certain and universal in its application, while also being flexible and able enough to respond to the challenges of particular projects.

Each of these "realities" of the context in which modern science is conducted merits separate consideration before a possible way forward can be proposed, as examined in the following three subsections.[13]

The Realities of the Varieties of e-Research Projects

The terms *e-science* and especially *e-research*—the newer, more encompassing label— are being applied liberally to network-enabled research rather than being restricted to those activities that are supported by a conjunction of ubiquitous computational resources and specific "collaboratory" technologies.[14] For present purposes, however, it is useful to distinguish among a broad set of collaborative research projects that can benefit from the support of digital networks. Such distinctions can be made on the basis of the main forms of interchanges they involve among researchers, rather than by reference to the particular digital information tools and services they might employ.

A proposed taxonomy of e-science projects developed on this principle has been found to be of value as a way both to fix ideas and to organize some available data on the characteristics of projects with labels such as *e-science*, *virtual laboratory*, and *collaboratory* (den Besten and David 2008a, 2008b).[15] Table 7.1 summarizes elements of this taxonomy of relevance here.

Table 7.1

A Taxonomy of e-Science Projects

Type	Key Characteristic
Community-centric	Projects bringing together researchers for synchronous or asynchronous information exchanges
Data-centric	Projects providing accessible stores of data drawn from different sources and the ability to edit and annotate them
Computation-centric	Projects providing high-performance computing capabilities, either by using servers that access supercomputers and parallel computing clusters or by making it possible for collaborators to organize peer-to-peer sharing of computation capacity
Interaction-centric	Projects enabling applications that involve real-time interactions among two or more participants for decision making, visualization, or the continuous control of instruments

Sources: den Besten and David 2008a, 2008b.

On the basis of table 7.1, activities belonging to the synchronous community-centric and the interaction-centric categories could be deemed to come closest to realizing the ambitions of those endeavoring to build an infrastructure for collaborative e-science. Yet it is precisely these types of projects that are most complex to organize in institutional terms, and they therefore are also likely to pose the most formidable technical challenges for the engineering of digital network middleware platforms and collaboration tools that meet the requirements of e-researchers who undertake such projects.

A sense of the size of the gap between the promise and the reality emerged clearly when this approach was applied to classify the twenty-three pilot projects funded by the U.K. e-Science Core Programme to develop middleware for the coming Grid environment. Among the twenty-three pilot projects examined in David and Spence 2003, only two featured middleware support for interaction-centric activities, and one of these projects was restricted to dyadic interactions. The data-centric branch of the taxonomic tree emerged as far and away the most densely populated, holding more than two-thirds (sixteen) of all the projects.[16] This result may be contrasted with the more uniform distribution found when the same taxonomic exercise was repeated for the much smaller number of pioneer collaboratory projects organized under public-funding programs in the United States during the late 1980s and early 1990s. The difference reflects in part the UK e-Science Programme's focus on the creation of middleware platforms and software tools, and in part the greater centrality of the roles that digital databases increasingly have come to occupy in the work of science and engineering communities.

Nevertheless, a suspicion remains that consideration of the greater administrative complexities that would have to be overcome in order to organize thoroughly interactive modes of collaboration among research groups located at various institutions within the United Kingdom has exerted some influence on the profile of the pilot project sample. This suspicion is further reinforced by the observation that the number of distinct component products among the "deliverables" of these e-science projects is often more or less the same as the number of "partnering" organizations. The natural supposition is that projects forming the vanguard of the e-science movement tended to be organized in ways that partitioned their tasks among the collaborating parties in order to minimize cross-institutional interaction and joint responsibilities. This tendency may reflect an extreme division of labor along the lines of specialized expertise, but it would be surprising if such specialization ran strictly along university lines and thereby obviated the need to form teams by mixing researchers from different institutions. If the reality is masked by the outward appearances of the projects' organization, one must again suspect that the latter was dictated by administrative considerations at the level of the host institutions.

As support for the foregoing interpretive speculations, it is relevant to observe that commercial developers of software for Grid services have focused their efforts on intra-organizational applications. They have marketed their "commercial off-the-shelf" (COTS) software packages primarily as tools that will yield significant cost savings through the dependable sharing of the geographically dispersed and heterogeneous computer clusters and databases that are under the buyer's control. The domain of commercially provided software tools for true peer-to-peer, interorganizational sharing of computational resources among business entities therefore remains quite sparsely populated. The provision of Grid solutions for these comparatively more complex and idiosyncratic collaborations has therefore been left usually to consultant-developers of customized software systems.

In a sense, the technical domain is the same one in which public-sector scientific research projects are building the means to work with colleagues, databases, and equipment at other laboratories and field research sites. Interorganizational conflicts among potential business partners over claims about intellectual property rights and trade secrets still remain less acutely present in most spheres of academic science. This means that the world of public research organizations may well prove to be a more accommodating environment in which to tackle many of the technical problems of collaboration system design.[17] Be that as it may, the example of eDiaMoND shows that the challenges of negotiating formal arrangements governing cooperative research can be far from trivial. Indeed, they are tending to become more complicated and more burdensome.[18]

The Realities of the Varieties of Social Context

A possibly more difficult source of challenges for the design of appropriate institutional infrastructures for e-research concerns the varieties of social context in which such projects are undertaken. The potential areas of dispute between the parties to an e-science project or between those parties and outsiders can involve: (i) the materials and personnel each party brings to a collaboration; (ii) the allocation of the resources, if any, to which the collaborative project gives rise; and (iii) apportionment of any liability that the collaborative project might incur.

Which of these potential disputes is more likely to hinder the establishment or effectiveness of any particular project depends on a variety of scientific, normative and institutional factors that vary with the social context in which the project is undertaken. Thus, one needs to consider the specific nature of the *scientific domain*(s) within which the research is conducted.

For instance, the ethical issues that are central to the feasibility of an e-science health project will be less important for an e-science project in astrophysics. The *normative context* in which the project is undertaken also must be considered. A project may be affected by norms of formal law (and these vary across a wide range of legal regimes).[19] What sometimes is known as "soft-law" (such as institutional policies and institutionalized procedures) is no less relevant, as are the informal social conventions that operate within particular stakeholder communities. An example of the latter are the often tacit understandings among researchers in a particular domain regarding the attribution of credits for contributions to the variety of specific forms in which project results may be disseminated—such as the order in which coauthors are listed.

Some norms among internationally distributed scientific communities have come to be more or less universally accepted, whereas others may vary among the countries whose scientists are being invited to form a global research network. Parallel differences in norms and conventions are generally more frequently encountered when researchers from various scientific domains and disciplinary communities are assembled to undertake multidisciplinary and interdisciplinary projects and programs.

The range of potential disputes that may arise within a given project also depends on the *institutional context* in which the project is being conducted—in particular, the array of different actors involved. Most obviously, public research institutions and their private-sector partners often have different incentives and different ways of working.

Public-sector research is characteristically different from its private sector counterpart. The former can involve higher levels of task uncertainty, be conducted by parties who have higher levels of autonomy, and be supported by public funds that have a two-part structure. The fact that researchers in the public sector enjoy a basic salary not dependent on research outcomes may exacerbate the effect of their higher levels of autonomy in determining their research goals and timetables. Most important, public-sector scientific research is traditionally "open" in the sense that it facilitates further research by making its findings and methods widely available as soon as possible among the community of scientific peers.[20]

This aspect of public-sector research contrasts sharply with the "proprietary" modalities based on intellectual property ownership and the preservation of trade secrets that are characteristic of the operations of corporate laboratories pursuing commercially oriented research and development, whether in search of process or product innovations that can be moved quickly into the market or in the exploration of future technological opportunities that may reshape the long-term strategy of their business enterprise. The ethos of open science (see chapter 11) and the behavioral norms it has supported were once tightly coupled with the culture of academic science and scholarship in the universities and public institutes in the West. That culture formerly had extended itself into the conduct of many government scientific and engineering research establishments linked with civilian agencies—institutes and service organizations that are engaged with questions arising in areas such as public health, experiments in plant and animal breeding, transport system engineering, materials testing, safety, and reference standard setting for weights and measures. Since the 1990s, however, there has been a visible trend in many scientifically advanced countries of government research organizations becoming "self-supporting" on a fee-for-service basis, in which commercial norms rather than the academic, open science ethos gains increased legitimacy. In academic research institutions, too, there has been much flux in the norms enjoining complete and timely disclosure, as well as in attitudes of "disinterestedness" on the part of investigators in the specific nonscientific implications of their research findings. Such changes have caused some conflicts within universities and greater uncertainty about current and future directions in institutional policies on this issue.

In the biomedical sciences and other frontier areas, exploratory studies are perceived to connect closely with opportunities for commercial innovation. Yet conflicts regarding adherence to traditional open-science norms are posed by the possibilities for private economic gain from academic patents and licensing of university "start-ups" based on publicly funded research results. Such conflicts and possibilities are also beginning to undermine the norms.[21] There remain important areas of exploratory investigation and fundamental inquiry in the mathematical, physical, and life sciences, where publicly funded research at universities and other public research organizations continues to accept open science precepts as the most appropriate. Although the survival of the open-science culture in the universities is certainly desirable, one of its effects must be recognized as further complicating the already challenging institutional context for complex and idiosyncratic collaboration agreements that are likely to involve research participants from both public and private business sectors, as was the case with the eDiaMoND project.

Intra-institutional Realities: Different Actors with Divergent Goals and Incentive Structures

Were the foregoing not complicated enough, it is necessary to recognize the complexities of inter-institutional realities affecting the conduct of scientific research. Although the difficulties of public–private partnerships in research are well known, it is not often fully appreciated that different actors within the same public-sector institutions (e.g., scientific departments, legal groups, research services, technology-transfer sections) will be operating with different incentives and under different constraints. The typical academic institution's policies and procedures in dealing with a given intricate, multifaceted, and multiplayer undertaking are often not coherently aligned. Thus, institutional tensions may arise, not only between public-sector researchers and their private-sector colleagues, but also among the various actors within the public-sector research organization. Thus, simply taking account of the interests of "the university" in designing institutional infrastructures for global research networks will turn out to be an insufficiently nuanced approach in most cases. Indeed, it would be rather naive to suppose that the optimal arrangements for collaborative public-sector science would automatically issue from leaving the matter exclusively within the hands of the advisory and administrative units to which universities typically assign the responsibilities for crafting agreements governing multiparty research projects (such as the office of the in-house counsel, the research services office, or the technology-transfer office).

Indeed, the core of many of the difficulties arising in the institutional organization of scientific collaboration is that although the actual work is to be done by individuals in laboratories, the agreements underpinning collaborations are usually made by others who are acting as the agents of the institutions that employ the researchers. It is quite appropriate that scientists should be relieved of the burdens of negotiating contract details and that this task should be undertaken by agents sensitive to institutional interests. This approach helps to avoid the risk that some individual researchers may seek to promote their personal self-interest over that of their institute, research group, university, or school. At the same time, however, a policy that takes contracting entirely out of the researchers' hands and reserves it to the university counsel's office carries risks of its own.

One likely difficulty is that the process of setting the terms of interinstitutional collaborations might be affected by the conflicting interests of the university or other host institution. This problem is often very real and may be exacerbated by the structures for obtaining legal advice that operate in most universities. For instance, legal counsels have the responsibility to protect the institution from the hazards of entering into collaborations. For university administrators or researchers, those hazards may include the risk of emerging from a collaborative undertaking with a smaller share of the gains than that received by the other contributing parties. In the calculus of "due diligence," the legal representatives—even with the best of intentions and the highest commitment to the value of research—are predisposed by their professional obligations to work to protect the immediate and palpable interests of their client, the university. This predisposition can frequently leave the researchers in the position of having to decide whether to argue for their own career interests, for their research unit's interests, or for the more transcendent and speculative benefits that society at large might derive from the proposed project.

In a collaboration in which the participating institutions are contributing complementary components, there is an understandable temptation for each of the parties to try to extract as large a portion of the anticipated fruits as they can. But this impulse is likely to reduce the efficiency of the project design as well as to initiate a protracted and costly bargaining process. Interinstitutional conflicts over research credits and intellectual property rights can only become more difficult if the parties try to anticipate the consequences of the increasingly mobile pattern of employment among academic researchers.

Perhaps the most formidable problems are likely to stem from the fact that the research university will find itself being called upon to enter into agreements about matters (such as the privacy of personal data) on which their powers to assure delivery are highly uncertain and which may leave the institution exposed to very considerable risks. The resultant quite reasonable nervousness on the part of responsible administrators and their respective legal counsels may adversely transform the traditional structure of the institutional relationships under which academics work. The effect of each party to the collaboration seeking to protect itself by shifting the burden of insuring against hazards of all sort at the expense of the others not only makes for more protracted negotiations, it tends to raise the costs of the entire undertaking when (and if) an agreement is eventually reached.

Balancing Certainty and Universality against Flexibility and Project Specificity

The third main source of difficulty in setting a standard for institutional e-research infrastructures is the need to achieve model infrastructures that are both sufficiently certain and sufficiently flexible. Large-scale collaborations need certainty, and lawyers and managers know that certainty requires foresight and careful planning. If all potential disputes are anticipated, and principled resolutions of them are determined in advance, then—to the lawyers and managers' way of thinking—institutional arrangements will be optimal.

Scientists are likely to take a different approach. They know that anticipating every dispute that might occur is unlikely to foster the type of trust on which effective collaboration depends. They also know that the world of scientific research is extremely fluid. Partners to collaborations are likely to change as researchers move between institutions as institutional research priorities change and as the nature of a given project develops. Institutional infrastructures for long-term fundamental research programs need to be able to accommodate the flux of joining and departing partners.

Finally, scientists know that projects develop in ways not quite anticipated at the outset. Thus, questions about the use to which material brought to the project will be put and the allocation of resources to which this use gives rise are likely to be far more complex than can be adequately anticipated.

A Possible Way Forward

The preceding discussion suggests that setting standards for institutional infrastructures means finding models that can take account of both the variety of e-research projects and the social contexts in which they are undertaken, as well as balancing the certainty and flexibility required for a successful collaboration. Arguably, this renders untenable two different and often-tried approaches to the provision of institutional infrastructures. First, solutions involving the imposition of "codes" should be resisted. Solutions involving codes might be legislative; they also might involve standard form contracts that are simply applied to a wide variety of projects. The beauty of codes is that they reduce transaction costs for individual participants. Scientists may not want to be bothered with institutional arrangements, so an off-the-shelf solution may seem attractive to help them get back to their research. Scientists generally do not want to be bothered with institutional arrangements, thus making an off-the-shelf solution seem very attractive when there is pressure to get on with the research. Standard-form agreements can also increase certainty by offering an invariant set of institutional arrangements. Once these arrangements are learned, they can be anticipated by repeat players.

Despite these benefits to some, we believe the imposition of such codes should be avoided. The danger with solutions involving codes is that they may be inappropriate to the particular context to which they are applied. Moreover, codes tend to have an ossifying effect similar to the way standard engineering specifications can restrict adaptations and innovations in technology.[22] Standard form contracts tend to work well in contexts such as domestic property conveyance or international shipping, where certainty is paramount and the large number of repeat transactions allows calculations of the probability distribution of net gains and losses. But research is different, and we are only beginning to understand how exploratory scientific collaborations might play out. Introducing a set of standard-form agreements in this context might not only harmfully distort the direction of the research but also hinder the development of more appropriate flexible institutional arrangements.

On the other hand, bespoke arrangements for every new e-research project also ought to be avoided. The parties involved in the eDiaMoND project, for instance, had to negotiate every aspect of their agreement, which was felt to be very burdensome even for a pilot project, and the burden was not made lighter by the differences in attitudes toward negotiation among the several groups of players. Bespoke solutions, because they are unique in at least some aspects, tend to increase uncertainty—for example, concerning the way particular features of the agreement might be interpreted by a court in the event of a dispute among the parties. One of the advantages of repeatedly used "codes" is that both their text and its interpretation can be settled within a given community or by external judicial bodies. Not only are the settled texts of the standard-form contracts used widely in activities such as international shipping, but the way in which those texts are read by courts has come to be relatively predictable—which tends to inhibit recourse to litigation in cases of dispute.

If public-funding bodies are to promote best practice in the institutional infrastructure for e-research collaborations, some approach needs to be found that avoids both the dangers of rigidly standard codes and the defects of bespoke arrangements for every new project. Proposals advanced to address this need include the use of template agreements, menus of model agreements for collaborative research, framework guides, and checklists for grant agreements and consortium agreements.[23] Most proponents emphasize the importance of having their particular template(s) used by the parties to structure their negotiations. Nevertheless, the menus of choices—typically drawn up on a priori principles by lawyers and administrators—tend to be collectively bewildering and individually overly restrictive. Where the guidelines are nonspecific, subgroups among the potential stakeholders have sought certainty and simplicity in their collaborative interactions by developing a standard contract.[24]

In light of our analysis, we argue that a better solution for this admittedly difficult problem might entail the establishment of a new public actor to promote best practice in institutional arrangements for various types of e-research projects (see also David and Spence 2003:section 3.2). In referring to this new entity, we will continue to use the name affixed to it for convenience when it first was proposed—the Advisory Board for Collaboration Agreements (ABCA). This body would function in effect as a "collaboration service," free of the pressures under which either public-sector institutions or their commercial partners operate, and with the goal of advancing collaboration in a context in which science is kept as open as possible.[25]

A New Public Actor: An Independent Nonprofit "Research Collaboration Service"
We believe the advisory board should address itself to three crucial questions regarding collaborative research arrangements: their legal shape, the substance of contractual commitments, and how they will be interpreted and enforced.

The Legal Shape of Collaboration Arrangements   The first question to which such a body should address itself is the legal shape that arrangements for different types of collaboration might take. Most discussion of such matters tends to assume that contractual arrangements among the parties to an e-research collaboration will provide the optimal formal structure for their governance. That overlooks the possibility that there will be many situations in which a project might best be incorporated as an independent legal entity—a "company." The latter designation does not imply a profit-making purpose; the entity equally could be a company limited by guarantee to operate on a not-for-profit basis, with individual scientists acting as guarantors. Such a company may be desirable in circumstances where issues of potential liability are important, or where there is a need to provide a stable mechanism for the arrival and departure of parties to the research and for continuous evolution of the research trajectory. It might also provide a repository for the assets contributed to or created by the project.

Alternatively, the collaboration might take legal form as a normal company with shareholdings for the partner institutions and a mechanism for distributing its profits. In this case, individual scientists can be involved as directors of the company to give them a clear hand in controlling its direction. Here, obvious questions would arise regarding potential serious conflicts of interests between the enterprise and the public research institutions whose employment ties with the academics-turned-entrepreneurs have not been completely severed. One role for the proposed independent collaboration service, therefore, would be to explore contexts in which incorporation is desirable for a large-scale project and to offer advice as to the appropriate form of its memorandum and articles of association.

The Substance of Contractual and Other Formal Arrangements   The second class of questions our new public actor (the ABCA) would address concerns the substance of either contractual arrangements or memoranda and articles of association. The independent service could work to build consensus between major research institutions and public (including charitable) funding bodies about the ways in which large-scale collaborations should be built. It could also develop model contractual clauses or memoranda and articles of association for use in particular contexts.

For example, although the copyright licensing of free and open source software has been found effective not only in promoting wider diffusion of reliable computer programs, and in facilitating customization of code to meet users needs, the benefits that this has yielded in the sphere of computer software would be much more difficult to achieve by analogous open source licensing of patents, say, in the area of biotechnology. Yet, it could be argued that a more hospitable situation for open source licensing is present in the emerging field of synthetic biology, where the essential basis of the science involves the manipulation of "code" based on DNA sequencing. The latter field of research therefore would allow greater scope for intellectual property licenses whose terms include "copyleft" provisions of the kind that distinguish the "GNU General Public License"[26] used by most large free and open-source software projects. Whether exploitation of that scope would be desirable, however, remains another question.[27]

Protection and expansion of the domain for open science may be an important priority for the future of e-research (as discussed in chapter 11), but so too is an understanding of which potential solution among the many currently on offer is the one that will best support effective modes of research cooperation. Another key task is the development of a body of experience based on careful legal work in structuring collaboration agreements and the licensing of property rights in order to provide and sustain effective access to research tools, materials, and published results.

The aspect of our proposed public actor's activities that involves promoting principles of best practice in establishing institutional arrangements might find a parallel in the work of a consensus-building entity such as the Basel Committee on Banking Supervision, which assists the governors of the Central Banks of thirteen countries to develop common principles for banking supervision.[28] This committee does not make laws of any kind, but it builds consensus between important actors in the international banking community, and its recommended standards are given effect by relevant national actors in their respective local contexts.[29] Such an approach has the advantage of flexibility, with principles emerging slowly rather than being imposed at what might be an inappropriate stage in their articulation. It is true that this group is working with a far smaller community than those involved in large-scale e-research projects, but the ABCA could begin by enlisting the cooperation of the major scientific research funding bodies, both public and private. If it were successful in doing so, then it is likely that its standards would develop normative force.

Our suggested organizational approach to consensus building, advice, and model clause development has begun to be employed in relation to dealing with the problems in collaborative science presented by intellectual property, particularly in relation to copyright. Standard licensing and contractual terms that facilitate access to research tools and materials—and that thereby support open science norms—are also beginning to emerge (chapter 11). Creative Commons and its Science Commons project are particularly promising developments in this regard.[30] However, intellectual property problems are, as we saw with the eDiaMoND project, only one among many different institutional issues facing the establishment of effective e-research collaborations.

The Interpretation and Enforcement of Arrangements   The final area of concern for an independent public actor would be the resolution of questions about the interpretation and enforcement of arrangements regarding collaborations in ways that are sympathetic to—and make use of—the informal codes and behavioral norms of the particular scientific communities involved. E-research and especially its transnational projects must find suitable forums for resolving disputes that take account of the often complicated and subtle features of the working cultures of productive scientific collaborations. They might do so in the same way that has been found effective in contracts for international shipping—by parties' habitually choosing the law of particular jurisdictions as the law governing their relationships and choosing the courts of particular jurisdictions as the fora in which disputes are to be heard.[31]

The independent collaboration service that we are proposing might alternatively develop specialized dispute-resolution mechanisms and venues to handle issues arising from e-research collaboration agreements. These fora would be well positioned to acquire particular expertise and to accumulate a body of documented experience regarding the sources of seriously disruptive conflicts, and as well as the means of resolving such conflicts expediently in a variety of institutional settings, digital information environments, and research domains.

In all these activities, the Advisory Board for Collaboration Agreements would need to harness expertise in particular areas of both scientific activity and the social sciences. Lawyers and economists who are committed to advancing the cause of open collaborative science, rather than to the causes of those entities they might represent in professional capacities, can play a particularly crucial role through the work of the new form of public actor that we are proposing. As we concluded in an Oxford Internet Institute report prepared for the Joint Information Services Committee of the UK Research Councils (David and Spence 2003):

What is required to meet the challenges of adaptive design of an appropriate institutional infrastructure, above all, is a guiding architectural vision, and sufficient resources to mobilize and maintain the necessary technical expertise: first, to select and standardize [particular patterns of institutional arrangement] . . . and then to assess the performance of the various collaboration [arrangements] that they have been used to construct. An entity able to sustain and assure continuity to those two, inter-twinning, tasks ultimately could exert a powerful influence towards realizing the . . . promise of [global research networks in] . . . e-Science.

Getting the social science of global research networks right from the outset is something that we cannot afford to fail to do.

Acknowledgments

We presented an early draft of this chapter in June 2007 at the e-Horizons Institute conference on worldwide science at which this book was developed. A subsequent presentation by Spence based on this draft was made to the Legal Framework for e-Research Conference organized by Brian Fitzgerald of Queensland University of Technology in July 2007. We are grateful for the useful comments received from other participants on those occasions. David's contribution to this work was supported during 2007–2008 by the U.K. Economic and Social Research Council–funded Oxford e–Social Science Project (RES-149-25-1022) at the Oxford Internet Institute and the Stanford Institute for Economic Policy Research.

Notes

1. For more on the e-Science Programme, see http://www.research-councils.ac.uk/escience/.

2. The description/definition of *e-science* by Taylor is cited by Hey and Trefethen (2002:1017).

3. For an overview of the e-Science Core Programme's connections among the U.K. e-Science Programme, Grid services, and generic middleware platforms, see Hey and Trefethen 2002. David and Spence 2003:appendix 1 also further explains terminology used in this chapter.

4. See http://www.research-councils.ac.uk/escience/ for more on the e-Science Programme.

5. Atkinson's comments on the e-Science Programme may be found at http://www.rcuk.ac.uk/escience/default.htm.

6. Within the U.K. Science and Innovation Investment Framework 2004–2014, the U.K. Office of Science and Innovation (2007) envisages future e-infrastructure development aimed at creating one or multiple "virtual research environments." Chapter 10 examines the use of terminology such as *virtual research environments* and *collaboratories*.

7. For more information on the U.S. Office for Cyberinfrastructure, see http://www.nsf.gov/dir/index.jsp?org=OCI.

8. The same may be said of the U.K. e-Science Programme's (2006) perception of the challenges to be met in promoting the growth of "virtual research communities."

9. Moore's Law is based on the prediction in 1965 by Intel cofounder Gordon Moore that the number of transistors on a chip will double about every two years.

10. Awareness of usability issues was heightened by the disappointing findings of systematic evaluations of the pioneering collaboratory projects that had been mounted in the United States during the early 1990s to explore the potentialities of the "virtual laboratory" concept (see Finholt 2003; David and Spence 2003:appendixes 1 and 2). Suzanne Iacono and Peter Freeman's (2005) presentation of the NSF cyberinfrastructure initiative from the perspective of sociotechnical system building argues that the prospective users of new collaboration tools should be studied and consulted by those who design and engineer such facilities. See also chapter 5 for an overview of e-research usability issues.

11. A major technical obstacle to database federation that e-DiaMoND had to overcome was the impact on the quality of information about breast tissue properties caused by the major differences that can be introduced into image properties by different equipment and centers. A solution to the problem was found by using the original image to parameterize a mathematical model of the passage of X-ray photons through breast tissue. This process, patents on which the University of Oxford owns, was then the only available adequate method of standardizing X-ray images. See also Brady, Gavaghan, Simpson, et al. 2002 on the technical basis of eDiaMoND and both Jirotka, Procter, Hinds, et al. 2004 and Jirotka, Procter, Hartswood, et al. 2005 on the social context of the proposed implementation.

12. The complex intellectual property rights issues surrounding the simulated mammography images are examined in Hinds, Jirotka, Rahman, et al. 2005, and D'Agostino, Hinds, Jirotka, et al. 2008.

13. The following sections draw heavily on material that is presented with more extensive documentation in David and Spence 2003:sections 2.1 and 2.2 and in David 2005. The many

contributions to Fitzgerald 2008 on the legal framework for e-research are also germane to this discussion.

14. A defining feature of collaboratories is that they involve an infrastructure with sufficiently large bandwidth and computational support to provide a multidimensional "virtual presence": research teams, their research instruments, and data repositories at spatially remote locations are able to work together interactively in real time. See the introduction and chapter 2 for further discussion.

15. Den Besten and David (2008a, 2008b) elaborate this taxonomy and its use in mapping the portfolio of projects drawing support from the U.K. e-Science Programme.

16. David and Spence 2003:appendixes 1 and 2, with the assistance of Matthijs den Besten, carries out the taxonomic classification of the U.K. e-Science Pilot Projects and compares the results with those found by applying the same schema to U.S. collaboratory projects. Den Besten and David 2008a and 2008b elaborate this framework and apply it to a larger array of U.K. e-Science projects.

17. With regard to public research organizations, it is somewhat surprising to find that the U.K. e-Science Programme's (2006) *Report of the Working Group on Virtual Research Communities* suggests that any future funding for public-sector developments of research tools for virtual research communities should aim "to learn from the experiences of companies developing solutions to collaborative working." See David 2005 for further discussion of the relevance of Grid service and other collaboration platforms developed for business enterprises on a bespoke basis.

18. See Heffernan and David 2007 as well as Heffernan and Kiel-Chisholm 2008 for findings of a detailed survey of Australian university researchers and research managers on legal and project agreement issues in collaboration and e-research. Although formal project agreements are found to be far less frequent than informal collaborative ones, about 31 percent of the respondents (mostly in science and technology disciplines) deemed formal agreements to be "always necessary" and reported duration times for the negotiations of between one to thirty months in cases involving large, complex, or multiparty collaborations. Heffernan and Kiel-Chisholm report a science and technology researcher's view of legal agreements as "the largest impediment to timely research" (2008:509). This is echoed in the quoted remark by a contract officer: "the legal and contractual process can often be much slower than the time it actually takes to complete the research" (2008:511).

19. See David and Spence 2003:28–44 for an overview of formal law relevant to research collaboration agreements, with special reference to the United Kingdom.

20. See chapter 12 and its references to the literature on open science.

21. On efforts to accommodate researchers and research universities' rising interest in patenting publicly funded research, see, for example, Owen-Smith and Powell 2001 regarding intradepartmental schisms and Murray forthcoming on the emergence of "hybrid" norms in biogenetics. David and Hall 2006 offers a more general treatment of these issues, and David 2007 looks specifically at the European policy context.

22. See David 1995 on the arguments for "metastandards" in fields where technology is undergoing rapid change and no clearly dominant design paradigm or trajectory of incremental advance has emerged.

23. Fitzgerald and Austin 2008 provides a very useful survey of the variety of such recommendations for "streamlining" collaborative research agreements, among them the 1996 Australian universities' B-HERT Collaborative Template Agreements; the 2003 menu of "model agreements" recommended by the United Kingdom's Lambert Review; and the U.S. University-Industry Demonstration Partnership TurboNegotiator project.

24. Fitzgerald and Austin 2008 discusses the case of the European Union's Framework Programme 7's 2007 Guidelines, which sought to create uniform agreements solely from guidelines. The latter did not provide any draft agreement for reference, but proposed that a coalition of stakeholders produce a simplified "consortium agreement" that purported to balance all interests of all partners in a project within the framework project.

25. The U.S. TurboNegotiator demonstration project is a software program that poses questions and uses the parties' responses to guide users through the selection of contractual clauses that best meet their needs (see Fitzgerald and Austin 2008 and http://www.osp.gatech.edu/TN/scripts/TN _DemoSurvey.php). It shares the modular approach to construction of a collaboration agreement, which is advocated in David and Spence 2003:section 4. But, it works from a static, preset list of clauses that are said to be consistent with the Guiding Principles for University-Industry Endeavors set by the U.S. National Cooperative Research Act of 1984. It lacks the features of independence from university administration interests and an adaptive capability based on feedback from field experience that can modify both the clauses and their indicated uses in specific project circumstances. These latter are features we believe to be critically important.

26. The Free Software Foundation's GNU General Public License is a free software license used by the majority of free software packages (see http://www.fsf.org/licensing/licenses/gpl.html). "Copyleft" is a general method for making a program or other work available for free, including the requirement that all modified and extended versions of the program be free as well (see http://www.gnu.org/copyleft/).

27. Although the example makes the point that solutions that fail to fit one scientific area could serve to meet the needs of another research domain, we do not think that open source licensing would be appropriate in the context of synthetic biology. The GNU GPL and similar licenses are founded upon the existence of copyrights in software, and to analogically follow that approach would entail extending IPR law to apply to information about biological processes that presently remains, and is best left, in the public domain.

28. The Basel Committee (see http://www.bis.org/bcbs/index.htm) is hosted by the Bank for International Settlements in Basel, Switzerland. It is best known for its international standards on capital adequacy, the Core Principles for Effective Banking Supervision, and the concordat on cross-border banking supervision. It has been considered a model in the context of developing a regulatory apparatus for e-commerce, although questions have been raised about the implications of its "self-regulation" stance in some contexts, such as those leading to the 2008 international

credit crisis. Its relevance to our proposed new body would be to argue for that body's independence, especially its insulation from pressures to serve the narrow and immediate interests of the institutions whose practices it is intended to guide.

29. Such a consensus-building process to develop codes that are not legally binding can rarely be better than the prevailing sentiment and technical knowledge of those involved in it. The more transparent the process, the less likely it is to be captured by the special interests of those to whom the recommended codes would apply.

30. See Wilbanks and Boyle 2006 and essay 11.2 in this volume on the range of Science Commons activities, which have extended into the successful streamlining of contracting among university labs and other research organizations to expedite material transfer agreements. One of this chapter's authors, Paul David, is a member of the Science Commons's Scientific Advisory Board.

31. David and Spence 2003:47 discusses the models provided by the Liverpool Cotton Association and the Grain and Feed Transport Association (GAFTA), focusing on the arbitration clauses in the GAFTA's array of standards contracts, which allow parties to use the GAFTA Dispute Resolution Service. That service has the advantage of being outside the legal system of any of the parties to these international shipping agreements. It also provides for the speedy and final resolution of disputes in an expert forum that is less expensive and quicker than traditional legal systems.

References

Atkins, D. E., K. K. Koegemeier, S. I. Feldman, H. Garcia-Molina, M. L. Klein, D. G. Messerschmitt, P. Messina, J. P. Ostriker, and M. H. Wright. 2003. *Revolutionizing science and engineering through cyberinfrastructure: Report of the National Science Foundation Blue-Ribbon Advisory Panel on Cyberinfrastructure.* Arlington, VA: National Science Foundation. Available at: http://www.community technology.org/nsf_ci_report/.

Brady, M., D. Gavaghan, A. Simpson, M. M. Parada, and R. Highnam. 2002. "eDiamond: A Grid-enabled federated database of annotated mammograms." In *Grid computing—making the global infrastructure a reality*, ed. F. Berman, G. Fox, and T. Hey. London: Wiley, 943–945.

D'Agostino, G., C. Hinds, M. Jirotka, C. Meyer, T. Piper, M. Rahman, and D. Vaver. 2008. "On the importance of intellectual property rights for eScience and integrated health record." Health Informatics Journal 14 (2):95–111. Available at: http://jhi.sagepub.com/cgi/content/abstract/14/2/95.

David, P. A. 1995. "Standardization policies for network technologies: The flux between freedom and order revisited." In *Standards, innovation, and competitiveness: The political economy of standards in natural and technological environments*, ed. R. Hawkins, R. Mansell, and J. Skea. London: E. Elgar, 15–35.

David, P. A. 2006. "Toward a cyberinfrastructure for enhanced scientific collaboration: Proving its 'soft' foundations may be the hardest part." In *Advancing knowledge and the knowledge economy*, ed. B. Kahin and D. Foray. Cambridge, MA: MIT Press, 431–454. Preprint available at: http://siepr .stanford.edu/papers/pdf/04-01.html.

David, P. A. 2007. "Innovation and Europe's universities: Second thoughts about embracing the Bayh-Dole regime." In *Perspectives on innovation*, ed. F. Malerba and S. Brusoni. Cambridge, UK: Cambridge University Press, 251–278. Preprint available at: http://siepr.stanford.edu/papers/pdf/04-27.html.

David, P. A., and B. H. Hall. 2006. "Property and the pursuit of knowledge—Issues affecting science: An introduction." *Research Policy 35* (6): 767–771.

David, P. A., and M. Spence. 2003. *Toward institutional infrastructures for e-science: The scope of the challenge*. Oxford Internet Institute (OII) Research Report no. 2. Oxford, UK: OII, University of Oxford. Available at: http://www.oii.ox.ac.uk/research/.

Den Besten, M., and P. A. David. 2008a. "Empirical mapping of e-science's path in the collaboration space." Paper presented to the e-Research Conference 2008, Oxford Internet Institute, University of Oxford, 11–13 September 2008. Available at: http://www.oii.ox.ac.uk/microsites/eresearch08/.

Den Besten, M., and P. A. David. 2008b. "Mapping e-science's path in the collaboration space: An ontological approach to monitoring infrastructure development." In *Proceedings of the 4th International Conference on e–Social Science*. Manchester: U.K. National e–Social Science Centre.

Finholt, T. A. 2003. "Collaboratories as a new form of scientific organization." *Economics of Innovation and New Technology 12*:5–25.

Fitzgerald, B., ed. 2008. *Legal framework for e-research: Realising the potential*. Sydney: Sydney University Press.

Fitzgerald, B. F., and A. C. Austin. 2008. *Legal strategies for streamlining collaboration in an e-research world*. Brisbane, Australia: Legal Framework for e-Research Project, Queensland University of Technology. Available at: http://eprints.qut.edu.au/17149/1/c17149.pdf.

Foster, I., and C. Kesselman, eds. 2001. *The Grid: Blueprint for a new computing infrastructure*. San Francisco: Morgan-Kaufmann.

Heffernan, M., and N. David. 2007. *Legal and project agreement issues in collaboration and e-research: Survey results*. Brisbane, Australia: OAK Law Project, Queensland University of Technology. Available at: http://eprints.qut.edu.au/archive/00008865/01/8865.pdf.

Heffernan, M., and S. Kiel-Chisholm. 2008. "Australian survey on legal issues facing e-research." In *Legal framework for e-research; Realising the potential*, ed. B. Fitzgerald. Sydney: Sydney University Press, 497–524.

Hey, T., and A. E. Trefethen. 2002. "The UK e-Science Core Programme and the Grid." Future Generation Computer Systems 18:1017–1031. doi:10.1016/S0167-739X(02)00082-1.

Hinds, C., M. Jirotka, M. Rahman, G. D'Agostino, C. Meyer, T. Piper, and D. Vaver. 2005. "Ownership of intellectual property rights in medical data in collaborative computing environments." Paper presented at the First International Conference on eSocial Science, U.K. National e–Social Science Centre, Manchester, UK.

Iacono, C. S., and P. A. Freeman. 2005. "Cyberinfrastructure-in-the-making: Can we get there from here?" In *Advancing knowledge and the knowledge economy*, ed. B. Kahin and D. Foray. Cambridge, MA: MIT Press, 455–479.

Jirotka, M., R. Procter, M. Hartswood, R. Slack, A. Simpson, C. Coopmans, C. Hinds, and A. Voss. 2005. "Collaboration and trust in healthcare innovation: The eDiaMoND case study." *Journal of Computer Supported Cooperative Work 14* (4):369–398.

Jirotka, M., R. Procter, C. Hinds, C. Coopmans, J. Soutter, and S. Lloyd. 2004. *Towards understanding requirements for eScience: The eDiamond case study*. Working Paper. Oxford, UK: Oxford University Computing Laboratory. Available at: http://www.allhands.org.uk/2004/proceedings/papers/225.pdf.

Murray, F. Forthcoming. "The Oncomouse that roared: Hybrid exchange strategies as a source of productive tension at the boundary of overlapping institutions." *American Journal of Sociology*.

Owen-Smith, J., and W. W. Powell. 2001. "To patent or not: Faculty decisions and institutional success in academic patenting." *Journal of Technology Transfer 26* (1):99–114.

Taylor, J. 2001. "Presentation at e-Science Meeting by the Director of the Research Councils," Office of Science and Technology, U.K. Available at: http://www.e-science.clrc.ac.uk/.

U.K. e-Science Programme. 2006. *Report of the Working Group in Virtual Research Communities (VRC)*. Swindon, UK: U.K. Research Councils. Available at: http://www.nesc.ac.uk/documents/OSI/vrc.pdf.

U.K. Office of Science and Innovation. 2007. *Developing the UK's infrastructure for science and innovation*. London: Office of Science and Technology. Available at: www.nesc.ac.uk/documents/OSI/report.pdf.

U.S. National Science Foundation (NSF) Cyberinfrastructure Council. 2007. *Cyberinfrastructure vision for 21st century discovery*. North Arlington, VA: NSF. Available at: http://www.nsf.gov/pubs/2007/nsf0728/nsf0728_1.pdf.

Wilbanks, J., and J. Boyle. 2006. "Science Commons: An introduction." Available at: http://science commons.org/wp-content/uploads/ScienceCommons_Concept_Paper.pdf.

7.1 Ownership of Medical Images in e-Science Collaborations: Learning from the Diagnostic Mammography National Database

Tina Piper and David Vaver

Understanding the Soft Infrastructure of e-Science

The global e-science infrastructure enabled by Grid technology holds the promise of a technically complex supercomputing infrastructure, distributed among geographically disparate locations and providing increased processing power and data storage.

Technical complexity is one thing; legal and social complexities are another. Although less tangible, the latter can be as difficult to isolate, analyze, and manage as engineering technologies. This essay suggests that as much attention should be paid to this "soft" normative infrastructure of e-science as to its "hard" physical counterpart. Otherwise, the promised benefits of Grid collaborations may not be fully realized. The essay illustrates this view through analysis of a case study[1] of the electronic Diagnostic Mammography National Database (eDiaMoND) pilot project, a £4.25 million interdisciplinary U.K. collaboration aimed at creating a database of digital mammography images using Grid technology.[2]

An Exemplar of Key e-Science Issues

The eDiaMoND project promised much: as a training tool, it would reduce regional disparities in diagnosing breast cancer, would improve surgical results by providing high-quality images to surgeons, and would be used as a research tool to enhance epidemiological and research knowledge. All three areas carried the eventual promise of internationalization.

As well as linking geographically dispersed users and physical collections, eDiaMoND connected institutions with widely differing mandates, funding sources, and internal norms. Distinctive features of this project were network members' coequal status, its promise of a grand virtual research infrastructure, and the novel use of Grid technology to effect this infrastructure. It would not merely provide a database of digital mammograms, but would also create a community of e-researchers. It therefore offered fertile ground to examine the soft infrastructure of e-science.

Evaluating Image-Ownership Aspects of eDiaMoND

The case study evaluating eDiaMoND was conducted by examining the legal relationships between the parties, focusing specifically on the intellectual property rights (IPRs) in databases and images in the project. Among other things, IPRs function as tokens that commodify and define veto rights between the parties. IPRs can also be used to generate financial rewards for their holders. Intellectual property law differs from corporation law, which defines the internal structures of organizations, and from the law of confidentiality and privacy, which helps determine relationships with third parties such as patients. IPRs directly engage project collaborators by artificially creating scarcity and forcing them into relationships of sharing, conflict, trust, and suspicion over how those tokens are created, distributed, and exploited for profit.

The study team hypothesized that just as property relationships lie at the root of the social contract and the modern state, IPRs may similarly lie at the root of the e-science community and its future organization. Therefore, the study researched instantiations of norms of intellectual property—mainly copyrights and database rights—between the parties, ranging from formal (e.g., legislation and contracts) to informal (practices and custom). No separate corporation was created to further eDiaMoND's purposes, and few written documents were concluded between the parties. Norms had to be deduced from institutional policies and procedures, governmental policies, and practices evident from interviews of participants.

Case Study Findings

The study on which this essay is based found that

1. Public U.K. National Health Service (NHS) Trusts[3] probably retained ownership of intellectual property in the physical and digital mammograms;
2. The commercial partners had an implied license for limited use of the images during the course of the development of eDiaMoND, but would not necessarily retain rights to use the mammograms after eDiaMoND ended;
3. Noncommercial eDiaMoND participants similarly had use rights in the images for the duration of the program but did not have reuse rights (largely because of the ethical clearances that would be required); and
4. NHS Trusts, universities, and some other participants retained and gained some database rights and copyrights in databases used in and created under eDiaMoND's aegis.

More legal certainty and coherence between the parties might have been achieved through written agreements that focused on the allocation and use of IPRs. Creating a separate legal identity for eDiaMoND and channeling contracts and management decisions through that identity would have provided a hub for the parties' legal relations.

Project coordinators, however, were reluctant to conclude formal contracts with non-commercial collaborators. For example, after a conflictual initial exchange of terms with one hospital, coordinators did not seek similar IPR agreements with the other hospitals. Neither did they reprioritize the exchange of contractual terms and certainty, which—much like a prenuptial agreement—they evidently thought could damage the spirit of collaboration.

Although the role that informal agreements played in nurturing the collaboration is unclear, uncertainty over IPR ownership was eventually blamed for making it impossible for the eDiaMoND collaboration to proceed past the pilot stage. Yet this stalemate seemed to have less to do with IPR ownership than with the fact that the parties could not agree on how their common endeavor should proceed. They had plainly not thought to establish Mertonian norms[4] of open science, in particular communality. The relationship could not generate norms to govern participants' conduct without common basic rules or values to guide their collaboration, not only in unanticipated situations but even in anticipated ones (such as how to proceed when the project formally terminated).

Building an Effective Technological Infrastructure and Working Culture

Although the deduced legal allocation of IPRs among the eDiaMoND parties generally met the parties' assumptions, following the law did not provide the community with the tools to evolve. Technology had allowed cooperation across great distances but had not provided the means to develop the underlying community relationships that would provide the basis of trust, agreement, and default rules. Although technology may be good at bridging physical gaps, it is not necessarily as effective in bridging social and commercial ones.

The case study therefore concluded that collaborations such as eDiaMoND should include, at their project design stage, plans for building a functioning working culture. This feature is essential where parties seek a long-term relationship and are geographically and institutionally diverse. It will be critical if a project becomes politicized with the involvement of important commercial partners and sensitive data. These challenges will magnify in international e-science endeavors, where norms of interaction may differ even more than they do within one country.

Bridging this divide may involve processes that include a range of tools and mechanisms:

1. Collaborators and project designers should spend time at the outset creating mechanisms to support relationship building, trust, and internal dispute-resolution techniques. Developing an agreed "statement of joint understanding" before concluding formal agreements might then be less polarizing. The joint statement can be attached

to the formal documents and assist in their interpretation. Community building would also create a process of informal norm development—norms that would fill in the gaps that necessarily follow formal agreement.

2. Formal contracts should be circumscribed documents defining how the parties are to proceed. Detailed rules of governance should be left to mechanisms such as negotiated codes of conduct, with penalties, rewards, and procedures that build the project community. For example, penalties might include limiting access to a peer-reviewed deliverable. Independent multistakeholder agencies can oversee governance and provide external oversight. Such work should precede the commencement of the project.

Future studies should seek to determine if e-science projects require sui generis norms of IPR governance unique to the e-science context. The allocation of and management rules relating to IPRs will be an important overture to the project—more than a sideshow, but a great deal less than the central plot.

Notes

1. In addition to the authors of this essay, the case study team comprised Marina Jirotka, Oxford e-Research Centre; Chris Hinds, Oxford e-Research Centre; Giuseppina D'Agostino, assistant professor, Osgoode Hall Law School; Charles Meyer, visiting professor of law, University of Pittsburgh; and Mustafizur Rahman, researcher in e-science, Oxford University. Results are published in D'Agostino, Hinds, Jirotka, et al. 2008.

2. The eDiaMoND project lasted two and a half years from the end of 2002 and involved a core of thirty to thirty-five staff spread over twelve locations in the United Kingdom. The participating entities included five universities, four U.K. National Health Service Trusts, a multinational company, and a rapidly expanding university spinout enterprise. Funding came mainly from the U.K. government, the U.K. Economic and Social Research Council, the private sector, and in-kind contributions from the universities and trusts. The legal and institutional background of eDiaMoND is discussed further in chapter 7.

3. NHS Trusts are responsible for the local management of health services in the United Kingdom.

4. Communalism, universalism, disinterestedness, originality, and skepticism, also known by the acronym CUDOS. First formulated by the sociologist Robert Merton (1973 [1942]).

References

D'Agostino, G., C. Hinds, M. Jirotka, C. Meyer, T. Piper, M. Rahman, and D. Vaver. 2008. "On the importance of intellectual property rights for e-science and the integrated health record." *Health Informatics Journal* 14:95–111.

Merton, R. K. 1973 [1942]. *The sociology of science: Theoretical and empirical investigations.* Chicago: University of Chicago Press.

7.2 The Value of Authorship in the Digital Environment: Producing and Protecting Scientific Information

Justine Pila

Law exists, among other things, to facilitate social interaction by creating the conditions necessary to enable people to trust each other sufficiently to interact.[1] To that end, it is part of a complex web of social mechanisms, variations in any part of which produce ripple effects in all others. Scholars of intellectual property have studied a variant of this web—modeled by Lawrence Lessig (1999:chap. 10) as laws, norms, and codes—to determine the impact throughout history of advances in reprographic technology on the copyright system. They have looked specifically at how such advances have affected the capacity of copyright law to fulfill its central purpose of maximizing the production and dissemination of creative and informational works. In so doing, they have demonstrated the importance of analyzing technology in its proper social and regulatory context in order to check that its potentialities are fully exploited without undermining the law's capacity to achieve its public-benefit ends.

Production and Protection of Digital Informational Works

The direct impact of digital technology on copyright doctrine has been well studied. Less well examined has been the impact of digital technology on the production of informational works and the institutional arrangements for their protection. One of the reasons for this relative inattention may be a lack of the requisite information, such as empirical information regarding the actual processes by which informational works are created and used. Generating that information with a view to analyzing these and other issues is a primary purpose of recent work by social theorists. A central idea explored in that work is the idea of "trust" as a norm in the regulatory web described earlier, with important implications for e-science.

For example, papers on the CalFlora[2] (Van House 2002) and Diagnostic Mammography National Database (eDiaMoND)[3] (Jirotka, Procter, Hartwood, et al. 2005) projects consider practices of trust in the production and protection of horticultural and medical information, respectively, and the implications for those practices of publishing the information in digital libraries. I review these studies elsewhere (Pila 2009) using concepts of authorship. Drawing on insights from intellectual property and social epistemology, I argue that an important aspect of the practices studied by Nancy Van House and by Marina Jirotka and her colleagues concerns the conventions by which sources of information are identified. My suggestion is that focusing on those conventions enhances our understanding of e-research and the regulatory issues it raises by revealing the central role of authorial attribution in managing the relationship between trust and skepticism in and across epistemic communities. In particular, by underlining the distinction between trust and integrity, proper use of attribution conventions helps direct our focus in the digital environment away from preserving existing practices of trust toward assessing those practices with a view to making our digital infrastructures not only trusted, but also trustworthy.

Authorship Issues

Running through this thesis is a wider argument regarding authorship. That argument concerns the need to dissociate copyright and science lest scientists be conceived as property owners and science itself as property (e.g., see Biagioli 2002). My suggestion is that this theme is unfortunate, for it encourages a myopic view of the author within copyright as an owner rather than as a creator and relieves the legislature and courts of the need to consider the wider social and legal consequences that designations of authorship attract. The result, in turn, is to limit the value of copyright jurisprudence as a source of policy standards and insights in discussions of science.[4]

In Anglo-American copyright law,[5] an author is a person who creates or makes a substantial and nonseverable intellectual contribution to the creation of a work, where a work includes most original literary, dramatic, musical, or artistic expressions of ideas or information, including the ideas or information but not the material forms in which they are fixed.[6] Although objects containing works are property, works themselves are not and therefore cannot be owned. In the United Kingdom, this conclusion was confirmed in *Donaldson v. Beckett* (1774, 2 Bro PC 129, 1 ER 837 [HL]), when the House of Lords held that in the era of statutory copyright, at least, authors have no common-law property in their literary creations. It follows that although an expression that possesses the evidential and substantial characteristics of a copyright work will attract property, the property that will be copyrighted is not synonymous with the work itself. In addition, the creators of the work will be the copyright's presumptive first owners, but their ultimate designation as such will be contingent and secondary to their designation as authors.

If an author at law is a person working in the shared and evolving tradition of a particular aesthetic or expressive tradition, who is a scientific author and how does s/he differ? According to Mario Biagioli (2002), a scientific author is a person judged by his or her peers to deserve credit and responsibility for a claim about nature. Although claims (like ideas) will almost always be expressed in a copyright work, they will never themselves be works, nor will they be property.[7]

This distinction raises an additional theme concerning the different conceptions of authorship protected by law. At law, authorship is both an act of creation protected by statute for the benefit of authors and a statement of origin protected by a combination of common law and statute for the alternative benefit of authors and readers (users). Underlying the patchy legal protection given to authorship in its latter conception is the uncertainty that has always plagued Anglo-American law regarding the relationship between works and their authors, and the consequent ability of acts and statements of authorship to be decoupled.[8] In the studies by Van House (2002) and Jirotka and her colleagues (2005), scientific works are cast as tethered to their authors. In my own work, I consider the implications of that tethering for e-science with reference to those studies, intellectual property jurisprudence, and ideas from social epistemology.

Notes

1. This essay is adapted from Pila, J. 2009. "Authorship and e-science: Balancing epistemological trust and skepticism in the digital environment." *Social Epistemology 23*: 1–24.

2. See http://www.calflora.org/.

3. See http://www.ediamond.ox.ac.uk/.

4. See Dreyfuss 2002 (especially pp. 1216–1227) for more on the use and value of intellectual property law as a source of default rules, policy, and public-interest safeguards in the regulation of science.

5. The relevant laws are the Copyright, Designs, and Patents Act of 1988 in the United Kingdom and the Copyright Act of 1976 (USC Title 17) in the United States.

6. The exception is for those types of artistic work that consist of an expression fixed in a material medium, such as paint.

7. Claims in this sense are akin to ideas, which are not works in which copyright subsists. Whether the copyright subsisting in works protects the ideas that those works contain is a separate question. In the United States, it does not, by virtue of U.S. Code Title 17 §102(b), which states that "[i]n no case does copyright protection for an original work of authorship extend to any idea, procedure, process, system, method of operation, concept, principle, or discovery, regardless of the form in which it is described, explained, illustrated, or embodied in such work." In the United Kingdom, as stated by Lord Hailsham in *LB (Plastics) Ltd v. Swish Products Ltd* ([1979] RPC 551 [HL] 629), it "all depends on what you mean by ideas" (quoted by Lord Hoffman in *Designer's Guild v. Russell Williams Textiles Ltd* [(2000) 1 WLR 2416 (HL) 2422]).

8. On the distinction between acts and statements of authorship and its theoretical basis, see Heymann 2005.

References

Biagioli, M. 2002. "Rights or rewards? Changing frameworks of scientific authorship." In *Scientific authorship: Credit and intellectual property*, ed. M. Biagioli and P. Galison. New York: Routledge, 253–279.

Dreyfuss, R. C. 2002. "Collaborative research: Conflicts on authorship, ownership, and accountability." *Vanderbilt Law Review 53*:1162–1232.

Heymann, L. 2005. "The birth of the authornym: Authorship, pseudonymity, and trademark law." *Notre Dame Law Review 80*:1377–1449.

Jirotka, M., R. Procter, M. Hartswood, R. Slack, A. Simpson, C. Coopmans, and C. Hinds. 2005. "Collaboration and trust in healthcare innovation: The eDiaMoND case study." *Journal of Computer-Supported Cooperative Work 14* (4):369–398.

Lessig, L. 1999. *Code and other laws of cyberspace*. New York: Basic Books.

Pila, J. 2009. "Authorship and e-science: Balancing epistemological trust and skepticism in the digital environment." *Social Epistemology 23*:1–24.

Van House, N. 2002. "The CalFlora study and practices of trust: Networked Biodiversity information." *Social Epistemology 16*:99–114.

8 The Politics of Privacy, Confidentiality, and Ethics: Opening Research Methods

William H. Dutton and Tina Piper

This chapter is about ethical principles in research and the implications for them of the developments in network-enabled research examined in this book. After discussing traditional research ethics and its related legal and administrative framework, highlighting the challenges that confront research ethics, we consider how technical change has forced researchers and policymakers to reconsider research ethics and practices (e.g., Fitzgerald 2008). Finally, we move from considering the challenges of e-research to examining its promise by proposing novel methods to enhance the administration of research ethics. The chapter is not a philosophical treatment of ethical principles, nor is its argument skeptical about the potential for e-research to be "ethical." We leave to other studies in-depth investigation of the possibility that e-research can be even more ethical than previous research, given some forethought and planning.

Traditional Research Ethics and Its Legal–Administrative Framework

Research ethics are fundamental to the training of scientists across the disciplines, and disciplinary codes of practice are often the most rigorous and effective controls over researchers' activities. However, ethics committees and institutional review boards in universities are often viewed as bureaucratic hurdles that brake or slow down innovative research, frequently because researchers see models from medical research being inappropriately imposed on all of the sciences. This view may change dramatically as network-enabled research collaborations force researchers to confront differences in practices across the disciplines and as university committees and review boards move into the new world of e-research.

Standard Ethical Issues

Privacy, confidentiality, anonymity, and informed consent are the accepted standard ethical issues involved between researchers and subjects (see box 8.1).

Box 8.1
Standard Ethical Issues of Research

Privacy   Human participants' right to control access to personal information about themselves that might lead to the unauthorized disclosure of that information or to intrusion on their private lives (e.g., the right to be left alone).

Confidentiality   The researcher's ability to restrict access to information about the subjects of their research, such as unauthorized access to the source of information or to quotations.

Anonymity   Maintaining any guarantees that human participants will remain anonymous as a condition for participation by not identifying the names of respondents or experimental subjects.

Informed Consent   People's ability to be informed about the details of a project (i.e., not to be deceived) and to have the opportunity to refuse to participate, including the avoidance of excessive inducements.

Source: Adapted from Ess and the AoIR Ethics Working Committee 2002; Anderson and Kanuka 2003:56–72; and Ess 2007.

Research ethics also engages with more systemwide concerns of ensuring that research serves the interests of individuals, groups, and society as a whole. This broader consideration raises questions about how far science (in particular data) should be open or proprietary in relation to

• the public funding of that research;
• how or whether the results of scientific research should be commercialized;
• the related roles of intellectual property rights and technology transfer;
• the distributive consequences of the digital divide between rich and poor nations; and
• broader issues concerning the justice of particular research pursuits (military technologies, "green" technologies, etc.).

The Legal Framework

E-research threatens the traditional jurisdictional grounding of determinations about what constitutes ethical behavior because in doing e-research, researchers from multiple jurisdictions may collaborate and draw data from multiple other jurisdictions. Ethically "challenging" situations sit within a complex national and international legal framework of legislation, directives, regulations, and decisions by judges, regulators, administrative tribunals, and review boards. These laws govern research subjects' privacy and dignity interests principally through data-protection legislation, but also by other means.

Data-Protection Laws and Regulations

Most developed nations active in e-research have some form of data-protection and confidentiality laws, enacted in response to the 1980 Organization for Economic Cooperation and Development (OECD) guidelines (OECD 1980) and the desire to exchange data within the European Union. Privacy in the European Union is governed by the 1995 Data Protection Directive,[1] which requires that specific and informed consent be given for data collection, that notice be given about data collected on individuals, and that individuals be allowed to opt out of data collection and to correct inaccurate data about themselves. It also importantly prohibits the transmission of information to countries with less-stringent data-protection laws, although there are concerns that loopholes allowing data transmission for public-security purposes overwhelm the protection provided by the directive.[2]

In many countries, data-protection laws impose stricter protections for highly sensitive personal information (e.g., health data or information regarding sexual orientation must be anonymized). International or supranational standards are implemented in national laws (such as the United Kingdom's Data Protection Act of 1988)[3] and then overseen by an administrative regime (such as the U.K. Information Commissioner's Office).[4] The regulatory regime is generally based on a collaborative, cooperative, nonlitigious philosophy that encourages and educates, penalizing only as a last resort. The requirements of data protection are particularized on an organizational or institutional level by corporate codes of conduct, university ethics guidelines, and other policy guidelines and documents.

Privacy Controls

In addition to data-protection legislation, many countries protect privacy in their constitutions. The right to privacy is enshrined in the Universal Declaration of Human Rights and the European Convention on Human Rights, including protection for "private and family life." The right to privacy is not explicitly established by the U.S. Constitution, but the Supreme Court has judged it to be a right derived from the First and Fourth Amendments—for example, in *Stanley v. Georgia* (394 U.S. 557 [1969]).[5]

On the national level, most developed countries have sophisticated systems of ethics review involving lay and professional members. These review processes include mechanisms to grant approval for research involving human subjects and to penalize researchers who engage in ethically unsound research. Similarly to data protection, ethics requirements are specified for institutions and disciplines as codes of conduct or guidelines.

As is evident from this description, the boundaries between laws and informal law making through codes, guidelines, and regulation are porous, particularly in the ethical regulation of research—often because of the novel challenges posed by new technologies and the diverse potential collaborations that make it impossible to craft a single law to deal with every possible situation.

In these circumstances, codes and regulations act as guidelines rather than as recipes. The dominant legal approach, therefore, is to accept the importance of discretion and local standards in making decisions about confidentiality, privacy, and other ethical issues while establishing baseline norms from which no deviation is allowed. National, regional, and disciplinary peculiarities remain in legal expressions of ethical standards, some of which are inconveniently left unwritten and merely encompassed in the practice of a particular board or official.

The boundaries between law making and ethical functions inevitably blur as laws become less directive and penal. Network-enabled research will pose significant challenges to the legal and ethical regulation of research. It will be critical to identify how, when, and where new "legal" norms are developed by the practice of e-research communities. For example, ambiguity remains about the privacy and confidentiality status of data concerning an avatar (a graphical, interactive image personifying a user or a software-generated entity) in a virtual world. One conclusion is that online codes of conduct in a virtual world will effectively become the "law" of that virtual jurisdiction. Interesting disputes will result when those norms conflict with the laws of a territorial jurisdiction.

Other Legal-Related Issues

A debate about who "owns" research (e.g., see essay 7.1) and in whose interests it should be mobilized further informs the context of this debate. Scientific research has been dogged at least since the early 1900s by contention over who owns the valuable products of scientific research funded by public dollars and how they should be commercialized. Open-source licensing, nonexclusive licensing, intellectual property concordances, public-domain dedications, new publishing models, and new metrics of public benefit for technology-transfer offices have encouraged a move away from traditional proprietary practices in research toward more open approaches. Further, public-science authorities and researchers have embraced the open-source and open-science methods enabled by collaboration and archiving technologies.

Opening science may ethically prioritize disclosure and accessibility over other values—thus leading to problems, for example, in the area of genomics research (essay 8.2). In tandem, so-called save-the-planet science initiatives have the potential to privilege the public-interest outcome of science projects over principles guiding the treatment of the participants in research. In the background has been a polarized, wide-ranging public discussion of the use of the Internet, the Web, media artifacts, and related inventions, often using the language of good and evil. For instance, Google's slogan "Don't be evil" perhaps implicitly brands its open-access projects (e.g., Google Books) and nonproprietary approach as "good."

Ethical Challenges in e-Research

Network-enabled research challenges research ethics on two levels: Internet technologies have changed how research is practiced and made available. These changes include:

- electronic instead of paper-based or face-to-face communication;
- enhanced archiving ability;
- technologies that combine data to yield new and different results;
- new types of data that are now readily available; and
- security and privacy issues arising from Web use and virtual research environments.

There is a potential at another level to transform the research enterprise and in the process to highlight underlying tensions. Ethical issues, such as privacy, are too often viewed as barriers to e-research, but ethical approaches can be designed into e-research if addressed early on and in their full complexity. This chapter argues later that new media can open up e-research methods to global accountability, complementing existing institutional review mechanisms in ways that can help identify and resolve conflicts. This change may reconfigure the boundaries and composition of real and virtual research organizations, facilitating collaboration between partners from different countries, disciplines, and types of organizations (government, university, private sector).

The Practice of Research and e-Research

In order to illustrate the range of ethical issues encompassed, this section focuses on e-researchers' key practices and how they operate in the new network-enabled research environment. These practices arise from overarching trends, in particular the ways that researchers deploy new technologies in new and established institutional and technical infrastructures of global e-research that encourage standardization across disciplines, cultures, and national and regional legal–administrative traditions. Standardization makes it increasingly difficult to exercise the discretion necessary to "do the right thing, for the right reason, in the right way, at the right time" (Ess and the AoIR Ethics Working Committee 2002:4).

Standardization is linked to a technoeconomic imperative to adopt e-research if a university or nation wishes to compete with the private sector or with other university or national initiatives. The increased speed and efficiency of e-research (for example, the economic efficiency of Web-based versus paper-and-pencil questionnaires) push scientists to adopt new research approaches that have potential ethical consequences. Beginning with the more familiar issues of data collection, this section traverses emerging issues of data capture, behavioral data, archiving, and virtual environments.

Quantitative Data Collection

Advances in information and communication technologies (ICTs) have enabled new forms of data collection, such as Web-based surveys, instead of traditional pen-and-paper questionnaires. In many respects, apart from making old methods more transparent, these methods take on such a different level of scale or complexity that they raise qualitatively different and new ethical issues. For example, many social scientists might not be aware of the risks of unauthorized access to research data stored on their personal computer, on a Web site, a Grid-enabled database, or "Cloud" computing utilities (essay 2.1). Aggregation of different data sets to create new databases raises ethical issues about "ownership" of the resulting database that are only partially resolved by the provisions of the European Database Directive.[6]

Cloud computing can blur jurisdictional boundaries. Its very virtue is to be able to benefit from the economies of scale offered by data centers and network utilities by moving computing functions and storage away from the desktop and into the "cloud" of services provided by major multinational firms. It may also, however, move communication and computational services away from universities and research institutes, with the potential loss of control over the privacy and confidentiality of data. Just as some firms are moving data centers to countries that provide greater protection of the privacy of their customers' transactions ("Computers without borders" 2008), universities may need to build data centers and shared computing facilities in their own national jurisdictions or in another nation with strict protections of the privacy and confidentiality of data.

Network-enabled research is also mobilizing computational power to enable social science researchers to study whole populations rather than relying on sample surveys. Advanced computational facilities make it easier to integrate and analyze data gathered about ever larger samples and entire populations. The prospect of access to national censuses—which may be combined with health, housing, and other demographic data—may obviate the usefulness of the traditional sample survey. Developments in this area may be restrained to control the kinds of questions asked and topics explored. However, with collaboration between government agencies and universities, sufficient control is possible, and the estimation of behavior, attitudes, and beliefs can be extremely fine-grained.

The new levels of concern over the adequacy of safe settings for research emphasize the need to prevent the unauthorized access to information about individuals and households. They also highlight the need for virtual safe settings that enable researchers to access sensitive data sets from remote locations (box 8.2).

Even fail-safe virtual security settings, however, might not be able to address researchers' ability to develop profiles of individuals on the basis of sophisticated data-mining techniques with larger population surveys. Privacy concerns will potentially be raised when data-mining techniques become increasingly "too" fine-grained.

Box 8.2
Virtual Safe Settings for Data Access and Analysis

Given the limitations of secure data transmission over electronic networks, many organizations share data with their colleagues and researchers situated at remote locations by transporting the data via physical storage media. Even physical media are not always safe, as demonstrated by a series of data breaches caused by lost laptops and memory devices. Despite guidelines to the contrary, sensitive data, often unencrypted and taken from the confines of secure research facilities, can often reside on laptops.

The tension between respecting confidentiality and providing research access to sensitive personal data has been an ongoing challenge for data custodians in the advancement of medical and social science. Upholding near absolute standards to protect privacy reduces the scientific value of the data, and breaches in confidentiality may lead to adverse consequences, including financial and legal sanctions against research agencies and individual researchers. Numerous agencies have been exploring different avenues to provide secure access to sensitive data via other means—for example, approaches that enable remote access to data by researchers from geographically distributed locations—while maintaining the data's confidentiality.

Source: Adapted from Rahman, Jirotka, and Dutton 2008.

The low cost and ease of network-enabled research, such as global Web-based surveys, mean that local institutional review processes will be increasingly challenged when assessing research methods that affect human participants around the world in varying normative settings. For example, more research may escape the attention of review processes if lower-cost e-research methods mean that projects will fall below the financial level requiring grant support and thus avoid the review process usually triggered by grants. Likewise, e-research may accelerate the pace of fieldwork and analysis, raising new kinds of decisions for researchers. A Web-based survey that contains scales of "suicidality" may give researchers some sense of a respondent's risk while he or she is completing the questionnaire, but researchers may then have to balance their obligation to protect the respondent's privacy and peace of mind with the need to recommend that a family physician be contacted, which may be disturbing to the respondent.

Qualitative Data Collection

Collecting qualitative data over the Internet raises ethical issues that are not different in kind from more traditional approaches, such as requiring informed consent and protecting anonymity (Parry and Mauthner 2004). However, the Internet and the Web present new opportunities for gaining access to qualitative data, through conducting online interviews and focus groups and observing online chat rooms, email listservs, and virtual environments such as *Second Life*. As with a quantitative data collection, these new settings can create particular local expectations of privacy and confidentiality. Researchers need to account for these expectations when deciding, for example, if and how they should gain informed consent from the participants. These requirements may also vary by the researchers and participants' national affiliation. Not surprisingly, therefore, many online discussions of Internet ethics concern the propriety of using particular content given the specific virtual setting.

Organizations have attempted to fill the online ethical vacuum with guidelines. The Ethics Working Committee of the Association of Internet Researchers has developed useful general ethical guidelines (Ess and the AoIR Ethics Working Committee 2002). These guidelines highlight the degree to which online media create new settings (e.g., chat rooms, email lists, or virtual environments) that foster particular and varying expectations of privacy or confidentiality on the part of their participants and where assumed identities pose distinct problems for obtaining informed consent.

Data Capture

Qualitative data collection often includes capturing digital audio and video. As Yorick Wilks and Matthijs den Besten explain in chapter 4, the capacity for storing, retrieving, and extracting information from distributed data sets is advancing rapidly. New technologies increase the use of and access to recordings of interviews, focus groups, and public events. This increase may seem to pose a greater risk to privacy, in the vein of concerns about the growth of a "surveillance society" that have shaped the British debate over the use of cameras in public spaces, including traffic speed cameras and security cameras positioned to help identify law breakers and to reduce crime in particular areas.

The use of these technologies, however, may challenge and then change norms about what constitutes ethical behavior. For example, the Access Grid permits multipoint video conferencing and digital recording of such sessions. As participants become accustomed to this medium—and as tools develop to better record, annotate, and analyze the content of such sessions (for example, to study group interaction)—the default expectation is likely to become that of being recorded. This shift potentially alters what would constitute a privacy violation in that setting.

Researchers already collect data through the use of passive global positioning systems (GPS), such as for the study of offenders or travel patterns. However, the tracking of an individual's movement is likely to be increasingly common and linked to other data, such as survey responses.

Behavioral Data: Webmetrics, Search, and Embedded Sensors

Audio-video is only one form of behavioral data that can be captured online. Other technologies include Webmetric (or Webometric) tools and embedded ICTs.

Webmetrics enable researchers to follow behavior online by using "cookies" (that authenticate the user of a service) to track browsing behavior and collect information about users. When a person uses a Web browser to access a server, such as to look at a news site, the server can send a cookie to the browser. The next time the browser contacts the same server, it can return the data contained in the cookie to show, for example, that the same person is returning to the site. Thus, cookies leave traces on individual browsers and servers that can be used to study behavior (e.g., Internet shopping or news reading habits). A log file on a personal computer provides similar information about user behavior, in-links and out-links from Web sites are also powerful ways of capturing user behavior. This information can pose significant privacy and confidentiality concerns if linked to individual users.

A newer form of Webmetric behavioral data focuses on the search terms users submit to Internet search engines to locate information, people, places, or services. The use or distribution of such behavioral data can generate major public issues. For instance, the chief technology officer at AOL resigned two weeks after releasing Internet search terms collected from more than half a million users.[7] Press accounts illustrated how search terms could be associated with individuals in ways that sparked criticism from privacy advocates and highlighted the role that corporations, as institutions, will play in the ethics debate.

Embedded ICTs include embedded sensor networks (essay 4.1) and the remote control of computers in ways that can generate requests and collect data, such as in studies of Internet content filtering. These new forms of gathering and capturing behavioral data enable researchers to change the timing (twenty-four hours a day, seven days a week) and scale of research (from a specific location to the globe), which cannot be replicated by traditional approaches. The use of embedded sensors in scientific domains such as "event-driven" marine science can be an efficient means of improving marine observation. However, analogous sensors to trigger event-driven social observation or intervention raise more sensitive personal and cultural issues. The use of video to study crowd movements in open public spaces, for instance, can enable researchers to develop models of potential events, such as a fight or a theft, which may trigger closer observation or intervention—but it has the distinct flavor of an authoritarian Orwellian surveillance state.

Archiving Quantitative and Qualitative Data

The collection and capture of new forms of data are complemented by a phenomenal increase in the capacity to store, annotate, curate, and otherwise archive digital data. The ability to store large quantities of data on ever smaller storage devices has driven many new policies on data archiving toward more-inclusive and less-selective collection and archiving. Increasing storage capacity and a push to open science in the interests of broader access and interdisciplinary inquiry have also encouraged archivists to

Box 8.3
Example of Ethical Tensions in an e-Research Project

One research project included findings from a pilot study using Webmetrics to study the linkages among a small sample of Web sites focused on an array of areas of current scientific research. The final report indicated that it would be wasteful to archive the results of these exploratory Webmetric analyses because they were based on small samples. It would be far better, the report stated, for any subsequent replication to draw new samples at the time of that research. However, the funding agency told the researchers that it might want the Webmetric results. More significantly, the agency noted that the final report mentioned qualitative interviews, and so it asked whether the researchers could provide the transcripts of these interviews with the scientists, along with any interview notes.

The researchers had recorded interviews with individual scientists across a range of disciplines and had promised that the scientists would remain anonymous and that their interviews would remain confidential. The researchers would quote only selectively from the interviews to illustrate themes and findings. Thus, the researchers felt they could not provide the funding agency with these qualitative interviews for archiving because doing so would violate their agreement with the participants.

store every data analysis conducted rather than merely the final tables that are usually presented in a published article.

The drive to archive everything in the interests of the "progress of science" and to protect public investment creates tensions with the ethical realities of individual research projects. One actual case of such tensions is summarized in box 8.3.

Three options appeared to be available to the project team facing the tensions outlined in box 8.3:

• Provide everything requested by the funding agency, although doing so might damage the researchers' reputations and violate agreements with interviewees.
• Anonymize the interview transcripts by shading out names and identifying information. However, this action would take time and render the interviews worthless because it would be impossible to interpret and make sense of the responses if one did not know who the scientists were and what they were referring to in their responses.
• The researchers might refuse to provide the interview transcripts that they had been told to provide, but this refusal would lead potentially to the withholding of the last payment of their grant and future "blacklisting" by the funding agency.

The team members eventually decided that they could not turn over the transcripts or anonymize them. Before it came to the point of an explicit refusal, they received a letter of reprieve indicating that the archive had decided that the results were not appropriate to archive, but providing no further reasons.

This real-world example shows the importance of recognizing and negotiating conflicting values underpinning research ethics. On one hand, there are calls for open science (chapter 11) and open access (Willinsky 2006); on the other, there are the longstanding concerns for privacy, confidentiality, and the protection of human research participants. Although national funding agencies and governments are responding to compelling calls to make the products of publicly funded research broadly accessible to the public, some data may be inappropriate to disclose (e.g., in cases where breaches in confidentiality might undermine the quality of social science by eroding trust in the interviewers, as the researchers in box 8.3 argued). As the push for open science becomes less of a social movement[8] and more balanced with other values shaping network-enabled research, there should be more room for considering ways to ensure that the quality of social science is not compromised by any single ethical guideline or principle.

The increased archiving of video and Webmetrics data also threatens a more difficult negotiation over informed consent as the scope of possible uses to which a participant may consent expands. Those who collect data (e.g., by video or by interpersonal interaction) are increasingly distanced from other researchers' use of these data at other points in time. In the United Kingdom's e–Social Science Programme (chapter 6), a project that used video recordings of interactions to study gestures (such as head nods) within a broader project studying interpersonal communication created the potential for others to use the same video for related studies, but not necessarily for research that the participants had consented to.[9] One rationale for archives to collect such qualitative data is the potential for later researchers to find new ways of looking at old data sets in order to address new research questions. Most research participants currently do not consent to as yet unknown ways in which researchers might wish to use the data provided. The very idea of informed consent is thus in jeopardy.

Virtual Experiments

It is unclear whether and how the normal rules in research ethics apply when experiments are conducted in virtual environments, as in *Second Life*. How should researchers conduct themselves within such environments? For example, it may be tempting for them to deceive others by not representing themselves as researchers or by inventing age, sex, or political affiliations in order to elicit more candid or reliable responses. Many research participants are also likely to be role playing, which raises issues about the authenticity and validity of experiments in virtual worlds, particularly because these results apply to real-life behavior. Such concerns highlight questions of informed consent that are not materially different from real-world ethical questions facing researchers.

More interestingly, using avatars means that researchers and participants can simulate human beings and their behavior without the physical, emotional, and material

Box 8.4
Example of Research Ethics in a Virtual Environment

A group of social psychologists has simulated in a virtual environment one of the most discussed set of experiments in the annals of research ethics: Stanley Milgram's (1963) and others' research to study whether subjects would administer painful shocks to human beings if instructed to do so by an appropriate authority figure. It was found that they *would* do so.

More recently, a research experiment with a similar objective was constructed to avoid asking volunteers to administer shocks to a real person if that person failed to give the correct answer. Instead, the volunteers were placed in a virtual environment where they were told to administer shocks to a virtual woman (Slater, Antley, Davison, et al. 2006; Smith 2006). Because volunteers were told that the woman was not real, the experimenters felt that the replication was not harmful. They found that although participants hesitated at times to administer shocks, tending to resist harming even a virtual person, they did so anyway. The outcome—the fact that the participants obeyed an authority figure—was as disturbing to the volunteers as it had been in the original Milgram experiments. In such ways, experiments in virtual reality should be subjected to the same questions posed regarding experiments in the laboratory.

---

consequences of real life. However, ethical determinations may require the treatment of a virtual person as a "real" person and, more explicitly, the consideration of the relationships between real people and avatars—as highlighted in the case in box 8.4.

Limits of the Substitution Paradigm in the e-Research Ethics Regime

The development of network-enabled research environments entails more than mere substitution of online for offline media. These technologies pose distinct challenges by changing the speed, geography, and scale of many research projects. For example, embedded sensor networks may be regarded simply as an extension of older forms of unobtrusive measures of human behavior, such as in monitoring the wear on flooring as an indicator of the popularity of different exhibits (Webb, Campbell, Schwartz, et al. 2000 [1966]). These new networks, however, extend observation in a manner that was never contemplated in 1966, when methodologists spoke of accessing actuarial records or observing natural erosion: the networks can be used to record who views what exhibit, for how long, and in what sequence. The diffusion of mobile phones and related devices with increasing geosynchronous monitoring capabilities means that communication networks will increasingly become embedded sensor networks.

In these ways, new technologies will challenge existing roles, particularly those of ethicists, researchers, institutions, and the existing administrative network of ethical review, as discussed in the following subsections.

New Roles for Ethicists

Ethicists are likely to play a key role in resolving conflicts posed by network-enabled research, but they may be poorly equipped to do so. Although the values threatened are often longstanding issues (such as privacy), e-research does pose some novel issues and conflicts across competing values. Figure 8.1 illustrates some of these competing values and their interconnections. It might not be possible to act in accordance with all of these values simultaneously, and the pursuit of some, such as open science, can conflict with others, such as confidentiality.

Ethicists provide us with a variety of ethical frameworks and answers that are of use in illuminating ethical dilemmas, but that do not necessarily resolve them (essay 8.1). Few believe that we should base decisions inflexibly on a single principle or should ignore principles in search of the greatest good for the greatest number. Research institutions, programs, and initiatives increasingly have their ethical specialists and defenders, just as they have their legal advisors, and these roles may overlap. Major projects in ethically complex areas, such as medical research and research on the human genome, will need an ethicist on board merely to defend their research. This development may increasingly shift ethicists from acting as philosophers to acting as advocates, which is already evident in controversial areas of medical and social research. The ethicist then becomes one more actor in the political process shaping decisions aimed at resolving ethical conflicts and value trade-offs.

The Researcher's Perspective

A range of ethical issues will impose themselves on the individual researcher who is faced with the continuing dilemma of deciding what is right in the circumstances of a particular set of subjects, data archivists, and so on. Researchers seek to "do no harm," which is often translated into efforts to "minimize risk of harm" to the subjects (Ess and the AoIR Ethics Working Committee 2002:8). Nevertheless, doing business in the new network-enabled research environment may require researchers to compromise some of their principles and more explicitly manage competing risks.

In the shorter term, e-research standards encourage interdisciplinary collaboration while at the same time exposing differences across the disciplines of individual researchers (essay 8.1). For example, guidelines for collecting and reporting qualitative interviews vary greatly by discipline: compare a political scientist interviewing a public official with a social anthropologist interviewing a homeless person. In particular, some researchers in the humanities may consider it their duty to respect their data

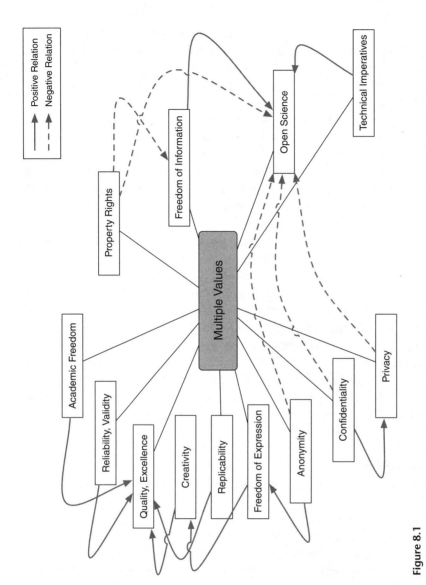

Figure 8.1
An ecology of academic values.

subjects as artists or authors who may own their contributions in these settings. Thus, these researchers may be far less concerned with privacy than with ownership. Expectations, risks, and disciplinary codes differ significantly across disciplines, and conflict arises when we treat data in similar or standard ways despite these differences. These problems raise serious questions relating to the principles guiding research and the governance of these ethical principles. Such questions need to be negotiated by and their resolution made accountable to the full range of actors involved in e-research.

Implications for Institutions and Administration

Negotiating the conflicts outlined here will have to expand to include disciplinary, institutional, and national boundaries as part of a broader political process. As worldwide science develops, the institutional arrangements in place to govern privacy, confidentiality, and related ethical issues will be dominated by local institutional review committees, albeit shaped by national and regional legal–administrative traditions.

The individual researcher is faced with a bewildering array of codes, guidelines, and review processes at local, national, professional disciplinary, and regional levels. This array encourages methodological conventions that have survived the gauntlet of review processes and may well discourage the development of innovative methods and data-collection efforts. It also encourages gaming of the review process as researchers learn how to push proposals through particular ethics committees or bypass them altogether. Ethics committees can also become conservative and fail to keep up with the state of the art in e-research, leading them either to block or to approve projects based on an incomplete understanding of the procedures and dilemmas, or making them unable to move outside culturally ethnocentric positions and appreciate all the cultural conventions of subjects who may be involved in network-enabled research.

Institutional and administrative processes of ethical review are partly a negotiation of a community's norms, values, and collective wisdom. This negotiation may be an appropriate locus for the application of distributed problem-solving strategies that move beyond such institutional limitations. Successful endeavors such as *Wikipedia*, Linux, and other open-source projects (Weber 2004) support the potential for geographically and intellectually distributed individuals to address sometimes complex common problems. Distributed networks may also show us one way of eliciting and defining the ethical standards in an interdisciplinary, international project. Here, a key problem is the accountability of e-research to a wide range of actors with competing priorities allocated to a variety of values that are at stake in the process and outcomes of research.

A Method for Opening Up the Ethical Review Process in e-Research

Can a process of distributed globalized accountability, when relevant, enable a wide range of expertise to be exploited to explain and expose risks, and force researchers to address those risks? Instead of or in addition to putting the results of science online, perhaps we should be putting proposals online. We should open methods, not just results. This proposal is not unprecedented. For instance, the *Journal of Visualized Experiments* has created a peer-reviewed, free-access forum to disclose in video format novel experimental techniques in biological research.[10]

The risks of opening methods are evident. It may facilitate criticism and objection to research, potentially creating a conservative influence. It may enforce a utilitarian ethic of the greatest good for the greatest number by demonstrating the relative weight of different opinions. It may lead to ridicule of research funders as the funding of weak proposals is exposed. An innovative proposal for research might be "stolen."

These objections themselves can be addressed by distributed review of proposals. Few proposals survive review processes in any case, and killing ethically flawed methodologies is as valid as rejecting proposals on other grounds. The potential for global social accountability of research might be great in shoring trust in the sciences, stimulating and informing debate about scientific and research methods, and discovering new approaches.

Distributed accountability of research, gained by opening all research proposals to a deliberative model of global scrutiny, might harness e-research tools in support of ethical processes and outcomes. It might act as a complement to rather than a substitute for institutional review.

Conclusions: Ethical Principles in Research

The critical perspective on the ethics of e-research outlined in this chapter provides a backdrop to issues emerging within the traditional ethics regime that addresses privacy, confidentiality, and related ethical issues with the growth of network-enabled research. Advances in ICTs are connecting library, information, and computer sciences with subject-matter disciplines in ways that enable a growing range of research practices, from data collection to publication and archiving. These interrelated technical, social, and institutional developments are reconfiguring scholars' research. In doing so, they are raising old ethical issues in new contexts, but also posing some genuinely new ethical dilemmas that must be balanced with opportunities created by these new technologies to "open" science and collaboration.

As we have illustrated in the chapter, e-researchers are likely to encounter ethical issues in areas as diverse as quantitative and qualitative data collection, data capture, behavioral data, archiving, and virtual experiments. Ethical questions may be resolved using existing paradigms or may require novel solutions. We propose the opening of research proposals as one mechanism to complement institutional review and to mobilize e-research tools to sustain and further develop ethical processes and outcomes.

Acknowledgments

We thank Annamaria Carusi, Paul Jeffreys, and Christopher Millard for their helpful comments on drafts of this chapter.

Notes

1. Details of the 1995 Data Protection Directive 95/46/EC (*Official Journal of the European Union* L 281 [23 November 1995]:31–50) are available at http://eur-lex.europa.eu/LexUriServ/LexUriServ .do?uri=CELEX:31995L0046:EN:HTML.

2. European Court of Justice Decision on Joined Cases C-317/04 and C-318/04.

3. For full details of the 1998 U.K. Data Protection Act, see http://www.opsi.gov.uk/Acts/Acts1998/ ukpga_19980029_en_1.

4. Background information on the U.K. Information Commissioner's Office is available at http:// www.ico.gov.uk/.

5. In *Stanley v. Georgia* (1969), Justice Marshall wrote: "Whatever may be the justifications for other statutes regulating obscenity, we do not think they reach into the privacy of one's own home. If the First Amendment means anything, it means that a State has no business telling a man, sitting alone in his own house, what books he may read or what films he may watch. Our whole constitutional heritage rebels at the thought of giving government the power to control men's minds."

6. Details of the 1996 Database Directive 96/9/EC (*Official Journal of the European Communities* L 077 [27 March 1996]:20–28) are available at http://europa.eu.int/smartapi/cgi/sga_doc?smartapi !celexapi!prod!CELEXnumdoc&lg=EN&numdoc=31996L0009&model=guichett.

7. Extensive press coverage includes Wiggins 2006 and Zeller 2006.

8. Many developments in computerization, including e-research, have had the characteristics of a "social movement," leading some to the analysis of what has been called "computerization movements" (Elliott and Kraemer 2008).

9. An example of such an application is the Mixed Media Grid, a project of the U.K. National Centre for e–Social Science. See http://www.ncess.ac.uk/research/video/mimeg/.

10. For the *Journal of Visualized Experiments*, see http://www.jove.com.

References

Anderson, T., and H. Kanuka. 2003. *e-Research: Methods, strategies, and issues*. New York: Pearson Education.

"Computers without borders: A special report." 2008. *The Economist 23* (October). Available at: http://www.economist.com/research/articlesbysubject/displaystory.cfm?subjectid=348909&story _id=12411854.

Elliott, M., and K. L. Kraemer, eds. 2008. *Computerization movements and technology diffusion: From mainframes to ubiquitous computing*. Medford, NJ: Information Today.

Ess, C. 2007. "Internet research ethics." In *Oxford handbook of Internet psychology*, ed. A. N. Joinson, K. Y. A. McKenna, T. Postmes, and U-D. Reips. Oxford, UK: Oxford University Press, 487–502.

Ess, C., and the Association of Internet Researchers (AoIR) Ethics Working Committee. 2002. *Ethical decision-making and Internet research: Recommendations from the AoIR Ethics Working Committee*. Available at: http://aoir.org/reports/ethics.pdf.

Fitzgerald, B., ed. 2008. *Legal framework for e-research: Realising the potential*. Sydney: Sydney University Press.

Milgram, S. 1963. "Behavioral study of obedience." *Journal of Abnormal Social Psychology* *67*:371–378.

Organization for Economic Cooperation and Development (OECD). 1980. *Guidelines on the protection of privacy and transborder flows of Personal data*. Available at: http://www.oecd.org/document/18/0,2340,en_2649_34255_1815186_1_1_1_1,00.html.

Parry, O., and N. S. Mauthner. 2004. "Whose data are they anyway? Practical, legal, and ethical issues in archiving qualitative research data." *Sociology 38* (1):139–152.

Rahman, M., M. Jirotka, and W. H. Dutton. 2008. "Lost in reality—the case for virtual safe settings." Paper presented at the Annual Conference of the National Centre for e–Social Science, University of Manchester, UK, 18 June. Available at: http://www.ncess.ac.uk/events/conference/programme/workshop1/?ref=/programme/thurs/2bRahman.htm.

Slater, M., A. Antley, A. Davison, D. Swapp, C. Guger, C. Barker, N. Pistrang, and M. V. Sanchez-Vives. 2006. "A virtual reprise of the Stanley Milgram obedience experiments." *PLoS One 1* (1):e39. doi:10.1371/journal.pone.0000039.

Smith, K. 2006. "Virtual reality shocker." News@Nature.com, 22 December. Available at: http://www.nature.com/news/2006/061218/pf/061218-17_pf.html.

Webb, E. J., D. T. Campbell, R. D. Schwartz, and L. Sechrest. 2000 [1966]. *Unobtrusive measures*. Rev. ed. Thousand Oaks, CA: Sage.

Weber, S. 2004. *The success of open source*. Cambridge, MA: Harvard University Press.

Wiggins, R. W. 2006. "AOL is caught in its own long tail." *Infotoday*, 14 August. Available at: http://www.infotoday.com/newsbreaks/nb060814-1.shtml.

Willinsky, J. 2006. *The access principle: The case for open access to research and scholarship*. Cambridge, MA: MIT Press.

Zeller, T. 2006. "AOL technology chief quits after data release." *New York Times*, 23 August.

8.1   Ethical and Moral Dimensions of e-Research

Michael Parker

This essay explores the ethical dimensions of distributed collaboration in e-research and makes suggestions for research strategies. It draws a distinction between morals and ethics, conceptualizing the "moral" as the commonly shared, normalized practices and values structuring everyday life and the "ethical" as situations where the moral is problematic, contested, and in need of deliberation, analysis, or critique. The ethical is the moral as an object of concern. Of particular ethical interest in relation to e-research are the ways in which the development of distributed collaboration has the potential to lead to the enactment of established moral relationships, expectations, and practices as objects of ethical concern.

Standardization and Shared Values

E-research involves diverse collaborations and networklike partnerships that bring together researchers from various academic disciplines, specialists in information technology, local collaborators (e.g., health professionals), professionals in distributed computing facilities, research funders, communities, and populations. This dependence on distributed collaborations across different disciplines, institutions, and research cultures means that key determinants of success are the establishment and maintenance of collaborative partnerships, shared values, and practices. Three main factors are of particular relevance to successful collaboration.

First, the effectiveness of e-research and the interoperability of electronic resources depend on standardization. Standardization is required in the construction of databases and in the selection, interpretation, and inputting of "data"—such as the selection of a digital image as falling into a particular category. It is not unproblematic. The chosen categories and modes of categorization may not fit easily with existing diversity of practice across institutions and disciplines. As a result, e-research collaborations may lead to the enactment of everyday practice as an object of concern in different ways for different partners. Systems of categorization are furthermore not morally or ethically neutral.

Second, the effectiveness of e-research depends on agreement across the consortium about key moral features of collaboration (e.g., those relating to the treatment of intellectual property, sharing of data, and publication). Agreement in these and other areas will be key to the establishment and maintenance of trust across the collaboration.

Third, in addition to the establishment of technological standardization and ideas about what is to count as good scientific practice, the success of collaborative e-research will depend on reaching agreement in response to important questions in other key areas of practice, such as: What is to constitute valid consent when obtaining permission from potential data subjects for the use of information about them? What are appropriate standards of confidentiality, anonymity, privacy, and security, and how are they to be maintained? What is an appropriate model of governance for access to, use of, and publication of data?

Finding answers to these questions is unlikely to be straightforward. The distributed nature of e-research means that different people and institutions with different approaches to good practice and different expectations will be involved. Questions will inevitably arise about how such expectations and practices are to be addressed and taken seriously. Trust in e-research will depend crucially on the achievement of some degree of clarity about good practice across networked relations.

Virtual Organizations and Distributed Collaboration

The Speciality of Responsibility

Reaching explicit agreement about what constitutes good practice is essential to successful and appropriate e-research, but such agreements and their embodiment in guidelines, policies, and statements are by themselves insufficient for the success of e-research. Good practice depends also on individuals' moral conduct (e.g., their sense of responsibility, integrity, what is expected of someone in their position, and what it is to be a good scientist). In e-research, the distributed nature of responsibilities for establishing and maintaining resources is of particular relevance in this regard.

Those who create and use such resources will be located within complex networks of overlapping and sometimes competing allegiances, affiliations, and research and other cultures. For example, those collecting health-related data and those using such data are likely to have different moral and institutional relationships to the "data subject." This difference suggests a "spatiality" of understandings of "responsibility," which may vary across the consortium so that individuals may find themselves the subjects of different types of complementary or conflicting obligations and responsibilities as they shift from institution to institution, from location to location, or from role to role. An additional feature of this spatiality of responsibility is that those who use and manage such resources may feel morally distant from the data subjects, data users, or their research collaborators.

The end users will have no knowledge of what resources they have used to process their data and in some cases will not know where the data itself came from. Their primary interest will be in the potential uses they can make of the resource.

Shifting Roles and Temporary Responsibilities

In addition to the distributed nature of e-research, a virtual organization is one in which individuals and institutions may have temporary or partial roles. An institution may contribute data or expertise to a virtual organization for a limited period of time, taking on and then relinquishing not only membership, but also the associated moral responsibilities in temporary and partial ways. Insofar as expectations of moral behavior are related to a sense of involvement, participation, community, and so on, this temporary, partial, or distant involvement may lead those involved to feel less sense of personal responsibility and allegiance, which has implications for their conduct and ultimately for trust in the enterprise.

The Spaciality of "Virtue"

It is sometimes argued that "virtuous conduct" is meaningful only in the context of well-established traditions and practices, and that high moral standards and practices are not sustainable without a sense of "role" or "belonging." This argument poses an interesting question for e-research, particularly in light of both the possibility of relatively easy access to sensitive data and the dependence of scientific collaboration on relationships of trust between collaborating scientists. To what extent is it possible that morality is simply incompatible with distributed collaborations and virtual organizations? To what extent is it possible to conceptualize trust and establish trustworthiness so that they make sense in the context of distributed, cross-institutional, and interdisciplinary collaborations?

The Possibility of Moral Architectures

Building and sustaining trust are key roadblocks to successful distributed collaboration. A significant technological challenge is thus the extent to which it may be possible to develop "moral architectures" such that moral behavior is encouraged by the structures and processes of the technology itself. In this way, users and collaborators might be enabled to have "confidence" in the architecture even if they do not trust their collaborators. Whatever the potentially useful role for the development of "moral architectures," it seems inevitable that trust, trustworthiness, and the achievement and maintenance of shared values will continue to be key factors in successful science research.

Conclusion: Mapping Trust and Meaning

This essay has briefly sketched some of the ethical features of e-research. These factors have the potential to act as barriers to e-research, which suggests that the development of successful and appropriate e-research will depend on interdisciplinary research into the identification and analysis of such factors. Ethnographic and other qualitative approaches have a significant role to play in understanding many of the ethical and social issues discussed because they arise in the context of the relationships between different and emerging research cultures, divergent understandings of key concepts such as "trust," and the meanings of research collaboration.

8.2 Data Sharing in Genomics—Is It Lawful?

Jane Kaye

Sharing Genomics Data as a Public Resource

Huge advances in the field of genomics have been enabled by the well-established scientific benefits of sharing sequence (genotype) data. This progress has been demonstrated by the creation of a range of community resources, including the International Human Genome Sequencing Consortium,[1] which is responsible for mapping the human genome, and the International HapMap Project,[2] a multicountry effort to identify and catalog genetic similarities and differences in human beings. Such projects seek to make sequence data freely available with unrestricted access to all scientists through the Web. However, none of these databases contains demographic, clinical, or other detailed lifestyle (phenotypic) information linked to the sequence information.

Based on these projects' success, major funding bodies around the world—such as the National Institutes of Health in the United States, the European Commission, and Medical Research Council in the United Kingdom—have put data-sharing policies[3] in place. The aim is to require sharing of *all* types of data generated through the research process—not just sequence data. The rationale behind such initiatives is to utilize publicly funded research data to the fullest extent by opening up such collections to other researchers, which will reduce unnecessary duplication of data sets, enable new lines of inquiry, and speed up the process of knowledge production. Other e-research initiatives share these aims, and the issues they raise are very similar to those encountered in genomics because they primarily concern the use of digital information.

The basic principle in these policies is that all data should be shared unless controllers of data sets can establish good reasons why they should not be. This essay focuses on the rights of the donor under European data-protection law and the implications for practice in light of funders and researchers' aims to share data for research purposes. The prime question is whether such data can be shared with third-party researchers without donors' consent. The legislative framework addressed is that based on the European Communities Directive 95/46/EC of 24 October 1995 on the protection of individuals with regard to the processing of personal data and on the free movement of these data (see European Communities 1997).[4]

Consent for the Processing of Medical Data

The basic principle underpinning Directive 95/46/EC is that the use and processing of sensitive identifiable data, such as medical information, is prohibited unless the donor has given explicit consent or the processing is required for a number of specific circumstances. The term *explicit consent* is not defined in the directive, although it is stated that "the data subject's consent" shall mean "any freely given specific and informed indication of his wishes by which the data subject signifies his agreement to personal data relating to him being processed" (Article 2[h]). This definition suggests that consent does not need to be in writing. However, for medical information, the directive's data-processing principles require that the individual be explicitly informed—with regard to any personal data relating to him or her—of the nature of the processing of that data, the particular type of data to be processed, the purposes of the processing, and any aspects of the processing that may affect the individual.

If data will be disclosed to a third person, the individual must also be informed of the identity of the third party, the purpose for which the information will be processed, the type of information that will be processed, and any other aspect of the processing that will make the processing fair (Article 11). However, there are exceptions to these requirements for different types of research, and the directive's principles will no longer apply if the data are anonymous.

The Exception Related to Secondary Use

For data being passed to a third party, such as another researcher, Article 11(b) of the directive allows identifiable data to be used for secondary scientific research reasons (e.g., for historical, statistical, or scientific purposes) without telling the individuals affected (Recital 40). This allowance would apply only if it is impossible to tell the person, if telling the person involves disproportionate effort, or if the recording or disclosure of the data is expressly laid down by law (Article 11[2], Recital 40). If these requirements were satisfied, the donor would therefore not have to be informed that the data were going to be employed for another research use or by another researcher. If these data were anonymous when they were passed to the third party, they would fall outside the directive's requirements. Processing to make the data anonymous—and therefore outside the mantle of the data-processing regime—would require the donor's explicit consent.[5] However, doing so would mean that anonymous data can be made available to third parties.

How the Secondary-Use Exemption Applies to Genomics Research

The key question in determining whether data sharing is lawful for genomic research is whether data sharing comes within the exception under Article 11(b) of Directive

95/46/EC.[6] This article exempts historical, statistical, or scientific purposes from the requirements that individuals need to be given information on the secondary processing of their personal data. It is not clear whether this exemption covers medical research and therefore the sharing of data sets created for genetic research purposes. The requirements for medical research are quite different from the requirements applied to statistical and historical research. In medical research, the principle has been that informed consent must be obtained for each new research project.[7] Large data sets that have been collected for medical research purposes occupy two different regulatory domains: medical research and statistics.

The purpose of data sharing is to allow epidemiological research to be carried out on these pooled data sets, and therefore the sharing is statistical in nature. For this exemption to apply, however, it would have to be established that a disproportionate effort would be involved in providing individual donors with the information that their data would be accessed by a number of other researchers. The amount of effort would be determined by "the number of data subjects, the age of the data, and any compensatory measures adopted" (Recital 40). Consideration of the effort involved would not be necessary if this use were laid down in law or if donors had already given their explicit consent.

Conclusion

If an activity can be categorized as falling under the exemption stipulated in Recital 40 of Directive 95/46/EC, then the individual who provides the data is no longer a key player in how the data are used or processed. Instead, this responsibility can be delegated to other third parties, such as scientists or statisticians (if the research is classified as statistical), or to other bodies stipulated in law.

When the directive was drafted (1995), the technological abilities to cross-reference large data sets was not at the scale that has subsequently become feasible. Although it is possible to use data for secondary research purposes if the data have already been collected, the directive still demands that certain conditions must exist for this use to be lawful. Therefore, the sharing of data sets by researchers as an aim established by funders is allowed under data-protection law related to this directive, even though it may not be acceptable under the principles of medical research.

Notes

1. See http://genome.wellcome.ac.uk/doc_WTD023572.html.

2. See http://snp.cshl.org/.

3. Initial data-sharing principles relating to sequence information were articulated in the 1996 Bermuda Principles (http://www.ornl.gov/sci/techresources/Human_Genome/research/bermuda .shtml#1) and later in the Fort Lauderdale Tripartite-Agreement of 2003.

4. All subsequent references in this essay to articles and recitals relate to this directive. An updated status report on the implementation of the directive is available at: http://ec.europa.eu/justice_home/fsj/privacy/law/implementation_en.htm.

5. See the definition of processing under Article 2(b).

6. This exemption is contained in Recital 40.

7. Recommendation No. R (97) 5 of February 1997 of the Committee of Ministers to Members States on the Protection of Medical Data CM (97) 18, para. 214.

References

European Communities. 1997. Directive 95/46/EC of 24 October 1995 on the Protection of Individuals with Regard to the Processing of Personal Data and on the Free Movement of Such Data. *Official Journal of the European Communities* L 281 (November 23):31–50. Available at: http://eur-lex.europa.eu/LexUriServ/LexUriServ.do?uri=CELEX:31995L0046:EN:HTML.

8.3 Protecting Confidentiality

Julia Lane

The empirical study of human and social behavior, traditionally reliant on the collection of data through surveys, administrative records, and direct observation, is now being transformed. Social scientists' new cyber-enabled ability to observe human interactions in cyberspace and to use technology to track what people do and when they do it has resulted in an explosion of rich new sources of research data. The resulting challenge is daunting: How can social scientists utilize this information while protecting the confidentiality of the human beings who are the objects of their research? Yet solving the problem is imperative: as Fran Berman and Henry Brady (2005) point out, "Many believe that the problem of finding ways to meet the legitimate privacy and confidentiality concerns of human subjects is the Achilles heel of the current data explosion."

Moving beyond Statistical Solutions

For many reasons, the traditional statistical ways of protecting confidentiality are no longer viable as the sole approach to disclosure limitation. Statistical techniques have not yet been developed that will deidentify video pictures, camouflage reidentifying information in emails, or protect personal information embedded in, for example, large-scale, longitudinal, linked, transaction-based data sets. The increasing availability of detailed personal identifying information (PII) online creates commensurately increasing potential for reidentification of data previously thought to be statistically anonymized. In addition, current statistical techniques often substantially reduce the utility of the data. For example, many techniques eliminate the very outliers that are often of most interest in explaining human behavior.[1] In addition, the long time required to apply and test the algorithms creates time lags that are increasingly unacceptable in a quickly changing social and economic environment.

However, there is no need to rely on a single method to reduce the risk of disclosure. It is vital that a research agenda be established that examines how a judicious combination of technological, statistical, operational, and educational approaches can be used to reduce the risk of subject reidentification. This agenda would examine how social scientists can work in conjunction with computer scientists to develop cyber-tools to provide broader access to confidential data on human beings. That research agenda would promote the replicability that is the essence of science. The long-term goal should be to develop a research data infrastructure similar to that being developed for other scientists, such as astronomers,[2] physicists,[3] and biotechnology researchers.[4]

The capacity already exists in the computer science community. Protecting databases against intruders has a long history in computer science (e.g., see the classic article by David Dobkin, Anita Jones, and Richard Lipton [1979]). Computer scientists themselves are interested in protecting the confidentiality of the data on which they do research (for example, the Abilene Observatory[5] supports the collection and dissemination of network data, such as Internet protocol addresses). The Trustworthy Computing initiative[6] of the U.S. National Science Foundation has established an entire research community that focuses on creating network computers that are more predictable and less vulnerable to attack and abuse (because they are developed, configured, operated, and evaluated by a well-trained workforce); it also educates the public in the secure and ethical operation of such computers. Similarly, the Privacy, Obligations, and Rights in Technologies of Information Assessment project[7] focuses on both the technical challenges of handling sensitive data and the policy and legal issues facing data subjects, data owners, and data users. The private sector—including IBM, Microsoft, Google, and eBay—has also developed open-source and interoperable identity technologies that decouple and blind PII so that subject privacy is protected while experimental data are collected and analyzed.

The precedents for such data access also exist in many other contexts. The U.S. Department of Defense has developed different levels of Web-based access using off-the-shelf technology, ranging from unclassified (nipr-net) to secret (sipr-net) to top secret (jwics-net).[8] The U.S. Department of Homeland Security has invested heavily in ways to share data on terrorists (Swire 2006), and the banking industry has a long history of accessing data in a secure manner while protecting confidentiality (Swire 2003).

Next Steps

Despite the transformational potential of such collaboration, the social science research community has not been proactive in changing the way in which data are accessed. Indeed, although the Conference on European Statisticians has developed a set of organizational, statistical, and legal guidelines for statistical agencies to follow in disseminating microdata,[9] the proposal does not exploit the new cybertechnologies that can be used to address the data-access challenges (e.g., see Weber 2005). Statements made by statistical agency heads indicate that a major reason for their hesitation is the difficulty of guaranteeing that researchers who access data remotely will protect the data as well as the difficulty of conveying this protection to their respondents. A focused approach to convincing respondents, data custodians, and policymakers that e-research advances can broaden researcher access without compromising confidentiality will be key to facilitating such access.[10]

Notes

1. Indeed, as Isaac Asimov noted, "The most exciting phrase to hear in science, the one that heralds new discoveries, is not 'Eureka!' (I've found it!), but 'That's funny'" (http://www.worldofquotes.com/author/Isaac-Asimov/1/index.html).

2. For example, see the U.S. National Virtual Observatory Web site at http://www.us-vo.org/.

3. For example, the Grid-enabled data infrastructure being developed for the Large Hadron Collider at the European Organization for Nuclear Research: http://public.web.cern.ch/Public/en/LHC/LHC-en.html.

4. For example, see the genotype and phenotype database at http://www.ncbi.nlm.nih.gov/entrez/query/Gap/gap_tmpl/about.html.

5. See http://www.internet2.edu/observatory/.

6. See http://nsf.gov/funding/pgm_summ.jsp?pims_id=503326&org=IIS&from=home.

7. The project's goals are to design and develop a next generation of technology for handling sensitive information that is qualitatively better than the current generation's and to create an effective conceptual framework for policymaking and philosophical inquiry into the rights and responsibilities of data subjects, data owners, and data users (see http://crypto.stanford.edu/portia/).

8. Carl Landwehr, now senior research scientist at the Institute for Systems Research at the University of Maryland, pointed out this application (see: http://en.wikipedia.org/wiki/SIPRNET).

9. See Lane 2003 and UNECE 2007.

10. The OECD (2007) has provided a very useful document on which such an approach can be based.

References

Berman, F., and H. Brady. 2005. *Final report: NSF SBE-CISE Workshop on Cyberinfrastructure and the Social Sciences*. Available at: http://vis.sdsc.edu/sbe/reports/SBE-CISE-FINAL.pdf.

Dobkin, D., A. Jones, and R. Lipton. 1979. "Secure databases: Protection against user influence." *ACM Transactions on Database Systems* 4:97–106.

Lane, J. 2003. "The uses of microdata." Keynote address to the Conference of European Statisticians, Geneva, Switzerland, June. Available at: http://www.unece.org/stats/documents/ces/2003/crp.2.e.pdf.

Organization for Economic Cooperation and Development (OECD). 2007. *At a crossroads: "Personhood" and digital identity in the information society*. Science, Technology, and Industry Working Paper 2007/7. Paris: Directorate for Science, Technology, and Society.

Swire, P. 2003. *Efficient confidentiality for privacy, security, and confidential business information*. Brookings-Wharton Papers on Financial Services. Washington, DC: Brookings Institution.

Swire, P. 2006. "Privacy and information sharing in the war on terrorism." *Villanova Law Review 51* (4):951.

United Nations Economic Commission for Europe (UNECE). 2007. *Managing statistical confidentiality and microdata access: Principles and guidelines of good practice*. Geneva: UNECE.

Weber, T. 2005. "Values in a national information infrastructure: A case study of the U.S. Census." Paper presented at the Fourteenth International Conference of the Society of Philosophy and Technology, Delft, the Netherlands, 20–22 July. Available at: http://crypto.stanford.edu/portia/pubs/articles/W2087827446.html.

IV   Implications for Research

The four chapters of this concluding part of the book highlight significant areas where e-research can challenge and change many long-established policies and practices in the sciences and humanities. These areas have deep implications across all disciplines, as discussed in chapter 9. One of the most distinctive features is the emergence of a new research paradigm that has the potential to reshape research collaborations—the theme of chapter 10. The nature and politics of the ways e-research can support and stimulate moves toward a more "open" mode of research are explored in chapter 11. Global implications of e-research for developing counties and regions is the subject of chapter 12, the book's last main chapter before a brief coda.

The part begins in chapter 9 with Jenny Fry and Ralph Schroeder's analysis of the diversity across the sciences and humanities, a characteristic often overlooked in scholarly debate on the implications of research-centered computational networks. These differences have been illustrated in many examples throughout the book. Fry and Schroeder draw together the key dimensions of such variations. They show how these variations influence the disciplines' boundaries, thereby reconfiguring the research landscape. In the one essay tied to this chapter, Paul Wouters focuses on the general implications of these developments for emerging shifts in research agendas, which he contends is more than just a question about the impact of technology. He identifies four other areas that are of particular significance for evolving agendas: funding levels for research; changing skill sets of the scientific labor force; the increasingly broad significance of the digital in many social domains; and a drive for greater scientific accountability.

A primary objective and expected impact of e-research use across the disciplinary spectrum is the deployment of a range of information and communication technologies (ICTs) to support collaboration across space, time, and disciplinary and institutional boundaries. The authors of chapter 10, Annamaria Carusi and Marina Jirotka, investigate the potential of these new forms of organizing research by looking in more detail at the widely applied concept of the virtual research environment (VRE), also known by the term *collaboratory* and other terms. They assess how and to what extent e-research can foster new approaches to collaboration by examining the relationship between VREs and research groups, communities, and organizations. They identify different types of such environments and discuss their implications for research practices across the disciplines. Their theme is pursued further in the essay related to this chapter, in which Matthew Dovey looks at the future of VREs. Although he says their emergent shape is uncertain, given the rapid pace of change in the Grid, Cloud computing, and other e-research technologies, he points to the enduring significance of key requirements for the effectiveness of these environments, such as their usability, adaptability, interoperability, and sharability.

A characteristic of the many new research avenues covered in this book is the potential for increasing "openness" in research. In chapter 11, Paul David, Matthijs den Besten, and Ralph Schroeder contribute an in-depth analysis of the underlying issues related to this trend. They explain how historical norms and practices of openness have been vital for scientific communities' work, but have often been in tension with technical and institutional restraints on access to research tools and information. The chapter clarifies the conceptual differences and similarities between e-science and open science, building on findings from a study of practices in U.K. e-science projects. The authors underscore a key conclusion: it is unwarranted to presume that the use of ICTs necessarily promotes more open global research collaboration. They propose a framework within which further empirical research can be undertaken to help establish where, when, and to what extent "openness' and "e-ness" in research may be expected to advance in harmony.

Two essays appended to chapter 11 extend the understanding of the main issues tied to the important topic of open access in e-research. The international politics of open access is the subject of the first essay, by Gustavo Cardoso, João Caraça, Rita Espanha, and Sandro Mendonça. Their broad perspective is based on a view that open access should be considered not just as being about alternative publishing models, but increasingly as a special kind of social movement that flourishes within the research community, across disciplines, and around the world. The next essay, by John Wilbanks and Hal Abelson, emphasizes that "open viewing" of journal articles online, free of charge, is insufficient to support the kind of participation in scientific research made possible by free public availability of scientific papers that includes the right to use the text of articles as data to software. They illustrate this point through the case of Neurocommons, an open platform for neuroscience that treats multiple biological databases and literature sources as a single database to deliver answers to questions within this field.

The global dimension implicit in this volume's main title, *World Wide Research*, is reinforced in its final chapter. This chapter examines the knowledge-production sectors of developing countries and regions using survey research and case studies in Ghana, Kenya, India, the Philippines, and Chile conducted by the chapter's authors, Marcus Ynalvez, Ricardo Duque, and Wesley Shrum. The authors discuss the impact of the

Internet on scientific collaboration and research productivity in such developing areas, arguing that the reaction to ICTs will depend on how researchers in specific localized contexts and with specific identities reconfigure the nature and dynamics of social interaction in general and of knowledge production in particular. Their central theme reinforces the foundations outlined in chapter 1: the key role that strategic choices play in using ICTs to reconfigure access to resources in ways that shape implications for worldwide research and the outcomes from those processes.

The editors offer a final coda that draws together some concluding themes. They reflect on a thread running through the contributions that points to the value in e-research development and the need to target the key ends of research, in particular its quality, rather than to focus on collaboration and other technically defined features and techniques that can lead to diverse outcomes in different disciplines and environments.

9 The Changing Disciplinary Landscapes of Research

Jenny Fry and Ralph Schroeder

As explored in this book, e-research encompasses the use of distributed and collaborative computing tools and data systems throughout the range of academic disciplines and fields. Key questions about it include: Will e-research pervade other disciplines or form one or more separate specializations of its own? What effect will it have on different disciplines in terms of shifting or reinforcing their boundaries or in terms of sidestepping them by becoming a separate domain outside of existing academic disciplines?

"Humanities computing," for example, is a tool-driven paradigm that applies modeling techniques to humanities data and spans a number of humanities disciplines, but is not a discipline in its own right, despite the fact that the community that formed around the core challenges of humanities computing has successfully established specialist channels of communication (e.g., the former journal *Computers and the Humanities* and the more recent *Digital Humanities Quarterly*), developed influential standards such as the Text Encoding Initiative, and generated a number of research institutes. As a comparison, although bioinformatics has also not become a discrete discipline and can be conceived of as a transdisciplinary research area, it has taken on at least the trappings of a subdiscipline in a variety of ways, with not only a recognizable community, conferences, journals, and research institutes, but also degrees and academic departments.

Thus, we can ask, in what ways the disciplinary landscape is changing in terms of boundaries; in researchers' movements and skill sets; in the formal links between departments and institutions, and whether e-research transcends boundaries or reinforces them by forming further specializations within fields, creating skills that apply only to narrow or specialized problems, and thus pushing resources farther into departmental or institutional silos.

In this chapter, we argue that there will be subdisciplinary specialization within computing (around Grids, for example) as well as subdisciplinary specialization within disciplinary-based configurations (e-research humanities, Grids for physics, and the like), together with many hybrids that can be seen as both or neither, such as text mining, the Semantic Web, and Webometrics (see essay 1.2). We discuss the likelihood that there will be more differentiation and dedifferentiation in the disciplinary organization of knowledge or that the techniques of e-research will become embedded and disembedded across different disciplines in the manner of other research technologies (as conceptualized in Shinn and Joerges 2002; see also Shinn 2005). Although e-research technologies might contribute to the reconfiguration of disciplines, the intellectual and social organization of disciplines will at the same time influence the diffusion and appropriation of e-research technologies. In short, the relationship between disciplinary cultures and e-research will be mutually shaping, but how that relationship will play out across different disciplines is not yet fully understood. Nevertheless, here we explore some possible scenarios based on the sociology of science and examples from e-research.[1]

The Components of Research Technologies and e-Research

The vision of e-research has been that the complexity of heterogeneous networks is black-boxed from users, with middleware—the software that sits between e-infrastructures and particular applications—mediating the interaction between users and the system. In practice, e-research is much more complicated, in part because the needs that individual disciplines have for infrastructures or other collaborative technologies are quite different, and in part because the image of a seamless network of heterogeneous systems or software tools and data management overlooks the fact that there will continue to be multiple overlapping and intersecting e-research networks that continue to coexist side by side and to be used in a variety of ways. Seamlessness will thus continue to be elusive, even if it can be achieved within and between different parts of e-research networks.

These different parts are in evidence in various ways among e-researchers. Some researchers may be trying to develop a common pool of resources that may advance an area of research, such as software tools, technical standards and protocols, new types of instruments and analytic tools, and what has been conceptualized as "infrastructure," or they may be trying to create critical mass in the form of virtual communities, community contribution systems, or distributed research centers (Bos, Zimmerman, Olson, et al. 2007). The distinction between infrastructures and communities or distributed groups can be made as a distinction on the organizational or social side, between groups organized top down via a central structure, as against a heterogeneous agglomeration of researchers organized from the bottom up.

The distinction, however, can also be made on the technological side, between a top-down centralized technical infrastructure on one side and a combination of various tools and data or resources on the other. Tools in this case are artifacts for manipulating research materials (data, instruments, visualizations, etc.), and data or resources are research materials that are available in support of research. We argue that the boundary between the social and technological sides is often blurred in e-research, but how different disciplines are developing one or the other (and thus contributing to or enabling access to the infrastructure) is a key difference between disciplines.

In any case, infrastructures, tools, and data (or other resources) can then be broken into several other types of activity that different disciplines are engaging in as part of e-research (where the term *materials* can be used as shorthand for *data* or *resources*):

• Digitizing material such as images or text or data to create a common data set or resource
• Making materials available as a shared online resource for search
• Enabling access to remote instruments or research materials
• Federating existing or collecting new digital materials
• Making the materials searchable or manipulable by means of a software tool
• Developing a means to combine data sources or exploit them in new ways with a tool
• Creating new tools to display and analyze data or resources
• Creating tools that combine existing databases or digital resources

This list is not exhaustive, but note that all of the items in it fit our definition of e-research insofar as they involve networks, shared and distributed research, and the software tools and sources of data or other resources that enable it.

Studying Disciplines and Emergent Paradigms

Outsider perspectives of scientific practice, such as those adopted by sociological studies of science, have used a range of concepts to delineate scientific communities. This variation in perspective reflects the multitude of overlapping social and institutional configurations within which scientific knowledge is produced (e.g., research groups, projects, invisible colleges, specialist fields, laboratories, academic departments, and disciplines), the boundaries of which are often blurred and not clearly separable (Fry 2006).

Derek de Solla Price (1963) and Diana Crane (1972) explored the notion of research-oriented scientific communities that identify themselves around comparable research problems or methods. The concept of the scientific or disciplinary community is often defined as rather idyllic and consensus oriented, and as such the concept has been criticized (Swales 1998). De Solla Price (1963) coined the concept of the "invisible college," which is based on a social network with a capacity membership of around two hundred scholars and a core of around twenty leading research scholars. Beyond this capacity, Price argued, a research area will become saturated, and groups will split off to form new specialist fields.

Researchers in a number of disciplines have explored and developed the concept of the "invisible college." For example, Crane (1972) built on Price's notion to show how knowledge is diffused through networks of scientific communities. Moving toward a less idyllic notion of scientific communities where competition and division of labor are central, Pierre Bourdieu (1988) introduced the notion of fields of intellectual inquiry. In his definition, fields are fluid entities based on the dynamics of competition rather than consensus as portrayed by the concept of "communities of practice" (Wenger 1998), whereby cohesive networked communities compete for the same problems and resources. Judy Klein has also argued that in the terminology of disciplinarity, the word *field* evokes intellectual inquiry independent of institutional dimensions such as the extent to which boundaries are clearly delineated and protected or whether they are in a more fluid emergent state (1996:5). Following Daryl Chubin (1976) and Klein (1996:5), therefore, we use the term *intellectual field* throughout the chapter as a feasible cultural entity whose numerous external representations more effectively capture the process of research than the more coarse-grained and institutional perspective embodied in the term *discipline*. Put differently, we use *field* when we do not want to prejudge the issue of whether an area is able to police its boundaries as a discipline or if it is in a more fluid state.

Toward the Institutionalization of e-Research

The extent to which e-research becomes embedded within disciplines will depend on patterns of diffusion and the ways in which it becomes institutionalized. Any discussion of the coevolution of e-research technologies and disciplines, therefore, needs to be placed in the context of intellectual, social, and institutional conditions.

The boundaries of an intellectual field may become delineated through a gradual process of "restricted institutionalization," such as via international journals, conference series, and postgraduate degree programs. The process is "restricted" because although the boundaries of e-research are transdisciplinary in terms of the research questions being addressed and the variety of disciplinary approaches used to address them, researchers who inhabit the e-research field also simultaneously inhabit intellectual fields aligned with a specific discipline (or set of disciplines) and some will remain closely-coupled to their parent discipline for recognition and reward. In the case of humanities computing, for example, researchers contribute to the humanities computing knowledge base and retain a disciplinary identity, such as history, linguistics, or literary studies for the purpose of establishing and developing their academic careers (e.g., tenure, promotion, and recognition and reward).

If the institutionalization of e-research reaches and remains at this level of maturity, the implication is not that a new intellectual field is emerging that establishes autonomy in the broader scientific system through primary mechanisms of institutionalization, such as the establishment of academic schools, professional chairs, and undergraduate programs that basically form a market monopoly for the production of that specific type of knowledge (Whitley 2000). Rather, what emerges will remain an interdisciplinary area with fluid boundaries and will be dependent on a set of parent disciplines for its coherence, autonomy, and direction.

These intellectual and social conditions might also make appropriation and the organization of work around a central infrastructure a more conservative process. This is because the mechanisms of institutionalization already occupied by a dominant discipline may be a source of resistance to the diffusion of innovation produced externally to the potentially adoptive field. The conservatism of intellectual fields thus depends on a number of cultural factors, not least of which is what Tony Becher and Paul Trowler (2001) describe as "intellectual pluralism." A field that is more pluralistic will support multiple perspectives and approaches, and organizational structures will consequently be quite fluid. For example, in some fields there will be a lack of hierarchical ordering of problems and goals as well as limited centralization of control over significance standards (Whitley 2000:136). Innovation will thus be more open to flexible interpretation, which, in turn, will act as an enabler for the transfer of innovation across field boundaries.

We can see these appropriation and adaptation patterns in the emergence of recent new fields, such as bioinformatics, genomics, and proteomics. For example, the transfer of techniques and tools such as X-ray crystallography and electron microscopy from chemistry and physics to genomics implies that the approaches and goals of chemistry and physics are also significant for genomics research. The genomics community has thus been able to leverage status in the wider scientific system by adopting well-established and trusted techniques and tools from highly coherent and autonomous disciplines and by applying them to new research problems—illustrating the contextual nature of the diffusion of innovation.

The adoption of novel technologies and approaches to a well-established field may conversely lead to a disruption of that field and may even harm the social concerns (e.g., tenure, promotion, and recognition and reward) of the scientists and scholars who inhabit it. In computing, for example, certain specialisms have waxed and waned over the years, and once high-prestige areas (artificial intelligence, hardware architecture) have become eclipsed by others (computer graphics, ubiquitous computing). This changing popularity has been apparent even when there is difficulty in deriving straightforward rankings of how it translates into academic recognition and reward.

Interdisciplinarity

As early as the 1960s, Donald Campbell argued that alternative social organizations that would permit the flourishing of narrow interdisciplinary fields were necessary for integrated and competent research areas (1969:348). Interdisciplinarity can also mean mutual appropriation of techniques and dedifferentiation of boundaries. This outcome can be observed in the coappropriation of community data systems and in the modeling techniques and visualization tools that are a necessary part of making sense of large-scale data (Bos, Zimmerman, Olson, et al. 2007) in areas such as the life and health sciences (e.g., the Protein Data Bank),[2] engineering (e.g., the U.S. National Science Foundation [NSF] TeraBridge Project), the geosciences (e.g., the NSF Network for Earthquake Engineering),[3] and many other fields.

It is often argued that e-research is inherently inter- or multidisciplinary. On the face of it, this statement seems a truism if we consider that the *e-* in *e-research* entails collaboration between at least two disciplines: computer science and a domain discipline. The exception might be if the research remains within the domain of computer science. Even in this case, however, e-research will still involve developing tools and data or resources and applying them to a particular domain of research—in this case, different subdisciplines within computer science, one of them relating to tool or resource development and another to research.

There is also considerable prima facie evidence of disciplines' engaging with each other in e-research even though such engagement would otherwise seem improbable. Here we can think about how researchers from various disciplines encounter each other at e-research conferences—for instance, physicists and humanities scholars who exchange ideas about how to solve software problems in access to Grids. Indeed, it seems that a number of issues confronted by different disciplines are common to e-research projects in many disciplines. For example, all disciplines need to explore how to design search interfaces, represent and make data reusable, and provide access to instruments at distributed sites.

Disciplines and the Push and Pull of Innovation

A prominent debate among e-research practitioners concerns the relation between computer science and domain disciplines. In other words, has e-research been driven by computer science or the other way around? This question can in turn be disaggregated into two parts. One is about research funding policy: Has computer science received the lion's share of the resources and in this way provided the push for e-research development? Separate questions concern the sociology of innovation (as distinct from the funding impetus), such as: Has the push for infrastructure or tool, data, and resource development come from e-research, or has the pull come from the domain sciences or disciplines?

These issues have been eagerly debated, mainly informally in discussions among e-researchers. To our knowledge, there is no systematic analysis of these issues for e-research, although there are extensive analyses of research funding policies, of the push and pull of technological innovation generally, and of the disciplinarity of innovative individual research projects.

Yet apart from innovation policy or funding policy discussions, these issues are often implicit in discussions among developers and e-researchers—for example, when it is often said that "the technology is ahead of the applications" and when it is asked, "We have the technology, but where are the users?" A different way of illustrating this point is by what e-researchers within computer science and within the individual domains often say, "We're not interested in the technology; we're interested in the science that can be done with it." Such statements may be sincere, but they also represent a misunderstanding about how science and research work—namely, via research technologies that may advance scientific agendas.

The reason for reporting these debates and discussions is not that we are able to present evidence for one or other of these positions, but that we would like to argue that these two questions are in an important sense wrongly framed. E-research is still in its early stages, so it may be premature to gauge how it is reconfiguring the landscape of innovation as a whole. Instead, we can ask whether there are any commonalities in the organizational forms of e-research initiatives and in the tools that are being developed, as well as how these initiatives and tools reshape and are being shaped by different disciplines.

Disciplines and Work Organization

Karin Knorr-Cetina has described large-scale collaboration of physicists, with 150 institutions and 1,500 scientists working on one experiment at the particle physics facility at the European Organization for Nuclear Research (CERN) (1999: 20; see also Shrum, Genuth, and Chompalov 2007). This is one extreme in terms of the size of a group working on a single research project. It points to a type of organization that is highly centralized—even though it also has many participating institutions and researchers—because the computing resources required in such a case need to be pooled and shared in order to tackle the high volumes of data that need to be processed. From a disciplinary perspective, then, the questions are whether the model of such large-scale efforts where communities collaborate around shared computing resources will continue within physics, and whether the model will rub off on other disciplines. In general, the answer to the latter question is that such a result is unlikely because other disciplines do not have such a well-defined and focused task.

At the other extreme, Becher and Trowler argue that the pattern of work organization in the humanities and social sciences has traditionally placed an emphasis on individual scholarship (2001:123). Although this pattern is shifting toward more and more collective activity, one question is whether e-research intensifies this shift as it creates more shared resources. In the humanities, in particular, one of the main efforts is to make materials available online, perhaps collecting together materials that were previously scattered, and to make them searchable and manipulable. To accomplish this task, organizations must pool resources, and one of the key issues is how availability will be sustained beyond the life of this shared effort. Yet, just as in physics, though on a smaller scale, both the organizational and the technological complexity in e-research with its shared computing tools and resources are greater than with individual researchers and stand-alone technologies.

Nathan Bos and his colleagues (2007) distinguish between informal, one-to-one collaborations, which have long been common between scientists, and more tightly coordinated, large-scale organizational structures, where there are considerable barriers to scientific collaborations supported via technologies. In a survey study of large-scale collaborations involving multidisciplinary groups and crossing boundaries between institutions, however, Jonathan Cummings and Sara Kiesler (2005) have shown that institutional boundary crossing is often a greater barrier than collaboration at a distance and across disciplines.

Legitimacy and status within disciplines derive primarily from publications; the outputs of e-research—for example, tool development, contributing to a common resource and the like—have so far failed to gain the recognition that publications have achieved within established disciplines. There have been many e-research publications, of course, but how they measure up to other publications remains an open question.

Reward and status relate not only to publications. Diane Sonnenwald (2006) has demonstrated, in the case of a particular multi-institutional distributed research project carried out over the course of several years, how the issue of academic rank and the status attached to participating in this type of collaboration can raise questions about the reward structure. For example, do younger researchers miss out on rewards, whereas more senior researchers have little incentive to participate actively even though they may derive rewards from being in charge of such projects?

It is also becoming increasingly difficult to separate e-research from related areas in terms of work organization because research tools are proliferating. Can setting up a common store such as a wiki be considered e-research? What about online project-management tools? Do collaborative projects without face-to-face meetings, such as collaboratories or virtual research organizations (see chapter 11), deserve to be counted as e-research? These and other modes of conducting research are becoming more common in all academic disciplines, although, as we have seen, to quite different degrees and in quite different forms.

Research Technologies

Perhaps e-research tools and resources can be conceptualized and appropriated as "research technologies" (Shinn and Joerges 2002; Shinn 2005). Terry Shinn and Bernward Joerges have argued that research technologies often transfer from across disciplines and foster innovation because they are "generic" or "open-ended and general purpose devices" that therefore span disciplinary boundaries (2002:212). They "operate like passports" (244) because they are typically developed outside of established disciplines and yet are eventually applicable in several areas of research. The development of research technologies is "a form of instrument design that consciously takes into account maximizing the variety and number of end-users whose local technologies can incorporate key features of a research-technology template" so that "communication between institutionally and cognitively differentiated groups of end-users" eventually develops" (212–213).

Whether the technologies in e-research do "operate like passports" in practice is, of course, an open question. However, examples can be found where this process is ongoing (Schroeder 2008). It remains to be seen whether the research technologies that have been taken up in different disciplines garner and maintain a large enough number of users such that they have a lasting impact across a number of disciplines and whether the research technologies become essential within these disciplines and are sustained and built upon in the course of time. But these questions can be asked of all technologies that are still in the making.

Disciplinary Differences

Against this background, it is possible to provide a few concrete illustrations of disciplinary differences in e-research.

An Infrastructure for Physics and Other Disciplines

Some disciplines are developing infrastructures within their domain. In physics, for instance, the project Enabling Grids for E-sciencE (EGEE)[4] can be seen as an illustration of infrastructure development. This initiative has built up a network for shared and distributed computing across many sites around the world that analyzes the data from the particle physics experiments at CERN. The aim in this case is to create a structure for distributed data analysis that will serve the community for some time.

But the EGEE project has also become something larger, extending to other disciplines—from life sciences and social sciences to the humanities—the software tools that were originally intended for physicists. This extension and addition to the initial infrastructure have been in part driven by funding, growing the potential for funding by the European Union to a broader pool of organizations and demonstrating that EGEE can serve a wider community of researchers and thus provide wider benefits. This extension has been driven by the notion that an infrastructure can serve multiple constituencies and achieve the benefits of scale and scope (Schroeder 2008). In the process, EGEE has become possibly the largest e-research initiative anywhere. However it develops, it will transform into an infrastructure serving various communities of researchers apart from the initial physics core.

Common Databases in Astronomy and Genomics

Other disciplines are developing common databases rather than focusing on computing infrastructures. In astronomy, for example, the initiative International Virtual Observatory Alliance (IVOA)[5] is creating a federated database from various national astronomy data sets and pooling them into a single online resource (Schroeder 2008). In the Genetic Association Information Network (GAIN),[6] benefits are similarly envisaged from sharing data sets of genotyping studies of diseases and other illnesses, including bipolar disorder (Meyer 2009). The aim of common databases can be different, however. Whereas IVOA is combining data to enlarge the scope of the data and share resources, GAIN hopes that new insights can be derived from the more powerful results when data sets are combined and can thus cover larger numbers of people who have the diseases and illnesses being studied. The tightly bounded research communities within astronomy and biomedical research confine these projects to intradisciplinary participation even if, as in the case of IVOA, the project is open to public (amateur astronomer) involvement or, as in the case of GAIN, requires intense collaboration between (genetic) researchers and database-management specialists with expertise in computer science.

Using a Wiki for Literary and Other Research

A different example is the Pynchon Wiki,[7] a project developed by nonacademic enthusiasts rather than by researchers. Created in order to annotate the novels of the contemporary American novelist Thomas Pynchon, this wiki can be seen as a contribution to literary research insofar as previous annotations, in book form, were produced by individual literary scholars, and insofar as both online and book annotations are aimed at supporting the study of the novelist's works. The Pynchon Wiki has drawn in hundreds of contributors. It has become a much more voluminous resource than the annotations in book form in terms of the numbers of entries and words covering the obscure topics that make Pynchon's novels into puzzles that require extensive detective work (Schroeder and den Besten 2008).

Yet in this case the tools used to create the wiki are off-the-shelf wiki tools, and the main effort to produce this resource took months of work by a single enthusiast who is not in an academic position (although he works in commercial Web design) and who requires no resources apart from a server on which to maintain the material. Although the Pynchon Wiki can be regarded as falling within literary studies, it can also be said to have opened the academic field of literary research to involvement from the public. This type of tool and form of annotation easily translates to other disciplines and fields—for example, in the life sciences, where community annotation is under way in projects such as WikiGenes,[8] although it faces quite different challenges in this arena.

Social Science Involving Public Participation

The Geographic Virtual Urban Environments project[9] falls within the social sciences and more specifically within mapping and visualization in geography (Hudson-Smith,

Milton, Batty, et al. 2007). The project has a number of parts. One is MapTube,[10] which allows the sharing and combining of maps of different kinds (its name echoes the name of the popular video-sharing site YouTube). MapTube includes, for example, maps related to the occurrence of crime, trends in the English population, post office locations, and transportation. Again, this project invites participation from the public. It also brings together various social science disciplines—indeed, any discipline, including environmental and health sciences—that use mapping techniques. Like the Pynchon Wiki, MapTube is aimed at researchers and a wider public, although, unlike the Pynchon Wiki, it has required considerable computer science skills in creating the Web site and the software to allow the combination of the various maps.

Academic and Commercial Collaboration

From biomedicine or life sciences, another project is the SwissBioGrid[11] project. This project may not be representative of the life sciences as a whole, but it provides an interesting study of how commercial collaboration in what was primarily an academic research project need not be an obstacle to success (den Besten, Thomas, and Schroeder 2009). SwissBioGrid, which developed software to harness the computing power of personal computers, consisted of two pilot projects: one for data analysis in proteomics (study of proteins) and the other for high-throughput molecular docking ("virtual screening") to find new drugs for neglected diseases (specifically, for dengue fever).

Many facets of this project highlight the relations between disciplines. Here, we mention just two. First, even though the project was successful in demonstrating benefits in the life sciences, the articles arising from the project are highly regarded as publications in computer science (and e-science), but not as publications in life sciences, which would have been more useful to the researchers who developed the software for SwissBioGrid. This problem is well known in e-science: there is little reward or status for software or tool development (Borgman 2007:esp. 179–224)—which is often a large part of e-science research—but greater reward or status in the domain discipline in which the e-research is being done.

Second, because the life sciences often operate like fiefdoms around particular labs (Knorr-Cetina 1999), there is as yet little standardization in the field (at least in this particular case) that would allow a coalescing of research effort around a single infrastructure. This mode of operation in part accounts for the fact that SwissBioGrid, although successful as a demonstration effort, has not been able to continue and build on its efforts as part of a larger Swiss or other infrastructure effort (although this status may change in the future). We can see that life sciences still have not developed a disciplinary reward mechanism or role for joint infrastructural efforts across the discipline—although these rewards and infrastructures are becoming established within e-science as an intellectual field.

Conclusions

This chapter has illustrated that within and across disciplines and intellectual fields, e-research takes different forms. Some fields are developing infrastructures that are intended for the long term and provide a critical mass of communities of scholars with common resources. Others are developing tools and resources from the bottom up for small-scale specialist research communities (or for a wider public), perhaps with the hope of sustaining them into the future, but without the aim of creating an established infrastructure that regularly provides services in a systematic or programmatic way. Still others may be aiming at longer-term and systematic solutions, but they are still in the phase of developing particular tools or resources or of providing access to data or to remote instruments for particular groups.

Although it would be premature to make generalizations about the relation between e-research and disciplinarity, it is possible to venture some hypotheses for future research:

• In disciplines or fields where there is high resource concentration or high task certainty or both, such as is typical, but not exclusive, to fields in the physical sciences, e-research is likely to develop specialized, top-down centralized infrastructures.

• In disciplines or fields where there is low resource concentration or a high degree of pluralism or both, such as is typical, but not exclusive, to fields in the humanities and social sciences with low task certainty, e-research is likely to take the form of a diverse set of nonoverlapping and bottom-up efforts at digitizing resources.

• In disciplines or fields where large-scale data sets are needed, but where the data sets are also quite heterogeneous, such as in the life sciences and in data-intensive social and health sciences, e-research efforts to combine the data sets within interoperable infrastructures are likely to depend on whether sociolegal and technical obstacles to integration can be overcome.

In short, e-research consists of a variety of technologies and technological systems, sometimes parts of larger wholes, at other times smaller in scale and more bounded. There are as yet only indications of how disciplines and e-research technologies will mutually shape each other—just indications because the technologies are still in the making and the disciplines are still in the process of becoming e-research enabled. It can already be seen that there is no "one-size-fits-all" model. The challenges and modes of organization and disciplinary practices with respect to tools and data are simply too diverse in different intellectual fields. What can be said with certainty is that different groups of researchers within intellectual fields have taken the opportunity to mobilize in order to develop different types of digital technologies for distributed and collaborative tools and data resources, and that these technologies are shaping or becoming embedded in intellectual fields and disciplines in different ways.

Disciplinary organization and uptake of new research tools therefore vary, and we have pointed to only some of the variations here, such as work organization. Others include level of resource intensiveness, to what extent resources are centralized or decentralized, and the degree of mutual dependence and task uncertainty (which formed for the basis for Richard Whitley's [2000] analysis of the intellectual and social organization of the sciences).

Hence, it is not yet possible to provide a comprehensive disciplinary landscape of e-research. One of the main drivers of collaborative research is that computing and other equipment has become ever more expensive in academic research, which is a good reason for sharing resources and making them more widely accessible. But to do both, disciplines need to be brought together. And although there have been widespread calls for multidisciplinarity on the front stages of research, among funding bodies, and in conference presentations, the argument for staying within the bounds of a discipline can typically be heard backstage, among researchers who regard research within their own disciplinary community as a priority in terms of status and the focus that research should have.

Seen from the point of view of the relation between disciplines, where the term *interdisciplinarity* is more appropriate, Julie Klein has argued that "interdisciplinarity is . . . caught in a larger debate about the growing collectivization and complexity of science" (1996:205). E-research can thus be seen as the ground on which these "turf wars," to use Becher and Trowler's (2001) phrase, are currently most prominently being played out. The grand visions of computer science colonizing other disciplines as well as the tales of how the computer science effort to do so "implodes" because there is no take-up of computer science tools and resources in other fields are thus bound to remain exaggerated.

Notes

1. Disciplinary differences in e-research have not so far been analyzed specifically from the point of view of the sociology of science. Samuelle Carlson and Ben Anderson (2007) and Christine Borgman (2007:179–226) have examined different types of data in relation to disciplinarity, and Michael Nentwich (2003) has analyzed disciplinarity in a detailed way, but for cyberscience or the use of the Internet in research generally, as opposed to e-research. Jonathan Cummings and Sara Kiesler (2005) analyze disciplinarity in relation to distributed and multi-institutional project collaboration.

2. See http://www.rcsb.org/pdb/home/home.do.

3. See http://www.nees.org/.

4. See http://www.eu-egee.org/.

5. See http://www.ivoa.net/.

6. See http://fnih.org/index.php?option=com_content&task=view&id=338&Itemid=454/.

7. See http://pynchonwiki.com/.

8. See http://www.wikigenes.org/.

9. See http://www.casa.ucl.ac.uk/projects/projectDetail.asp?ID=57.

10. See http://www.maptube.org/.

11. See http://www.swissbiogrid.com/.

References

Becher, T., and P. Trowler. 2001. *Academic tribes and territories: Intellectual inquiry and the culture of disciplines* 2d ed. Milton Keynes, UK: Open University Press.

Borgman, C. 2007. *Scholarship in the digital age: Information, infrastructure, and the Internet*. Cambridge, MA: MIT Press.

Bos, N., A. Zimmerman, J. Olson, J. Yew, J. Yerkie, E. Dahl, and G. Olson. 2007. "From shared databases to communities of practice: A taxonomy of collaboratories." *Journal of Computer-Mediated Communication 12* (2). Available at: http://jcmc.indiana.edu/vol12/issue2/bos.html.

Bourdieu, P. 1988. *Homo academicus*. Trans. Peter Collier. Stanford, CA: Stanford University Press.

Campbell, D. 1969. "Ethnocentrism of disciplines and the fish-scale model of omniscience." In *Interdisciplinary relationships in the social sciences*, ed. M. Sherif and C. W. Sherif. Chicago: Aldine, 328–348.

Carlson, S., and B. Anderson. 2007. "What are data? The many kinds of data and their implications for data re-use." *Journal of Computer-Mediated Communication 12* (2). Available at: http://jcmc.indiana.edu/vol12/issue2/carlson.html.

Chubin, D. 1976. "The conceptualization of scientific research specialties." *Sociology Quarterly 17*:448–476.

Crane, D. 1972. *Invisible colleges: Diffusion of knowledge in scientific communities*. Chicago: University of Chicago Press.

Cummings, J., and S. Kiesler. 2005. "Collaborative research across disciplinary and institutional boundaries." *Social Studies of Science 35* (5):703–722.

Den Besten, M., A. Thomas, and R. Schroeder. 2009. "Life science research and drug discovery at the turn of the 21st century: The experience of SwissBioGrid." *Journal of Biomedical Discovery and Collaboration 4* (5). Available at: http://www.uic.edu/htbin/cgiwrap/bin/ojs/index.php/jbdc/index/

Fry, J. 2006. "Studying the scholarly Web: How disciplinary culture shapes online representations." *Cybermetrics: International Journal of Scientometrics, Informetrics and Bibliometrics 10* (1). Available at: http://www.cindoc.csic.es/cybermetrics/vol10iss1.html.

Hudson-Smith, A., R. Milton, M. Batty, M. Gibin, P. Longley, and A. Singleton. 2007. "Public domain GIS, mapping, and imaging using Web-based services." Paper presented at the Third International Conference on e–Social Science, Ann Arbor, MI, 7–9 October. Available at: http://www.casa.ucl.ac.uk/working_papers/paper120.pdf.

Klein, J. T. 1996. *Crossing boundaries: Knowledge, disciplinarities, and interdisciplinarities*. Charlottesville: University of Virginia Press.

Knorr-Cetina, K. 1999. *Epistemic cultures: How the sciences make knowledge*. Cambridge, MA: Harvard University Press.

Meyer, E. T. 2009. "Moving from small science to big science: Social and organizational impediments to large scale data sharing." In *E-research: Transformation in scholarly practice*, ed. N. Jankowski. New York: Routledge, 147–159.

Nentwich, M. 2003. *Cyberscience: Research in the age of the Internet*. Vienna: Austrian Academy of Sciences Press.

De Solla Price, D. J. 1963. *Little science, big science*. New York: Columbia University Press.

Schroeder, R. 2008. "E-sciences as research technologies: Reconfiguring disciplines, globalizing knowledge." *Social Science Information (Paris) 47* (2):131–157.

Schroeder, R., and M. den Besten. 2008. "Literary sleuths online: E-research collaboration on the Pynchon Wiki." *Information, Communication, & Society 11* (2):167–187.

Shinn, T. 2005. "New sources of radical innovation: Research technologies, transversality, and distributed learning in a post-industrial order." *Social Science Information (Paris) 44* (4):731–764.

Shinn, T., and B. Joerges. 2002. "The transverse science and technology culture: Dynamics and roles of research technology." *Social Science Information (Paris) 41* (2):207–251.

Shrum, W., J. Genuth, and I. Chompalov. 2007. *The structures of scientific collaboration*. Cambridge, MA: MIT Press.

Sonnenwald, D. 2006. "Collaborative virtual environments for scientific collaboration: Technical and organizational design frameworks." In *Avatars at work and play: Collaboration and interaction in shared virtual environments*, ed. R. Schroeder and A-S. Axelsson. Dordrecht, Netherlands: Springer, 63–96.

Swales, J. M. 1998. *Other floors, other voices: A textography of a small university building*. London: Lawrence Erlbaum Associates.

Wenger, E. 1998. *Communities of practice: Learning, meaning, and identity*. Cambridge, UK: Cambridge University Press.

Whitley, R. 2000. *The intellectual and social organization of the sciences*. Oxford, UK: Oxford University Press.

9.1   The Agenda-Setting Role of e-Research

Paul Wouters

Understanding How e-Research Affects Researchers' Questions

The agenda of publicly funded scholarly and scientific research is the result of a complex institutional and intellectual arrangement (Shove and Caswill 2000). Many different actors influence the kind of issues addressed by academics in their research projects. As outlined in this book, e-research may dramatically change the landscape of academic work. A relevant question would then become, In what ways will e-research affect the setting of research agendas?

The discussion about e-research has surprisingly taken little time to address this problem of its implications for the substance of research agendas (e.g., see Hine 2006; VKS 2008). Instead, attention has been drawn mainly to the conditions under which researchers work, with e-research usually being concerned primarily with issues such as the system of scholarly publishing, the sharing of data and information, the building of collaboratories, and the creation of large networked data infrastructures.

E-science started as a particular agenda that interfered with already existing research agendas by claiming to revolutionize all the sciences and humanities. For example, the U.K. e-Science Programme in 2001 and U.S. cyberinfrastructure initiatives dating from the mid-1980s (see the introduction) are fine examples of research-agenda setting that can be seen as interventions in existing agendas. They were initiated mainly by a relatively small but powerful group of physicists and computer scientists based on their particular research agenda and a strong tradition of large-scale research instrumentation. In this way, the group has mobilized interests in information technology and industry for a radical restructuring of scientific and scholarly research.

Implications for Research Agendas

Understanding how these developments will influence research agendas is, in the first place, a question not about technology impact, but rather about the modulation of existing processes of agenda setting. Of the many ways in which this modulation will take place, four areas are of particular interest: research funding and competition for resources, technological and informational skills of the scientific labor force, the rise of the digital as a specific dimension of the social domain, and scientists' accountability to their peers and to society at large.

Research Funding and Resources

Working at the frontier of research increasingly requires advanced research instrumentation and specialized technological environments. A potential effect of e-research is an acceleration of this development. It will mean not only that more and more research money will be spent on advanced information environments for research, but also that the share of total research funding invested in e-research will rise. If both happen, there will be less funding available for other research activities and personnel. E-research projects may start to dominate as a result of this trend.

Of course, such implications will vary by discipline and country, which is itself an interesting domain of research. However, it seems reasonable to expect that the greater investment in e-research may sharpen the competition over resources. We can therefore expect an increasing concentration of resources, stronger dominance of big science, and penetration of large, technologically advanced research consortia in the humanities and social sciences. These outcomes may lead to a certain standardization of research agendas modeled after data-driven studies.

The risk is that the possibilities for serendipitous discoveries and radically new philosophical approaches may diminish, at least in some fields. The challenge here is twofold:

• To study to what extent these expectations do indeed play out, and
• To build e-research infrastructures in such a way that they accommodate all varieties of research styles, including more solitary work practices, while abstaining from a priori foregrounding particular styles over others.

New Skills Requirements

A second area of interaction between e-research and the broader research agenda is that of the skills that new generations of researchers possess. We are witnessing the entry into the workforce of doctoral students and technical assistants who from their early youth have played with and within new media. All of them may not be technically savvy, but the share of "advanced users" in the workforce will increase significantly. This increase may be accompanied by a partial shift in orientation from text to visual media. Gaming, visualization, and simulation may also become more prominent as modes of research, a shift that, in a sense, amounts to resurrecting and strengthening an old tradition: the analogical style of research (Crombie 1994). Research styles implicate styles of reasoning and thinking, and it is clear that shifts in styles will have important but unpredictable effects on the type of questions that scholars and scientists will ask in the near future.

Social and Economic Implications of the New Digital Domain

The rise of the digital as an important aspect of the social domain has already created a whole set of fresh research questions about the new media's roles and their effects on social and economic processes and behavior. The digital domain is, moreover, a playground for mathematicians and network scientists because it allows for the externalization and algorithmic construction of mathematical models. In social science (sociology and psychology), new forms of online experiments are breaking through the limitations of small-group experiments and traditional surveys.

It is not yet clear, however, whether these methodological changes will lead to new research agendas. This shift may actually still take a long time, if it happens at all. If these online methodologies lead to new research agendas, they should include far more sophisticated social theorizing than we have so far seen in this kind of research.

New Forms of Social Accountability for Researchers

Changes introduced by e-research in the communication between scholars and lay audiences and in the way scholars are made accountable may be particularly influential. Whether we will witness the rise of new forms of public scholarship (Graubard 2004), in which "amateur" or lay experts are coproducers of knowledge rather than consumers, will depend on whether we can eliminate the rigid publication system that is often driven more by an academic's need to establish a publication record than by the need to reach important audiences.

A highly technical set of output forms remains necessary for specialists, but the overall impact of research will in the end rely on interpretation. The current cyberinfrastructure and its increasing variety of social-networking and communication tools may support this reliance in new ways by being turned into a vast resource for scientific and scholarly story-telling, which may mean that a good story will become the quintessence of e-research.

References

Crombie, A. C. 1994. *Styles of scientific thinking in the European tradition.* London: Duckworth.

Graubard, S. 2004. *Public scholarship: A new perspective for the 21st century.* New York: Carnegie Corporation of New York.

Hine, C., ed. 2006. *New infrastructures for knowledge production: Understanding science.* Hershey, PA: Information Science.

Shove, E., and C. Caswill. 2000. "Introducing interactive social science." *Science and Public Policy* *27* (3):152–157.

Virtual Knowledge Studio (VKS) (P. Wouters, K. Vann, A. Scharnhorst, M. Ratto, I. Hellsten, J. Fry, and A. Beaulieu). 2008. "Messy shapes of knowledge—STS explores informatization, new media, and academic work." In *New handbook of science, technology, and society*, ed. E. Hackett, O. Amsterdamska, M. Lynch, and J. Wajcman. Cambridge, MA: MIT Press, 319–352.

10   Reshaping Research Collaboration: The Case of Virtual Research Environments

Annamaria Carusi and Marina Jirotka

The Context and Significance of Virtual Research Environments

A wide variety of information and communication technologies (ICTs) and tools are becoming available to facilitate and support researchers in working together in virtual collaborations that reach beyond traditional boundaries. For instance, a virtual collaborative organization (VCO) enables researchers with common interests to function as a coherent unit even though they are distributed geographically and temporally, drawing membership from different legal entities to pursue common research goals. A related popular context in which researchers are using ICTs to reconfigure access to colleagues, data, software, and other services and resources is the virtual research environment (VRE) (see also essay 10.1). A VCO may make use of a VRE in order to undertake and share research, and a VRE may include tools to assist in the management of a VCO, but the two are different. VREs typify both the growing range of e-tools and technologies available for research purposes and—crucially—the implications of their use for research practices. They are therefore regarded as a suitable focus in this chapter for analyzing how ICTs are being applied more broadly in e-research activities and the wider implications arising from this change.

Terms and Definitions

It is not an easy matter to define the term *virtual research environment* and related terms (such as *collaboratories, cyberinfrastructure, e-science,* and, as in this book, *e-research*) in a way that easily distinguishes one from the other (see Borda, Careless, Dimitrova, et al. 2006).

Virtual research organizations, collaboratories, and VREs have emerged around the new capabilities of cyberinfrastructure that are potentially exploitable by researchers and research institutions. The thrust of these converging terms is toward creating cyberinfrastructures that are real to researchers and are emerging as part of their research resources in a form that impacts on their routine research practices within the institutions in which they work. The challenges of creating cyberinfrastructures capable of connecting distributed individual researchers and the broader institutional environments in which they function are not negligible. In this chapter, we focus on the significance this kind of virtual environment can have for the research or epistemic practices of researchers operating within their individual disciplinary research cultures.

The term *collaboratory*, a blend of *collaboration* and *laboratory*, was the first to take root in this field. It was first used by William Wulf (1989) in a White Paper that informed the U.S. National Research Council report *Toward a National Collaboratory*. This report has been profoundly influential in defining a vision for research that enables researchers to collaborate beyond the confines of their own physical locations. Wulf describes a collaboratory as a "center without walls" in which "the nation's researchers can perform their research without regard to geographical location—interacting with colleagues, accessing instrumentation, sharing data and computational resources, and accessing information in digital libraries" (1989; e.g., see U.S. National Science Board 2000:chap. 9).

One attempt to distinguish the specific characteristics of a collaboratory is to see it as essentially referring to the software that composes such a "center without walls." As Wulf puts it in another article,

The physical infrastructure of the collaboratory is the worldwide collection of networked computers augmented by instrumentation interfaced to the network (such as that at Sondre Stromfiord in Greenland). The essence of the collaboratory, however, is not this physical infrastructure. Rather, it is the software that enables scholars to use remote libraries, collaborate with remote colleagues, interact with remote instruments, analyze data and test models—all with nearly the facility they now enjoy locally. (1993:854)

In contrast, the term *virtual research environment* emerged in the United Kingdom, where it was defined as

a set of online tools, systems and processes interoperating to facilitate or enhance the research process within and without institutional boundaries. The purpose of a Virtual Research Environment (VRE) is to provide researchers with the tools and services they need to do research of any type as efficiently and effectively as possible. This means VREs will help individual researchers manage the increasingly complex range of tasks involved in doing research. In addition they will facilitate collaboration among communities of researchers, often across disciplinary and national boundaries. The research processes that a VRE will support include: resource discovery, data collection, data analysis, simulation, collaboration, communication, publishing, research administration, and project management. (Borda, Careless, Dimitrova, et al. 2006)

In the remainder of the chapter, we use "VRE" for general reference to the range of related terms covering similar capabilities, although we make it clear when we are discussing a VRE's or a collaboratory's special characteristics.

Despite the apparent clarity in these descriptions of VREs and collaboratories, the difficulty in pinning down precise definitions is unsurprising in an area of scientific and technological development that is in a state of unpredictable flux. For example, even though Wulf's "vision" of the collaboratory was a major inspiration for a program of technological research that resulted in several pilot projects (e.g., see Bos, Zimmerman, Olson, et al. 2007), he is careful to note the difficulty of making predictions (1993:855). As VREs and collaboratories are designed, developed, and implemented, it also becomes increasingly clear that they are similar to other entities such as virtual communities.

Relationships between VREs, Groups, and Communities

The Instrumentalist View and Its Limitations

In the original definition of a VRE, collaboration was not mentioned as an essential characteristic. However, in the 2006 clarification, collaboration is highlighted as one of the activities facilitated ("In addition, they will facilitate collaborations"). This determination was arrived at over a period beginning with the launch of the U.K. Joint Information Systems Committee VRE program in July 2004, with the aim of developing "the infrastructure and tools for collaborative e-research environments."[1]

Research undertaken in projects within this program showed that supporting collaboration among researchers was a central aspect of all VRE development (Carusi and Jirotka 2006). However, this definition uses the word *facilitate* rather than *support*. In essence, the idea is similar to that initially put forward by Wulf: the technologies that compose a collaboratory or VRE are seen as being secondary to the research activities they support and are defined or determined by scientists' research activities. In other words, it may be argued that the relationship is presented in a classically instrumentalist way wherein the technology is understood as neutral and serves a humanly controlled purpose formed independently of the technology (e.g., MacKenzie and Wajcman 1985; Feenberg 1999).

This way of viewing the relationship between collaboration and research practices in the development of VREs is problematic. Studies in computer-supported collaborative work have shown that collaboration is extremely difficult to define (Galegher, Kraut, and Egido 1990; Luff, Hindmarsh, and Heath 2000). This difficulty has also been evident in the requirements-gathering process and user-engagement activities of VRE development that have attempted to elicit from researchers a characterization of their collaborations.

Researchers who are undertaking research in a VRE or collaboratory have very different conceptions of the notion of collaboration (Carusi and Jirotka 2006). This assessment holds true for both researchers who claim to collaborate and those who claim not to. In addition, collaborations do not necessarily exist before the ICT that is developed to support them. New collaborations and, more important, new forms of collaboration can emerge from use of the ICTs, and existing forms of collaboration may sometimes recede into the background. Both are standard occurrences, with email and texting being popular recent examples in communication technologies.

The "laboratory" part of the collaboratory vision renders the instrumentalist view problematic for a further reason. The notion of a laboratory nested in "collaboratory" demonstrates its origin in the world of natural-science research and an environment of laboratories. Other forms of research are not necessarily excluded, but they also may not fit the paradigm of research that has inspired the vision. VREs have similarly been seen as a way of extending e-research across the academy, even though the form of science presupposed by the term *e-science* was of natural sciences in the first instance. Here, the idea of a laboratory is a metaphor that may—as other metaphors do—have a formative role on research in other domains, most notably the social sciences and humanities. In these cases, the extension of the notion of collaboratory into the social sciences will mark yet another stage in the long and sometimes difficult relationship between these two forms of science. The humanities also have their own unique set of issues related to the imposition of the paradigm of science.

Implications of Adopting a Laboratory Metaphor for VREs

The underlying perceptions indicated by the laboratory metaphor are a further reason to be cautious of the instrumentalist view. Consider two scenarios: where the laboratory metaphor serves as a tacit model for collaboratory design and where it does not. In the former case, the lack of neutrality with respect to the type of research envisioned as being supported, which is modeled on the natural sciences, may be embedded into the design of the technologies themselves. This relationship is most clearly evident in the very emphasis on collaboration. Styles of collaboration vary enormously across disciplines, with large-scale empirical natural sciences having the most clearly defined set of collaborative practices. This form of collaboration may be designed into the technology in a unidirectional manner, obscured by the instrumentalist view.

The second scenario is one that acknowledges that technologies will be deployed in contexts that do not share the same understanding of collaborative research and where there is often not a clearly defined preexisting sense of collaboration to draw upon. For these reasons, the relationship between the technologies and collaborative research is formative in both directions: in the understanding of collaborative research as embedded in the framework for technology development and in the understanding of collaborative research as occurring between potential users of the technology. In the reciprocal tensions caused by the pull in these two directions, the result is optimally one of coevolution of technology and research; otherwise, there may be a lack of progress, uptake, or sustainability of pilot projects.

In both these scenarios, the instrumentalist view is untenable. However, the possibility of the first scenario's being actualized is real—unless awareness is built up of the

complex interrelationships between technologies and practices. A naive instrumental-
ism diminishes the chances of sustaining a diverse array of research practices adequate
for the full range of modes and objects of knowledge. Careful work is needed to understand better how this diversity can be respected—for example, through investigating
the opportunities afforded by adopting a more coevolutionary approach.

Codefinition of the Collaboration–Technology Relationship

The discussion so far of the process of collaboratory development points to a potential
underestimation of the complexity of the collaboration–technology relationship. A
number of large-scale attempts to build computer-supported scientific collaboration
environments were based on the collaboratory vision set out by Wulf and others. However, Nathan Bos and his colleagues observe that "only a few of these efforts have
succeeded in sustaining long-distance participation, solving larger-scale problems,
and initiating breakthrough science." In the light of their analysis, it is interesting
to note their definition of collaboratory: "A collaboratory is an organizational entity
that spans distance, supports rich and recurring human interaction oriented to a
common research area, and fosters contact between researchers who are both known
and unknown to each other, and provides access to data sources, artifacts, and tools
required to accomplish research tasks" (2007:653, 656).

This definition represents a notable shift to discussing "an organizational entity,"
away from the previous focus on a set of tools and technologies or software that support collaboration or research. This shift is indicative of a movement from seeing "tools
and technologies" and "groups and activities" as two distinct entities, one of which is
in a relation of support to the other. Rather, it acknowledges that what needs to occur
is a two-way relationship, whereby the tools and technologies and the activities they
support codefine each other. For instance, the absence of a group of researchers who
can act as user-developers at the outset is generally indicative of an e-research environment where it is difficult to achieve uptake for digital tools and technologies. For this
reason, VREs can only fairly artificially be defined as a set of tools and technologies
interoperating to facilitate or enhance the research process. In fact, this definition can
have meaning only by reference to researchers in their positioning in groups, such as
communities or organizations.

Typologies of Collaboratories

Developing typologies of VREs and related concepts may be useful to gain a better understanding of networked research in order to inform policy and to identify
strengths and challenges of different approaches. Bos and his colleagues (2007) have
proposed a typology of collaboratories using a "landscape sampling" or a bottom-up

Table 10.1
A Typology for Collaboratories

Collaboratory type	Entity held in common	Technological issue	Organizational issue
Shared instrument	Scientific instrument	Synchronous communications and remote-access technology	Allocating access
Community data system	Information resource	Data standardization	Motivating contributors
Open community contribution system	Research problem	System that operates across platforms without sacrificing usability	Maintaining quality control
Virtual community of practice	Research area	Usability	Sustaining participation
Virtual learning community	Knowledge in context of learning and education	Disparities in technology infrastructure in different educational institutions	Aligning educational goals and assessments
Distributed research center	Cross-institutional common topics of interest or joint projects	Same as for other collaboratory types and need for technologies for workplace awareness	Same as for other types and [dealing with] questions of cross-institutional intellectual property [and] career issues of younger participants
Community infrastructure project	Infrastructure for a particular domain	New field standards for data and data-collection protocols, data provenance	Negotiat[ing] goals among disciplinary partners, manag[ing] structures, [adapting to] younger researchers

Source: Bos, Zimmerman, Olson, et al. 2007.

method, which depends on what is held in common by those using it. They have gone on to discuss the technological and organizational issues relating to each of these typologies. Their findings form a useful basis for developing a broader VRE typology (table 10.1).

These authors also provide a diagnosis of the kinds and degrees of difficulty encountered by the types discussed previously. This diagnosis is summarized in table 10.2, about which they comment that collaborations "become more difficult to manage and sustain" when moving "from the top left of the table to the bottom right" because it is "more difficult to share knowledge than data or tools, and it is more difficult to co-create than to aggregate" (Bos, Zimmerman, Olson, et al. 2007:668).

Table 10.2
Collaboratory Types by Resource and Activity

Type	Tools (instruments)	Information (data)	Knowledge (new findings)
Aggregating across distance (loose coupling, often asynchronously)	Shared instrument	Community data system	Virtual learning community, virtual community of practice
Cocreating across distance (requires tighter coupling, often synchronously)	Infrastructure	Open community contribution system	Distributed research center

Source: Bos, Zimmerman, Olson, et al. 2007:668, table 1.

Creating and Sharing Knowledge: The Key Impacts on Research Practices

We would add the following to the set of findings highlighted in tables 10.1 and 10.2: it is at the level of creating and sharing knowledge that the important impacts of these technologies on central/fundamental research or epistemic practices will be found in collaboratories and VREs. All the definitions observed have included the term *research*, but have left it relatively unanalyzed. Because it is with respect to research that collaboratories and VREs are distinguished from other networking environments, we need more detailed understanding of the actual practices through which research is conducted.

By the term *research practices*, we mean those activities that are necessary for knowledge claims to be made and justified within particular disciplinary or scholarly areas: the practices of dissecting, segmenting, relating, measuring, counting, comparing, interpreting, and so on. These practices share the qualities of a common language of a group of researchers who have a shared research area or discipline. Some research practices are also *epistemic practices*; that is, they provide the means to achieve the key knowledge goals of an area of inquiry. These means are akin to "tools of the trade."

For the purposes of this chapter, we refer to both forms of practices as *research practice*, in the broader term. These practices must be held in common for researchers to communicate with each other and to form groups, communities, or other collectives. A consideration of research practices thus enables us to keep in view some of the essential characteristics of groups or communities of researchers and to consider how these characteristics figure in the development of tools and technologies for research via a set of common activities. Thus, to attend to research practices in a collaboratory or VRE is at the same time to attend to essential features of virtual communities.

In addition, a consideration of these research practices is essential for an evaluation and assessment of the extent to which collaboratories and VREs meet the epistemic objectives that are claimed for them by programs and visions of research. Finally, in order to be properly understood, these central research practices need to be placed in the context of the technologies that are required for them and of the groups of researchers who hold them in common.

Central Research Practices for VREs

Based on our research findings[2] in this field (Carusi and Jirotka 2006), this section outlines four research practices that are central to the VREs discussed in this chapter. These practices relate to

• Defining a canon of scholarly work;
• Mapping an object of research;
• Mapping and operating on personal interactions;
• Performative processes.

Practices Defining a Canon of Scholarly Work

The data deluge (chapter 4) is often claimed to be a major motivation for e-research. Although this deluge is an important factor across the research arena, it is not the same for all disciplines. In the natural and physical sciences, there are usually large quantities of data of the same type (e.g., experimental data sets); in other domains, it is access to different types of data that makes a difference. There are also "niches" of data that were previously inaccessible for a variety of reasons.

Scholarship generally works with authorized texts, the standard editions or the translations of major works, with other editions or translations not being easily accessible. Disciplinary scholarship is also clustered around the canon of major works (a list or group of texts, documents, scripts, art or musical works) that is considered to set the standard for the discipline. Such canons are sources of authority for disciplines, playing a central role in defining what is and what is not studied as well as the norms or criteria of what constitutes scholarship in the discipline. By their very nature, canons exclude some objects that are, by the nature of things, also difficult to access. In this way, the canon is "solidified."

However, canons are also historical and change over time. The feminist challenge of the canon in all humanities and social science disciplines is a good example of a large-scale historical shift that is still occurring. Digitization of research material means that more previously excluded, marginalized, or difficult to access material is becoming available. A good example of a VRE that has capitalized on this point relates to the "History of Political Discourse 1500–1800" project (box 10.1).

Access to previously excluded or marginalized documents can be a powerful force in reshaping a research area. Such access can profoundly affect the very existence of

Box 10.1
The "History of Political Discourse 1500–1800" VRE

Starting in September 2008, the School of History at the University of East Anglia and the Department of History at the University of Hull in the United Kingdom have provided a master's degree in the history of political discourse from 1500 to 1800 based on a VRE.[a] Its starting point was the availability of noncanonical material (such as political pamphlets) in digital form that enabled the building of an environment to support new teaching opportunities. In turn, this program may build up critical mass for virtual environments and their tools, technologies, and modes of access as master's students who have been taught in the virtual environments progress to become doctoral students and researchers.

Note:
a. See http://www.earlymoderntexts.org/ for details of the "History of Political Discourse 1500–1800" project.

canons because it would enable the emergence of disciplinary areas that do not solidify into canons as easily as others that have utilized the affordances of paper text. The dissolving of the canon—and obviously of the authority structures that go with it—is also likely to have a deep effect on the mode and style of interaction around documents dealt with by the individuals involved (teachers, researchers, students). Together with the distributed access to and interpretation of texts in a VRE, this dissolution is set to make an important difference to the course of research.

Digitization similarly enables access to ancient documents that were previously inaccessible because they are too fragile or too degraded. It makes possible both the deciphering and the interpretation of these documents. For instance, although fragments of a document are globally dispersed, they can be brought together digitally. In this way, the object of study—the meaningful document as well as the physical text—is at least partially constructed in the digital domain.

A further instance of how computational resources associated with e-research can play a role in constructing a document is stereoscopic imaging, which has been used to make visible and legible the script on stone (Bowman, Brady, and Tomlin 1997). The important point here is that the legibility or decipherability of the script occurs at the same time as it becomes visible: each informs the other.

The different ways of making a text available in digital form for distributed access by researchers have the potential to make a substantial difference to what is considered to be a text or document and to the practices of reading and interpretation around them. One way is through collaboration with computer scientists and others to bring about a legible document. Such collaboration subjects researchers to questions about reading and interpretation practices or may change these practices in some way, thereby shaking up interpretive paradigms. In addition, the very existence of a digital rendition of documents that were originally in papyrus and stone has alternative implications for interpretive orientation.

Mapping an Object of Research

The previous section shows how new collaborations and disciplinary reshapings can occur with the availability of previously excluded or difficult-to-access objects of research. Another form of emergent collaboration occurs when objects of research not only are accessed through the infrastructural resources of a cyberinfrastructure such as a VRE, but are mapped in such an environment. The difference is subtle but notable.

In these cases, texts and documents may be accessed via a VRE—but nothing more than accessed. In other cases (and sometimes in other aspects of the same VRE), the environment in some way maps the entity or process that is being studied. This aspect of VREs has a representational and organizational role with respect to the object of study in a research area. A good example is the archaeological Silchester Roman Town VRE project (box 10.2).

The map in figure 10.1 is particularly interesting because of the type of research and collaboration that it enables. It is the output of the real spatial disposition of the excavation site as well as the result of a complex process of research, beginning with on-site data gathering, the physical movements of on-site excavators with hand-held computers, and curators and researchers' interpretive and identification processes on and off site. It is both a continuation of existing practices of archaeologists in the style and genre of the map and a modification thereof in the new virtual forms of interactivity within the VRE.

The possibility of mapping a physical entity in such a virtual representation can play a major role in research that is highly dependent on location and spatiality. It has the potential to bring into play more wide-ranging collaborations in that it will be possible

Box 10.2
Silchester Roman Town VRE

> In the development of a VRE relating to an archaeological excavation of the Silchester Roman town in northern Hampshire, England,[a] one aim has been to connect on-site data gathering from the excavation site with collaborative research domains. These domains are essentially maps of the excavation site in that they represent the site itself through a combination of iconic, indexical, and symbolic means (Moriarty 2005:229ff).
>
> *Note*:
> a. The Silchester Roman Town VRE is a University of Reading Department of Archaeology project (http://www.silchester.rdg.ac.uk/).

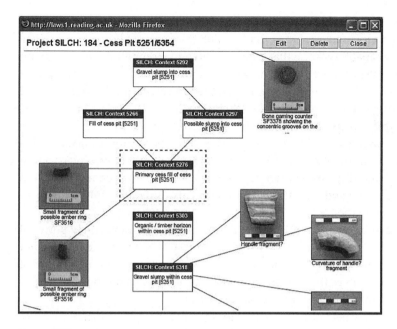

Figure 10.1
Identification of objects found in Silchester building.

for globally distributed experts to collaborate on the identification and interpretation of objects. In this respect, it can also play an important subsidiary role in providing a research discovery service as experts converge upon specific areas. One of the most important aspects to be considered in this manifestation of a VRE is the nature of the map because it plays a knowledge-management and research role as well as a representational function.

The map's organization and disposition on the screen as well as its manipulability and interactivity will not be cognitively or epistemologically neutral. It will optimally reflect the cognitive and epistemological practices of the user community of researchers; however, it is well known that such practices are not homogeneous and are sometimes contentious. How VREs affect the representational, organizational, and knowledge practices of a research area is an important question. In order to be generic, VREs have tended to standardize practices. In this process of standardization, the same debates need to be held as have emerged from general contestations of the neutrality of standardized ontologies (e.g., see Bowker and Star 1999). In this context, however, the debates may need to take into consideration the physical medium in which information is embedded (e.g., visual, aural, textual) and the spatial and temporal arrangements of information that this medium allows for because they are powerful aspects of the meaning-making process.

Practices Involved in Mapping and Operating on Personal Interactions

The previous section focused on that aspect of a VRE that maps a physical entity. Here we look at another capability—one that maps interactions. Some VREs operate not on a particular knowledge area, but on interactions among researchers—for example, at meetings or conferences. Different kinds of such environments are illustrated by the Meeting Memory Technology Informing Collaboration (MeMeTIC, box 10.3) and Integrating Web Information Using the Semantic Web (IUGO, box 10.4) VREs.

Convergences between MeMeTIC and IUGO were developed to form the Collaborative Research Events on the Web (CREW) project.[3] CREW seeks not only to make it possible to search and find disparate content relating to research and teaching events, but also to enable the replay and annotation of these events using MeMeTIC's Compendium concept mapping tool.

The combined toolkits within CREW offer the potential for an extremely powerful research and teaching intervention, where students and conference attendees need not rely only on their notes (or even on their presence) in order to gain all the benefits of these events. It also enables the replay and operation of these recordings to analyze, organize, arrange, and generally map interactive events.

Here we see another aspect of a VRE that maps interactions. This VRE not only provides new possibilities for collaboration, but also creates new ways of operating on

Box 10.3
The MeMeTIC VRE: Helping to Develop the Access Grid

The Meeting Memory Technology Informing Collaboration (MeMeTIC)[a] aimed to develop further the potentialities of the Access Grid (see the introduction to this volume), which has become a staple of many researchers' lives (e.g., as a technology for holding distributed meetings and seminars). The Access Grid is often used in much the same way as video conferencing, and many researchers' experience of it will be very similar. However, it has several other capabilities, including that of sharing material such as documents. It also allows for digital recordings to be created of events held using its capabilities. MeMeTIC adds components such as Screen Streamer, which allows participants at meetings to share their computer screens with others at the meeting, and Compendium, a concept-mapping tool that essentially allows the meeting to be mapped as it proceeds. Together with the ability to record Access Grid meetings, these tools allow participants to replay a meeting. A central purpose of this type of VRE is to render ephemeral events durable so that they can be better exploited.

Note:

a. MeMeTIC is a collaboration between the University of Manchester, Open University, University of Southampton, and University of Edinburgh (see http://www.memetic-vre .net/).

Box 10.4

The IUGO VRE: Integrating Web Information Using the Semantic Web

IUGO is a Semantic Web application using a VRE.[a] It aims to integrate Web-based information on research events such as conferences and workshops. This information may include
anything from public items, such as calls for papers and details of research programs, to
more restricted items (participant lists, blogs, and photographs posted on the Web, or
recordings of sessions, slides, and handouts). It would also be possible to search across
events and thereby track people or research themes across events.

Note:

a. IUGO is centered at the University of Bristol (see http://iugo.ilrt.bris.ac.uk/).

those collaborations to facilitate the rendering of previously unobtainable aspects of
research interactions. These kinds of VRE tools open collaborations to unprecedented
levels of self-reflectiveness. Researchers will be able not only to access others' talks, but
also to reflect on their own interactions because these interactions are recorded and
annotated.

However, despite the apparent neutrality and flexibility of the concept-mapping system, there is still some concern about the basic ontology built into many of these tools
because they can delineate items that are picked out (questions, ideas, attitudes for, attitudes against, etc.) and relations among them. Leaving aside the question of whether
this capability may or may not suit all types of human interactive processes, there
remain doubts about whether for any particular event or community, the mode of
mapping chosen will be neutral with respect to the interaction or will play a formative
role in shaping the way the event or community is remembered or understood.

Increased levels of self-reflectiveness, together with a concept-mapping tool that
guides that reflectiveness, have the potential to change collaboration at research and
teaching events in ways that are unpredictable. It remains uncertain whether this
increase will result in research communities' becoming better at understanding their
own interactions by means of these tools or in the tools' co-construction of the interactions and behaviors. How will the use of such tools for research collaborations be supported if it is the case that communities are not always good at realizing how their own
interactions are not simply supported and co-constructed by the tools they use, but also
coevolve with them?

Research Practices Relating to Performative Processes

Research practices often include making, doing, or performing activities. Among the
examples we have considered, archaeological research is extremely physical in its interactions with a real environment in order to gather and explore data. Scientific research

can similarly incorporate many aspects of physical interaction, such as setting up and running the apparatus and data for experiments. In the arts, creative works and performances are the outcomes of a "research"[4] activity. Artworks and performances essentially involve doing, making, and performing processes. Here, these research activities are labeled "performative" processes in that they are ways in which research is accomplished by actions performed.[5]

A subdivision between two types of performative process is necessary to account for the array of VREs observed:

• Research practices relating to performing experiments, found mainly but not only in scientific experimentation
• Research practices relating to the humanities and arts

Performing Experiments   One way in which the scientific process of experimentation is embedded within VREs is through enabling the sharing of experimental work flows— for example, in projects such as MyExperiment (box 10.5) and the Integrative Biology VRE (box 10.6).

Performative processes are particularly challenging for a VRE. They are not only discursive, thus requiring more than voice or text, but also usually multisensory (requiring a combination of visual, tactile, and aural perception, as well as kinetic and spatial input). In addition, they usually require copresence with the object being acted upon or with others who are cooperating or collaborating. It is not a novelty to see technologies

Box 10.5
MyExperiment: Sharing of Research Work Flows and Resources

MyExperiment is a VRE that allows researchers to share their work flows as well as other research objects and data.[a] These work flows must be standardized in order to be shared, which implies abstraction from "real" processes and formalization. This abstraction, in turn, normally implies an increase in discrete knowledge, but a decrease in contextual or narrative knowledge. The VRE combines the formal and the informal, providing opportunities for blogs describing the nonformal and unformalizable detail around the real conditions in which experiments are carried out. When combined with Web 2.0 technologies, the sharing of work flows and other research objects allows for the creation of mash-ups. In this process, there is a back-and-forth shift between physical and digital objects, physical and digital spaces, as well as a simultaneous respecification of each object or space.

Note:
a. MyExperiment is a joint project between the University of Manchester and the University of Southampton (see http://www.myexperiment.org/).

Box 10.6
Integrative Biology VRE: Sharing Computational Simulation Work

The Integrative Biology VRE (IBVRE) enables the sharing of work flows involving computational simulations *(in silico* experiments).[a] Here, the physical space of the laboratory has been shifted into the computer, and physical events (e.g., electrical currents in animal hearts, data for which has been gathered in real "wetlab" conditions) are abstracted into digitally rendered parameter values and algorithms. IBRVE allows biologists and others in the life sciences who do not share the computational and mathematical background of pioneers of computational biology to run *in silico* experiments for themselves, bypassing the mathematics. It offers an important arena for the reshaping of life science epistemic practices into a more formal, quantified, and mathematicized way of conducting science than these researchers are used to or have been prepared to accept (e.g., see Galison 1997).

Note:
a. IBVRE is based at the University of Oxford (see http://www.vre.ox.ac.uk/ibvre/).

responding to these multisensory demands, often in ingenious and interesting ways (e.g., long-distance surgery using advanced digital communications). VREs are rising to this challenge—for instance, through projects such as the Collaborative Stereoscopic Access Grid Environment (CSAGE) (box 10.7).

The Value of the Humanities and Arts in Performing Experiments in VREs   The way artists can push technologies beyond any specific predefined purpose was illustrated in a CSAGE application that used a VRE both to record a real-world dance performance (for teaching purposes) and to perform dances in virtual space, where dancers perform with three-dimensional images of other dancers who may or may not be dancing at the same time at another location.[6] This performance involves a real-time rendered world of three-dimensional shapes that have the appearance of being in front of and surrounding a dancer when viewed with passive polarized glasses. The dynamic nature of the changing shape and forms from the virtual world, together with the performer's movement and expression in response to these forms, provides a completely new set of opportunities for performance.

Such arts-based experimentation may offer a specific research niche where it is difficult to draw conclusions concerning what may be transferable to other domains. However, it is clear that VRE technologies such as CSAGE can create an opportunity for a very different kind of collaboration, where the coperformance of dance can potentially be exemplary of what is entailed in collaboration in other fields. It is also exemplary as a human-technical system or environment in that neither the dancers' specific practices nor the technology's capabilities were predefined, but coevolved as

Box 10.7

The Collaborative Stereoscopic Access Grid Environment

The Collaborative Stereoscopic Access Grid Environment (CSAGE) has built on Access Grid technologies by the use of semi-immersive stereoscopic facilities to create an increased level of "presence" within the Access Grid environment.[a] It offers a variety of capabilities, such as recording, commenting, and annotating Access Grid meetings. In addition, the use of three-dimensional stereoscopic capabilities has resulted in particularly interesting uses, including the facial reconstruction of an archaeological skull carried out in a distributed environment over the Access Grid, along with many other uses for geologists, paleontologists, and other researchers for whom spatial information is crucial to their research.

Note:

a. The Universities of Manchester and Southampton are joint partners in the CSAGE project (see http://www.kato.mvc.mcc.ac.uk/rss-wiki/SAGE). Discussion of the project here is based on an interview with the project manager, Martin Turner.

the interrelationship between technology and performance were explored over several iterations.

The use of three-dimensional stereoscopic imaging, together with the other capacities of the Access Grid, go beyond recording and mapping; they move toward a form of "cyberinteracting" that makes participants more present to each other in the interaction. Echoing Wulf's words on collaboratories, one participant in the dance experiment described this enhanced Access Grid environment as "a seminar room without walls" because it enables participants to communicate with others in different spaces and to feel as though they are in the same space. The exploration of the potential for achieving this space through dance is one of the ways in which the technology can be improved.

Should this type of capability become generally available, it would provide a rich experience of colocation and copresence. As a participant in the dance experiment put it, one ideal for a VRE is to be an environment for people to get on with their work with the minimal intrusion from technologies. This view is challenging and attractive. However, it is important to consider how these naturalistic effects are embedded in technological design because, in their apparent transparency, they may hide the artifices through which the activity was accomplished—and those artifices sometimes have a hidden formative effect on behaviors, in this case on research practices.

Many disciplines in the humanities (e.g., history of art and literary criticism and theory) have a great deal of knowledge of how such naturalistic effects are achieved and at what cost. CSAGE is an example of why it is worthwhile to look to the full range of disciplines that collaboratories and VREs are meant to include and to be open to influences from disciplines other than the natural science "laboratory" model.

Conclusion

The previous sections identified four ways in which VREs, collaboratories, and related concepts may shape epistemic and research practices by virtue of the tools and technologies developed for them, thus showing the close connection between research practices and the development of tools and technologies for conducting that research. Because of the collective nature of research practices, the disciplinary, social, or community dimension of research is fully recognized as being implicated in the development of these research tools and technologies in an ongoing process of coevolution.

Tools and technologies for research have the potential to reshape the research landscape, not only opening out some spaces, but also closing others—making some stand out and others unrecognizable. This potential reshaping is not value neutral either for the societies upon which research impacts or for the researchers in their interrelationships with institutions and each other. Susan Leigh Star has coined the term *orphans of infrastructure* for those "individuals groups and forms of social and professional practice that fit uneasily or not at all within the emerging infrastructural paradigm."[7] A similar phenomenon can be identified in the case of research practices that are or are not fostered by VREs and collaboratories. It is not specific to these new technologies, but is an integral part of the history of communication technologies in their relation to knowledge.

It is essential to consider the impact of VREs and collaboratories on central or fundamental research practices in order to be in a position to evaluate and assess these technologies for their epistemic outcomes in relation to knowledge development and understanding, as well as for their social, institutional, and organizational outcomes.

Notes

1. See http://www.jisc.ac.uk/uploaded_documents/TownMeeting20040719.ppt#259,4,Context.

2. Our research draws largely on projects in the U.K. Joint Information Systems Committee VRE Programme.

3. IUGO and MeMeTIC have been combined to form CREW (http://www.crew-vre.net/?page _id=8).

4. The quotation marks around "research" here are due to academic artists' own questioning of whether what they produce, in addition to their journal articles and conference presentations, should count as research.

5. See J. L. Austin's (1962) discussion on performative utterance in speech act theory.

6. See http://kato.mvc.mcc.ac.uk/rss-wiki/SAGE/StereoBodies.

7. As explained in Susan Leigh Star's talk entitled "Orphans of Infrastructure: A New Point of Departure" at the Oxford Internet Institute's conference "The Future of Computing: A Vision," 29–30 March 2007, University of Oxford.

References

Austin, J. L. 1962. *How to do things with words*. Oxford, UK: Clarendon Press.

Borda, A., J. Careless, M. Dimitrova, M. Fraser, J. Frey, P. Hubbard, S. Goldstein, C. Pung, M. Shoe-bridge, and N. Wiseman. 2006. *Report of the Working Group on Virtual Research Communities for the OST e-Infrastructure Steering Group*. London: U.K. Office of Science and Technology. Available at: http://eprints.soton.ac.uk/42074/.

Bos, N., A. Zimmerman, J. Olson, J. Yew, J. Yerkie, E. Dahl, and G. Olson. 2007. "From shared databases to communities of practice: A taxonomy of collaboratories." *Journal of Computer-Mediated Communication 12* (2):652–672. Available at: http://jcmc.indiana.edu/vol12/issue2/bos.html.

Bowker, G. C., and S. L. Star. 1999. *Sorting things out: Classification and its consequences*. Cambridge, MA: MIT Press.

Bowman, A. K., J. M. Brady, and R. S. O. Tomlin. 1997. "Imaging incised documents." *Literary and Linguistic Computing 12* (3):169–176.

Carusi, A., and M. Jirotka. 2006. "Building virtual research environments and user engagement." In *Proceedings of the Second International Conference on e–Social Science, Manchester, UK, June 2006*. Available at: http://www.ncess.ac.uk/research/social_shaping/oess/presentations/20060630_carusi _VREUserEngagement.pdf.

Feenberg, A. 1999. *Questioning technology*. London: Routledge and Kegan Paul.

Galegher, J., R. Kraut, and C. Egido. 1990. *Intellectual teamwork: Social and technological foundations of cooperative work*. Mahweh, NJ: Lawrence Erlbaum Associates.

Galison, P. 1997. *Image & logic: A material culture of microphysics*. Chicago: University of Chicago Press.

Luff, P., J. Hindmarsh, and C. C. Heath, eds. 2000. *Workplace studies: Recovering work practice and informing system design*. Cambridge, UK: Cambridge University Press.

MacKenzie, D., and J. Wajcman, eds. 1985. *The social shaping of technology: How the refrigerator got its hum*. Milton Keynes, UK: Open University Press.

Moriarty, S. 2005. "Visual semiotics theory." In *Handbook of visual communication: Theory, methods, and media*, ed. K. Smith, S. Moriarty, S. Barbutsis, and K. Kenney. Mahwah, NJ: Lawrence Erlbaum Associates, 227–242.

U.S. National Science Board. 2000. *Science & engineering indicators—2000*. Arlington, VA: National Science Foundation (NSB-00-1).

Wulf, W. A. 1989. "The national collaboratory—a White Paper." Appendix A in J. Lederberg and K. Uncaphar (eds.), *Towards a national collaboratory*, a report of a National Science Foundation invitational workshop held at Rockefeller University, New York, 17–18 March 1989. Washington, DC: National Science Foundation.

Wulf, W. A. 1993. "The collaboratory opportunity." *Science 261* (5123):854–855.

10.1   The Future of Virtual Research Environments

Matthew Dovey

Antecedents and Motivations behind Emerging Virtual Research Environment Concepts

Fundamentally, a virtual research environment (VRE) is a location where researchers go to find and use the information and communication technology (ICT) tools needed for their research. This concept is far from new, and earlier similar initiatives have occurred under such headings as a "scholar's workstation" or "collaboratory."

The VRE concept traces its heritage from virtual learning environments (VLE). Although initial VLEs were monolithic Web applications, there has been a movement to modularize them—separating the framework from the tools and linking VLEs together using standards such as those emerging from the portal world.[1] Some of the tools (e.g., communication and scheduling) were generic enough to be applicable to research as much as to teaching, so the idea emerged of exploring what might be achieved by using frameworks being developed by the VLE community to host research-oriented tools— taking the L for "learning" out of "VLE" and replacing it with R for "research."

We consistently see various tensions regarding the "correct" approach to building computer-based environments, as well as oscillations between one side and the other. Some of the key tensions are:

• *Monolithic versus modular*   A single "do everything" application clearly raises issues about being locked into a monolithic system. However, the alternative modular collection of tools based on the adage that "the whole is greater than the sum of its parts" does not automatically apply to a miscellaneous collection of tools—which can remain just a miscellaneous collection of tools.

• *Solo versus group work*   The scholar's workstation approach tended to be oriented around tools needed by a single researcher. Collaboratories, in contrast, concentrate on environments for collaborations between multiple researchers, driven by the growth of the network form and the resultant growth of possibilities from it.

• *"Thin" versus "thick" clients*   A significant tension oscillates between making the most use of the processing and storage power of the user's client (e.g., a laptop or laboratory workstation) and reducing the support costs (in terms of installing or maintaining software or ensuring local data are backed up). Various approaches range from "thin" clients with a relatively low level of resources (e.g., "dumb" terminals linked to traditional mainframes or Web-based applications) to "thick" clients with higher resource levels that move the balance away from the network servers (e.g., "virtualization" systems that share the resources of one computer across multiple environments, such as VMWare,[2] Citrix XenSource,[3] and Microsoft's SoftGrid[4] and Hyper-V[5]).

For all of these tensions, there is no universally "correct" approach that will accommodate all users or even a single user in all circumstances. Rather, the middle line, or the ability to mix and match, will lead to successful solutions; these tensions are thus really spectrums rather than simple dichotomies.

Key Issues in VRE Developments

There are four key areas in which VREs need to develop: usability, adaptability, interoperability, and sharability.

Usability

Unless your research field happens to be ICT innovation, how the tool can be used is most likely far more important to you than how innovative it is. The user interface continues to evolve, with an increasing focus on immersive, three-dimensional, and mixed reality techniques (see chapter 8). For instance, immersive environments can be used for performing virtual medical operations; semitransparent liquid-crystal display panels can overlay digital views onto physical locations, as in overlaying past architecture onto an historical site; and three-dimensional virtual worlds (e.g., *Second Life*) and spatialized audio can assist in teleconferencing and videoconferencing. The tension between usefulness and adaptability in such user contexts can become distracting, however.

Adaptability

Given the inherently unpredictable nature of research, tools' adaptability is essential. However, adaptability is in tension with usability. To most users, the easiest interface would be a button marked "Do what I want." Unfortunately, without reams of confusing configuration options behind it, such a button is hardly very adaptable. The most adaptable user interface is a programming language; however, for many, a programming language is not particularly usable. It is important to remember that there is no universally "correct" solution here and that complex tasks will inevitably require complex interfaces.

What is needed is an "onion" model of user interfaces—each layer exposing slightly more complexity, but slightly more functionality. A task will then be as complex or as simple to perform as it needs to be. For example, some systems for managing work flows have visual point-and-click editors that work directly off visually generated work flows. An approach would be to have the user interface generate a script, then have the script run by the application engine to perform the work flow. Users then have the choice, depending on their preferences or the context in hand, of working with a visual representation or a script of the work flow (or even of working with both). Natural-language engines are likely to become more common and will be most useful if they generate scripts that can be accessed and modified if required.

Interoperability

Interoperability is the necessary ingredient to ensure that a miscellaneous collection of tools becomes more than the sum of its parts. In this area, there has always been tension between the adoption of a single standard and the building of translations and gateways between standards (which tends to be inevitable in most cases). Although interoperability has always been the holy grail of computing, the unpredictable nature of research makes it even more difficult to achieve because many standardization processes run at a much slower timescale than research. Web 2.0 ideologies may offer a solution by publishing the programming interfaces and data formats, and by being prepared (and having the appropriate tools) to cope with multiple programming interfaces and formats rather than attempting to standardize toward particular ones.

Sharability

A key driver behind the use of Web-based portals for VLEs and VREs has been the ability to access your environment from anywhere and with any operating system. This ability includes not just sharing data, but also sharing a snapshot of your virtual environment (e.g., tools and configured collections of tools) between machines, operating systems, and people. Virtualization enables this sharing with client-side applications to create the ability to select and run a collection of applications and tools within a virtual machine—and to snapshot that entire machine's state/memory and disk in a way that can be used to reproduce that environment on another machine.

Virtualization also allows windows from different virtual machines (on both client and remote machines) to appear together as if under the same machine. Such virtualization is being increasingly embedded in both the processors and operating systems. However, issues about security and licensing still need to be resolved in this area.

Summary of Key Issues

Very few, if any, of the issues described here are unique to research. Usability, adaptability, interoperability, and sharability are all requirements that any user of computers would benefit from, and so they should become features aspired to by all computer platforms.[6] However, it is still a very open question whether the computing platform of the future will ultimately be the operating system, the browser, the network, the Grid, the Cloud (see essay 2.1), or something else. In this respect, such a research environment is just the same platform anyone else uses for his or her work, but with a choice of tools (some specialized, some generic) suitable for a particular type of research.

Trends in VRE Developments

Typical VREs will continue to develop by combining underlying resources via published programming interfaces. For some disciplines, this combination will occur through well-defined user interfaces; for others, it will occur via Web 2.0 mash-ups that allow quick composition of the resources and services (sometimes purely on an experimental basis) in a manner familiar to those who combine Unix tools via the "pipe"[7] command. These VREs will also take advantage of Web 2.0 social-networking tools to aid collaboration. The underlying e-infrastructure resources will be a mixture of traditional resources—data repositories, publications, scientific instruments, computation farms, and so on—and more on-demand resources (e.g., Cloud computing).

In the longer term, as a computing platform that fully supports the broad ICT aspirations outlined here, VREs may even eventually cease to exist as such, with researchers using the same platform as anyone else. If that comes about, the VRE would still have been a useful and effective exercise because it would have become, in the way of Wittgenstein's Tractatus, a ladder to be thrown away once you have achieved your goal—in this case, understanding what researchers require in a computing platform. VREs are thus best viewed as a phenomenon rather than as a technology—a shorthand for the research tools and their context, but one that importantly enables the key issues to be recognized, discussed, cogitated, and perhaps solved.

Notes

1. For example, see the OASIS Web Services for Remote Portlets at http://www.oasis-open.org/committees/tc_home.php?wg_abbrev=wsrp) and Java Specification Requests (JSR-168/JSR-286 at: http://jcp.org/en/jsr/detail?id=168 and http://jcp.org/en/jsr/detail?id=286).

2. See http://www.vmware.com/.

3. See http://www.xensource.com/Pages/default.aspx.

4. See http://www.microsoft.com/systemcenter/softgrid/default.mspx.

5. See http://www.microsoft.com/windowsserver2008/en/us/virtualization-consolidation.aspx.

6. For instance, advanced systems such as Microsoft Live Mesh (http://www.mesh.com/) aspire to these principles.

7. In Unix-like computer operating systems, a "pipeline" is the original software pipeline: a set of processes chained by their standard streams so that the output of each process (stdout) feeds directly as the input (stdin) of the next one. See http://en.wikipedia.org/wiki/Pipeline_(Unix).

11 Will e-Science Be Open Science?

Paul A. David, Matthijs den Besten, and Ralph Schroeder

The Importance of Global Collaboration to e-Science

Much that has been written about e-research is occupied with the engineering and application of an enhanced technological infrastructure for the transmission, processing and storing of digital data and information (e.g., Hey 2005). This chapter, like others in the book, steps back to consider different, nontechnological requirements for attaining the ostensible goal of network-enabled research—augmenting the scale and effectiveness of global collaboration in scientific research. This takes many forms, but from the various initiatives around the world (see chapter 2) a consensus is emerging that collaboration should aim to be "open"—or at least that there should be a substantial measure of "open access" to the data and information underlying published research and to communication tools.

For example, the Atkins Committee, in a seminal U.S. National Science Foundation report that set the stage for research on cyberinfrastructure in the natural sciences and engineering in the United States, advocated "open platforms" and referred to the Grid as an "infrastructure for open scientific research" (Atkins, Droegemeier, Feldman, et al. 2003:4, 38). In a follow-up report expanding that vision to include the social sciences, Fran Berman and Henry Brady likewise stress the need for a "shared cyberinfrastructure" (2005:19).

In the United Kingdom, the e-science Core Program has required that the middleware being developed by its projects be released under open source software licenses, and has established the Open Middleware Infrastructure Institute (OMII). The e-Infrastructure Reflection Group, which is a high-level European body formed in 2003 to monitor and advise on policy and administrative frameworks for Grid computing, data storage, and networking resources, has gone farther (see Leenaars, Karayannis, et al. 2007). It has issued an "e-infrastructure roadmap" that calls for: open standard Grid protocol stacks; open source middleware; transparent access to relevant Grid data sources; the sharing of run-time software and interaction data including medical imagery, high-resolution video, and haptic (tactile) information; and public funding of scientific software development because current intellectual property rights (IPR) solutions "are not in the interest of science" (Leenaars, Karayannis, et al. 2007:13).

Provision of enhanced technical means of accessing distributed research resources is neither a necessary nor a sufficient condition for achieving open scientific collaboration (David 2006; David and Spence 2008; chapter 7 in this volume). Collaboration technologies—both infrastructures and specific application tools and instruments—may be used to facilitate the work of distributed members of "closed clubs." Such clubs include government labs engaged in secret defense projects and corporate R&D teams that work with proprietary data and materials, guarding their findings as trade secrets until they obtain the legal protections granted by IPR. Nor do researchers' tools, as such, define the organizational character of collaboration, as is evident from the fact that many academic researchers who fully and frequently disclose their findings, and collaborate freely with colleagues on an informal, noncontractual basis, nonetheless employ proprietary software and patented instruments and publish in commercial scientific journals that charge high subscription fees.

The availability of certain classes of tools, and the ease with which they may be used by researchers within and across scientific domains, are quite likely to affect organizational decisions and shape the ethos and actions of the work groups that adopt those tools. Some basic collaboration technologies—notably network-enabled research infrastructures such as Grid services and middleware platforms—are particularly potent enablers of distributed multiparticipant collaborations. They may significantly augment the data, information, and computational resources that can be mobilized by the more loosely organized, "bottom-up" networks of researchers engaging in "open science." The availability of access to those resources on share-and-share-alike terms can induce researchers' participation in passive as well as active collaboration arrangements, acquainting them with benefits of cooperation and thereby reinforcing the ethos of open science.

This chapter presents our understanding of the term *open science* and its significance in studying the relationships between institutional structures, working procedures, and the formation of scientific knowledge. It also discusses ways in which this concept may be applied to assess the "openness" of certain structural features and organizational practices observable in programmatic e-science initiatives and particular projects. We then consider some results from our preliminary empirical enquiries, intended primarily to illustrate the empirical implementation of our proposed conceptual framework. Although these findings are based as yet only on our limited sample of U.K. e-science projects, other similar findings based on structured interviews and responses with research project directors support our contention that further investigation along the conceptual and methodological lines explored will prove to be both feasible and illuminating.

What Is Open Science?

Many of the key formal institutions of modern science are quite familiar to academic researchers in all disciplinary fields, not only to specialists concerned with the economics and sociology of science, technology, and innovation. It is a striking phenomenon, well noted in the sociology of science, that there is a high degree of mimetic professional organization and behavior across the diverse cognitive domains of academic endeavor. Whether in the mathematical and natural sciences, in the social sciences, or in the humanities, each discipline has its professional academies and learned societies, journal refereeing procedures, public and private grant programs, peer panels for merit review of funding applications, organized competitions, and prizes and public awards. The outward forms are strikingly similar, even if the details of the internal arrangements may differ.

The Norms of Open Science

The norms of the "Republic of Science" were first articulated by Robert Merton (1973 [1942]) and summarized by the mnemonic *CUDOS*—for communalism, universalism, disinterestedness, originality, and skepticism:[1]

- *Communalism* emphasizes the cooperative character of enquiry;
- *Universalism* stresses the need to keep entry into scientific work and discourse open for all persons of "competence";
- *Disinterestedness* highlights researchers' neutrality vis-à-vis the nature and impact of the knowledge that they contribute;
- *Originality* is the basis on which collegiate reputations are built and rewards are based; and consequently
- *Skepticism* is the appropriate attitude towards all priority claims that are made.

These five key norms constitute a clearly delineated ethos to which members of the academic research community generally subscribe, although their individual behaviors may not always conform to its strictures. Separately, as well as systemically, these norms lead to the functional allocation of resources in an idealized research system. A complete functionalist explanation can be provided for the existence of the "open" part of the institutional complex of modern research, by focusing on its economic and social efficiency properties in the pursuit of knowledge and making explicit the supportive role played by norms that tend to reinforce cooperative behaviors among scientists (Dasgupta and David 1987, 1994; David 1998, 2003). This rationale highlights the "incentive compatibility" of the key norm of disclosure within a collegiate reputation-based reward system grounded upon validated claims to priority in discovery or invention.

Rapid disclosures assist rapid validation of findings, reduce excess duplication of research effort, enlarge the domain of complementarities, and yield beneficial "spillovers" among research programs. It is the difficulty of monitoring research *efforts* that makes it necessary for both the open science system and the IPR regime to tie researchers' rewards in one way or another to priority in the production of observable "research outputs." The latter can be submitted to validity testing and valorization (to place a value on the research)—whether directly by peer assessment, or indirectly through their application in the markets for goods and services.

The specific functionality of the information-disclosure norms and social organization of open science rests on the greater efficacy of data and information sharing as a basis for the cooperative, cumulative generation of eventually reliable additions to the stock of knowledge. Treating new findings as tantamount to being in the public domain exploits fully the "public goods" properties that permit data and information to be concurrently shared in use and reused indefinitely, and thus promotes faster growth of the stock of knowledge. This practice, and its effect, contrasts with those of the information control and access restrictions that generally are required to allow private appropriation of material benefits derived from the possession of knowledge. In the proprietary research regime, discoveries and inventions must either be held secret or be "protected" by gaining monopoly rights to their commercial exploitation. Otherwise, the unlimited entry of competing users might destroy the private profitability of investing in research and development.

Sociologists and philosophers of science continue to wrestle with the relationship between the conduct of the scientific research process as seen from the epistemological perspective and the norms perceived by Merton both to underlie and to receive reinforcement from the institutionalized organization and stratified social structure of scientific communities. Indeed, this subject has occasioned some internal disciplinary struggles as well as the usual difficulties in cross-disciplinary communication. Still, reviewing the evolving literatures in the philosophy and social science of scientific research reveals broadly shared agreement that a reciprocal interdependence exists between the ethos and normative structures of research communities and the informal and institutionally reinforced conditions of access to research findings, underlying data, and methodologies.[2]

The possibilities of coordination and effective collaboration are shaped by the norms and rules affecting communications through personal networks and broadcast channels, as well as by the interchange of personnel among scientific workgroups. These norms and rules thereby impinge on the efficiency of research projects' internal use of resources, and of resource allocation among the members of separate projects who constitute "invisible colleges." The resulting, rather amorphous collaborative associations are distributed across academic departments, institutes, and universities, transcending national and regional boundaries, and extending even into research laboratories of business corporations and government agencies.[3]

Degrees of "Openness" in the Organization and Practice of Research

The considerations just reviewed provide strong reasons to regard the formal and informal institutional arrangements governing access to scientific and technical information as being no less critically influential than physical research facilities, instruments, and materials in determining how fully e-science is able to realize the potential of network-enabled research in advancing reliable knowledge. Questions concerning the actual extent of openness of contemporary research processes therefore ought to address at least two main sets of issues pertaining to the conduct of open science.

The first set concerns the terms on which individuals may enter and leave research projects. Who is permitted to join the collaboration? Are all participating researchers able to gain full access to the project's databases and other key research resources? How easy is it for members and new entrants to develop distinct agendas of inquiry within the context of the ongoing project, and how much control do they retain over the communication of their findings? What restrictions are placed (formally or informally) on the uses that participating researchers may make of data, information, and knowledge in their possession, after they exit from the research collaboration?

The second set of questions is more extensive and concerns the norms and rules governing disclosure of data and information about research methods and results (see box 11.1).

The questions posed in box 11.1, and still others, can be formulated as a simple checklist, such as the one devised by Stanford University (1996) to provide guidelines for faculty compliance within its "openness in research" policy. The Stanford checklist, however, is too limited in its scope for our present purposes, having initially been designed primarily to implement rules against secrecy in sponsored research. We report here on the development of a fuller, more specific set of questions (inspired by the Stanford list but designed for the purpose of gathering research data on U.K. e-science projects). These questions have provided an empirical framework that has been field-tested in a small number of structured interviews and subsequently in a more extensive Web survey of e-science project leaders.[4] But, the questions are not intended to be comprehensive, and they focus on selected salient aspects of openness and collaboration in academic science research that could be illuminated by similar systematic surveys conducted on a much wider scale.

E-science as Open Science: Evidence from Empirical Research

Researchers in public-sector science and engineering organizations historically have been at the forefront of many basic technological advances underlying new paradigms

Box 11.1
Disclosure of Information about Research Methods and Results

How fully and quickly is information about research procedures and data released by the project?

How completely is that information documented and annotated so as to be not only accessible, but also usable by those outside the immediate research group?

On what terms and with what delays are external researchers able to access materials, data, and project results?

Are findings held back rather than being disclosed in order first to obtain IPRs on a scientific project's research results? If so, for how long is it usual for publication to be delayed (by researchers or their respective host institutions)?

Can research partners in university–business collaborations require that some findings or data not be made public?

When IPR on research results is obtained, will that use be licensed to outsiders on an exclusive or a nonexclusive basis?

Do material transfer agreements among university-based projects impose charges (for cell lines, reagents, specimens) that require external researchers to pay substantially more than the costs of making the actual transfers?

In publicly funded research groups, are the rights to use such legally "protected" information and data conditional on payment of patent fees or copyright royalties in ways that mean the members of the group have some discretionary control? Or is control exercised by external parties (e.g., the group's host institution or the funding sources)?

---

of digital information creation and dissemination. Their pressing needs for more powerful information processing and communication tools have led to many of the key enabling technologies of the "information society"—including its mainframe computers, packet-switched data networks, Internet and Web protocols, proliferating markup languages, and other continuing advances such as the Semantic Web (essay 4.3). These technologies facilitate the distributed conduct of collaborative research, and with the same motivation research communities throughout the world are now active in developing not only technical infrastructure-tools like the Grid and middleware platforms but also a new array resources for shareable digital data and information dissemination. The latter class of information resources includes public-domain digital data archives and federated open data networks, open institutional repositories, open-access electronic journals, and open-source software applications (see, for example, Arzberger, Schröder, Beaulieu, et al. 2004; Dalle, David, Ghosh, et al. 2005; David and Uhlir 2005, 2006; Schroeder 2007; and Uhlir and Schröder 2007).

Here, we focus on one of these efforts in particular: the U.K. e-Science Programme (chapter 2), which has given rise to a number of high-profile projects. A close look at these projects and the responses of leading participants provides a first impression of the degree of openness in e-science in order to answer, at least in part, the questions that have been outlined here. We draw on a recently published study by Jenny Fry, Ralph Schroeder, and Matthijs den Besten (2009) based on a series of structured interviews with a small group of the principal investigators (PIs) in those projects. The interviews were designed to assess both the perceptions and the practices relating to the openness of the projects that the interviewees headed.

On the basis of the experience gained in conducting the structured interviews, den Besten and David (2009) developed and implemented a related questionnaire for an online Internet survey in an email-targeted survey of a larger population of PIs on U.K. e-science projects. The results obtained from that study are broadly congruent with the detailed and more nuanced impressions drawn from the structured interviews.

Insights from Specific e-Science Projects' Experiences

This subsection looks in some detail at the conduct of three U.K. e-science projects affecting aspects of openness:

1. the electronic Diagnostic National Mammography Database (e-DiaMoND), a Grid-enabled prototype system intended to support breast cancer screening, mammography training, and epidemiological research;
2. the MixedMediaGrid (MiMeG), which aims to produce software for the collaborative analysis and annotation of video data of human interactions; and
3. CombeChem, a test-bed that integrates existing sources of chemical structure and properties data, augmenting them within a Grid-based information and knowledge environment.

None of these quite-different projects have developed income-generating activities that might occasion direct conflicts with their adherence to open-science norms, but it is striking that all three nevertheless have confronted other difficult issues related to control rights over data and information.

E-DiaMoND—Unresolved Problems of Sharing Images

The central problems for e-DiaMoND surrounded issues of the control of mammography images, many of which remained unresolved when this "proof of concept" project reached its scheduled end (see Jirotka, Procter, Hartswood, et al. 2005 and essay 7.1 in this volume). The researchers' original intentions—to distribute standardized images for research and diagnostic purposes over electronic networks—clashed with clinicians' concerns about professional responsibilities to patients, protecting patient privacy, and assuring ethical uses of the data. In practice, it proved to be less straightforward than expected to convince clinical practitioners to trust the researchers and, at the same time, engineering a comprehensive and adequately flexible security system. Surprising difficulties were encountered even in developing a clear legal framework to fairly address the needs of patients, clinicians, researchers, and project participants with commercial interests in the systems being developed and deployed (Hinds, Jirotka, Rahman, et al. 2005).

MiMeG—Ethical Concerns about Abuse of Trust in Collaborative Analysis

MiMeG encountered similar problems to e-DiaMoND.[5] The researchers who employed the tool for collaborative analysis of video streams felt that the trust of the persons whose images they were studying would be violated by archiving the collaboration's data and making them available for reuse by other researchers, quite possibly for purposes other than the one for which consent originally had been obtained. Approaches to satisfying ethical concerns about privacy and the informed consent of experimental subjects would require careful consideration in future projects of this kind, in which a key objective is to permit sharing research data via the Grid or other e-infrastructures (chapter 8).

MiMeG moved from the project's initial intention to analyze video collaboratively via e-networks to then focus more on the development of video-analysis tools for other researchers to use. This MiMeG research software is being released under the GNU General Public License (GPL) and distributed at minimal cost for noncommercial use.[6] This policy resulted at least in part from the use of some GPL components to build the project's software tools. In addition, however, the MiMeG team is encouraging external users to participate in further developing its video-analysis software tools. In these respects, the project has been able to go forward in the collaborative open-science mode.

CombeChem—An Exemplar of Open Science Practices

The CombeChem project at Southampton University includes several departments and related projects.[7] The many organizational features of this complex collaboration include important aspects that are clearly "open" (see box 11.2).

CombeChem's interrelated e-science activities, highlighted in box 11.2, illustrate four facets of open science practice:

1. use of Globus-based Web services and open-source Grid software;
2. providing Web access to shared resources for a diverse research community;
3. open-access archiving and dissemination of results through an open repository; and
4. formatting of information using open standards.

Like other publicly funded academic research, the project interacts easily with the world of commercial scientific publishing: fee-charging journals that adhere to subscriber-only access policies provide readers with links to the CombeChem data

Box 11.2

Open Aspects of the CombeChem Project

CombeChem utilizes the pre-existing Engineering and Physical Sciences Resources Council National Crystallographic Service, which has allowed remote users from U.K. universities to submit samples of chemical compounds to the laboratory at Southampton for X-ray analysis (Frey 2004:1031). CombeChem accepts submitted samples and returns them via a Globus-based Grid and Web services infrastructure (Coles, Frey, Hursthouse, et al. 2005:appendix B; see also chapter 2 in this volume). In addition to demonstrating and developing this Grid implementation, a major project goal is to increase the archiving of analyzed samples, thereby averting the loss of nonarchived information and the consequently wasteful repetition of crystallographic analyses.

Chemical analysis results yielded by these techniques were previously "archived" by virtue of their publication in research journals, most of which were available on a subscription-only basis. CombeChem makes it possible to have results available in open-access repositories via the Open Archives Initiative,[a] as well as deposited in e-BankUK archives and ePrints publications (Coles, Frey, Hursthouse, et al. 2005). Because the archived results are put into Resource Description Framework and other standard metadata formats, they are searchable via the Semantic Web. With only 20 percent of data generated in crystallographic traditionally reaching the public domain (Allen 2004), and not all of it being readily searchable, this service extension is an important open-science advance (Frey 2004).

Note:

a. For details of this initiative, see http://www.openarchives.org/.

---

archive. Moreover, as is the case for other collaborative projects that fit the traditional open science model, CombeChem has been able to draw some sponsorship support from industry—IBM having been interested in this deployment of a Grid service.[8]

Open Science in e-Science—Policy or Contingency?

Fry, Schroeder, and den Besten (2009) report the findings from their use of structured, in-depth interviews about the relationships between collaboration in e-science and open science. These interviews were conducted with twelve individuals who had roles as principal investigators, project managers, and developers engaged in e-science projects in the United Kingdom during 2006.[9] The interview questions covered research inputs, software development processes, access to information resources, project documentation, dissemination of outputs and by-products, licensing issues, and institutional contracts. A focal point of the study's approach was the juxtaposition of research project leaders' descriptions of their local practices at the project level with their descriptions of their views on research governance policies at the institutional level. Here, we summarize briefly the main thrust of the study's findings.

The interviews with the study's sample of university-based project leaders indicate that the desirability of maintaining conditions of openness in doing academic science is part of a generally shared research ethos. More specifically, those interviewed were cognizant of, and receptive to, the U.K. e-science Pilot Programme's strong policy stance favoring open-source software tools and the sharing of information resources.

Nevertheless, many uncertainties and unresolved issues surround the practical implementation of the informal norms and formal policies supporting open science practices. Making software tools and data available to external users might mean simply putting these research outputs online, but that need not be the same as making them sufficiently robust and well-documented to be widely utilized.[10] For those with leadership responsibilities at the project level, the most salient and fundamental challenges in resolving issues of openness in practice and operating policies—and thereby moving toward coherent institutional infrastructures for e-science research—appear to involve the coordination and integration of goals across the diverse array of e-science efforts.[11]

By comparison, much less concern was voiced about the resolution of tensions between IPR protections and the provision of timely common-use access to research tools, data, and results. This contrast is not surprising when the context of the survey is considered. Although IPR-related issues have been very much at the center of public discussions and debates about the effects of the growth of "academic patenting" on the openness of publicly funded research,[12] the U.K. e-Science Core Programme was strongly focused on the development of software tools in support of research. Furthermore, EU policy has circumscribed the patenting of software without eliminating the patenting of embedded algorithms and a wider class of "computer implemented inventions." In the United Kingdom, for example, government-funded e-science projects have explicitly prohibited university grant and contract recipients from filing software patents that would impair the open source licensing of their outputs of middleware and applications software.

The foregoing impressions, albeit drawn from interviews conducted with only a small, nonrandom sample of project leaders, are nevertheless quite informative—inasmuch as these observations are reinforced by the findings from an online survey that sought responses from the entire population of PIs on U.K. e-science projects. This will be seen from discussion of those results in the next section.

Contract Terms and Openness in Research

Findings of an Online Survey of e-Science Projects
Systematic and detailed data at the individual project level about the openness of information and data resources remain limited as regards to actual practices and to the priority assigned to these issues among the other concerns of project leaders. A glimpse

of what the larger landscape might look like is provided by the responses to the online survey conducted among PIs contacted by email on the basis of National e-Science Centre (NeSC) data on the projects and their principal investigators (see den Besten and David 2009 for full details of the survey).

Of the 122 PIs contacted, 30 responded with detailed information for an equal number of projects.[13] A comparison of the distribution of the projects for which responses were obtained and the distribution of the entire population of NeSC projects showed remarkable similarities along the several dimensions on which quantitative comparisons could be made—including project grant size, number of consortium members, and project start dates. This provides a measure of confidence that the picture formed from this admittedly restricted and self-selected sample is representative of the whole.

Research Undertaken within Formal Agreements
Formal agreements governing the conduct of publicly funded university research projects may involve explicit terms concerned with the locus and nature of control over data and publications and with the assignment of IPR based on research results, especially when the collaborating parties include several host institutions and business organizations. The survey sought to elicit information about project leaders' understandings of these matters and the importance they attach to the ways these matters can affect the terms of their respective project's policies regarding information access. It posed questions that probed the extent of a participant's knowledge of the circumstances of the project's contractual agreemen, by asking about the identities of the parties responsible for the agreement's initial drafting and subsequent modifications (if any) as well as about the origins of some of the contract's specific terms.

The survey results suggest that in general these projects are:

• free from positive contractually imposed restrictions on the participation of qualified researchers;
• not burdened by significant restraints upon participants' access to critical data resources; and
• not placing noteworthy restrictions on their eventual ability to make public their research results.

A substantial proportion of project members appear not to be informed about the specifics of the project agreements under whose terms they are working. This is not surprising because many scientists express disinterest, if not outright impatience, regarding such matters. Instead, they wish to get on with their work without such distractions, therefore leaving it to others—including some among their fellow PIs—to deal with legal aspects of governance if and when problems of that nature intrude into the scientific conduct of the project. Therefore, in this context it could be taken as a healthy indication that issues involving restrictive provisions in projects' contractual terms intrude infrequently on the researchers' work and so have remained little discussed among them.

As encouraging as that would be, the absence of formal, contractually imposed restraints on disclosure and access to scientific information and data resources leaves a substantial margin of uncertainty in how closely the norms of open science are approximated by the operating practices and informal arrangements typically found within these projects. Probing into those important areas of "local" policy and practice is possible by examining the results obtained from a different set of the survey's questions.

Information Access in e-Science Projects: Practices and Policy Concerns

What stands out most clearly from the online survey's findings is that high-level policy guidelines, set by the funding agency, can exert a potent influence on the pattern of adoption of open access archiving of scientific research products (den Besten and David 2009). In this instance, there was an important early policy commitment by the UK e-Science Core Programme that middleware "deliverables" from its pilot projects would be made available as open source code. This requirement for the research projects has been maintained—even through there has been a notable evolution away from the original expectations of open source release of code (under the GNU GPL) once they had passed through the OMII's enhancement and repacking process.[14]

The extent to which the provision of access to data and information at the project level is perceived to be matters of explicit policy concern varies with the project's roles in e-research. This is only to be expected, particularly in view of the varied nature of the projects' deliverables and the existence of higher-level policy regarding the software being created. A clear pattern of covariation is evident in the responses to the question, "Was the provision of access to data and information to members of the project a matter of particular concern and discussion in your project?" as well as to a parallel question referring to "external researchers" (see den Besten and David 2009:questions 16 and 17). Among the projects engaged in middleware development, none expressed a concern for access within the project—presumably because the organization of the project and the ubiquity of open-access code repositories meant that this matter had largely been settled. In contrast, one third of the respondent PIs from the projects developing middleware saw the issue of external access to be an important project concern. One-third of the respondents from projects involved with user-communities and database resources, especially those from the latter group, expressed this concern.[15]

The responses relating to a question about obstacles encountered by the project in achieving openness (den Besten and David 2009:question 18) are consistent with the survey's finding regarding actual practices and policy concerns at the project level, for they indicate that providing access to information to people within the project was not an issue deserving mention. All but two PIs indicated that their respective projects had established at least one type of common repository to which participants were given access. Open access repositories are provided almost only where access by external research parties is seen as important to the purposes of the project (which is the case for about one-third of the projects covered in the survey).

Project participants are not always instructed to contribute to the repositories, when they have been provided, and it appears to be generally assumed that they will do so spontaneously. Among the respondents who stated that providing outsiders with access to project results was an important project goal, almost two-thirds listed one or more obstacles that had been encountered in achieving that goal. Among those who stated that such provision was not a project concern, however, almost half volunteered that they had personally encountered practical obstacles to external dissemination of their research output.

Conclusions

The research reported in this chapter has examined both the rationale and key identifying characteristics of collaborative open science, which carry important implications for the wider landscape of e-research examined in this book. It also began to explore ways of mapping the regions of practice where e-science and open science coincide, and where they do not. Many e-science tools could support distributed projects that conduct research in ways that accord more or less closely to open science norms. But, this does not provide assurance that such congruence will emerge wherever collaborative research is pursued under the name of e-science. Even academic e-science projects that have leaders who subscribe to the ethos of openness in research and undertake to implement some concrete "open access" practices may fall well outside those norms in one or more respects. This seems to be the case especially in regard to effective sharing of data resources and timely external disclosure of research findings.

The research summarized here has shown that e-science projects, like those in e-research more generally, are far from homogeneous. Variations in information-sharing policies and practices need to be understood in context, by taking into account the diversity of scientific purposes, the technical nature of tasks, and the details of organizational structures.

We regard the empirical studies reviewed here as trial steps in conceptual framework building, data collection, and analysis toward what we envisage as a far broader and longer-term program of systematic inquiries into the evolving global conduct of e-research in general and of e-science in particular.

Acknowledgments

We thank Anne Trefethen, Jenny Fry, Jeremy Frey, and Mike Fraser for their contributions. The preparation of this chapter, and of most of the research on the underlying data, has been supported by Economic and Social Research Council grant RES-149-25-1022 for the Oxford e-Social Science (OeSS) Project on Ethical, Legal, and Institutional Dynamics of Grid-Enabled e-Sciences. We gratefully acknowledge the institutional support provided by the Oxford Internet Institute and the Oxford e-Research Centre, and David also acknowledges support of the Program on Knowledge, Networks, and Institutions for Innovation at the Stanford Institute for Economic Policy Research (Stanford University). We claim sole responsibility for the judgments expressed and any mistakes and misinterpretations that may be found herein.

Notes

1. *CUDOS* was introduced as a mnemonic by Merton's (1973 [1942]) essay on the normative structure of science. The association of the "O" with *originality* was a subsequent modification that has become conventional.

2. For more background, see, for example, Barnes 1974, 1977; Bloor 1976; Latour and Woolgar 1979; Knorr-Cetina 1981; Shapin 1994; and the survey in Callon 1995. More on the epistemology of science can be found in Kuhn 1970 [1962], Kitcher 1993, and Fuller 1994. Regarding the sociology of science, see Cole and Cole 1967, Crane 1972, and Cole 1978. Den Besten, David, and Schroeder 2009 briefly examines the relationship of the "new economics of science" to the foregoing disciplinary developments.

3. See Schroeder 2008 and Fry, Schroeder, and den Besten 2009 for discussions of the distinction between generic research technologies and narrowly defined research tools, and of its bearing on the potential for openness in e-science.

4. For a report on the structured interviews, see Fry, Schroeder, and den Besten 2009. David, den Besten, and Schroeder 2006 presents a preliminary version of the framework of questions from both the structured interview protocol and the subsequent online survey questionnaire that was developed. Reference is made later to the tabulated responses to certain question in the Web survey, which can be examined, along with the Web layout of the entire survey instrument, in den Besten and David 2009.

5. For more on MiMeG, see http://www.ncess.ac.uk/research/video/mimeg/.

6. For more on GNU, see http://www.gnu.org/.

7. For more on CombeChem, see http://www.combechem.org/.

8. See Fry, Schroeder, and den Besten 2009, based on an interview with Jeremy Frey, the PI at CombeChem.

9. The structured interview protocol described in Fry, Schroeder, and den Besten 2009 elaborated and modified the extended questionnaire proposed by David, den Besten, and Schroeder (2006).

10. As Fry, Schroeder, and den Besten (2009) point out, "The effort to make the tools or data suitable or robust enough to make them into a commonly used resource may be considerable, and

thus represents a Catch-22 situation for researchers: a large effort can be made, which may not be useful, but if it is not attempted, then it cannot be useful in the first place. Nevertheless, all projects expressed the aspiration to contribute to a common resource, even if this was sometimes expressed as a hope rather than [as] a certainty or foregone conclusion."

11. Coordination and integration problems calling for solutions that take the form of interoperability standards posed particularly difficult challenges for ongoing projects in the U.K. e-science Pilot Programme. The same applies to complying with standards, ontologies, and metadata that are still in the process of development.

12. On issues relating to academic patenting on the openness of publicly funded research, see for example David and Hall 2006 and David 2007. However, much of the discussion on this topic has focused on the implications of the patenting of research tools and and *sui generis* property right specific to the legal protection of databases. These covered, for example, the patenting of computer software (in the United States) and computer-implemented inventions (in the European Union), as well as fields such as genomics, biogenetics, and proteinomics (in the European Union) and nanotechnology research tools. Although these have been very active fields of academic science research, which have seen growing university ownership of patents, they are not represented in the U.K.'s e-science Core Programme and so do not appear among the projects included in either the structured interview or the survey samples discussed here.

13. The number of responses represented just over 10 percent of the projects listed by NeSC, implying a project response rate of 25 percent. The existence of projects that appear more than once in the NeSC database and had multiple (co)PIs also contributes to reducing the apparent rate of "project" responses.

14. See David, den Besten, and Schroeder 2006, 2009 on the evolution of OMII's policy on the licensing of its releases of middleware.

15. Providing access to researchers outside the project was a significant concern for almost two-thirds of the data-centric projects and for one-third of community-centric projects.

References

Allen, F. H. 2004. "High-throughput crystallography: The challenge of publishing, storing, and using the results." *Crystallography Review 10*:3–15.

Arzberger, P., P. Schröder, A. Beaulieu, G. Bowker, K. Casey, L. Laaksonen, D. Moorman, P. Uhlir, and P. Wouters. 2004. "Promoting access to public research data for scientific, economic, and social development." *Data Science Journal 3*:135–152.

Atkins, D., K. K. Droegemeier, S. Feldman, H. Garcia-Molina, M. Klein, D. Messerschmitt, P. Messina, J. Jostriker, and M. Wright. 2003. *Revolutionizing science and engineering through cyberinfrastructure: Report of the National Science Foundation Blue-Ribbon Advisory Panel on Cyberinfrastructure.* Arlington, VA: National Science Foundation.

Barnes, B. 1974. *Scientific knowledge and sociological theory.* London: Routledge and Kegan Paul.

Barnes, B. 1977. *Interests and the growth of knowledge*. London: Routledge and Kegan Paul.

Berman, F., and H. Brady. 2005. *NSF SBE-CISE Workshop on Cyber-infrastructure and the Social Sciences. Final Report*. San Diego: San Diego Supercomputing Center.

Bloor, D. 1976. *Knowledge and social imagery*. London: Routledge and Kegan Paul.

Callon, M. 1995. "Four models for the dynamics of science." In *Handbook of science and technology studies*, ed. S. Jasanoff, G. E. Markle, J. C. Petersen, and T. Pinch. London: Sage.

Cole, S. 1978. "Scientific reward systems: A comparative analysis." In *Research in sociology of knowledge, sciences, and art*, ed. R. A. Jones. Greenwich, CT: JAI Press, 167–190.

Cole, S., and J. Cole. 1967. "Scientific output and recognition." *American Sociological Review* 32:377–390.

Coles, S., J. G. Frey, M. B. Hursthouse, M. E. Light, K. E. Meacham, D. J. Marvin, and M. Surridge. 2005. "ECSES—examining crystal structures using 'e-science': A demonstrator employing Web and Grid services to enhance user participation in crystallographic experiments." *Journal of Applied Crystallography* 38:819–826.

Crane, D. 1972. *Invisible colleges: Diffusion of knowledge in scientific communities*. Chicago: University of Chicago Press.

Dalle, J-M., P. A. David, R. A. Ghosh, and W. E. Steinmueller. 2005. "Advancing economic research on the free and open source software mode of production." In *How open is the future? Economic, social, and cultural scenarios inspired by free and open-source software*, ed. M. Wynants and J. Cornelis. Brussels: VUB Press, 395–624. Preprint available at: http://siepr.stanford.edu/papers/pdf/04-03.html.

Dasgupta, P., and P. A. David. 1987. "Information disclosure and the economics of science and technology." In *Arrow and the ascent of modern economic theory*, ed. G. Feiwel. New York: New York University Press, 519–542.

Dasgupta, P., and P. A. David. 1994. "Toward a new economics of science." *Research Policy 23*: 487–521.

David, P. A. 1998. "Common agency contracting and the emergence of 'open science' institutions." *American Economic Review 88* (2):15–21.

David, P. A. 2003. "The economic logic of 'open science' and the balance between private property rights and the public domain in scientific data and information." In *The role of the public domain in scientific and technical data and information: An NRC symposium*, ed. J. Esanu and P. F. Uhlir. Washington, DC: Academy Press, 19–34.

David, P. A. 2006. "Towards a cyberinfrastructure for enhanced scientific collaboration: providing its 'soft' foundations may be the hardest part." In *Advancing knowledge and the knowledge economy*, eds. B. Kahin and D. Foray. Cambridge: MIT Press, 431–454.

David, P. A. 2007. "Innovation and Europe's universities: Second thoughts about embracing the Bayh-Dole regime." In *Perspectives on innovation*, ed. F. Malerba and S. Brusoni. Cambridge, UK:

Cambridge University Press, 251–278. Preprint available at: http://siepr.stanford.edu/publications profile/1889/.

David, P. A., M. den Besten, and R. Schroeder. 2006. "How 'open' is e-science?" In *E-Science '06: Proceedings of the IEEE 2nd International Conference on eScience and Grid Computing, Amsterdam*, eds. P. A. M. Sloot et al. Los Alamitos, CA: IEEE Computer Society, 33–41. Available at: http://ieeexplore .ieee.org/stamp/stamp.jsp?arnumber=04031006. Preprint available at: http://siepr.stanford.edu/ publicationsprofile/1847/

David, P. A., M. den Besten, and R. Schroeder. 2009. *Collaborative research in e-science and open access to information.* Stanford Institute for Economic Policy Research (SIEPR) Discussion Paper no. 021. Stanford, CA: SIEPR, January. Forthcoming in *The international handbook of eResearch*, ed. J. Hunsinger, M. Allen, and L. Klastrup. New York: Springer. Available at: http://siepr.stanford.edu/ papers/pdf/08-21.html.

David, P. A., and B. H. Hall. 2006. "Property and the pursuit of knowledge: An introduction." *Research Policy 35*:767–771.

David, P. A., and M. Spence. 2008. "Designing institutional infrastructures for e-science." In *Legal and policy framework for e-research: Realizing the potential*, ed. B. Fitzgerald. Sydney: University of Sydney Press, 55–146.

David, P. A., and P. F. Uhlir. 2005. "Creating the global information commons for e-science: Workshop rationale and plan." CODATA International Workshop Program. UNESCO, Paris, 1–2 September: http://www.codata.org/archives/2005/UNESCOmtg/workshopplan.html. Also available at: http://www.oii.ox.ac.uk/microsites/oess/papers/.

David, P. A. and P.F. Uhlir. 2006. "Creating global information commons for science: An international initiative of the Committee on Data for Science and Technology (CODATA)," unpublished, 17 April. Prospectus of the Global Information Commons for Science Initiative (GISCI) launched at WSIS-Tunis, November 2005. See: http://www.codata.org/wsis/sessions/session-iwata.html.

Den Besten, M., and P. A. David. 2009. *Data information access in e-research: Results from a 2008 survey among UK e-science project participants.* Oxford Internet Institute (OII) Research Report no. 18. Oxford, UK: OII. Available at: http://ssrn.com/abstract=1323812.

Den Besten, M., P. A. David, and R. Schroeder. 2009. "Research in e-science and open access to information and data." In *The international handbook of e-research*, ed. J. Hunsinger, M. Allen, and L. Klastrup. New York: Springer.

Frey, J. G. 2004. "Dark lab or smart lab: The challenges for the 21st century laboratory software." *Organic Research and Development 8* (6):1024–1035.

Fry, J., R. Schroeder, and M. den Besten. 2009. "Open science in e-science: Contingency or policy?" *Journal of Documentation 65* (1):6–32.

Fuller, S. 1994. "A guide to the philosophy and sociology of science for social psychology of science." In *The social psychology of science*, ed. W. Shadish and S. Fuller. New York: Guilford Press, 403–409.

Hey, T. 2005. "E-science and open access." In *Berlin 3 Open Access: Progress in implementing the Berlin Declaration on Open Access to Knowledge in the Sciences and Humanities*. Southampton, UK: University of Southampton. Available at: http://eprints.rclis.org/archive/00003520/03/04-Hey.pdf

Hinds, C., M. Jirotka, M. Rahman, C. Mayer, G. D'Agostino, and T. Piper. 2005. "Ownership of intellectual property rights in medical data in collaborative computing environments." Paper presented at the First International Conference on e–Social Science, June 22–24.

Jirotka, M., R. Procter, M. Hartswood, R. Slack, A. Simpson, C. Coopmans, and C. Hinds. 2005. "Collaboration and trust in healthcare innovation: The eDiaMoND case study." *Journal of Computer-Supported Cooperative Work 14* (4):369–398.

Kitcher, P. 1993. *The advancement of science: Science without legend, objectivity without illusions*. Chicago: University of Chicago Press.

Knorr-Cetina, K. 1981. *The manufacture of knowledge: An essay on the constructivist and contextual nature of science*. Oxford, UK: Pergamon Press.

Kuhn, T. S. 1970 [1962]. *The structure of scientific revolutions*. 2d ed. Chicago: University of Chicago Press.

Latour, B., and S. Woolgar. 1979. *Laboratory life*. Beverly Hills, CA: Sage.

Leenaars, M., F. Karayannis, et al. 2007. *E-infrastructures roadmap 2007*. 2d ed. E-Infrastructure Reflection Group Technical Report. The Hague: e-Infrastructure Reflection Group (e-IRG). Available at: http://oldsite.e-irg.eu/roadmap/.

Merton, R. K. 1973 [1942]. "The normative structure of science." In *The sociology of science: Theoretical and empirical investigations*, ed. N. W. Storer. Chicago: University of Chicago Press, 267–278.

Schroeder, R. 2007. "E-research infrastructures and open science: Towards a new system of knowledge production?" *Prometheus 25* (1):1–17.

Schroeder, R. 2008. "E-sciences as research technologies: Reconfiguring disciplines, globalizing knowledge." *Social Science Information (Paris) 47* (2):131–157.

Shapin, S. 1994. *A social history of truth*. Chicago: University of Chicago Press.

Stanford University. 1996. "Openness in research." In *Stanford University research policy handbook*. Stanford, CA: Stanford University, chap. 2.6. Available at: http://www.stanford.edu/dept/DoR/C-Res/ITARlist.html.

Uhlir, P. F., and P. Schröder. 2007. "Open data for global science." *Data Science Journal 6*:OD1–OD3.

11.1 The Politics of Open Access

Gustavo Cardoso, João Caraça, Rita Espanha, and Sandro Mendonça

Open Access as a Social Movement

The international Budapest Open Access Initiative declares: "By open access to this literature, we mean its free availability on the public internet [*sic*], permitting users to read, download, copy, distribute, print, search, or link the full texts of these articles, crawl them for indexing, pass them as data to software, or use them for any other lawful purpose, without financial, legal, or technical barriers other than those inseparable from gaining access to the internet itself. The only constraint on reproduction and distribution, and the only role for copyright in this domain, should be to give authors control over the integrity of their work and the right to be properly acknowledged and cited."[1]

Our argument in this essay is that in order to understand open access, we should not consider it merely as a discussion toward alternative publishing models, but increasingly as a social movement (Castells 2004). Indeed, it is a special kind of social movement: one that flourishes not outside academia in other fields of social life, but rather within the very scientific community, across disciplines, and around the world.

The Web is a huge repository for the ongoing and past history of what we call the "open-access movement." This history ranges from stances promoting the benefits of open access (e.g., BioMed Central[2] and its Open Access Now[3] campaign or Peter Suber's "What You Can Do to Promote Open Access"[4]) to the countering of such positions by some leading journal publishers.

Tracing Open-Access Ideas

Three Historical Phases

Open access can be traced back as far as the 1960s, to Ted Nelson's (1987 [1974]) hypertext system, or the early 1970s, to Michael Hart's Gutenberg Project.[5] However, until the birth of the Web and the launch of the first browsers in the 1990s, the lack of a technological apparatus capable of delivering codified knowledge at low cost to vast audiences had confined open-access initiatives to relatively small audiences.

In order to analyze open access, we define three different historical stages:[6]

1. The "paleoconceptual" phase began in 1963 with Ted Nelson and lasted to 1979 with the birth of Usenet, the pioneering distributed Internet discussion system. This phase is characterized by the early developments of networked digital technology and the mutual influence of developments in science and conceptual communication thought.
2. The "neoexperimental" phase encompasses the two decades from 1980 to 2000. This period was characterized by experimentation and the social diffusion of what Pekka Himanen, Linus Torvalds, and Manuel Castells (2001) termed the "hacker ethic." Experimentation of technological possibilities, under a trial-and-error approach, led to the development of applications and their diffusion to large audiences, fostering large-scale online cooperative work. Examples can be found in the operating system Linux, the Human Genome Project, *Wikipedia*, and academic journals born during these two decades.
3. The "social movement" phase of open access can be said to have started with the Budapest, Bethesda, and Berlin initiatives in 2002 and 2003.[7] These three events constitute a decisive turning point; they defined what open access stands for, a definition subsequently diffused throughout the international scientific community. These events also signaled the existence of two complementary strategies within the open-access movement: open-access journals and institutional repositories.

The Key Strategies

Both open-access journals and institutional repositories seek to increase accessibility to academic publications. Because academic journals are the main scientific communication instrument, the open-access movement chose them to be the spearhead of a movement that seeks to lower the barriers of price, legal access, and technology. In the twenty-first century so far, open-access journals have flourished within the international community,[8] and many traditional publishers have adopted, partially or fully, the overall principles by also changing their business models in this direction.

If the open-access journal is the present and future of scholarly publication, the institutional repository is a tool designed to work as a facilitator of access for past published works of academic origin—not just to articles, but also books, theses, and every other publishable instrument of scientific knowledge. Two key functions are ascribed to the repository: to allow, despite the short life of media and rapid obsolescence of hardware, the preservation of publications in electronic format; and to provide access to content first published in Web sites or other publishing sites that might not guarantee future access.

Developments in the Open-Access Movement

Castells (2004) argues that social movements must be understood in their own terms—that is, through their actions, their discursive practices, and their impact on social structures. What defines a social movement is its identity: what it declares itself to be, its adversaries, whom or what it aims to confront, and its vision, social model, or societal goal. These dimensions for open access are clearly enunciated and easily found not just in the founding declarations such as the Budapest Open Access Initiative, but also in the editorials of both scientific journals and repositories published by academic institutions, research centers, and new business ventures in the field of scholarly publications.

The open-access movement is therefore a movement dedicated to promoting access to knowledge, in particular scientific knowledge. It proclaims to identify its adversaries either in the barriers raised by some business models of academic publishing, in the use of a legal apparatus to stop general access to works, or under the unequal diffusion of digital technologies of access. At the same time, this movement defines its societal goal as achieving an intellectual commons through open access (Suber 2004). This goal involves a wide change within royalties-free literature, the small category of literature that authors consent to distribute without payment or for which they are paid salaries by their employees rather than by their publishers (e.g., peer-reviewed journal articles and their preprints).

Future Directions

Open access implies a more open science within its peer community. Institutional and international publishers have begun to look at open access not as a threat, but rather as an opportunity. Scientists also seem to be increasingly using open access for publishing and for the retrieval of published papers (Machado and Ortellado 2006). Open access also implies a more open science because it allows a larger choice of publishing strategies for scientists. The model that seems to be designing itself is one where both open and nonopen access share the publishing landscape. Within this landscape, authors can choose, according to the audience they wish to reach, to publish in paper-only journals, in both electronic and paper journals, or just in electronic format.

Our scientific publishing environment is also becoming a place where scientists can publish preliminary "beta" versions of their work in one journal and afterward, when the work is completed, publish a final version in another journal. Open access also promotes change by allowing journals originally published in non-English-speaking countries to join the international scene by allowing authors to choose the scientific community they intend to reach with a paper. For example, under the same journal one can target the international research community by publishing in English, one's own national research community by publishing in one's mother tongue (if that is not English), or scholars outside one's national community who share one's knowledge of a given language (Cardoso and Espanha 2007).

As shown by the Science Commons initiative[9] (see the introduction and chapter 7), a social movement based in openness will not confine itself to the publishing and preservation of knowledge. Science Commons can be viewed as a "second-stage" mobilization strategy within the overall open-access movement. Through their licensing project, Science Commons aims to simplify and speed up research procedures. For example, the use of a "research commons" public attribution can help research on neglected diseases by allowing funded research to specify that publications about it must be available to all researchers in the field.

Conclusion

Understanding the political economy of open access implies understanding a globalization of science production, dissemination, and social appropriation by a large set of social actors and institutions—an understanding that has little resemblance to any idyllic historical view of science being closed behind the walls of a university campus, apart from the pervasive action of overall societies, institutions, and cultural and economic trends. Science is one of the core elements of modernity. Consequently, change in science, like change in its communication systems, must surely also be reflected in societal change at large.

Notes

1. See http://www.soros.org/openaccess/.

2. BioMed Central is a publisher of peer-reviewed open-access journals (http://www.biomed central.com/).

3. See http://www.biomedcentral.com/openaccess/.

4. See http://www.earlham.edu/~peters/fos/do.htm.

5. See http://promo.net/pg/.

6. See http://www.earlham.edu/~peters/fos/timeline.htm.

7. See http://www.soros.org/openaccess/initiatives.shtml.

8. See, for example, the Directory of Open Access Journals (http://www.doaj.org/) and the Public Knowledge Project (http://pkp.sfu.ca/?q=ojs).

9. See, for example: http://sciencecommons.org/.

References

Cardoso, G., and R. Espanha, eds. 2007. Editorial observatorio (OBS*). Available at: http://obs .obercom.pt/.

Castells, M. 2004. *The power of identity*. Oxford, UK: Blackwell.

Himanen, P., L. Torvalds, and M. Castells. 2001. *The hacker ethic and the spirit of the information age.* London: Vintage.

Machado, J., and P. Ortellado. 2006. "Direitos autorais e o acesso às publicações científicas." *Revista da Associacao dos Docentes da Universidade de S. Paulo 37* (August). Available in Portuguese at: http://www.adusp.org.br/revista/37/r37a01.pdf.

Nelson, T. 1987 [1974]. *Computer lib.* Redmond, WA: Tempus.

Suber, P. 2004. "Creating an intellectual commons through open access." Paper presented at the Workshop on Scholarly Communication as a Commons, Workshop in Political Theory and Policy Analysis, Indiana University, Bloomington, 31 March–2 April. Available at: http://dlc.dlib.indiana.edu/archive/00001246/.

11.2 Open Access versus "Open Viewing" for a Web of Science: The Neurocommons Example

John Wilbanks and Hal Abelson

The Right to Open Access

Debates over open access to the scientific literature are frequently cast in terms of letting the public view journal articles online free of charge. That's an admirable goal, but "open viewing" alone is insufficient to support participation in scientific research. Genuine open access, as called for by the 2002 Budapest Open Access Initiative (see essay 11.1), is the free availability of scientific papers on the public Internet, including, notably, the right to pass the text of articles as data to software. That right is crucial because the rate of knowledge creation in the twenty-first century is rendering traditional journal-based publishing inadequate as a platform for science unless it is amplified by new methods of automated processing.

The biomedical literature provides a good example of the issues raised by the open-access concept. Imagine a researcher trying to keep up with the literature on a popular target of study—for example, the protein P53, which plays a central role in tumor suppression. Searching the U.S. National Library of Medicine's PubMed[1] database in 2008 yielded about 50,000 citations, including more than 5,700 review articles alone. And the number of citations was growing at about 10 per day.

For any corpus like this one to remain tractable as the scientific enterprise expands, researchers will need tools that treat journal articles not simply as stand-alone independent works, but as nodes in a "web of science." From such a perspective, journal articles become information sources that can be aggregated and correlated. These sources can be linked to other articles as well as to the databases that hold the results of experiments, analyzed with text-mining software, and translated into multiple data formats and multiple languages.

This kind of extended integration capability is something Web users take for granted when it comes to Web pages and news articles, thanks to search engines. But it has simply not been available in the sciences—and it should be. In the age of the Web, the web of science should provide seamless connection of information from multiple sources worldwide. Researchers should easily be able to draw upon that information to derive novel hypotheses that can readily be tested and then feed the results back into the information stream. Some of that ability exists in limited domains and within the walled gardens of large companies. Yet it can be available to everyone. Realizing this vision requires genuine open access to the scientific literature, not just "open viewing" of individual journal articles.

The Neurocommons Open-Access Platform

Even though much of the scientific literature is still locked up behind copyright walls, enough open digital resources are available to support prototypes and proofs of concept. One of these resources is the Neurocommons,[2] an open platform for neuroinformatics created by Science Commons[3] as a demonstration of what the power of e-science can be in a world of open access energized by Web technology.

The Neurocommons platform lets scientists treat multiple biological databases and literature sources as a single database, asking precise questions and getting precise answers unavailable anywhere else on the Web. For instance, a researcher might ask for a "list of genes involved in signal transduction that are related to pyramidal neurons." It is formidably awkward to get an answer to this question, which pertains to potential drug targets for Alzheimer's disease, using traditional Web tools. Typing the question into a popular general search engine is likely to result in tens of thousands of hits, primarily titles of scholarly papers, but with no list of genes evident and not even a sense of why those particular papers were listed. With the Neurocommons, the question can be formulated as a single database query, which returns a list of genes. Neurocommons has the long-term potential to move beyond abstracts to full articles.[4]

The underlying technology for Neurocommons is provided by the Semantic Web,[5] which expresses relations as triples—subject, predicate, object—in the World Wide Web Consortium's Resource Description Framework (RDF) language.[6] Some of the effort going into implementing the Neurocommons[7] involves creating new predicates for expressing biological concepts, such as the idea of a gene being "involved in" a process, as in the query given previously. Other work goes into database integration, building on such efforts as the SenseLab[8] project being pursued at the Yale Center for Medical Informatics, which exports data from neuroscience databases into RDF format. Still other work involves using text-mining software to extract assertions from PubMed abstracts and express these assertions as RDF triples. This kind of experimental automated text mining is complemented by extensive (and expensive) manual curation of the biomedical literature in the U.S. National Library of Medicine,[9] the Jackson Laboratories,[10] and other repositories.

Wider Implications of Neurocommons

The basic Neurocommons approach is not novel. Pharmaceutical companies have been investing in this capability for years, under the rubric "knowledge management." What's new is that this capability can be available to the public as well as to researchers in university laboratories. Moreover, because the Neurocommons is an open system, one can hope to link in more and more data sources. These sources may even include services that create systems where the physical tools of science can be accessed directly from search results. For example, one might access the catalogs of organizations such as Addgene,[11] which provides DNA plasmids under standard contracts, manufactured and mailed on demand.

The Neurocommons project demonstrates that such infrastructures can be put in place. As with similar informatics research projects, however, Neurocommons rests squarely on top of the ability to access—not just "view"—the scholarly literature.

Notes

1. See http://www.ncbi.nlm.nih.gov/PubMed/.

2. The Neurocommons project is creating an open-source knowledge-management platform for biological research (http://sciencecommons.org/).

3. Science Commons seeks to identify and ease key barriers to the movement of information, tools, and data through the scientific research cycle (http://sciencecommons.org/).

4. By 2008, the Neurocommons integrated (for more limited abstract services) information across a dozen databases, including a database derived from automated text mining of 750,000 abstracts in PubMed's freely available corpus of biomedical abstracts.

5. See http://www.w3.org/2001/sw/.

6. See http://www.w3.org/RDF/.

7. In 2008, Neurocommons had more than 300 million RDF triples.

8. See http://senselab.med.yale.edu/.

9. See http://www.nlm.nih.gov/.

10. See http://www.jax.org/.

11. See http://www.addgene.org/pgvec1.

12   Shaping Research in Developing Areas

Marcus Antonius Ynalvez, Ricardo B. Duque, and Wesley Shrum

The globalization of research presents emergent social realities. Both developed and developing societies are increasingly knowledge based.[1] As discussed in this book, many social analysts suggest that this globalization of knowledge is a result, either directly or indirectly, of innovations in information and communication technologies (ICTs). To understand these new globalizing technologies, we must attend to the nature and dynamics of research institutions not only in developed areas, but also in developing areas. This chapter examines these institutions in terms of access, utilization, and consequences of ICTs, focusing on the question, How and to what extent will these technologies globalize science? To answer this question, we review research that began in 1994 with surveys of scientific communication in Kenya, Ghana, India, the Philippines, and Chile, using qualitative interviews, surveys, and newer video ethnographic methods.

Implications of ICTs for Knowledge Production

Our overarching interest is whether new ICTs (such as the Internet) will change the nature of knowledge production in the long term as they diffuse in developing areas. There are three competing perspectives on this issue (see Davidson, Sooryamoorthy, and Shrum 2002; Duque, Shrum, Barriga, et al. 2008):

• *Modernization*   The Internet has been viewed from a modernization perspective as the much-needed "elixir" that will free the developing world from its relative isolation.[2]
• *Dependency*   A dependency perspective conversely views innovations such as the Internet as an "affliction" that might exacerbate global inequality and lead to yet another dimension of social stratification: a digital divide within the scientific community. Unequal access to the Internet might lead to even greater inequalities in global science in terms of access to knowledge, social networks, and productivity between the scientifically strong and scientifically weak countries.
• *The "Teething" Argument*   From a more global perspective, a "teething" hypothesis argues that science in less-developed areas absorbs these innovations asymmetrically in

the short term. However, with appropriate transnational partnerships, these communities may successfully incorporate the Internet over time.

Because scientists in developed countries were the innovators of the Internet, its diffusion in the scientific communities of Africa, Asia, and Latin America is a crucial issue for understanding the production and institutionalization of knowledge in a global context.[3] Knowledge production is intrinsically collaborative both in the sense that knowledge building is a communal activity and in the way that multiple actors are increasingly required for the conduct of research. The Internet is similarly related to collaboration in two respects:

1. As a technology, the Internet changes the conditions of physical presence and time delay that previously characterized knowledge production.
2. As an initiative, the Internet is itself a form of collaboration. It is a technology designed in the developed world for asynchronous interpersonal communication and subsequently for information retrieval. The Internet has therefore dramatically increased the potential for most types of collaboration, including those focused on knowledge production and dissemination of expertise.

We argue that the concept of "development" does not accurately depict the changes that take place in developing areas as a result of initiatives (i.e., financial and technical assistance, capacity building, and resources) emanating from developed areas.[4] As Wesley Shrum (2005) has argued, the concept of "development" can usefully be replaced with the notion of "reagency," a process of redirection involving a contingent reaction among places and identities. We illustrate the efficacy of the notion of reagency with empirical findings on Internet diffusion in the knowledge-production sector of developing areas. The original notion was that the Internet may reagentize science in developing areas more effectively than prior development initiatives. Its efficacy emanated from a shift in communication and collaborative patterns that had little to do with the ideology of participation and much to do with the maintenance of online interactions.

Methods Used in Our Research Analysis

This chapter is based on three complementary approaches to research: network survey methods, qualitative interviews, and video ethnography. We initially adopted these approaches serially, but now employ them together. Although we base most of the empirical material on studies conducted between 2000 and 2005, these studies build on communication network surveys of the research system in Ghana, Kenya, and Kerala (India) that began in 1994, sponsored by the Dutch government. Those surveys were relatively comprehensive but thin, covering a large number of university departments and research institutes, but relatively few respondents in each organization.

The constant struggle of collecting the data and the photographic evidence that accompanied our journeys made us aware that the situated context was not adequately captured through the network surveys alone. Qualitative interviews were conducted through the intervening years until the U.S. National Science Foundation began sponsoring a series of panel surveys in 2000 that continue through the present.

These studies—the results of which we review later in this chapter—involve fewer organizations but seek to be comprehensive in covering the respondents within those organizations. Located generally around the capital city of a region (Nairobi, Kenya; Accra, Ghana; and Thiruvananthapuram, Kerala), we selected the major research institutes and university departments, and targeted an interview with every scientist every five years. In the intervening years, we conducted a smaller number of qualitative interviews, adding Chile and the Philippines in 2005 to our group of countries for better global coverage. Although qualitative interviews were an improvement and provided a new way of understanding research networks in the developing world, they were nevertheless inadequate. We therefore began, in 2002, to employ consumer camcorders not only for interviews, but, more important, to capture the process of research and development as we pursued our own connectivity initiative. Video ethnography, or the use of audiovisual technology to supplement traditional ethnographic methods, has been an invaluable tool.[5] The following analyses draw on all three sources—surveys, interviews, and video ethnography—for insight on the dynamics of reagency.

We discuss the Internet as a reagentive force in the globalization of science. In one sense, the Internet is reagentive as a potential for collaboration that is independent of collaborators' location in geophysical space and social structure. Yet the Internet's effects on scientific collaboration in developing areas must also be seen as a potential in specific localized contexts because variations in place and identity have much to do with the realization of the new ICTs' capability for symmetrical collaboration. We then summarize results from empirical studies of the research sector in the developing areas of sub-Saharan Africa, India, Southeast Asia, and Latin America that suggest the Internet's reagentive role in the globalization of science.

In our discussion, we show the complexity of the concepts of "use" and "access" in the developing world and describe a paradox generally unrecognized in both academic and policy studies of collaboration: the social conditions that undermine any straightforward relationship between collaboration and scientific productivity in developing areas also undermine the Internet's collaborative benefits. The existence of such a paradox indicates differences between the knowledge-production process in developed areas and that process in developing areas. These differences emanate from the typically unpredictable consequences of interaction between foreign initiatives and specific local contexts.

The Internet's Reagentive Role

We argue that new ICTs, specifically the Internet, have the potential to reagentize science in developing areas more effectively than past development initiatives (e.g., capacity building, technical assistance). This potential to reagentize the structure and process of knowledge production comes from a shift in patterns of collaboration that have very little to do with the ideology of participation and much to do with the maintenance of online relationships and interaction. The Internet holds great potential for modifying the temporal and spatial aspects of social interaction through its capacity to facilitate multiway global communication via information interchange and retrieval through high-speed search engines (Hamelink 1999; Rogers 1995; Stehr 2000; Castells 2000).

Social Interaction in the Network Society

In the hypothesized "network society," the spatial aspect of social interaction is morphed to remove mutual exclusiveness among different domains, the temporal is "compressed," and interaction among identities takes place simultaneously no matter where they are geographically located (Sassen 2000). Hence, it is claimed that social interaction occurs not only in real time and in real space, but also in cybertime and in cyberspace (Castells 2000). With the advent of the Internet, interacting identities are more dispersed, less contiguous, and increasingly heterogeneous. In other words, the local contains much that is global, and the global is increasingly penetrated and reshaped by myriad locales.

Because the Internet is a medium uniquely capable of integrating modes of information and communication, it constitutes an important research site for examining theories of social interaction and principles of social networks. More specific examples include technological adoption (DiMaggio, Hargittai, Neuman, et al. 2001), knowledge production, and the network analysis of research systems. Indeed, the Internet's potential to alter temporal and spatial aspects of interaction and networks encourages us to test the adequacy of traditional sociological concepts in explaining current social phenomena (DiMaggio, Hargittai, Neuman, et al. 2001).

As a tool in the generation, production, and dissemination of scientific knowledge, the Internet has the potential to aid scientists by providing

• links to colleagues, information, and databases;
• opportunities for sharing results with other members of the (national, international, or transnational) scientific community; and
• opportunities for building personal and organizational networks that are crucial for access to material and nonmaterial resources (Crane 1972; Schott 1993).

The Internet and Knowledge Production

The nexus between the Internet and science is anchored on the notion that the scientific knowledge–production process is itself a form of social interaction. On the one hand, the Internet is a facility for social interaction for actors who are not colocated. On the other, the norms of science allude to a scientific knowledge–production process that requires both intensive and extensive forms of social interaction, including formal and informal communication, local and foreign collaboration, national and international conferences, and consultations that are and are not colocated. Both Manuel Castells (2000) and Saskia Sassen (2000) allude to the connection between the Internet and science and speculate about the Internet's role in the global integration of science.

Yet the Internet's impact on knowledge production in general and on the nature and dynamics of science in developing areas in particular remains in dispute. Proponents of the elixir argument contend that the Internet will revolutionize scientific communication by improving and increasing the frequency of informal communication among scientists who are not colocated, thus narrowing the "communication gap" and helping to integrate disadvantaged scientists (Castells 2000; DiMaggio, Hargittai, Neuman, et al. 2001; Uimonen 2001; Davidson, Sooryamoorthy, and Shrum 2002; Barjak 2004:2). The affliction argument holds that the Internet forms a new basis for social differentiation and evaluations that can exacerbate existing divides and create new forms of social inequities on a global scale (Hamelink 1999; DiMaggio, Hargittai, Neuman, et al. 2001; Davidson, Sooryamoorthy, and Shrum 2002).

We view the Internet as neither an elixir nor an affliction. For us, the Internet is reagentive: its impacts are not readily predicted, and its trajectory is largely conditioned by the characteristics of places and the attributes of identities that populate these places. Although new ICTs are increasingly essential in generating, producing, and disseminating scientific knowledge (Bijker 1995; Rogers 1995; Duque, Ynalvez, Sooryamoorthy, et al. 2005; Ynalvez, Duque, Mbatia, et al. 2005), they are readily constructed as a barrier or threshold that must be overcome for collaborators in developing areas. Although Internet diffusion can lead to enhanced scientific communication and collaboration among scientists in developing areas, deficient and sporadic electronic communication and shifting communication regimes can make collaboration at a distance difficult to sustain and fraught with problems (Olson and Olson 2000; Olson, Zimmerman, and Bos 2008). Commitments to collaborative tasks in such cases are especially difficult when vast distances, wide spaces, and different time zones separate actors. The introduction of any new actor—human or nonhuman—into the social landscape must be assessed in terms of fresh action versus its alternatives.

Communication among scientists requires three levels of analysis (Schott 1993): the collegial circle of an individual scientist, the national scientific community, and the global scientific community. Thomas Schott holds interpersonal ties to be more common at the local or national levels and to be rare at the global level. However, this feature of scientific communication networks may have shifted with the advent of new ICTs. It may no longer make sense to view the Internet as simply an "optional technology," but as a "required technology" for doing science.

As the Internet increasingly becomes a prerequisite for scientific research and transnational scientific collaboration, it is essential to understand its impact on scientific communities in developing areas (Davidson, Sooryamoorthy, and Shrum 2002; Duque, Ynalvez, Sooryamoorthy, et al. 2005; Ynalvez, Duque, Mbatia, et al. 2005). Although studies of Internet diffusion in developing areas have elicited interest and gained momentum, the diffusion of the Internet and its actual and potential impacts on scientific culture and practice in developing areas need to be investigated more systematically. The study of Internet adoption and its effects on science in developing areas requires attention to communication, collaboration, productivity, professional involvement, and personal networks.

The Internet and Science in Developing Areas

Because we view the Internet as reagentive to global scientific interaction, our studies seek an empirical understanding of its diffusion and consequences in developing areas. How does the connectivity initiative impact the behavior of identities in places with lower macroeconomic and social indicators in comparison to societies in Australia, North America, and western Europe? Because socioeconomic ranking and the technoscientific level of societies are highly correlated, our study can also be viewed as an attempt to describe the Internet's role in shaping the nature and dynamics of knowledge production in places populated by identities often considered "isolated."

We have examined the dimensions of connectivity in developing areas and sought to describe how these dimensions condition scientific productivity in domestic and foreign outlets. We also discuss a paradox associated with collaborative research in developing areas: the conditions that make the relationship between collaboration and productivity problematic in these areas may undermine the new ICTs' collaborative benefits (Duque, Ynalvez, Sooryamoorthy, et al. 2005). We attribute this paradox to the process of reagency. Because knowledge production in developing areas is generally carried out in state universities and in government research institutes, with little private-sector involvement, our sample was drawn from these sectors within each of our main study locations: the state of Kerala in India, Kenya, Ghana, the Philippines, and Chile.

Kerala, India

The distinctive model of development established in Kerala emphasizes such factors as education, literacy, and equality (Iyer and MacPherson 2000). As a result, Kerala's level of social development exceeds its level of economic development (Parayil 1996). However, because of Kerala's reputation for labor unrest and often Communist-led state government, capital investment and economic growth is low and unemployment high, even for those individuals with advanced education. At the same time, social indicators (e.g., demographic trends, literacy rates, presence of social programs, and women's status) suggest a social situation akin to that of many developed countries.

The state government has its own independent system of research institutes apart from those affiliated with the Indian government. Although the low level of external investment might seem to predict a reduced rate of ICT diffusion compared with the Indian national average, Kerala scientists exhibit high levels of awareness and interest in ICTs. Indeed, Kerala rates near the top in many ICT indicators. In comparison to other states within India, it is high in telephone density, mobile phone usage, and volume of Internet connections.

Kenya

For about twenty years after independence in 1964, Kenya was seen as the success story in Africa. Its average annual gross domestic product growth rates stood at 6.5 percent, the economy was buoyant, investments were high, and international donor support was generous (World Bank 2003). Kenya also possessed one of the largest scientific communities in the region. With the expansion of its university system in the 1970s, its scientific output continued to increase. However, by the 1980s, Kenya experienced an economic downturn. The 1990s witnessed the steady decline of foreign development assistance owing to the national government's poor governance and mismanagement of both public resources and development aid (World Bank 2003). Widespread government corruption coupled with the tribal politics so evident in the political violence of 2008 persisted despite the donor community's efforts to stimulate reforms. Nevertheless, Kenya is one of a handful of African countries with strong competition among Internet service providers.

Ghana

Among sub-Saharan countries, Ghana was the first to gain independence, but also one of the first to experience violent military takeovers and to witness the decline of promising developmental prospects through economic depression (Dzorgbo 2001). However, since the early 1980s, its military leadership has made it possible to impose the stringent financial measures required to receive continuous structural adjustment loans. Scientific and research infrastructures were handed over from the colonial period, but worsening socioeconomic and political situations in the 1980s resulted in the emigration of scientists, researchers, and technicians, which resulted in a significant decline in scientific productivity and output. Ghana is a regional leader in the liberalization of its telecommunications sector and by 2004 had a very small aperture terminal connection that provides an international Internet backbone through two-way links between a ground station and very small satellite dish antenna.

Philippines

In 2006, there were nearly fifty Internet service providers and about 3.5 million users in the Philippines, concentrated mainly in the national capital and other major cities.

In terms of scientific development, the Philippines is still classified as low performing, and its research capability and infrastructure are far behind those in East Asian countries such as China, Japan, Singapore, South Korea, and Taiwan. Much of Philippine scientists' contribution to international science is in the agricultural sciences.

Although the extent of Internet diffusion in the Philippines has been largely uneven, with government research institutes having more access than state universities, the increase in the number of Internet shops has been significant (Ynalvez and Shrum 2006). Nevertheless, by 2005 relatively few scientists used the Internet, and they used it mainly for financial, technical, and personal reasons. For instance, many report financial constraints against using the Internet in shops, technical problems such as unstable connections or slow connect times, or even fear of being stigmatized by going to places frequented by youths and high school students (Ynalvez and Shrum 2006).

Chile

Chile was once known for its oppressive military government, but since 1989 has returned to a democracy, enjoyed steady economic growth, and actively promoted Internet use nationwide (Duque 2007). It has also experienced a dramatic increase in scientific publication and international collaboration during the first decade of global Internet diffusion (Mullin, Adam, Halliwell, et al. 2000; Hill 2004). Yet in Chile, as in many developing nations, there exists an endogenous dislocation among sectors that challenges the effective translation of scientific discovery into marketable products and economic development (Krauskopf and Vera 1997). Even so, its scientific community consistently ranks as among the most productive in the region.

The introduction of a competitive funding process has affected the research sector, with government research institutes no longer being guaranteed funding. Instead, they must compete with academic and private-sector research-and-development departments. Government funds are also more contingent on results. Access to and use of the Internet are ubiquitous, resulting in the expansion of professional networks among Chilean scholars.

Our Studies' Methods and Data

Our quantitative study employs repeated network surveys of scientific communication in the research sectors of the areas discussed. The first wave was carried out in 1994, the second wave between 2000 and 2002, and the third in 2005. The 1994 surveys aimed at achieving relatively comprehensive coverage of a wide range of scientists and scientific organizations.[6] The most recent wave aimed at obtaining better coverage of fewer organizations in order to maximize the sample that could be generated with available resources. The 1994 questionnaire was redesigned in 2000 with new questions on ICTs. This revised questionnaire consisted of about two hundred items on sociodemographic factors, professional networks and activities, scientific collaboration, research productivity, organizational structure, and access to and use of ICTs. Respondents represented a variety of research fields: agriculture, biological sciences, engineering, mathematics, information technology, chemistry, physics, geology, and social sciences. These fields cover two organizational types: government research institutes and academic departments.

Our combined samples from Kerala, Kenya, and Ghana (the 2000–2002 wave) and from the Philippines and Chile (the 2005 wave) consist of approximately fifteen hundred scientists, about half from universities and half from research institutes.[7] As indicated earlier, these survey data have been augmented by qualitative interviews and video ethnographic research, which began in 1994 and has been augmented by the most recent interviews conducted in the summer of 2008. This qualitative research proved invaluable for interpreting the findings from the surveys, especially in documenting unique histories of Internet adoption by scientists and as a visual record of the often constrained conditions under which researchers in less-developed regions employ Internet technologies.

Results

Our analysis initially attempted to answer the following questions:

- To what degree have research communities in Africa, Asia, and Latin America "adopted" the Internet?
- How can we best characterize disparities in Internet adoption in these communities?
- To what extent is Internet adoption associated with research productivity?
- Is collaboration associated with productivity?
- Does the Internet reduce research problems associated with collaboration?

In answering these questions, we quickly recognized that the concepts of "Internet adoption" and "productivity" were problematic. The practice of conceptualizing Internet adoption in terms of binary dimensions (e.g., access/nonaccess, user/nonuser) was clearly inadequate. We began to use more meaningful and content-valid terms:

- *Current user* An individual who defines himself or herself as such, regardless of the frequency or practice of use.
- *Ready access* Another perceptual measure, based on how individuals define themselves as having accessible, available, and reasonable connectivity within their immediate environment.
- *Internet experience* The period of time during which an individual has used the Internet.
- *Internet practice* The variation among individuals in terms of the ways they use the Internet.

We came to conceptualize research productivity in terms of two distinct dimensions: productivity in foreign outlets and productivity in local outlets. We measured these dimensions in terms of self-reported number of publications in foreign journals and in local journals in the five years prior to the survey. The conceptual bifurcation between foreign and local productivity yielded an analysis that is more sensitive to the preferences, priorities, and orientation of scientific actors in developing areas.

The following sections summarize our main findings in relation to our key research questions.

To What Degree Have Researchers in the Developing World Adopted the Internet?

In answering this question, we view place in three contexts: physical location, organizational setting, and the immediate workplace and its characteristics. Our analysis is sensitive to the variations in socioeconomic level, organizational culture, and amenities of the immediate working environment. Our results show that there are variations among locations and between organizational settings in hardware (the presence of personal computers, or PCs) and connectivity (the Internet), showing that level of socioeconomic development and organizational setting play a role in conditioning the diffusion of innovations. These observations are consistent with the concept of reagency, wherein the trajectory of foreign initiatives is conditioned by characteristics of place through identities and interactions as they embed in local context and is influenced through the connectivity initiative's interaction with local culture. Two points deserve particular attention.

First, the acquisition of computers is a necessary prior technology in connecting to, accessing, and using the Internet. In our study locations, PCs are still not "personal" in these communities, but rather "public" computers, given that the user–PC ratio is relatively high (Ynalvez, Duque, Mbatia, et al. 2005). The notion of a PC as understood and experienced in the research systems of developed areas is far different from that in developing areas. To illustrate, each PC was used by more than five scientists on average. Although most scientists have access to a computer at work, with the exception of Chilean researchers, only a minority has one in his or her personal office. Indeed, many scientists in our African sample were without ready access to the technology that makes connectivity possible. Further, if only a few have PCs in their personal office and share them with several others, then most are in workplaces that do not provide researchers with the needed "architectural privacy" that would allow them to experiment on and intensively use the Internet.

Second, there is a large gap between scientists' self-image as Internet current users and the extent to which they actually have the opportunity to use the Internet for ready access. In the early part of the twenty-first century, nine in ten scientists considered themselves current users, but only six in ten actually reported reasonable access. The large discrepancy between user definition and access further supports the assertion that current use is largely realized through sharing of Internet-connected PCs. The low user–PC ratio we found results in low individual usage, which directly impacts the development of sophisticated Internet practice and extensive Internet experience. In developing areas, a scientist may be an "email user" without the implication of being able to engage in any form of scientific collaboration that requires continuous and reliable Internet access.

How Can We Best Characterize Disparities in Internet Adoption?

When viewed within a reagency framework, the issue of disparities in Internet adoption is interpreted as an inquiry across contexts of place and categories of identities about the patterns of Internet adoption (current use, ready access, Internet practice, and experience). By "categories of identities," we refer to two key attributes of the scientists in our sample: "ascribed" (age, gender) and "achieved" (marital status, children, education, degree from a developed country, and membership in professional organizations).

With respect to place, we found significant disparities in Internet adoption across locations. We observed large differences in use, access, practice, and experience that are associated with differences in socioeconomic and technoscientific development. Again, this result is consistent with the reagency framework in that initiatives trigger unforeseen reactions. These initiatives generally produced outcomes far from those initially predicted by the authors of initiatives introduced in places where the lack of resources is the rule rather than the exception. In some countries, organizational context (research institute or university) has a significant impact on the level of adoption and connectivity.

In the context of the workplace, we observed that having PCs in personal offices enhances the likelihood of sophisticated Internet practice and extensive Internet experience. This observation seems intuitive given that having a PC in one's personal office translates to a considerable degree of architectural privacy that serves as a facilitating condition to explore, experiment, and familiarize oneself with the Internet's various functionalities. Our results show that characteristics of location and workplace configure the Internet's impacts in peripheral scientific communities, whereas organizational context has a marginal impact on "digital inequality."

Gender remains a durable source of digital inequality with respect to ascribed and achieved attributes of identities: men have higher current use, Internet practice, and experience. Despite the deference provided to older and married members of society in these locations, age and marital status do not constitute major sources of digital inequality in research communities. As far as achieved attributes of identities are concerned, education is perhaps the most consistent dimension defining the digital divide among scientists in developing areas, especially so in terms of Internet practice and experience. We also observed that place of graduate training is a significant factor in determining the "absorption capacity" of identities for initiatives such as connectivity. It is likely that scientists trained in the United States or Europe from 2000 on would have used the Internet as a significant part of their training experience. Two main advantages of such direct interaction are (1) learning and modeling from those who use the Internet and (2) the acquisition of a network of communication partners.

Membership in professional organizations also favors sophisticated Internet practice and extensive Internet experience. Professional involvement translates into opportunities for interaction with other scientists, who may exchange information at the same time that they hone Internet skills. We observe increasing disparities among aspects of place and categories of identity as one moves from current use to ready access, then to practice, and finally to experience. We conclude that digital inequality pertains more to aspects of practice and experience than to access and use. Current use and ready access may become less-relevant aspects of digital inequality as developing areas become increasingly knowledge-based societies.

To What Extent Is Internet Adoption Associated with Research Productivity?
The notion of reagency does not presuppose any enhancing effect of technology on research output. Proponents of conventional development views tend to believe that the diffusion of the Internet in developing areas' research communities will enhance productivity through the rapid acquisition and exchange of information. Greater productivity will indirectly enhance the visibility of scientists from the developing world throughout the international scientific community. However, our results show that the Internet has no consistent effect on research productivity. Rather, its effect is conditioned by differences in location (e.g., Ghana or the Philippines) and organizational setting (e.g., state universities or government research institutes). Research communities—the combination of places and identities—differ substantially, and the circumstances surrounding and constraining scientific production generate conditions that may not favor any detectable impact by the Internet.

The joint effects of level of development (socioeconomic and technoscientific) and organizational setting condition the volume of scientific output disseminated through foreign journals. Nevertheless, international productivity varies between organizational settings in each location, even as one moves from less- to more-developed areas. In African locations, there is a general tendency for scientists in academic settings to be more productive than their counterparts in the government research sector, but the opposite holds true in Indian locations, and no significant difference appears in the Philippines. Local productivity is sensitive to variations in levels of development, but not to organizational setting. Locations situated at both extremes of the development spectrum generally exhibit higher local publication productivity.

These results support the reagency thesis that the consequences of applying initiatives from developed areas to developing areas do not translate to predicted and expected outcomes. Such initiatives develop their own trajectories, which are distinct from their originators' expectations, when imported to different local contexts and absorbed by local identities. As can be gleaned from the Internet's effects on research productivity, these trajectories are unpredictable and largely conditioned by idiosyncrasies of place and by the collective behavior and practices of identities to which these initiatives are introduced.

Is Scientific Collaboration Associated with Research Productivity?

In the knowledge-production sites of developed areas, collaboration is positively associated with publication productivity. Our research in developing areas, except for Chile, shows that no such general relationship exists, however. With results disaggregated by organizational setting, we found a weak positive association between collaboration and productivity for academic scientists, and a negative association for scientists in research institutes. This finding indicates that variations in organizational setting shape the nature of this relationship. The same can be said about the mediating effect of location, where a positive association is evident only in Kenya. Analyses by location and sector show that different combinations of identity attributes influence productivity in domestic and foreign outlets.

No single general model can adequately capture the essence of the relationship among place, identities, collaboration, and productivity. Generalized statements about the importance and benefits of collaboration, which policymakers typically adopt without critical understanding in planning development initiatives and programs, should be viewed with skepticism. Although every initiative is reagentive and will generate unexpected outcomes, we argue that explanatory work must focus on the characteristics of place and the attributes of identities situated in the flow of time.

Does the Internet Reduce Research Problems Associated with Collaboration?

Claims that Internet access reduces problems of collaboration imply that scientists in developing areas will also gain the benefits of connectivity. If the dynamics of the research process are similar in developed and developing areas, this thinking goes, then access to email should also be expected to reduce coordination difficulties in developing areas. Indeed, our study location that reports the highest access to email (Kerala) reports the fewest difficulties in research. However, it may not be inferred that scientists with access to email report fewer problems of coordination, when other background factors are held at constant level. We found scant evidence that collaboration was related to research difficulties per se. Although collaboration is associated with research problems, problems of collaboration itself are largely an effect of local context. Hence, it seems premature to speculate about the Internet's impacts on knowledge-production processes without paying close attention to differences in locations and organizational settings.

Conclusions: Understanding Key Development Dimensions and Dynamics

Moving Away from Expecting Development to Be Linear and Predictable

This chapter has described the basis for our view that the Internet is reagentive, given its capacity to bring about a series of reactions in the research communities of developing areas. The Internet includes the connectivity initiative itself: it has trickled through a series of donor-funded projects that bring computers, cables, and bandwidth to organizational settings in the developing world where research is conducted. Once installed, at whatever low bandwidth or sporadic functionality, the Internet also includes the capacity to send an email or browse the Web. However, reactions and responses to connectivity are typically not in the direction and magnitude anticipated by foreign donors, whose expectations are based on a concept of development that is linear and predictable.

Instead, we examine the relationships among location, collaboration, and productivity, with ICTs as a new factor, but without preconceived notions of benefits. Scientists in our Indian location have much greater Internet access, which may explain their low level of perceived research difficulties and which has paved the way for increased collaboration. However, these scientists do not seem to take much advantage of this "opportunity," with relatively few of them collaborating. Nevertheless, they produce twice the output of their African counterparts.

African scientists, in contrast, make limited use of the Internet to reduce research problems, but use it instead to generate and pursue "collaborations for development" that help them overcome the continual day-to-day economic difficulties they and their families experience. First and foremost, they search for consultancy jobs and internationally funded projects for these much-needed supplements, given that their salaries are painfully small. As they continue to participate in many projects and collaborations to sustain family needs, they incur an increasing number of difficulties resulting from conflicting schedules, deadlines, reports to write, and—most important—the need to find the next consultancy.

In these ways, African scientists undermine potential gains in productivity by incurring additional research projects and problems. When current projects near completion, the scientists refocus their energies on the search for new collaborations, even before they can submit terminal reports to sponsoring agencies. As a consequence, there is little effort to translate collaborative projects into the conventional scientific outcomes of productivity in domestic and foreign journals, mainly because this stage of the collaboration signals the end of income and the need to migrate to greener pastures.

A Paradox Facing Researchers in Development Areas

Our analysis has therefore revealed that scientific collaboration presents a paradox for scientific communities in developing areas. For instance, the research systems in sub-Saharan Africa, where collaborative work has seemed to hold the greatest returns, are the least equipped to benefit because the very conditions that problematize the relationship between collaboration and productivity undermine the benefits the Internet was expected to produce. Although collaboration may enhance productivity in developed areas, our study suggests that no general relationship can be expected where donors initiate collaborations from developed to developing areas. Initiatives from afar (donor-funded and international collaborative projects) are reagentive rather than developmental. The chain reactions that initiatives trigger typically take far from expected trajectories and ricochet in ways shaped by the characteristics of place and the attributes of identities.

Once foreign donors place initiatives such as connectivity in less-developed areas, they lack the ability to control them, and their expectations are largely conditioned by the use and experiences of the technology in (their own) developed areas. In developing areas, however, use and experience of the technology are constructed by new actors through new conditions and attributed meanings consistent with the orientation of new identities. The recipients' interests are not generally congruent with the donors' interests, although the former are readily able to adopt the discourse of participation. Our results show that the Internet's impact on the nature and dynamics of science in developing areas is far more complex than a simple model of diffusion would predict. We observed that the Internet's movement into African, Asian, and Latin American settings is characterized by important attributes of identity and place. Even its impact on scientific productivity yields patterns that are far from those experienced in developed areas.

Insights from the Reagency Concept

The concept of reagency sensitizes us to the myriad patterns that result when initiatives from developed areas are introduced into developing areas. Further, the reagency framework provides science and technology studies with a mode of understanding and a conceptual tool that mindfully considers the unexpected outcomes emanating from the interaction among initiatives, identities, and place. It shies away from prescribing generic and universal action and reaction schemes and from viewing knowledge production as an institutionally isomorphic process that is independent of identities, places, and meanings. Instead, it allows for the analysis of unexpected reactions, which is far more salient than the setting of predicted reactions and consequences. It doesn't imply a wayward stance without a clear-cut objective or goal, but an "always ability" to change the approach and continuously negotiate the complicated terrain of sociotechnical interaction.

On a more empirical level, our reagency perspective does not involve an ICT "elixir," which contrasts with the view held by traditional institutions of development that a universal advantage will come with the diffusion of ICTs such as the Internet. Our research has indicated that the Internet has the potential to alter the nature and dynamics of science. But it also shows that this potential is far from realization—and that the realization will be far different from what donors expect.

Notes

1. In this chapter, we use the terms *developing world*, *less-developed areas*, and *developing areas* interchangeably, although this usage is not precisely correct.

2. The increased visibility and inclusion of scientists from the developing world in global scientific communities would constitute a major change in the nature and structure of science that has existed since the seventeenth century.

3. It should be emphasized at the outset that the diffusion of ICTs in Africa reflects the standard pattern of innovation in economically advantaged groups such as professionals (Polikanov and Abramova 2003). In one extreme case, a 1999 survey of women in two East African regions showed that more than 99 percent of them had not heard of email (Khasiani 1999). About one-third of these women had never been to school, and fewer than half had more than a primary education.

4. Modernization theory views "development" as a uniform evolutionary path from traditional, rural, agricultural forms to modern, urban, and industrial forms (Escobar 1995; Shrum 2000). Societies engaged in the process of development follow a determinate, predictable, and linear sequence of developmental stages (Chirot and Hall 1982:82) with predictable and manageable consequences. Development can also be pictured as a set of initiatives that originate in international, nongovernmental, and academic organizations in developed areas, with consequences for identities in developing areas.

5. See http://worldsci.net/movies.htm and http://worldsci.net/papers.htm#methods.

6. The 1994 survey entailed selecting scientists from a relatively large sample of research institutes, universities, nongovernmental organizations, and international research centers. However, owing to the effort, time, and expense involved, the sample was relatively small, and only a few (generally two to four) scientists could be interviewed at each organization.

7. For sampling purposes, and because staff size is often similar, we defined "organizations" as either a university department, a stand-alone research institute, or a subinstitute, where an overarching body (e.g., the Kenya Agricultural Research Institute) was purely administrative, without research activities in the body itself.

References

Barjak, F. 2004. *On the integration of the Internet into informal science communication*. Series A: Discussion Paper DPW 2004–02. Solothurn: University of Applied Sciences, Solothurn Northwestern, Switzerland.

Bijker, W. E. 1995. "Sociohistorical technology studies." In *Handbook of science and technology studies*, ed. S. Jasanoff, G. E. Markle, J. C. Petersen, and T. Pinch. Thousand Oaks, CA: Sage, 229–256.

Castells, M. 2000. *The information age: Economy, society, and culture: The rise of the network society.* Vol. 1. 2d ed. Malden, MA: Blackwell.

Chirot, D., and T. Hall. 1982. "World-system theory." *Annual Review of Sociology* 8:81–106.

Crane, D. 1972. *Invisible college: Diffusion of knowledge in scientific communities.* Chicago: University of Chicago Press.

Davidson, T., R. Sooryamoorthy, and W. Shrum. 2002. "Kerala connections: Will the Internet affect science in developing areas?" In *The Internet in everyday life*, ed. B. Wellman and C. Haythornthwaite. Malden, MA: Blackwell, 496–519.

DiMaggio, P., E. Hargittai, W. R. Neuman, and J. P. Robinson. 2001. "Social implications of the Internet." *Annual Review of Sociology* 27:307–336.

Duque, R. B. 2007. "Internet Golpe in Chile." In *Past, present, and future of research in the information society*, ed. W. Shrum, K. Benson, W. Bijker, and K. Brunnstein. New York: Springer, 198–206.

Duque, R. B., W. Shrum, O. Barriga, and G. Henriquez. 2008. "Internet practice and professional networks in Chilean science: Dependency or progress." *Scientometrics.*

Duque, R. B., M. Ynalvez, R. Sooryamoorthy, P. Mbatia, D-B. S. Dzorgbo, and W. Shrum. 2005. "Collaboration paradox: Scientific productivity, the Internet, and problems of research in developing areas." *Social Studies of Science* 35 (5):755–785.

Dzorgbo, D. B. 2001. *Ghana in search of development: The challenge of governance, economic management, and institution building.* Aldershot, UK: Ashgate.

Escobar, A. 1995. *Encountering development: The making and unmaking of the Third World.* Princeton, NJ: Princeton University Press.

Hamelink, C. 1999. *ICT and social development: The global policy context.* Geneva: United Nations Research Institute for Social Development.

Hill, D. I. 2004. *Latin America shows rapid rise in S&E articles info brief: Science resource statistics.* Washington, DC: Directorate of Social, Behavioral, and Economic Sciences, U.S. National Science Foundation.

Iyer, S. R., and S. MacPherson. 2000. *Social development in Kerala: Illusion or reality?* Aldershot, UK: Ashgate.

Khasiani, S. 1999. *Needs assessment of Isukha central location in Kakamega District and Nguumo location in Makueni District.* Nairobi, Kenya: Family Support Institute.

Krauskopf, M., and M. I. Vera. 1997. "Assessment of scientific profiles and capabilities of PhD programs in Chile: A scientometric approach." *Scientometrics* 40 (3):569–577.

Mullin, J., R. M. Adam, J. E. Halliwell, and L. P. Milligen. 2000. *Science, technology, and innovation in Chile.* Ottawa, Canada: IDRC Books.

Olson, G. M., and J. S. Olson. 2000. "Distance matters." *Human-Computer Interactions* 15:28–36.

Olson, G. M., A. Zimmerman, and N. Bos, eds. 2008. *Scientific collaboration on the Internet*. Cambridge, MA: MIT Press.

Parayil, G. 1996. "The Kerala model of development: Development and sustainability in the Third World." *Third World Quarterly 17*:941–957.

Polikanov, D., and I. Abramova. 2003. "Africa and ICT: A chance for breakthrough?" *Information, Communication, & Society 6* (1):42–56.

Rogers, E. M. 1995. *Diffusion of innovations*. New York: Free Press.

Sassen, S. 2000. *Cities in a world economy*. Thousand Oaks, CA: Pine Forge Press.

Schott, T. 1993. "World science: Globalization of institutions and participation." *Science, Technology, and Human Values 18* (2):196–208.

Shrum, W. 2000. "Science and story in development: The emergence of non-governmental organizations in agricultural research." *Social Studies of Science 30* (1):95–124.

Shrum, W. 2005. "Reagency of the Internet, or, how I became a guest for science?" *Social Studies of Science 35* (5):723–754.

Stehr, N., ed. 2000. *Modern societies as knowledge societies*. Thousand Oaks, CA: Sage.

Uimonen, P. 2001. *Transnational.Dynamics@Development.net: Internet, modernization, and globalization*. Stockholm, Sweden: Elanders Gotab.

World Bank. 2003. *World development report 2003*. New York: Oxford University Press.

Ynalvez, M., R. B. Duque, P. Mbatia, R. Sooryamoorthy, A. Palackal, and W. Shrum. 2005. "When do scientists 'adopt' the Internet? Dimensions of connectivity in developing areas." *Scientometrics 63* (1):39–67.

Ynalvez, M., and W. Shrum. 2006. "International training and the digital divide: Computer and email use in the Philippines." *Perspectives on Global Development and Technology 5* (4):277–302.

Coda: The Ends and Means of World Wide Research

William H. Dutton and Paul W. Jeffreys

The Quality of Information and Research

In our introduction to this book, we agreed with Jacques Ellul's (1964) critique of the increasing confusion of the means of technological progress with the ends being sought from its uses. The technocratic view underpinning this confusion "entails a belief in the worth of scientific and technological innovations as ends in themselves" (Marx 1997:14). Understanding the dynamics of the relationship between the means of conducting e-research and their expected ends has been a central theme cross-cutting the contributions to this volume.

Contributors to this book have shown that outcomes on collaboration, data sharing, and open science were the ends targeted by early proponents of e-research (chapter 2). The many examples of such objectives given in the book are typified by a comment John Taylor made when he was director general of the U.K. Research Councils: "e-Science is about global collaboration . . . and the next generation of infrastructure that will enable it."[1] These kinds of collaboration have also been characterized and defined as requiring "access to very large data collections, very large scale computing resources and high performance visualization back to the individual user scientists."[2]

Such aims were generally chosen because they seemed to be not only desirable, but also inherent and predictable outcomes of the technological shifts described and analyzed in this book. However, the book's focus on how information and communication technologies (ICTs) can reconfigure access provides a framework for understanding why these outcomes are socially shaped and not inevitable (chapter 1). They are dependent on numerous decisions and on different research, social, and institutional settings, which can lead to many different outcomes in different environments. Hence, many contributors emphasize the social shaping of technical change and its impacts in their attempts to understand the nature of the changes and transformations they discuss (e.g., chapters 5 and 7).

The ultimate end is to create higher-quality research outcomes to enhance theory, policy, practice, and broader social and economic well-being. Because this research needs to be based on higher-quality information, the central questions for e-research are:

• To what degree are the new technologies and the practices they enable leading to improvements in the quality of information?

• Are researchers able to be more creative and productive in their research in ways that improve the quality of information in order to advance "genuine, that is to say *social*, progress" (Marx 1997:15), rather than focusing on the trajectory of technological progress as such and assuming that the social and institutional changes will flow in its wake?

Collaboration, data sharing, open science, and other outcomes of e-research may or may not enhance the quality of research in particular circumstances. For instance, social scientists who use research-centered computational networks may be as likely to be lone researchers as they are to work in collaborative teams (chapter 6). If this view is correct, these networks may support many approaches to collaboration, or open research in some cases may undermine quality (chapter 8).

It is because the impact of e-research on the quality of information cannot be taken for granted that many of its potential benefits have failed to materialize in the ways proponents might have expected, such as open science (chapter 11). Moreover, there are reasons to question whether all applications of new techniques are yielding better information (e.g., the proliferation of Web-based questionnaires). Despite forward strides in e-research, we continue to be faced with urgent questions about whether we should trust the quality of information being stored, processed, and delivered electronically. Can we trust knowledge and information drawn from the growing stores of data available at the fingertips of anyone with access to these electronic technologies? Will it be possible for e-research to avoid the emergence of a world "lost in information," to echo T. S. Eliot's words quoted in our introduction?

The Early Stages of e-Research Maturity

Our contributors have provided a wide-angle lens snapshot of the evolution of e-research about a decade after this phenomenon first emerged. They have covered a broad spectrum of technologies and research as well as of social and institutional settings—from satellites in space (chapter 1) to libraries of historical manuscripts (chapter 3), and from personal computers in developing regions (chapter 12) to the most advanced "big science" flagships, such as at the European Organization for Nuclear Research (chapter 2). This wide-ranging analysis has demonstrated how the design, development, and use of these technologies are being shaped by social, institutional, and technical factors, and with what implications for research.

The driving forces behind the development and application of these technologies have sometimes come from the top down, through national and regional initiatives (chapter 2). At other times, they have come from bottom up, as when infrastructures enable domain scientists and other users to create applications that meet their needs for scholarly research (e.g., chapter 6). Both innovation pathways have shortcomings. National policymakers may support certain initiatives one year, but then move on to new priorities in subsequent years, making resource availability unpredictable and short term. User communities with the expertise and collaborative partners to build from the bottom up are relatively few, feeding the skepticism of those who do not see the relevance of new technologies to their research. One of this book's themes (particularly in chapter 5) is the need to develop technology that is more usable and that has lower barriers to use.

The range and scale of innovation in ICTs and computational networks applied to research have been remarkable so far, but we are aware that our snapshot was taken in the early phases of what may become a profound transformation in research, across disciplines and around the world. E-research is diffusing globally and across the disciplines, but not evenly, and the degree of maturity is far from consistent. E-science has been a frontier buster, followed increasing by e–social science initiatives. Despite notable exceptions, some of which have been discussed in this book, the take-up in the arts and humanities was only beginning to emerge toward the 2010s. And some countries in the West have built far more e-research experience and expertise than developing countries. However, slow starters can build on the West's experience with developing and using e-research technologies in the early phase in order to "catch up," and those more advanced can use that same experience to help bring about further breakthroughs.

Emerging applications of ICTs enable the undertaking of research that might not otherwise have been feasible, such as in new ways of observing objects in outer and microscopic spaces, detecting environmental changes, studying human behavior, and preserving and viewing creative works. Key future developments that will help to achieve such advances include Grid and Cloud computing, advances in artificial intelligence, Webmetrics, visualization technologies, virtual research environments, and the Semantic Web. All these developments and more have been explored in this book together with their actual and potential applications, such as helping to create, survive, adapt to, and prosper from the data deluge unleashed by the new ICTs.

The tangible examples and case studies in this book have sought to help anchor readers while our contributors explore the wide landscape opened by the application of these technologies. The social and institutional shaping and implications of e-research show unique challenges within individual research disciplines and in interdisciplinary research methodologies (e.g., chapters 6 and 9). These challenges are complemented by generic issues, which allow innovations in one area to be adopted later or to provide a foundation for innovation in a different domain (chapter 1).

Advances have occurred despite recognized social, ethical, and institutional limitations. Social scientists have helped to identify the centrality of the "soft" institutional infrastructures required to facilitate the formation and conduct of, for instance, collaborative public-sector research projects that are truly global in scope (chapter 7). Open collaborative methods may lead to the need for changes in institutional arrangements to better protect ethical standards through revisions to ethical review processes and other arrangements.

The implications of these kinds of change defy easy characterization. They may not be erasing or bridging disciplinary boundaries, but they are creating new subdisciplines in an evolving research landscape (chapter 9). Research-centered computational networks are also being shaped by the codes of disciplines and have enabled researchers who are geographically and institutionally distributed to collaborate and to share large-scale data sources (chapter 4). However, as already explained, the same set of e-research technologies can usually support many forms of collaboration, so such support does not predetermine how the technologies will be applied in a given setting. It also does not automatically lead to data sharing, as indicated by many initiatives' failure in their attempt to achieve this goal, as in the case of some collaboratories (chapter 10). E-research might provide a global infrastructure for research, but many developing areas are still on the fringes of the possible positive transformations that can be brought to their research (chapter 12).

The Next Challenge: Demonstrating Improvements in Research Outcomes

The next mission is to move beyond showing the technical feasibility of e-research to demonstrably enhancing the quality of research and the information it employs. This enhancement would generate a virtuous cycle by facilitating major advances in research-centered network innovations that will foster true advances across research disciplines. In turn, that cycle will then feed back to support further valuable innovation.

Reflecting on the status of e-research and what has been achieved, key technological landmarks and developments can be seen. National e-infrastructures have been created, and researchers are using resources and practices that were not available even a decade ago. This process is accelerating at a rapid pace, breaking through the bounds of our snapshot while we write. But it is not the technological capabilities themselves that are determining their effects. It is the way researchers use them to reconfigure access to information, expertise, and experience in ways that can either support or undermine the quality of research.

That is why it is critical for all those involved in e-research to focus attention on the quality, creativity, and impact of research when they make choices and define strategies for the design and application of research-centered computational networks.[3] Researchers need to adapt these networks to their research areas to cope with the flood of digital data (chapter 4) and to promote more effective sharing of information—for example, by using the emerging Semantic Web (essay 4.3). Further advances in design and development are required, such as lowering barriers to use by improving the technologies' usability and by better exploiting the potential of social-networking facilities.

This book serves as a roadmap charted at a particular point in the progress of e-research, with signposts to likely future dynamics and issues. The scene it depicts is patchy. Some countries have embraced e-science more than others. Some disciplines have been prepared to deploy the technologies we have highlighted, whereas others have focused on low barriers to entry. Given this timing, many of the book's examples present early-stage surveys, prototypes, and proof-of-concept projects. More comprehensive e-research analyses will need to be undertaken as the field continues to mature.

In editing and contributing to this book, we have been convinced that the continued development and application of research-centered computational networks will be of increasing value to innovation in the sciences and humanities. However, the quality of research—the primary outcome of e-research—will be shaped by the wider range of social and technical factors highlighted by our contributors. This social and technical shaping of e-research choices and strategies will affect what researchers know, what they can observe, with whom they collaborate, how they conduct their analyses, and when and how they communicate their methods, data, and findings.

We hope the book will contribute to the development of this field by giving a greater focus to the ends of e-research, even while recognizing the significance of the immense advances made in the means for reaching these goals.

Notes

1. See http://www.nesc.ac.uk/nesc/define.html and essay 2.3.

2. See "Defining e-Science" at http://www.nesc.ac.uk/nesc/define.html.

3. This recommendation is not simply for others, but for ourselves as well. A focus on the quality of research is at the heart of a new phase of our own research, through the Oxford e-Social Science Node within the U.K. National Centre for e–Social Science (Economic and Social Research Council grant RES-149-25-1082).

References

Ellul, J. 1964. *The technological society*. New York: Alfred A. Knopf.

Marx, L. 1997. "Does improved technology mean progress?" In *Technology and the future*, 7th ed., ed. A. H. Teich. New York: St. Martin's Press, 3–14.

Glossary

Note: Italicized words point to a related item in the glossary.

Access Grid   An ensemble of resources supporting group-to-group visual and audio interactions across the Internet.

Advanced Research Projects Agency Network (ARPANET)   Established by the U.S. Department of Defense's Advanced Research Projects Agency to support the sharing of computing facilities among computer scientists and engineers. Became the foundation of the Internet beginning around 1969.

artificial companion   Intelligent software or a physical embodiment (e.g., an avatar) that can become a "companion" to its user-owner by learning about her or his preferences, habits, and wishes (e.g., to filter information on the Web based on familiarity with its owner's preferences).

avatar   A graphical, interactive image that personifies a computer user or a software-generated entity.

Bermuda Principles   Guidelines for sharing research data on gene sequences, first drawn up in Bermuda in 1996.

blog   A combination of the terms *Web* and *log*. Personal content posted on a Web site, such as a diary of progress on a research project, comment, criticism, advice, and other types of information. A typical *Web 2.0* capability.

blogosphere   General term for the virtual space on the Internet created by blogging Web sites.

Budapest Open Access Initiative   A statement of principle and strategy aimed at accelerating progress in the international effort to make research articles in all academic fields freely available on the Internet (see *open access*). It has been signed by many individuals and organizations from around the world.

captcha   An automated test to distinguish between machines and humans online, such as by asking the user to enter a password to a Web site using characters presented on the screen in a manner that cannot be read automatically (e.g., as wavy distortions of the characters).

Cloud computing   An approach in which dynamically scalable and often virtualized computing resources are provided as a service over the Internet to enable users to run their applications without having control over the technological infrastructure that supports them.

collaborative network organization   Arrangements, typically spanning organizational boundaries, based on the use of an *ICT*-enabled infrastructure that allows individuals (e.g., researchers) to participate as and when they wish in collaborations and communication with others.

collaboratory   Digital network that allows groups of people to form communities of interest to help them cooperate to create new ideas, information, knowledge, and artifacts, and to address interdisciplinary areas of research. Similar to a *virtual research environment.*

computational science   The use of computers to analyze and solve scientific and engineering problems with the aid of mathematical models and numerical solution techniques. Sometimes called "scientific computing."

copyleft   A general licensing method, as used in the *General Public License,* for making a program or other work free (e.g., requiring that all modified and extended versions of the program also be free).

Creative Commons   A not-for-profit organization focused on defining the spectrum of possibilities between full copyright and free access in the public domain (e.g., see *Science Commons*). Also used as a generic term for initiatives promoting *open access.*

cyberinfrastructure   The digital networks and range of other software, data, and hardware resources offering access to a wide variety of powerful computing and communication services to support *e-research* collaborations. A term developed within the U.S. National Science Foundation's cyberinfrastructure vision.

data deluge   The high volume of data and information processed and communicated through digital networks.

data mining   Techniques to help researchers dig deep into the details of large data sources to try to detect patterns, trends, anomalies, and other information.

digital object   A document, text message, *blog*, video, audio, or other entity that can be processed and reused in a digitized format.

disintermediation   The removal or otherwise substantial alteration of the role of traditional mediators—for example, by using network-enabled research to challenge the role of academic publishers in mediating between researchers and their audiences.

distributed computing   Approaches to providing *ICT*-enabled services that coordinate the resources of many computers wherever they are located in order to optimize the use of available resources in working toward a common purpose (e.g., the *Cloud* and *Grid computing*).

e-humanities   Adapts *e-research* technical innovation to the humanities, such as in libraries, rare manuscript collections, and the storage, analysis, and presentation of artworks.

e-infrastructure   The digital networks and range of other software, data, and hardware resources offering access to a wide variety of powerful computing and communication services to support *e-research* collaborations. A term developed within the U.K. Research Councils' e-Science Programme.

embedded sensor network   An electronic network encompassing many sensors that are physically embedded in the environment in order to monitor, collect, and transmit large volumes of information for analysis (e.g., relating to the environment, large manufacturing operations, or chemical-processing plants).

e-research   Research across the disciplines conducted via distributed collaborations using digital networks that offer access to powerful computing and data-management capabilities, typically based on large-scale *research-oriented computational networks* such as the *Grid*. Also encompasses the research and development to provide the associated *e-infrastructure*.

e-science   *E-research* mainly in the "hard" sciences. A term initially used with reference primarily to large-scale projects.

e–social science   Employing *e-research* technologies within the social sciences.

firewall   A system (hardware or software or both) that creates a boundary to help secure a network or computer from access by unauthorized users.

General Public License (GPL)   A free license of the Free Software Foundation's GNU operating system, which is one of the most widely used forms of license enabling authors to provide their software, publication, or other work for free under certain licensing conditions. See also *copyleft* and *open access*.

giga   Measure of computing speed and storage capacity to a scale of one billion (10^9).

global positioning system (GPS)   A satellite-based system using communication signals to determine accurately the location of a receiver.

Grid   A *distributed computing* approach based on the sharing of powerful computing, communication, and storage resources to support the solving of often large-scale *e-research* problems using components selected from a standard set. The name is a metaphor for making substantial computing capabilities as simple to access as plugging electrical equipment into a utility power grid.

hyperlink   Web-based connector in an electronic document that anchors a point in one *hypertext* document to another point in the same or another document on the Web. A click on a hyperlink typically moves the user to the anchor in the related document.

hypertext   Information in documents held in electronic form on the Web, including *hyperlinks*.

hypertext markup language (HTML)   The language used to create documents on the Web. See also *hypertext*.

information and communication technologies (ICTs)   A wide range of electronic ICTs used to store, analyze, process, and transmit text, sounds, visual, and other information in digital forms (e.g., the Internet and the Web, high-performance computational centers, *embedded sensor networks*, and *personal computers*).

information extraction   An automatic method for locating facts in electronic documents and storing them in a database for processing, based on techniques such as *data mining* or the use of software products such as spreadsheets and report generators.

information retrieval   Methods of searching for particular texts or documents according to a set of search criteria.

in-links   The *hyperlinks* directed toward a Web site. See *out-links*.

listserv   An electronic mailing list that can be used as an aid for discussion groups by facilitating the electronic distribution of messages to members.

log-file analytics   The study of files that log activities related to a site on the Web.

machine translation   The use of computer software for automatically translating one natural language into another, in contrast to human translation.

mash-up   The easy combination of content from different Web sites—for example, by overlaying statistical information on the digital map of an area.

mega   Measure of computing speed and storage capacity to a scale of one million (10^6).

metacomputing   An early term for what has become known as *e-infrastructure*, or *cyberinfrastructure*.

metadata   Contextual information (i.e., data about data) describing the environment, content, and structure of records and their management through time, such as aspects of actual data items (their name, format, and so on).

middleware   Components of software that interconnect higher-level applications with lower-level operating system software, including a set of enabling services that allow multiple processes to run on one or more machines that interact across a network.

open access   When as much information as possible is made available for free, such as through online networks (e.g., as defined in the *Budapest Open Access Initiative*). See also *Creative Commons* and *Science Commons*.

open source   A form of software licensing that makes the program's source code available for use or modification by users and other developers. This software is typically (but not always) made available for free to anyone who wants to use it. See also *copyleft* and *GPL*.

out-links   The hyperlinks directed from a Web site. See in-links.

parallel computing   Running computer applications across a number of separate processors at the same time, rather than sequentially.

personal computer   Desktop and portable computers used by individuals for their own purposes, including for linking to networks such as the Internet.

peta   Measure of computing speed and storage capacity to a scale of 10^{15}.

Pretty Good Encryption   The technique used in the Pretty Good Privacy (PGP) software program for encrypting and decrypting email over the Internet, based on the nonproprietary OpenPGP standard of the Internet Engineering Task Force.

requirements engineering   A systematic approach to the gathering, analysis and specification of the requirements (e.g. for user interaction) that should be met by an engineered artifact, such as an information system.

research-centered computational network   Digital information and communication network that links computational and networking facilities to support research applications.

Resource Description Framework (RDF)   A standardized approach to describing entities held in digital form, especially information available on the Web. It is used, for example, for the Semantic Web.

Science Commons   A *Creative Commons* project built on the promise of *open access* to scholarly literature and data. Seeks to identify and ease key barriers to the movement of information, tools, and data through the scientific research cycle.

scientometrics   A research field concerned with measuring the outputs of science to evaluate scientists and to shed light on the dynamics of the growth of disciplines and specialisms.

search engine   Computational tools that enable users to find information located on the Web.

Semantic Web   An approach aimed at making it easier to find, share, and combine information on the Web by moving away from the traditional Web of interlinked *HTML* documents to a Web of linked data, underpinned by a series of technologies and standards.

Simple Protocol and RDF Query Language (SPARQL)   The standard query language and protocol for interrogating *RDF* data. Designed for the *Semantic Web*.

social networking   A *Web service* that facilitates interactions between individuals who choose to join an online virtual community. A typical *Web 2.0* capability.

spam, spammers   Unwanted email, analogous to unsolicited "junk" mail.

telescience   Use of advanced information, communication, and optic technologies to observe and analyze outer space and microscopic worlds.

tera   Measure of computing speed and storage capacity to a scale of 10^{12} (one trillion).

text mining   Technique used by researchers to dig deep into information to look for patterns within complex data.

trusted computing   A set of standards supporting secure computing environments that help to protect their information assets from compromise through external software attack and physical theft. Overseen by the nonprofit Trusted Computing Group.

trusted computing base   The core of a computer-based system (hardware, software, data management, and services) that needs to be trusted to ensure the security and integrity of the whole system. An element in *trusted computing*.

twitter   An electronic communication through the quick exchange of brief messages.

ubiquitous computing   The trend for people to interact with a dynamic set of small, networked computers, often embedded in everyday objects (e.g., hand-held devices and high-capability mobile cellphones) and in *embedded sensor networks*.

user-generated content   The ability for any user to contribute text, images, music, and other content to a Web site. A typical *Web 2.0* capability.

virtual collaborative organization   An organizational form that enables researchers with common interests to function as a coherent unit, even though they are distributed geographically and temporally. Enables members from different legal entities to pursue common research goals.

virtual research environment   Digital network creating a community of researchers in different locations and institutions who can use the network to collaborate on research work. Similar to a *collaboratory*.

visual analytics   A specialized field that uses visualization techniques to enhance the analysis of data and its communication to wider audiences (e.g., by helping to discover patterns within massive and dynamically changing information spaces).

visualization technologies   *E-research* approaches that enhance the presentation of data analyses and research results by using a variety of visual media, such as graphs, animation, and video.

Web 2.0   A broad name for a second generation of Web-based applications (following the first generation of information sharing through *HTML*-based document linking). Typified by the promotion of user participation and collaboration through services such as *blogs*, *social networking*, *user-generated content*, and *wikis*.

Webmetrics   Techniques based on monitoring and measuring activity on a Web site to analyze patterns of use; referred to by some as *Webometrics*.

Webometrics   A term sometimes used in place of *Webmetrics*.

Web service   A software system that supports interoperable machine-to-machine interaction over a network.

wiki   A Web site that supports collaboration by allowing users to add, remove, and modify content; the *Wikipedia* online encyclopedia is the most prominent example. A typical *Web 2.0* capability.

Abbreviations

AI	artificial intelligence
ARCS	Australian Research Collaboration Service
ARPANET	Advanced Research Projects Agency Network (U.S. Defense Department)
BADC	British Atmospheric Data Centre
Blog	Web log
Captcha	completely automated public Turing tests to tell computers and humans apart
CENS	Center for Embedded Networked Sensing (U.S. National Science Foundation)
CERN	European Organization for Nuclear Research
CHASTE	Cancer, Heart, and Soft Tissue Environment
CNGrid	China National Grid
CREW	Collaborative Research Events on the Web (United Kingdom)
CSAGE	Collaborative Stereoscopic Access Grid Environment
CSCW	computer-supported collaborative work
CUDOS	communalism, universalism, disinterestedness, originality, skepticism
DAMES	Data Management through E–Social Science (NCeSS node)
D-Grid	German Grid Initiative
DOI	Digital Object Identifier
e-CAT	e–Content Analysis Tool
e-DiaMoND	electronic Diagnostic Mammography National Database (U.K. e-Science project)
EGEE	Enabling Grids for E-sciencE (CERN project)
e-IRG	e-Infrastructure Reflection Group
GAIN	Genetic Association Information Network (US)
GNU	GNU's Not Unix
GPL	General Public License (for GNU)
GPS	global positioning system
IBVRE	Integrative Biology Virtual Research Environment
ICT	information and communication technology

IE	information extraction
IP	Internet protocol or intellectual property
IPRs	intellectual property rights
IR	information retrieval
ISO	International Standards Organization
IVOA	International Virtual Observatory Alliance
JISC	Joint Information Systems Committee (UK)
LHC	Large Hadron Collider (CERN)
MiMeG	MixedMediaGrid (NCeSS node)
MT	machine translation
NASA	National Aeronautics and Space Administration (United States)
NCeSS	National Centre for e–Social Science (United Kingdom)
NeSC	National e-Science Centre (United Kingdom)
NHS	National Health Service (United Kingdom)
NIH	National Institutes of Health (United States)
NLP	natural-language processing
NSF	National Science Foundation (United States)
OAI	Open Archives Initiative
OeRC	Oxford e-Research Centre
OeSS	Oxford e–Social Science project
OGSA	Open Grid Services Architecture
OII	Oxford Internet Institute
OGSI	Open Grid Services Infrastructure
OMII	Open Middleware Infrastructure Institute (for the United Kingdom and Europe)
PC	personal computer
PGP	Pretty Good Privacy program, including Pretty Good Encryption
PIPII	principal investigatorPersonal Identifying Information
PMHQA	Protocol for Metadata HarvestingQuestion Answering (NLP technique)
RCN	research-centered computational network
RDF	Resource Description Framework
RFID	radio frequency identification
SPARQL	Simple Protocol and RDF Query Language
TPM	trusted platform module
URI	uniform resource identifier
VCO	virtual collaborative organization
VLE	virtual learning environment
VO	virtual organization
VRE	virtual research environment

Index

Abbott, Andrew, 85, 92–93
Abelson, Hal, 14, 254, 322–324
Abilene Observatory, 250
Academic research libraries, 84–87
Access. *See also* Open access; Privacy
  data rich/poor nations and, 27–28, 32–33
  developing areas and, 325–340
  digital choices and, 25–35
  digital object identification and, 126
  ethics and, 33–34, 223–238
  libraries and, 83–94
  multiple actors and, 25–31
  open science and, 299–313
  reconfiguration of, 21–37
  user control over, 30–31
Access Grid, 103, 169, 230, 292
Ackland, Robert, 19–20, 48–50
Adam, R. M., 332
Addgene, 324
Adler, Moshe, 49–50
Advanced Research Projects Agency Network
  (ARPANET), 5, 9
Advisory Board for Collaboration Agreements
  (ABCA), 204–207
Agendas, 272–275
Agile approaches, 144–145
Albert, Réka, 48
Allan, R., 69
Allen, F. H., 307
Amazon.com, 28
American Council of Learned Societies (ACLS),
  62

Ancient manuscripts, 79, 102–105, 140–141
Andrews, S., 69
Antley, A., 234
AoIR Ethics Working Committee, 227, 235
Archaeology, 102–105
Archives
  core purpose of, 93
  data webs and, 98–101
  ethics and, 231–233
  image repositories and, 98–101
  libraries and, 83–94
  long-term data curation and, 90–92
  Open Archives Initiative Protocol for Meta-
    data Harvesting and, 98
Arnab, A., 127
Artificial intelligence (AI), 111–117
arXiv, 87, 91, 93
Arzberger, P., 304
Association of Research Libraries, 84
Astronomy, 265–266
Atkins, D. E., 120, 192, 299
Atkinson, Malcolm, 192
Atwood, M. E., 136
Australian Research Collaboration Service
  (ARCS), 59
Authentication, 53, 61, 126, 187, 231
Authorship protection, 218–220

Bagnall, R. S., 102
Baidu, 189
Bannon, L., 135
Barabási, Albert-László, 48

Barga, Roger, 20, 65, 67–71
Barjak, F., 47, 86, 171, 329
Barnard, P. J., 136
Barriga, 325
Basel Committee on Banking Supervision, 205, 210n28
Batty, M., 167, 169, 267
Beaulieu, A., 304
Becher, Tony, 261, 263, 269
Bell, G., 70
Bement, Arhen L., 193
Berger, A., 113
Berlin, 318
Berman, Fran, 3, 52, 62, 249, 299
Bernabeu, M. O., 145
Berners-Lee, Timothy, 13, 80
  CERN and, 5
  data webs and, 98
  Semantic Web and, 130–133
Bethesda, 318
Better-not-perfect principle, 73–74
Biagioli, M., 219
Bibliothèque Nationale, 84
Big science, 122
Bijker, W. E., 329
BioMed Central, 317
Birkin, M., 167, 169
Bishop, A. P., 122
Black, A., 107
Blair, A., 89
BLAST, 69
Blogs
  access and, 21, 26
  Cloud computing and, 68, 70
  data deluge and, 110
  libraries and, 83, 86
  social networks and, 29, 73, 157, 185, 188, 289–290
Blomberg, J., 137
Blum, M., 110
Borgman, Christine L., 13, 80, 267
  access and, 22–23
  bottom-up innovation and, 165

embedded network sensing and, 120–124
  libraries and, 85, 90
Bos, Nathan, 329
  access and, 22–23
  bottom-up innovation and, 167, 179
  changing disciplinary landscapes and, 258, 261, 264
  usability designs and, 135
  virtual research environments and, 279, 281–282
Bourdieu, Pierre, 260
Bowker, Geoffrey C., 19, 40–44, 62, 109, 287
Bowman, Alan, 13, 79, 102–106, 285
Boyd, D., 157–158
Brabazon, T., 28
Brady, Henry, 62, 249, 299
Brady, J. M., 103, 285
Brand, Steward, 40, 43
Brin, Sergey, 113
British Atmospheric Data Centre (BADC), 91
BROADEN project, 57
Brown, Peter, 113
Budapest Open Access Initiative, 317–319, 322
Building a Virtual Research Environment for the Humanities project, 140–141
Büscher, M., 142
Buttenfield, B. P., 122

Cairncross, F., 3
Caldas, A., 48, 177
Campaigns, 121
Campbell, Donald, 234, 261
Cancer, Heart, and Soft Tissue Environment (CHASTE), 145
Canterbury Tales (Chaucer), 102
Captchas, 110
Caraça, João, 14, 254, 317–321
Card, S., 136
Cardoso, Gustavo, 14, 254, 317–321
Carr, N., 5, 28, 174
Carusi, Annamaria, 14, 253–254, 277–294
Castells, Manuel, 41, 317–318, 328–329

Center for Embedded Networked Sensing (CENS), 120–121
Certainty trough, 171
Chandler, A. D., 41
Chat, 157
Chile, 254, 325, 327, 330, 332–334, 337
China, 13, 32, 332
  bottom-up innovation and, 162, 179
  e-Content Analysis Tool (e-CAT) and, 188–189
  e–social science and, 188–190
  free online services and, 189
  Grid computing and, 188
China Grid Supporting Platform, 59
China National Grid (CNGrid), 59
China NSF, 59
China R&D Over Wide-Area Network, 59
Chompalov, I., 263
Christensen, M., 142
Chubin, Daryl, 260
Citations, 45–47
CiteULike, 157
Citrix XenSource, 296
CLEANER, 121
Climate change, ix, xi, 21, 25–28
climate*prediction*.net, 155
Clock of the long now, 40
Cloud computing, 13, 20–21, 61, 65
  computational services and, 68
  data services and, 68
  domain-specific services and, 68
  ends and means of, 345
  ethics and, 228
  industrialization and, 174
  pervasive deployment and, 74
  research platforms in, 67–71
  scholarly communication and, 69
  scientific services and, 69
  social networking and, 67–68
  software plus services and, 69
  technical services and, 69
  virtual research environments (VREs) and, 254, 297–298

ClustalW2, 69
Coalition for Networked Information, 91
Cockburn, A., 143, 145
Cognitive models, 136
Coles, S., 307
Collaborative Research Events on the Web (CREW) project, 288
Collaborative Stereoscopic Access Grid Environment (CSAGE), 291–292
Collaboratories
  typologies of, 281–283
  virtual research environments (VREs) and, 277–284, 292–293
CombeChem, 29, 132, 306–307
Commercial off-the-shelf (COTS) software, 198
Commission on Cyberinfrastructure for the Humanities and Social Sciences, 62
Communalism, universalism, disinterestedness, originality, and skepticism (CUDOS), 301
Communities of practice, 260
Community intelligence, 73–74
Completely automated public Turing tests (captchas), 110
Computational biology, 145
Computers and Humanities journal, 257
Computer-support cooperative work (CSCW), 136–138, 149
Comte, Auguste, 41
Condor project, 53
Conference on European Statisticians, 250–251
Consumption capital, 49
Cookies, 231
Cooper, J., 145
Copyright, 35, 304
  authorship and, 218–220
  bottom-up innovation and, 162
  digital technology and, 101, 105
  open access and, 317
  ownership and, 215, 323
  public sector and, 205–206, 210n27
Core Programme, 59, 191, 197, 208n3, 308, 310, 313n12

Cornell University, 87

Cortada, J. W., 41

Cost structures, 26–28

Cowie, J., 112

Crabtree, A., 138, 140

Crane, Diana, 259–260, 328

Creative Commons, 206

Crombie, A. C., 273

Cross-language IR, 113

Cryptography, 154–155

CUAHSI, 121

Cultural norms, 33–35

Cummings, Jonathan, 138, 264

Curran, S. 107

Curse tablets, 103

Cyberinfrastructures, 2, 6, 21. *See also*
  E-infrastructures

Cloud computing and, 67–71

data webs and, 98–101

development of, 57–61

eDiaMoND project and, 194–198, 200, 203,
  206, 208n11

government initiatives and, 57–61

image ownership issues and, 214–217

long now of, 40–43

Moore's law and, 193–194

Next Generation Cyberinfrastructure Tools
  and, 167

NSF vision of, 192–194

open science and, 299–313

as organizational practices, 41–42

real-world challenges and, 194–195, 198–200

shared, 299

social dimensions of, 41–42

superstars and, 48–50

technology and, 41–42

virtual research environments (VREs) and,
  277–293

Cyberinfrastructure Vision, 59

Cybernetics and Society (Wiener), 41–42

Cyc, 116

Dalle, J.-M., 304

Dasgupta, P., 301

Data

artificial intelligence and, 111–117

behavioral, 230–231

cameras and, 110

captchas and, 110

cookies and, 231

daily amount of, 107

as different from information, 107

digital object identification and, 125–128

digital technology and, 107–117

embedded network sensing and, 120–123

e–social science and, 171–172

ethics and, 223–238

examiners of content and, 111

genomic, 245–248, 265–266

indexing and, 70, 92, 113–117, 317

information-extraction (IE) technology and,
  108

interdisciplinarity and, 261–262

log-file, 142–143

making sense of, 110–111

medical, 245–248, 265–266, 322–324

metadata and, 70, 88–91, 98–103, 111, 122,
  125–128, 132, 187, 307, 313n11

naturally occurring, 185

newspapers and, 108

ontologies and, 72, 88, 100, 115, 122, 131,
  287, 289, 292, 313n11

personal identifying information (PII) and,
  249–251

processing of, 107–117

quantification of, 107–108

radio frequency identity (RFID) tags and, 110

retrieval rates of, 107–108

secondary use and, 246–247

text mining and, 116

Databases, 41–42

Data capture, 230

Data-centric e-research, 88–89

Data deluge, 80, 107, 116–117

blogs and, 110

characteristics of, 108–109

defined, 108–109

discussion forums and, 110

dreams and, 110
e–social science and, 185–186
forces driving, 109–110
libraries and, 89–90
making sense of, 110–111
management technologies for, 111
threats and, 109
transience and, 109
virtual research environments (VREs) and, 284
Data mining, 9–10
Data webs, 79, 98–101
David, Paul A., 14, 162, 254
institutional infrastructures and, 191–211
open science and, 299–316
Davidson, T., 325, 329–330
Davison, A., 234
Dead Sea Scrolls, 102
Defense Advanced Research Projects Agency (DARPA), 114
de la Flor, Grace, 13, 80, 135–152
den Besten, Matthijs, 13–14, 80, 254, 266
digital technologies and, 107–119
open science and, 299–316
privacy and, 230
public sector and, 196
de Roure, David, 5, 9, 13, 20, 72–74, 131
de Solla Price, Derek, 259–260
Developing areas
adaptation in, 334–335
dependency and, 325
development concept and, 325
disparities in, 335–336
e-science and, 329–332, 337
Internet and, 325–340
knowledge production and, 325–326
modernization and, 325
productivity and, 336–337
public computers and, 334
reagency and, 325, 327–330, 339–340
shaping research in, 325–340
study data from, 332–340
teething hypothesis and, 325–326
Digg, 157

Digital choices, 22
access proximity and, 28
ancient documents and, 79
changing cost structures and, 26–28
network architecture restructuring and, 28–29
power redistribution and, 29–30
reconfiguring access and, 25–35
social factors shaping, 31–35
user control over content and, 30–31
Digital Curation Centres, 86
Digital Humanities Quarterly, 257
Digital libraries, 122–123
Digital object identification, 125–128
Digital Replay System, 143
Digital technology
ancient manuscripts and, 102–105
authorship protection and, 218–220
data deluge and, 185–186
data processing and, 107–117
image ownership issues and, 214–217
Moore's Law and, 193–194
potential of, 185
virtual research environments (VREs) and, 277–293, 295–298
Dillon, A., 92
DiMaggio, P., 328–329
Disciplines
academic/commercial collaboration and, 267
common databases and, 265–266
data resources and, 259
emergent paradigms in, 259–260
humanities computing and, 257
infrastructures for, 265 (see also E-infrastructures)
innovation and, 262–263
interdisciplinarity and, 261–262
invisible college and, 259–260
public participation and, 266–267
research institutionalization and, 260–261
research technologies and, 258–259, 264–265
subdisciplinary specialization and, 257–258, 268
use of term, 260

Disciplines (cont.)
 Wikis and, 266
 work organization and, 263–264
Discussion forums, 110
Disease, ix, 9, 100, 194, 266–267, 320, 323
Disinterestedness, 301
Distributed Aircraft Maintenance Environ-
  ment (DAME) project, 57
Distributed computing, 3
Dix, A., 141
Dobkin, David, 250
Donaldson v. Becket, 219
Dovey, Matthew, 254, 295–298
Draper, S., 137
Dretske, F., 107
Droegemeier, K. K., 120, 299
Dubin, D., 126
Duque, Ricardo B., 14–15, 254, 325–342
Dutton, William H., 19
 bottoms-up innovation social sciences and,
   161, 165–184
 e-research concept and, 1–17
 e-research maturity and, 344–346
 ethics and, 223–240
 improving research outcomes and, 346–347
 information quality and, 343–344
 privacy and, 223–240
 reconfiguring research access and, 21–39
Dzorgbo, S., 331

e-BankUK, 307
eBay, 250
Economic and Social Research Council, 169
Economic issues, 14–15
 Central Banks and, 205
 changing cost structures and, 26–28
 commercialization of Internet and, 33–34
 consumption capital and, 49
 data deluge and, 110
 developing conception of, 51–65
 fee-for-service approach and, 200
 funding and, 7, 11 (*see also* Funding)
 gatekeepers and, 29

 global financial crisis and, ix
 innovation and, 9–10
 open access and, 84–88, 111
 resource strategies and, 32–33
 social factors shaping, 32–33
 superstars and, 48–50
e-Content Analysis Tool (e-CAT), 188–189
Edge, D., 178
Edwards, Paul N., 19, 40–44
Egido, C., 279
E-humanities, 5–6. *See also* E–social science
 Building a Virtual Research Environment for
   the Humanities project and, 140–141
 Text Encoding Initiative, 257
 virtual research environments (VREs) and,
   291–292
 Webometrics and, 45–47
e-Infrastructure Reflection Group, 59, 299
E-infrastructures, 2, 161–163
 access proximity and, 28
 effects of digital choices and, 25–35
 capabilities of, 61
 changing cost structures and, 26–28
 data deluge and, 80
 data webs and, 98–101
 description of, 58–61
 development of, 57–61
 disciplines and, 265–267
 eDiaMoND project and, 194–198, 200, 203,
   206, 208n11
 gatekeepers and, 29
 government initiatives and, 10, 57–61
 Grid computing and, 2–3, 52 (*see also* Grid
   computing)
 image ownership issues and, 214–217
 information and knowledge layer and, 60
 institutional infrastructures and, 191–211
 long now of, 40–43
 Moore's law and, 193–194
 multiple actors and, 25–31
 nation-states and, 77–78
 network architecture restructuring and,
   28–29

open science and, 299–313
power redistribution and, 29–30
reconfiguring access to information and,
    21–37
social factors shaping, 31–35
social sciences and, 185–187
spatiality and, 34–35
storage and, 21
user control over content and, 30–31
Electron microscopy, 261
Eliot, T. S., 2, 344
Ellison, N., 157–158
Ellul, Jacques, 1, 343
Email, 5, 117, 166, 185
access and, 29–30
Cloud computing and, 68–69
developing areas and, 335–338, 340n3
libraries and, 83–84, 86
long now and, 42–43
open science and, 305, 309
privacy and, 229–230, 249
social networking and, 157–158
spam and, 110
trusted computing platforms and, 153–154
virtual research environments and, 280
Enabling Grids for E-sciencE (EGEE), 265
End-user programming, 143–145
Engineering
embedded network sensing and, 120–123
e-Science Programme and, 191
Network for Earthquake Engineering and, 262
NSF vision of, 192–194
requirements engineering and, 136–138,
    140–142, 147, 149, 158
Engineering and Physical Sciences Resources
    Council, 307
Enyedy, N., 122
Era of x-ology, 41
E-research, x
agenda-setting role of, 272–275
benefits of, 6–7
changing disciplinary landscapes of, 257–269
citations and, 24

collaborative network organizations and,
    175–176
components of research technologies and,
    258–259
data-centric, 88–89
data deluge and, 107–108 (*see also* Data
    deluge)
defined, 6
designing for usability and, 135–149
developing areas and, 325–340
digital object identification and, 125–128
early stages of maturity and, 344–346
effects of digital choices and, 25–35
embedded network sensing and, 120–123
empowerment and, 73–74
ends and means of, 1, 343–347
ethics and, 223–238, 241–244
fostering, 7–10
foundations of, 12–13
funding and, 7, 11, 24 (*see also* Funding)
future policy for, 64–65
government support and, 10
Grid computing and, 2–4, 9–10 (*see also* Grid
    computing)
growth of, 55–57
herd effect and, 24
ICTs and, 102 (*see also* Information and com-
    munication technologies (ICTs))
implications for, 253–255
improvements in outcomes of, 346–347
increased scale of content and, 72–73
information quality and, 1–2, 343–344 (*see
    also* Information)
institutional strategies and, 75–77, 191–211,
    260–261
interdisciplinarity and, 261–262
intrinsic social nature of, 35–37, 61–62
invisible college and, 259–260
libraries and, 83–94
limits of substitution paradigm and, 234–237
middleware and, 27, 54–56, 59–61, 64–65,
    131, 144, 148, 155, 172, 191, 197, 258, 299–
    300, 304, 308, 310

E-research (cont.)
more efficient sharing and, 73
multidisciplinarity of, 6–9
new environment of, 7–9, 72–74
new skills requirements and, 273–274
ownership issues and, 214–217, 226
participation diversity and, 72–73
politics and, 75–78
reconfiguring access to information and, 21–37
revolution of, xi–xii
risks of, 1–2, 11, 75–78
Semantic Web and, 130–133
shaping developing areas in, 325–340
social context and, 198–200
social networking and, 157–159
standard practices and, 283–293
subdisciplinary specialization and, 257–258, 268
superstars and, 48–50
types of researchers and, 174–175
variety of types of, 196–198
virtual collaborative organizations (VCOs) and, 63–64
virtual research environments (VREs) and, 277–293, 295–298
vision of, 21, 55–57
winner-take-all effect and, 24
E-science, xii, 6–7, 14, 20, 254
data-centric e-research and, 88–89
developing areas and, 329–332, 338
developing e-research conception and, 51–65
embedded network sensing and, 120–123
Enabling Grids for E-sciencE (EGEE) and, 265
formal agreements and, 309–310
global collaboration and, 35
image ownership and, 214–217
importance of global collaboration to, 299–300
information access and, 310–311
institutional infrastructures and, 191–211
invisible college and, 259–260
legal issues and, 35
libraries and, 84
long-distance collaborations and, 139
NSF vision of, 192–194
online survey of, 308–309
as open science, 299–313
OpenScience and, 9
participation diversity and, 72–73
realities of, 194–195
social context and, 198–200
soft infrastructure of, 214
superstar scientists and, 48–50
virtual collaborative organizations (VCOs) and, 63–64
virtual research environments (VREs) and, 277–293, 295–298
visions of, 191–194
Webometrics and, 45–47
e-Science Diagnostic Mammography National Database (eDiaMoND)
authorship protection and, 218
e-research conception and, 62–63
image ownership and, 214–217
open science and, 305–306
public sector and, 194–195, 198, 200, 203, 206, 208n11
e-Science Pilot Programme, 308
e-Science Programme, 2, 6, 55, 272
bottom-up innovation and, 162
broadening of, 192
Core Programme and, 59, 191, 197, 208n3, 308, 310, 313n12
funding for, 192
Grid and, 191
long now and, 43n1
open science and, 304–305
public sector and, 192, 208n8, 209n17
E-social science, 2, 6, 62–63, 161
bottoms-up innovation for, 165–182
certainty trough and, 171
Chinese, 188–190
collaborative network organizations and, 175–176
commercial issues and, 173
community emergence and, 171–172
data deluge and, 185–186

data poor/rich nations and, 27–28
defining, 167–170
distraction and, 177
e-infrastructure for, 185–187
elitism and, 174
empowerment and, 173
free online services and, 189
global divides and, 173, 175–176
Grid computing and, 165–176, 179
high-end approach and, 188
implications for norms in, 172–176
industrialization of, 173–174
key directions for, 179–180
legal issues and, 170
limits of, 179
low-end approach to, 188–190
methodological issues and, 173
National Centre for e-Social Science (NCeSS) and, 169
Next Generation Cyberinfrastructure Tools and, 167
observations of social phenomena and, 176–177
personal computers and, 166
potential of, 179
public participation and, 266–267
quality of, 176–178
research capacity and, 173
risk minimization and, 177–178
Semantic Web and, 132
sustainability and, 171–172
tool diffusion and, 171–172
types of researchers and, 174–175
usability and, 170
winner-takes-all effect and, 177
Espanha, Rita, 14, 254, 317–321
Ess, C., 227, 235
Ethics, 11, 244
  access and, 33–34
  archiving and, 231–233
  behavioral data and, 230–231
  commercialization of Internet and, 33–34
  confidentiality and, 224
  cookies and, 231

cultural norms and, 33–35
data capture and, 230
European Convention on Human Rights and, 225
genomic data and, 245–248
hackers and, 318
informed consent and, 246
key practices and, 227–234
legal issues and, 223–226
limits of substitution paradigm and, 234–237
Milgram experiment and, 234
moral architectures and, 243
new forms of accountability and, 274
new roles for ethicists and, 235
OECD guidelines and, 225
opening up review process and, 237–238
open science and, 306
personal identifying information (PII) and, 249–251
qualitative data collection and, 229–230
quantitative data collection and, 228–229
researcher's perspective and, 235, 237
responsibility and, 242–243
shared values and, 241–242
shifting roles and, 243
spaciality of responsibility and, 242–243
standard issues of, 223–224
standard practices and, 241–242
traditional, 223
virtual experiments and, 233–234
virtue and, 243
Ethnographies, 145–147
European Commission, 245
European Communities Directive, 245–247
European Convention on Human Rights, 225
European Organization for Nuclear Research (CERN), xii, 5, 344
  access and, 21, 33
  changing disciplinary landscapes and, 263, 265
  e-research concept and, 55, 61
  Grid computing and, 61
  information overload and, 89–90
  Large Hadron Collider and, 55, 89–90
Evans, J. A., 24

Facebook, 67, 111, 157, 159
Factoids, 80
Feenberg, A., 279
Feldman, S. I., 120, 192, 199, 299
Fielding, R. T., 99
Finholt, T. A., 138
Fitzgerald, B., 223
Flickr, 111, 157
Flores, Fernando, 137
Foster, Ian, 3, 53–54, 191
Fox, Geoffrey, 3, 52, 144
Fraser, Michael A., 80, 125–129
Freidberg, S., 146
Frey, J., 307
Friedman, B., 3
Fry, Jenny, 13–14, 79
  bottom-up innovation and, 170
  changing disciplinary landscapes of research
    and, 253, 257–271
  libraries and, 83–97
  open science and, 305, 307
Funding, 7, 11, 59–60, 253, 273, 332
  access and, 24, 33
  bottom-up innovation and, 162, 167–169, 178
  changing disciplinary landscapes and, 262,
    265, 269
  China and, 190
  Cloud computing and, 67
  data sharing and, 245
  e-infrastucture and, 185
  libraries and, 84
  long now, 40
  open science and, 299–301, 304, 310
  ownership and, 214, 217n2
  privacy and, 224, 232–233, 238
  public sector and, 192–197, 204–206, 209n17
  superstars and, 50
  usability and, 139, 146–147
  webometrics and, 45

Gaizauskas, R., 114
Galegher, J., 279
Gapminder, 169
Gardin, Jean Claude, 115

Gatekeepers, 29
Gavaghan, D. J., 138, 140
GÉANT, 5
GenBank, 69
Genetic Association Information Network
  (GAIN), 266
Genomics, 245–248, 265–266
Genuth, J., 263
Geographic Virtual Urban Environments
  project, 266–267
GEON, 121
German Grid Initiative (D-Grid), 59
Ghana, 254, 325–327, 330–331, 333, 336
Ghosh, R. A., 304
Ginsparg, P., 87, 91, 122
Globalization
  developing areas and, 325–340
  national strategies and, 76–77
  open science and, 299–300
Global positioning system (GPS), 9, 110, 230
Globus, 53–54, 306
GNU General Public License, 205, 210nn26–
  27, 306, 310
Goble, C., 74
Goddard, J., 34
Gold, A., 88
Goldin, Ian, ix–x
Goodwin, C., 138
Goodwin, M. H., 138
Google, 28, 46
  e-Cat and, 189
  hyperlink algorithms and, 113
  open-access and, 226
  privacy and, 250
Google Books, 226
Google Earth, 89
Google Friend Connect, 159
Google Generation, 93–94
Google Maps, 89
Google Scholar, 94
Gorman, M., 92
Government
  basic objectives of, 77–78
  e-infrastructure initiatives and, 57–61

institutional strategies and, 76–77
Webometrics and, 45–47
Grain and Feed Transport Association
  (GAFTA), 211n31
Graubard, S., 274
Gray, J., 70, 136
Graziadio, B., 115
Green, 136, 146
Grid computing, 2–4, 9–10, 13, 19
  BROADEN project and, 57
  China and, 188
  Collaborative Stereoscopic Access Grid Envi-
    ronment (CSAGE) and, 291–292
  commercial off-the-shelf (COTS) software
    and, 198
  DAME project and, 57
  decreased effects of distance and, 53
  deployment of, 54–55
  development of, 54–55
  effective resource use and, 53
  Enabling Grids for E-sciencE (EGEE) and, 265
  ends and means of, 345
  e-Science Programme and, 191
  e-social science and, 165–176, 179
  ethics and, 228
  Globus Toolkit and, 53–54
  image ownership issues and, 214–217
  importance of, 52–53
  industrialization and, 173–174
  institutional infrastructures and, 191–194,
    197–198
  I-WAY project and, 52–53
  Large Hadron Collider Computing Grid and,
    55
  middleware and, 54, 56, 61
  MixedMediaGrid and, 305–306
  Moore's law and, 193–194
  National Grid Service and, 55, 58
  OGSA standards and, 54
  OGSI and, 57
  open science and, 299–300, 304–307, 312
  open standards and, 53
  reconfiguring access of information and, 21–
    23, 26–28, 33

  resource sharing and, 53
  secure access and, 53
  security and, 154–155
  Semantic Web and, 55, 131–132
  subdisciplinary specialization and, 257–258,
    268
  superstars and, 50
  TeraGrid and, 55
  trusted platform module (TPM) and, 154–155
  various countries' approach to, 59
  virtual research environments (VREs) and,
    254, 291–292, 296–298
Gross, Maurice, 115
Grudin, J., 136
Gutenberg Project, 317

Hacker ethic, 318
Hahn, K. L., 85
Halfpenny, P., 169, 171
Hall, Wendy, 13, 80, 130–133
Halliwell, J. E., 332
Hamelink, C., 328–329
Hannerz, U., 146
Hansen, K. M., 142
Hargittai, E., 328–329
Harper, R., 138–139
Harries, G., 86
Hart, Michael, 317
Hartswood, M., 135, 218, 305
Harvard, 35, 84–87, 90
Heath, C. C., 137–138, 140, 149, 279
Hendler, J. A., 98, 131
Herculaneum, 102
Herd effect, 24
Hewlett Packard, 138
Hey, Antony, 3, 20, 172, 299
  Cloud computing and, 67–71
  data processing and, 107
  embedded network sensing and, 120
  e-research concept and, 51–52, 65
  libraries and, 88
  public sector and, 191
  usability and, 135
Hill, D. I., 332

Himanen, Pekka, 318
Hindman, M., 48
Hindmarsh, M., 279
Hinds, C., 306
Hine, Christine, 11, 22–23, 146, 272
History of Political Discourse 1500–1800
　project, 284–285
Hocks-Yu, H., 126
Holt, Robert, 173
Home brew computers, 34
Hubble telescope, 7
Hudson-Smith, A., 266–267
Hughes, J., 137
Human-computer interactions, 136
Human Genome Project, 318
Human Genome Sequencing Consortium,
　245
Humanities. *See* E-humanities
Huntington, P., 85
Hursthouse, M. B., 307
Hutchison, A., 127
Hyperlinks, 46–48, 113
Hypertext, 317

IBM, 113, 194, 250
Images, 98–101, 105
　digital object identification and, 125–128
　e-DiaMoND and, 62–63, 194–195, 198, 200,
　　203, 206, 208n11, 214–216, 217n2, 218,
　　305–306
　Flickr and, 111
　improving ICT access to, 103
　interpretation of, 110
　medical, 104
　multispectral imaging and, 102
　ownership issues and, 214–217
　Riya and, 111
　usability and, 140–141
Indexing, 70, 92, 113–117, 317
India, 254, 325–327, 330–331, 336, 338
Industrial Revolution, 174
Inference, 115–116
Informal communications, 86

Information
　access and, 21–27, 310–311 (*see also* Access)
　ancient manuscripts and, 79, 102–105,
　　140–141
　artificial intelligence and, 111–117
　authorship protection and, 218–220
　blogs and, 21, 26, 29, 68, 70, 73, 83, 86, 110,
　　157, 185, 188, 289–290
　community intelligence and, 73–74
　data as different from, 107
　data rich/poor nations and, 27–28, 32–33
　data webs and, 98–101
　developing areas and, 325–340
　digital authorship and, 218–220
　disclosure and, 304
　e-Cat and, 188–189
　ethics and, 223–238
　examiners of content and, 111–116
　factoids and, 80
　gatekeepers and, 29
　hyperlink algorithms and, 113
　informed consent and, 224
　institutional infrastructures and, 191–211
　interdisciplinarity and, 261–262
　invisible college and, 259–260
　language models and, 113
　libraries and, 83–94
　linguistics and, 42
　machine translation (MT) and, 112–117
　medical, 245–248, 265–266, 322–324
　natural-language processing (NLP) and,
　　112–117
　ontologies and, 72, 88, 100, 115, 122, 131,
　　287, 289, 292, 313n11
　overload of, 80, 89–90, 185–186 (*see also*
　　Data deluge)
　ownership issues and, 214–217 (*see also* Intel-
　　lectual property rights (IPRs))
　personal identifying information (PII) and,
　　249–251
　quality of, 1–2, 176, 343–344
　question-answering (QA) and, 113
　reagency and, 325, 327–330, 339–340

relevance feed back and, 113
searches and, 111–116
Semantic Web and, 130–133
social factors shaping, 31–35
superstar scientists and, 48–50
templates and, 113–116
text mining and, 116
user control over content and, 30–31
Webometrics and, 45–47
Wikipedia and, 111
Information and communication technologies
   (ICTs), 13–14, 19–20, 161, 253–255
access proximity and, 28
analysis and, 25
ancient manuscripts and, 102–105
behavioral data and, 230–231
bottoms-up innovation for social science
   and, 165–182
broader user bases and, 7, 9
changing cost structures and, 26–28
Cloud computing and, 67–71 (*see also* Cloud
   computing)
cookies and, 231
dependency and, 325
designing for usability and, 135–149
developing areas and, 325–340
digital choices and, 25–35
distribution and, 25
effects of digital choices and, 25–35
embedded network sensing and, 120
ends and means of, 343–347
experience technologies and, 171
expertise and, 24
gatekeepers and, 29
Grid computing and, 2–4, 9–10 (*see also* Grid
   computing)
home brew computers and, 34
improving access to document images and,
   103
institutional strategies and, 75–77
Internet and, 5
intrinsic social nature of, 35–37
modernization and, 325

multiple actors and, 25–31
network architecture restructuring and, 28–29
new perspective on impacts of, 23–24
observation and, 24
power redistribution and, 29–30
public funding and, 192
RCNs and, 2–6 (*see also* Research-centered
   computational networks (RCNs))
reconfiguring access to information and,
   21–37
shaping research in developing areas and,
   325–340
significance of, 1–2
spatial issues and, 34–35
teething hypothesis and, 325–326
usability and, 80–81
user control over content and, 30–31
virtual research environments (VREs) and,
   277–293, 295–298
workflow and, 10
World Wide Web and, 5
Information-extraction (IE) technology, 108,
   113–116
Information layer, 60
Information retrieval (IR), 111–117
Information revolution, 40
Information society, 304
Informed consent, 224, 246
Infrared spectrum, 102
In-links, 48
Innis, H., 28
Innovation, 56. *See also* Technology
bottoms-up, 165–182
broader user bases and, 7, 9
creating virtuous cycle of, 2–4
disciplines and, 262–263
economic issues and, 9–10
ends and means of, 343–347
e–social science and, 165–182
fostering, 7–10
implications of, 9–10
institutionalization and, 260–261
market competition and, 77

In silico experimentation, 132, 140
In situ sensing, 121–122
Institute for Prospective Technological Stud-
    ies, 46
Institutional infrastructures, 161
  challenge of designing, 195–200
  commercial off-the-shelf (COTS) software
    and, 198
  contracts and, 205–206
  divergent goals and, 200–202
  eDiaMoND project and, 194–198, 200, 203,
    206, 208n11
  enforcement issues and, 206–207
  e-science and, 191–211
  e-Science Diagnostic Mammography Na-
    tional Database (eDiaMoND) and, 194,
    208n11
  fee-for-service approach and, 200
  flexibility and, 202–203
  formal arrangements and, 205–206
  funding of, 197
  GNU General Public License and, 205,
    210n27
  Grid computing and, 191–194, 197–198
  incentives for, 200–202
  independent research collaboration service
    for, 204–207
  legal issues and, 194–195, 204–205, 209n18
  multiple actor issues and, 200–202
  NSF vision of, 192–194
  possible methodology for, 203–207
  project specificity and, 202–203
  research collaboration service and, 204–207
  social context and, 198–200
  softer parts of, 195–200
  universality and, 202–203
  varieties of e-research projects and, 196–198
  virtual laboratories and, 191
Institutions
  codes for, 35
  competitive advantage and, 76–77
  digital object identification and, 125–128
  disciplines and, 260–261

  ethics and, 237
  market competition and, 77
  nationality of, 76
  open science and, 299–313
  regulations and, 35
  strategies for, 75–77
Integrating Web Information Using the Se-
    mantic Web (IUGO), 288–289
Integrative Biology Virtual Research Environ-
    ment project, 140
Integrative Biology VRE, 290–291
Intel, 138
Intellectual pluralism, 261
Intellectual property rights (IPRs)
  archiving/reuse issues and, 89
  copyright and, 35 (see also Copyright)
  digital authorship and, 218–220
  disintermediation of scholarship process and,
    87–88
  Donaldson v. Beckett and, 219
  e-research concept and, 24, 34–35
  globalization and, 76–77
  image ownership issues and, 214–217
  institutional strategies and, 76–77
  legal issues and, 35
  libraries and, 79, 83–94
  open access and, 84–88, 299–300, 302, 304,
    309
  ownership and, 215–217, 304
  privacy and, 24, 34–35, 215–217, 304
Interdisciplinarity, 261–262
International HapMap Project, 245
International Standards Organization (ISO),
    136
International Virtual Observatory Alliance
    (IVOA), 265–266
Internet, 322
  ARPANET and, 5
  blogs and, 21, 26, 29, 68, 70, 73, 83, 86, 110,
    157, 185, 188, 289–290
  Cloud computing and, 13 (see also Cloud
    computing)
  commercialization of, 33–34

developing areas and, 325–340
development of, 5
e–social science and, 167–170
free online services and, 189
Grid computing and, 2–3, 28 (*see also* Grid computing)
knowledge production and, 328–330
modernization and, 325
reagency and, 325, 327–330, 339–340
research revolution of, xi–xii
retrieval rates of, 107–108
security and, 153–156 (*see also* Security)
trusted computing platforms and, 153–156
Webometrics and, 45–47
Internet of Things (ITU), 128
Invisible college, 259–260
I-WAY project, 52–53
Iyer, S. R., 330

Jackson, Steven J., 19, 40–44
Jackson Laboratories, 323
Jamali, H. R., 85
James Martin 21st Century School, ix
Japan, 32, 332
Jeffreys, Paul W.
  developing conception of e-research and, 51–66
  e-research concept and, 1–17
  e-research maturity and, 344–346
  improving research outcomes and, 346–347
  information quality and, 343–344
Jelinek, Frederick, 113
Jirotka, Marina
  authorship and, 218–210
  e-research concept and, 13–14, 62
  open science and, 305–306
  usability and, 80, 135–152
  virtual research environments (VREs) and, 253–254, 277–294
Joerges, Bernward, 258, 264
John, B. E., 136
Johnson, J., 48
Joint Information Systems Committee, 107

Jones, Anita, 250
Jones, B. F., 88
Journal of Visualized Experiments, 238

Kahn, R., 125
Kao, A., 116
Karayannis, F., 299–300
Katz, J. S., 139
Kaye, Jane, 245–248
Kenya, 254, 325–327, 330–331, 333, 337, 340n7
Kertcher, Z., 171
Kesselman, Carl, 3, 53–54, 191
Kiesler, Sara, 138, 264
King, V., 137
Klein, Judy, 260
Klein, Julie, 269
Knobel, Cory, 19, 40–44
Knoblauch, H., 140
Knorr-Cetina, Karin, 263, 267
Koegemeier, K. K., 192
Krauskopf, M., 332
Kraut, R., 279
Kuzuoka, H., 138

Lacunose manuscripts, 102
Lafferty, J., 113
Lagoze, C., 125
Landscape sampling, 281–282
Lane, Julia, 163, 171, 249–252
Langford, J., 110
Language models, 113
Large Hadron Collider (LHC), 89–90
Lasilla, O., 98
Leenaars, M., 299–300
Legal issues, 11, 165
  anonymity and, 224
  authorship protection and, 218–220
  copyright and, 35, 101, 105, 162, 205–206, 210n27, 215, 218–220, 304, 317, 323
  data-protection laws and, 225
  Donaldson v. Beckett and, 219
  e-social science and, 170

Legal issues (cont.)
  ethics and, 223–238
  European Communities Directive and,
    245–247
  genomic data sharing and, 245–248
  GNU General Public License and, 205,
    210n27
  image ownership issues and, 214–217
  informal law and, 225–226
  informed consent and, 224, 246
  institutional infrastructures and, 194–195,
    204–205, 209n18
  OECD guidelines and, 225
  ownership, 214–217, 226
  personal identifying information (PII) and,
    249–251
  privacy and, 223–226
  public policy and, 35
  secondary use and, 246–247
  Stanley v. Georgia, 225
Leibniz/Clarke exchange, 42
Lele, S. R., 122
Lenat, D., 116
Lessig, Lawrence, 218
Li, Xiaoming, 13, 161, 188–190
Libraries, 79, 344
  academic research, 84–87
  archiving/reuse and, 89
  core purposes of, 93
  data-centric e-research and, 88–89
  digital object identification and, 125–128
  digital preservation and, 83–84
  disintermediation of scholarship and, 87–88
  embedded network sensing and, 122–123
  e-research policies for, 92–94
  e-science and, 84
  future roles for, 93–94
  informal communications and, 86
  information overload and, 89–90
  long-term curation strategies and, 90–92
  new emerging roles for, 83–84
  open access and, 84–87
  as publishers, 85–88

Licklider, Joseph, 51, 62
Lieberman, Henry, 143
Lin, Y., 169, 171
Linguistics, 113–116
Link counts, 36–37
Linux, 318
Lipton, Richard, 250
Little science, 122
Liverpool Cotton Association, 211n31
Lloyd, Sharon, 13, 80, 135–152
Lloyds Register, 108
Log-file data, 142–143
Lone researchers, 175
Long Now Foundation, 40
Long Term Ecological Reserve System, 121
Luff, P., 137–140, 149, 279
Lynch, Clifford, 89, 91–92

Machado, J., 319
Machine translation (MT), 112–117
MacKenzie, Donald, 171, 279
MacPherson, S., 330
Madsen, Christine, 13, 79, 83–97
Making Tea approach, 142
MapTube, 267
Marcus, G., 145
Martin, Andrew, 81, 139, 153–156
Marx, L., 343–344
Mash-ups, 110
Mateos-Garcia, J., 111
Mauldin, Michael, 115
Mauthner, N. S., 229
May, J., 136
Mayernik, M. S., 90, 122–123
Mbatia, P., 329–330, 334
Medical data, 245–248, 265–266, 322–324
Medical Research Council, 245
Meeting Memory Technology Informing Col-
  laboration (MeMeTIC), 288
Mendonça, Sandro, 14, 254, 317–321
Menturp, A., 47
Merton, Robert, 301–302
Mesch, G., 48, 177

Metadata, 187, 307, 313n11
ancient manuscripts and, 103
Cloud computing and, 70
data processing and, 111
digital object identification and, 125–128
embedded network sensing and, 122
image repositories and, 98–101
libraries and, 88–91
Semantic Web and, 132
Metasearch, 188–189
Meyer, Eric T., 13, 79, 161
bottom-up innovation social sciences and, 165–184
changing disciplinary landscapes and, 266
libraries and, 83–97
Microsoft, 28, 46, 91, 138, 250, 296
Middleware, 27, 258
bottom-up innovation and, 172
e-research concept and, 54–56, 59–61, 64–65
Open Middleware Infrastructure Institute (OMI) and, 299
open science and, 299–300, 304, 308, 310
public sector and, 191, 197
Semantic Web and, 131
trusted computing platforms and, 155
usability and, 144, 148
Milgram, Stanley, 234
Milton, R., 267
Mirada Solutions, 194
Mitchell, R., 84, 87
MixedMediaGrid (MiMeg), 305–306
Mobile devices, 153
Moore's law, 193–194
Moran, T., 136
Moriarty, S., 286
Mullin, J., 332
Multidisciplinarity, 6–9
Multisited ethnography, 145–147
Multispectral imaging, 102
myExperiment, 144, 290
myGrid project, 132
MySpace, 157

Nardi, B., 139
National Aeronautics and Space Administration (NASA), 55
National Centre for e-Social Science (NCeSS), 132, 169, 187
National Crystallographic Service, 307
National e-Science Centre (NeSC), 309
National Grid Service, 55
National High-tech R&D Programme, 59
National Institutes of Health (NIH), 35, 84, 245
National Science Foundation (NSF), 55, 59, 61
Atkins Committee and, 299
developing areas and, 327
Directorate for Social, Behavioral, and Economics Sciences program and, 167
Directorate of Computer and Information System Engineering and, 192
e-social science and, 167
interdisciplinarity and, 262
Network for Earthquake Engineering and, 262
Next Generation Cyberinfrastructure Tools and, 167
NSFNET and, 5
TeraBridge Project, 262
Trustworthy Computing initiative and, 250
virtual organizations and, 193
Workshop on Cyberinfrastructure and the Social Sciences and, 62
Natural-language processing (NLP), 112–117
Nelson, Ted, 317, 318
Nentwich, M., 22
Neuman, W. R., 328–329
Neurocommons, 9, 322–324
Newell, A., 136
New e-research, 72–74
Newspapers, 108, 114
Next Generation Cyberinfrastructure Tools, 167
Nicholas, D., 85
Nichols, D., 140
Nielsen, J., 137
Norman, D. A., 137

Obbink, D., 102
O'Brien, J., 140
Observatory networks, 121
O'Hara, Kieron, 13, 80, 130–133
Olson, G. M., 22–23, 135, 167, 179, 258, 261, 279, 282, 329
Olson, J., 135, 258, 261, 279, 289, 329
Ontologies
  data processing and, 115–116
  embedded network sensing and, 122
  image repositories and, 100
  libraries and, 88
  new e-research and, 72
  open science and, 313n11
  Semantic Web and, 131
  virtual research environments and, 287, 289, 292
Open access, 14
  developments in, 318–319
  future directions and, 319–320
  Gutenberg Project and, 317
  hackers and, 318
  hypertext and, 317
  key strategies and, 318
  libraries and, 84–88
  neurocommons and, 322–324
  open viewing and, 322–324
  ownership issues and, 214–217, 226
  politics of, 317–320
  Semantic Web and, 323
  three historical phases of, 317–318
Open Access Now, 317
Open Archives Initiative Protocol for Metadata Harvesting, 98
Open Grid Services Architecture (OGSA), 54
Open Grid Services Infrastructure (OGSI), 57
Open Middleware Infrastructure Institute (OMI), 299, 310
Open Science, 9, 29. *See also* E-science
  abuse of trust and, 306
  Atkins Committee and, 299
  bottom-up networks and, 300
  closed clubs and, 300

CombeChem and, 306–307
communalism and, 301
contingency and, 307–308
contract terms and, 308–311
degress of openness and, 303
disinterestedness and, 301
e-DiaMoND and, 305–306
empirical evidence for, 303–305
epistemological perspective on, 302
ethics and, 306
formal agreements and, 309–310
Grid computing and, 299–300, 304–307, 312
image sharing and, 305–306
importance of global collaboration and, 299–300
incentive compatibility and, 301
information disclosure and, 304
intellectual property rights (IPRs) and, 299–300, 302, 304
MiMeG and, 306
norms of, 301–303
originality and, 301
rapid disclosures and, 302
research practices and, 303, 310–311
Semantic Web and, 304
skepticism and, 301
specific experiences in, 305–307
universalism and, 301
Open source software, 111, 205, 210nn26–27, 306, 310
Open viewing, 14, 322–324
Organization for Economic Cooperation and Development (OECD), 225
Originality, 301
Ortellado, P., 319
Ownership issues, 214–217, 226
Oxford, 11, 194, 207

Page, Larry, 113
Palaeography, 102–105
Palimpsests, 103
Pan, X., 103
Paperless office, 34

Papyri, 102–105
Parallel computing, 51–52
Parastatidis, Savas, 20, 65, 67–71
Parayil, G., 330
Park, H. W., 176
Parker, Michael, 162–163, 241–244
Parry, O., 229
Passports, 264–265
Passwords, 110
Pasteur, Louis, 84
Paternó, F., 143
Payette, S., 125
Payne, S., 136
Perseus Digital Library, 92
Personal identifying information (PII), 249–251
Philippines, 254, 325, 327, 330–333, 336
Pictures. *See* Images
Pierce, M., 144
Pietrosanti, E., 115
Pila, Justine, 14, 218–221
Piper, Tina, 13–14, 63, 162
  ethics and, 214–217, 223–240
  image ownership and, 214–217
  privacy and, 223–240
Pitt-Francis, J., 145
Plowman, L., 138
Policy, xi, 20
  Data Protection Act and, 225
  digital object identification and, 125–128
  e–social science and, 170 (*see also* E–social science)
  ethics and, 223–238
  future, 64–65
  institutional and, 76–77, 191–211
  legal issues and, 35
  open science and, 307–311
Politics, 77–78
  ethics and, 223–238
  global financial crisis and, ix
  institutional identity and, 75–76
  privacy and, 223–238
Porter, T. M., 42

Poteet, S. R., 116
Power, 73–74
  access control and, 21–37
  e–social science and, 173
  multiple actors and, 25–31
  parallel computing and, 51–52
  redistribution of, 29–30
Power laws, 48
Prakash, M., 116
Preece, A., 131
Price, D. J. D. S., 122
Principal investigators (PIs), 305, 308–310, 313n13
Privacy, 24, 35, 75, 202
  anonymity and, 224
  archiving and, 231–233
  behavioral data and, 230–231
  bottom-up innovation and, 161–162, 173
  captchas and, 110
  commercialization of Internet and, 33–34
  confidentiality and, 224
  controls for, 225–226
  cookies and, 231
  cryptography and, 154–155
  data capture and, 230
  data-protection laws and, 225
  e-research concept and, 4, 7, 11, 14, 70
  ethics and, 223–238
  gatekeepers and, 29
  genomic data and, 245–248
  informed consent and, 224, 246
  intellectual property rights (IPRs) and, 24, 34–35, 215–217, 304
  legal issues and, 35
  long now and, 42
  OECD guidelines and, 225
  passwords and, 110
  personal identifying information (PII) and, 249–251
  power redistribution and, 29–30
  protecting confidentiality and, 249–251
  qualitative data collection and, 229–230
  quantitative data collection and, 228–229

Privacy (cont.)
Semantic Web and, 132
social networking and, 159
Stanley v. Georgia, 225
statistics and, 250–251
telephones and, 29–30
trusted computing platforms and, 153–156
Trustworthy Computing initiative and, 250
usability and, 140
U.S. Constitution, 225
virtual experiments and, 233–234
Privacy, Obligations, and Rights in Technologies of Information Assessment project, 250
Procter, Rob, 13, 62
authorship and, 218
bottom-up innovation and, 167, 169, 171
e-infrastructures and, 185–187
open science and, 305
Semantic Web and, 132–133
usability and, 135, 140
Protein Data Bank, 262
Provenance, 126–127
Psychology, 234
Publishers, 85–88, 218–220
PubMed, 69, 84, 87, 322
Pynchon, Thomas, 266
Pynchon Wiki, 266, 267

Quals, 175
Quants, 175
Question-answering (QA), 113–114

Radio frequency identity (RFID) tags, 110, 127
Rahman, M., 306
Ramage, M., 138
Randall, D., 138–139
Reagency, 325, 327–330, 339–340
Real-time Observatories, Applications, and Data Management Network, 121
Reid, R. H., 33
Relevance feedback, 113
Renear, A., 126

Requirements engineering, 136–138, 140–142, 147, 149, 158
Research. *See also* E-research
agendas and, 272–275
broader implications for, 14–15
digital network dangers and, ix–x
ethics and, 223–238
ICTs and, 1 (*see also* Information and communication technologies (ICTs))
information quality and, 1–2
new environments for, 7–9
ownership issues and, 214–217, 226
revolution in, xi–xii
social change and, 4
technical change and, 4
types of computational networks for, 4–6
Research-centered computational networks (RCNs)
benefits of, 6–7
digital choices and, 25–35
e-research concept and, 2–6, 11, 13, 15
parallel computing and, 51–52
reconfiguring access to information and, 21–37
risks of, 11
scope of, 21
social factors shaping, 31–35
user control and, 30–31
Research collaboration service, 204–207
Resource Description Framework (RDF), 98–100, 130, 323
Reusability, 126
Richardson, R., 34
Risk. *See also* Security
e-social science and, 177–178
social networking and, 159
trusted computing platforms and, 153–155
Riya, 111
ROADNet, 121
Robinson, S. A., 47
Robotics, 120
Rock, The (Eliot), 2
Rodden, T., 62, 137, 140
Rogers, E. M., 328–329

Rogers, Y., 138
Rosen, Sherwin, 48–49
Rouncefield, M., 138–139

Sabel, Charles, 174
Salton, Gerald, 113
Sassen, Saskia, 329
Sawyer, S., 27
Schmidt, K., 135
Schott, Thomas, 328–329
Schraefel, M. C., 141
Schröder, P., 304
Schroeder, Ralph
  access and, 21
  bottom-up innovation and, 170, 176–177
  changing disciplinary landscapes of research
    and, 253–254, 257–271
  e-research concept and, 14, 62
  open science and, 299–316
  superstars and, 48
Schwartz, R. D., 234
Science Commons, 319–320, 323
Scott, S. V., 173
Secondary-use-exemption, 246–247
Second Life environment, 230, 233
Security. *See also* Privacy
  authentication and, 53, 61, 126, 187, 231
  commercialization of Internet and, 33–34
  cryptography and, 154–155
  digital authorship and, 218–220
  ethics and, 223–238
  image ownership and, 214–217
  mobile devices and, 153
  trojans and, 153
  trusted computing platforms and, 153–156
  viruses and, 153–155
  vulnerability of Internet and, 153–154
Seismology, 121
Sellen, A. J., 149
Semantic Grid, 131–132
Semantic Web, 55, 80, 258, 347
  basic technologies of, 130–131
  building on, 132–133
  data deluge and, 110

image repositories and, 98
information retrieval and, 112
Integrating Web Information Using the Se-
  mantic Web (IUGO) and, 288–289
open access and, 323
open science and, 304
research value of, 131–132
Serres, Michel, 41
SETI@home, 155
Shackel, B., 136
Shadbolt, Nigel, 13, 80, 130–133
Shepherd, A., 116, 171
Shin, E., 125
Shinn, Terry, 258, 264
Shotton, David, 13, 79, 98–101
Shrum, Wesley, 14–15, 254, 263, 325–342
Signal processing, 120
Silchester Roman town, 286–287
Simple Protocol and RDF Query Language
  (SPARQL), 100, 101n5, 131
Simpson, A., 135
Singapore, 332
Situated evaluation studies, 142–143
Skepticism, 301
Slater, M., 234
Smith, K., 92, 234
Social, behavioral, and economic (SBE) sci-
  ences, 62
Social issues, 13–14
  access control and, 21–37
  effects of digital choices and, 25–35
  change in research and, 4
  cultural norms and, 33–35
  data rich/poor nations and, 27–28, 32–33
  developing areas and, 325–340
  developing e-research conception and,
    51–65
  digital choices and, 25–35
  ethics and, 223–238
  Grid computing and, 2–3, 9–10 (*see also* Grid
    computing)
  Hubble telescope and, 5
  ICTs and, 1–2 (*see also* Information and com-
    munication technologies (ICTs))

Social issues (cont.)
informed consent and, 224
innovation and, 9–10 (*see also* Innovation)
institutional infrastructures and, 191–211
privacy and, 223–238 (*see also* Privacy)
superstar scientists and, 48–50
virtual collaborative organizations (VCOs)
and, 63–64
virtual research environments (VREs) and,
277–293
Webometrics and, 45–47
Social networking
Cloud computing and, 67–68
profile pages and, 157
rise of, 1157–159
risks of, 159
Social norms, 33–34
Social Science Computer Review journal, 166
Software plus services, 69
Soguo, 189
Sonnenwald, Diane, 264
Sooryamoorthy, R., 325, 329–330
South Korea, 332
Spammers, 110
Spärck Jones, Karen, 112
Spatiality
access and, 34–350
responsibility and, 242–243
virtue and, 243
Webometrics and, 45–47
Specificity, 202–203
Spence, Michael, 14, 162, 191–211, 300
SPSS, 166
Stanford University, 303
Stanley v. Georgia, 225
Star, Susan Leigh, 287, 293
State-istics, 42
Statistics, 40, 45–47
Stehr, N., 328
Steinmueller, W. E., 111
Sterling, Bruce, 127
Stonecutters, 103
Storage Resource Broker, 53
Suber, Peter, 317, 319

Subject-predicate-object form, 130
Substitution paradigm, 234–237
Suchman, Lucy, 137–138
Superstar scientists, 48–50
Swales, J. M., 259
SwissbioGrid project, 267
Szalay, A., 70

Tagging, 110, 127
Taiwan, 332
Taper, M. L., 122
Task action grammars, 136
Taylor, John, 13, 20, 75–78, 135, 191
Taylor, Robert, 51, 62
Team players, 175
Technology, 158
ancient manuscripts and, 79, 102–105,
140–141
ARPANET and, 5
artificial intelligence (AI) and, 111–113
change in research and, 4
Cloud computing and, 67–71 (*see also* Cloud
computing)
competitive advantage and, 76–77
constraints and, 33
data management, 111
designing for usability and, 135–149
developing areas and, 325–340
digital, 15, 102–105, 107–117, 185–186, 193–
194, 214–220, 277–293, 295–298
digital object identification and, 125–128
disciplines and, 257–269
effects of digital choices and, 25–35
Ellul's warning on, 1
embedded network sensing and, 120–123
enablers and, 33
ends and means of, 343–347
global positioning systems (GPS) and, 9, 110,
230
Grid computing and, 2–3, 52 (*see also* Grid
computing)
home brew computers and, 34
Hubble telescope and, 7
human-computer interactions and, 136

ICTs and, xii (*see also* Information and communication technologies (ICTs))
institutional infrastructures and, 191–211
institutional strategies and, 76–77
Internet and, 5 (*see also* Internet)
inward transfer and, 76–77
Moore's law and, 193–194
multispectral imaging and, 102
natural-language processing (NLP) and, 112–113
parallel computing and, 51–52
radio frequency identity (RFID) tags and, 110
reconfiguring access to information and, 21–37
requirements engineering and, 136–142, 147, 149, 158
research-centered computation networks (RCNs) and, 2–4
research revolution and, xi–xii
Semantic Web and, 130–133
virtual research environments (VREs) and, 277–293, 295–298
wireless sensing, 120–123
World Wide Web and, 5 (*see also* World Wide Web)
Teething hypothesis, 325–326
Telephones, 29–30
Templates, 113–116, 204, 265
TeraBridge Project, 262
TeraGrid, 55
Terras, M., 103–104
Terrorism, 109
Text Encoding Initiative, 257
Texting, 34
Text mining, 116
Thelwall, Michael, 12–13, 19
libraries and, 81, 86
social networking and, 157–159
Webometrics and, 45–47
Thompson Scientific database, 45
Tomlin, R. S. O., 103, 285
Torvalds, Linus, 318
Toward a National Collaboratory (National Research Council), 278

Translation models, 113
Trefethen, A. E., 51, 88, 107, 120, 135, 172, 191
Trigg, R. H., 137
Triples, 130
Trojans, 153
Trowler, Paul, 261, 263, 269
Trusted computing platforms, 153–156
Trusted platform module (TPM), 154–155
Tsioutsiouliklis, K., 48
Tuecke, Steve, 53
Tufekci, Z., 157
Tufte, Edward, 31
Turner, John, 173
Twittering, 84, 94n1

Uhlir, P., 304
Uimonen, P., 329
U.K. Department of Trade and Industry, 194
U.K. Engineering and Physical Sciences Research Council, 194
U.K. Information Commissioner's Office, 225
U.K. Joint Information Systems Committee, 279
U.K. Medical Research Ethics Committee, 195
U.K. Office of Science and Innovation, 56, 58, 64, 192
U.K. Research Councils, 85, 207, 343
Uniform resource identifiers (URIs), 130–131
United Kingdom
BROADEN project and, 57
Cloud computing and, 67
Data Protection Act and, 225
Donaldson v. Beckett and, 219
e-infrastructure and, 2
e-Science Diagnostic Mammography National Database (eDiaMoND) and, 62–63, 194–198, 200, 203, 206, 208n11, 214–216, 217n2, 218, 305–306
e-Science Programme and, 2, 6, 43n1, 55, 59, 162, 191–192, 197, 208n3, 208n8, 209n17, 272, 304–305, 308–310, 313n12
National Centre for e-Social Science (NCeSS) and, 169, 187

United Kingdom (cont.)
 National Grid Service and, 55, 58
 open access and, 84–85
 open science and, 300–305
 Roman era of, 103
 Technology Programme and, 57
 Virtual Workspace for the Study of Ancient
  Documents and, 103
United States, 32
 Atkins Committee and, 299
 Cloud computing and, 67
 cyberinfrastructure and, 2 (*see also*
  Cyberinfrastructure)
 institutional infrastructures and, 197
 libraries and, 84
 Next Generation Cyberinfrastructure Tools
  and, 167
 open access and, 84–85
 Stanley v. Georgia, 225
 virtual research laboratories and, 7
Universalism, 301
Unix, 298
Usability
 agile methods and, 144–145
 approaches to, 137
 cognitive models and, 136
 components of research technologies and,
  258–259
 computer-supported cooperative work
  (CSCW) and, 136–138, 149
 defined, 135
 Digital Replay System and, 143
 end-user development and, 143–145
 e–social science and, 170
 ethnographies and, 138, 145–147
 fieldwork and, 139–141
 future policy for, 147–149
 human-computer interaction and, 136
 institutional infrastructures and, 191–207
 International Standards Organization (ISO)
  and, 136
 large-scale distributed project management
  and, 135

 Making Tea approach and, 142
 multiple user requirements and, 139, 141
 myExperiment and, 144
 network-enabled research and, 139–147
 reconceptualizing, 136–139
 requirements engineering and, 136–142, 147,
  149, 158
 situated evaluation studies and, 142–143
 situated workplace studies and, 137–138
 small-group interactions and, 138
 task action grammars and, 136
 virtual research environments (VREs) and,
  296
U.S. Constitution, 225
U.S. Department of Defense, 5, 7, 9
U.S. Department of Energy, 55
Usenet, 318
User-modeling approach, 137
U.S. National Library of Medicine, 322–323
U.S. National Research Council, 278
U.S. National Science Board, 278
Uzzi, B., 88

Van House, Nancy, 122, 218–220
van Rijsbergen, K., 114
Vaver, David, 63, 14, 214–217
Vellum, 102
Venters, W., 173
Vera, M. I., 332
Virtual collaborative organizations (VCOs),
  63–64, 277
Virtual experiments, 233–234
Virtual learning environments (VLEs), 295, 297
Virtual research environments (VREs), 7, 14,
  58, 61, 64, 253–254
 adaptability and, 296–297
 Cloud computing and, 298
 collaboration-technology relationship and,
  281
 Collaborative Research Events on the Web
  (CREW) project and, 288
 Collaborative Stereoscopic Access Grid Envi-
  ronment (CSAGE) and, 291–292

collaboratories and, 277–284, 292–293
commercial network servers for, 296
context of, 277
data deluge and, 284
defining scholarly work and, 284–286
definitions for, 277–279
e-humanities and, 291–292
future of, 295–298
Grid computing and, 55 (*see also* Grid
    computing)
group/community relationships and,
    279–281
History of Political Discourse 1500–1800
    project and, 284–285
impacts on research practices and, 283–293
instrumentalist view and, 279–280
Integrating Web Information Using the Se-
    mantic Web (IUGO) and, 288, 288–289
Integrative Biology and, 290–291
interoperability and, 297
laboratory metaphor for, 280–281
landscape sampling and, 281–282
mapping on object of research and, 286–287
Meeting Memory Technology Informing Col-
    laboration (MeMeTIC) and, 288
MyExperiment and, 290
performative processes and, 289–292
personal interactions and, 288–289
sharability and, 297
significance of, 277
Silchester Roman town and, 286–287
terms for, 277–279
thick/thin clients and, 295–296
typologies of collaboratories and, 281–283
usability and, 296
Web 2.0 and, 297–298
Virtual screening, 267
Virtual Workspace for the Study of Ancient
    Documents, 103
Virtuous cycle, 2–4
Viruses, 153–155
Visual analytics, 31
Vitiello, G., 127

VMWare, 296
von Ahn, Luis, 110

Wajcman, J., 279
Wallis, J. C., 90, 122–123
Warr, Andrew, 13, 80, 135–152
WATERS Network, 121
Web 2.0, 64, 81
    end-user programming and, 143–145
    social networking and, 157–159
    virtual research environments (VREs) and,
        297–298
Webb, E. J., 234
Weber, T., 237, 250
Webometrics, 19, 45–47, 230–232, 258
Weinberg, A. M., 122
Wellcome Trust, 84
Welsh, E., 138, 140
Wenger, E., 260
"What You Can Do to Promote Open Access"
    (Suber), 317
Whitley, R., 260–261
Wiegand, G., 171
Wiener, Norbert, 41–42
Wikipedia, 111, 237, 318
Wikis, 73, 83, 266–267
Wilbanks, John, 14, 322–324
Wilensky, R., 125
Wilkinson, D., 86
Wilks, Yorick, 13, 80, 107–119, 230
Williams, R., 178
Willinsky, J., 233
Wilper, C., 125
Wilson, B., 107
Windows Live Search, 46
Winner-takes-all effect, 24, 177
Winograd, Terry, 137
Wireless communications, 120
Wogan, P., 147
Wooden stylus tablets, 103
Woolgar, S., 34, 171
Workplace studies, 137–138
World Bank, 331

World Wide Web, 40
  Berners-Lee and, 5, 80
  blogs and, 21, 26, 29, 68, 70, 73, 83, 86, 110,
    157, 185, 188, 289–290
  data webs and, 98–101
  development of, 5
  Grid computing and, 2–3
  hyperlink algorithms and, 113
  newspapers and, 108
  research revolution of, xi–xii
  social science and, 166
  Webometrics and, 45–47
World Wide Web Consortium (W3C), 323
Wouters, Paul, 272–275
Wuchty, S., 88
Wulf, V., 143
Wulf, William, 278–279, 281, 292

Xerox, 138
X-ray crystallography, 261

Yahoo!, 28, 94
Yale Center for Medical Informatics, 323
Yang, X., 69
Yates, JoAnne, 41
Ynalvez, Marcus Antonius, 14–15, 176, 254,
    325–342
YouTube, 67, 267
Yuan, H., 144

Zeitlin, Jonathan, 174
Zhu, Jonathan J. H., 31, 161, 188–190
Zimmerman, A. S., 329
  access and, 22–23
  bottom-up innovation and, 167, 179
  changing disciplinary landscapes and, 258,
    261
  embedded network sensing and, 122
  usability and, 135, 139
  virtual research environments and, 279, 282
Zittrain, J., 110